Refugees

Philosophical Projections

Series Editor: Andrew Benjamin, Distinguished Professor of Philosophy and the Humanities, Kingston University, UK, and Professor of Philosophy and Jewish Thought, Monash University, Australia

Philosophical Projections represents the future of Modern European Philosophy. The series seeks to innovate by grounding the future in the work of the present, opening up the philosophical and allowing it to renew itself, while interrogating the continuity of the philosophical after the critique of metaphysics.

Titles in the Series

Refugees

Towards a Politics of Responsibility

Nathan Bell

ROWMAN & LITTLEFIELD
Lanham • Boulder • New York • London

Published by Rowman & Littlefield
An imprint of The Rowman & Littlefield Publishing Group, Inc.
4501 Forbes Boulevard, Suite 200, Lanham, Maryland 20706
www.rowman.com

6 Tinworth Street, London SE11 5AL, United Kingdom

British Library Cataloguing in Publication Information Available

Library of Congress Cataloging-in-Publication Data

Names: Bell, Nathan (Lecturer), author.
Title: Refugees : towards a politics of responsibility / Nathan Bell.
Description: Lanham : Rowman & Littlefield, [2021] | Series: Philosophical projections | Includes bibliographical references and index.
Identifiers: LCCN 2020053263 (print) | LCCN 2020053264 (ebook) | ISBN 9781786614186 (cloth) | ISBN 9781786614209 (epub) | ISBN 9781538179871 (pbk)
Subjects: LCSH: Refugees—Government policy—Moral and ethical aspects. | Refugees—Legal status, laws, etc. | Government accountability. | Human rights—Philosophy.
Classification: LCC JV6346 .B45 2021 (print) | LCC JV6346 (ebook) | DDC 172/.2—dc23
LC record available at https://lccn.loc.gov/2020053263
LC ebook record available at https://lccn.loc.gov/2020053264

Contents

Acknowledgements

I have many people – colleagues and students, friends and family – to thank for their support, encouragement, and provocations to thought over the ten-year period which I have dedicated (between my PhD, completed part-time, and the subsequent writing of this book) to the following question: how should the right to asylum be understood and acted upon?

I must start by thanking Professor Andrew Benjamin, whose generosity cannot be overstated. The present work reflects the constancy of a dialogue with Andrew that has been incredibly rewarding and challenging. His influence is virtually everywhere in the text that follows, and not only in those places where his work is explicitly engaged. This generosity is all the more remarkable for the fact that I was never his formally enrolled student – testament to his pure dedication in supporting all those pursuing the life of the mind.

Similar thanks must be extended to the supervisors of my PhD and constant mentors over this past decade (and prior to that), Dr Michael Janover and Dr Paul Muldoon. Their gracious wisdom and gentle guidance, while at the same time always pushing me to clearer explication and challenging me where necessary, was invaluable. They have also given me my start in academic teaching, as both tutor and lecturer, and for that I will always be enormously grateful. I also want to thank my colleagues in the Philosophy Department at Monash University who have supported and challenged me in my growth as a philosopher. Particular thanks to those I have worked with the most these past years, Professor Robert Sparrow, Dr Robert Simpson, and Dr Suzy Killmister. Thanks are also owed to my former colleagues at CEVIPOF Sciences Po in Paris, where I spent a year and a half on scholarship during my PhD – an experience which was essential in allowing me to work full-time on the project and to grow as a scholar.

Thanks also to my students, in human rights and political theory and political philosophy, who have been a joy to teach, and who have also taught me a great deal. It has been the honour of my career to have a role in the development of their intellectual journey. Also to those I have met at conferences at home and around the world, thank-you for your probing questions and insights; in particular, thanks to Richard Cohen and Jolanta Saldukaityte for having me at their annual Levinas seminar, and to Claire Higgins and other organizers for my membership and participation in the Kaldor Centre Emerging Scholars Network at UNSW. Thanks to Asher Hirsch for educating me on how the law works (or doesn't) in relation to asylum.

I must thank all those who read drafts of the chapters of this book and provided invaluable feedback: Johannes Bennke, Richard Cohen, Sue Hempel, James Kent, Suzy Killmister, Paul Muldoon, Robert Simpson, Rozemund Uljée, Michelle Boulous Walker. Special thanks to Valentin Cartillier who went above and beyond in reading multiple chapter drafts, and George Cox for both reading chapters and editing assistance. Michelle has also been a constant champion of the project, thanks for all your kindness and generosity Michelle!

Great thanks to Frankie Mace and Scarlet Furness at Rowman & Littlefield for their kind patience in tolerating my many delays in completion of the work. This book quickly outgrew the project of being a rewrite of my PhD, becoming an entirely new argument, which made finishing it on time difficult; their support has been very much appreciated. Thanks also to those who provided reader reports on the book proposal, especially Peg Birmingham whose comments were incredibly encouraging, and who indeed helped me to clarify exactly what I was seeking to articulate with this book. I wish also to extend my gratitude to the cover design team – I find it elegant and evocative. My only request was that the colour be ocean blue, as a reflection of the dangerous sea journeys endured by so many. As Hans Blumenberg is quoted in the book, 'both progress and sinkings leave behind them the same peaceful surface'. As will be seen, this theme of the invisible aspect of reality, of the calamities that hide beneath the calm exterior of all that is, can be understood as a central theme of the book. The cover makes me think also of accounts of sea crossings where all the lights on the boat are turned off to avoid detection, where the only light is literally the light of the moon.

In a more personal vein, thank you to my three sisters Jodie, Megan, and Laura for all their love and kindness. To my father David Bell for awakening my political instincts in a progressive direction and for all our conversations about politics over the years. To my late Grandparents Bill and Joan Bell, who were always kind to me. To Kath, Seb, Josh and Sarah; to my aunts and uncles and cousins on both sides of the family, thanks for your love and support. To Martin and the Harkess family for all their support. To my best friend James Townsend, my constant brother-in-arms through all these years, and to Peter Newbigin, who is trying to make the world a better place in his development work around the world (Robinsons Attack!).

I want to make special mention of my recently departed and dearly loved Nanna, Audrey Hill, who took me to *Schindler's List* when it was released in the cinema and thus awakened my conscience to those events, which form an integral part of the meditations of this book. George Steiner summarized it well: '*Schindler's List* was, despite *kitsch* elements, a clarion call to awareness'. Parts of it are infuriating (that bloody icicle scene!, pulling an icicle off the side of the train to give to the children, a Hollywood sign of hope on the transport when in actuality significant numbers of people died from the train journey alone, enduring days without food and water, before ever reaching the camps), but the penultimate scene, where Schindler breaks down because he 'could have got more out', the recognition of a responsibility without limit and of all those who could have been saved but were not, is the only thing that never fails to make me cry. I know of these things because of the emphasis on the importance of education in our family, which has led me to become who I am. As Nanna used to say to her children, 'I don't care if you're a street-sweeper, as long as you're an *educated* street-sweeper'. Thank you, Nanna, to you and Grandpa, Arthur Hill, for all your unconditional love. I miss you.

Finally, this book is dedicated to my mother, Julie Margaret; if I have learned to care for others, it is because I learned it from her loving example. I cannot even put in words my admiration for her.

There are only two solutions left . . . the natural solution, which would be for the Messiah to turn up on a cloud and take us there with a flap of his wings, and the supernatural solution, which would be for civilized nations to actually do something, however small.

– André Schwarz-Bart, *The Morning Star*

Introduction

> But if we take seriously the inability to choose with whom we cohabit
> the earth, then there is a limit to choice, a kind of constitutive unfreedom
> that defines who we are and even, normatively, who we must be.[1]
>
> – Judith Butler, *Parting Ways: Jewishness*
> *and the Critique of Zionism*

Nothing has changed, nothing has been learned, nothing has been remembered. The nothing grows, a nothing that nihilates, nihilism as the absence of meaning, a world astray in an endless nothing that 'can entail only world catastrophes'.[2] And yet, such a populous nothing! The number of stateless persons[3] in the world now exceeds that at the time of the Second World War. That previous calamity *should* have been a permanent reminder to the world not to look away or fail to act. However, not only does the pile of wreckage and bodies continue to grow under the horrified gaze of Walter Benjamin's Angel of History, but the world is every day more replete with the ghosts of those who could have been saved, but were not; lives lost because they were deliberately exterminated, or drowned, or excluded from access to asylum via *non-entrée* policies that violate the obligation to uphold the principle of *non-refoulement*, or turned back to murder or prison, or immiserated for decades, without hope, in camps. This calamity is set to exponentially increase with the hastening effects of climate change.[4] A numerous nothing, then, perhaps like a disaster, a disaster of numbers and yet beyond numbers and beyond all counting in its endless expansion, a disaster which, as Maurice Blanchot put it, does not even have the ultimate for a limit, but bears the ultimate away in the disaster, a disaster 'related to forgetfulness', a failure to remember, to care and to think.[5] A failure of politics and those who make it, but also of those who think it. For while one can and should judge the failures of politicians, the poverty of political philosophy is also manifest in its temperate, pragmatic, liberal-democratic iterations, the inexcusably 'tepid temperature' of 'every calculation of prudence', to borrow from Nietzsche, when the fire alarm is clanging so loudly.[6] Disaster past and perhaps greater disaster to come, if disaster can even be measured, and if nothing is done: 'Before the spark reaches the dynamite, the lighted fuse must be cut'.[7]

The argument to be established concerns a novel concept of the political centred on an *ethos of responsibility* that would posit a *guarantee* of the right to asylum as the *realization* of politics. This argument is necessary because both the theory and practice of asylum stand at an impasse, stranded in the tension between human rights and sovereignty, at best, and criminally negligent at worst. Since 1994, global resettlement of displaced persons has never exceeded 1% of their total number.[8] This has resulted in the indefinite, lifelong suffering of people in exile, where they can exercise only limited agency in insecure camp conditions, or are forced by desperate need to attempt journeys that are often dangerous and uncertain, where they risk death in transit or at a border (which are violent constructions – thousands of people die at borders every year).[9] A new way of approaching these problems is required that goes beyond the tension between rights and sovereignty, on the one hand, or the recapitulation of tenets of Marxist thought on the other, where answers are predetermined and all that remains is to realize the revolution, or to remain within a dynamic of struggle (necessary to be sure, but which requires a novel orientation). To proceed via fidelity to existing axiomatics in this context would be symptomatic of what Benjamin called 'left melancholia', a failure to move outside of existing political paradigms in seeking to combat oppression.[10] Such an approach would not actually constitute a *response* worthy of the name, to the exigencies of today, the lessons of the past, or the presentiments of disasters to come.

Emmanuel Levinas once wrote of his generation, which endured two world wars and a Great Depression, the Shoah, and many other calamities, that 'at no other time has historical experience weighed so heavily upon ideas', a sentiment that resonates in the present.[11] *Never again*, the vital imperative of Holocaust remembrance, should be invoked not only against reoccurrences of genocide and crimes against humanity but also in relation to the fate of contemporary refugees, whose twentieth century forerunners were produced by that other disaster and were to a significant extent not saved from that disaster when they could have been; this failure to render the world other than it is by the failure to take responsibility is the *tertium comparationis* across disparate experiences. Samuel Moyn has noted the delayed reception of the Holocaust (what is better termed the Shoah[12]) into human rights discourse – it was not emphasized or even well known in the immediate post-war period. When it did emerge, it was at a time in the late twentieth century when paradigms of reform or possibilities of more radical change were waning, and concerns about atrocities and the need for humanitarian intervention came to the fore: 'It was not the Holocaust in itself that drove the contemporary salience of human rights, but belated memories of it in new circumstances.'[13] Moyn laments this form of human rights discourse as too focused upon 'preventing a *summum malum* rather than conceiving of a *summum bonum*'.[14] However, it is possible that the lessons to be drawn, if actualized, might represent the fulfilment of both ambitions. One could argue that as it relates specifically to refugees, the lessons of the Shoah are still yet to be fully absorbed, or certainly, are yet to be *honoured*, in the double sense of paying tribute – first by way of recognition, and second by attending to obligation, as the honouring of a historical debt. For amongst the terrible calamities of human history, it is paradigmatic of the *lethal* consequences that can attend the failure to grant asylum.[15] While every disaster, every historical epoch of unjust suffering and death is *sui generis*, what Walter Benjamin called the 'tradition of the oppressed' suggests that there is also a universal history of injustice which persists throughout time: 'The tradition of the oppressed teaches us that the "state of emergency" in which we live is not the exception but the rule'.[16] His much-discussed image of the 'Angel of History' blown backwards into the future, staring in paralysed and mute horror at the wreckage of the past, is a *continuous* experience, the angel a witness to a pile of destruction that is always increasing: 'Where a chain of events appears before us, he sees one single catastrophe'.[17] How history appears from 'the standpoint of the defeated', while varied in experience, is in other ways constant. The mutual imbrication of past, present, and future and the lessons for asylum that follow from this and other disasters (the Palestinians and *al-Naqba*, Rwanda, Syria, Myanmar, a list that could be extended indefinitely) will be a persistent theme in what follows.

Hannah Arendt, in articulating what she meant by the task of understanding, made affirmative reference to the value of indignation, as a move beyond dispassionate argumentation that engages with the world and responds to it. She thought a place should be retained for indignation, but distinguished it from moralizing or sentimentality; thus, she explained, if she used the metaphor of Hell to describe conditions on earth, it is because the stylized depiction of Hell in the Western tradition has been realized in actuality, and that this had to be reckoned with: 'To describe the concentration camps *sine ira* [without anger] is not to be "objective", but to condone them.'[18] Indignation is thus an important element of the intellectual work of understanding: 'If I describe these conditions without permitting my indignation to interfere, I have lifted this particular phenomenon out of its context in human society and have thereby robbed it of part of its nature, deprived it of ones of its important inherent qualities'; concomitant to this she writes, 'the question of style is bound up with the problem of understanding'.[19] As Derrida queries in *Archive Fever*, 'In works said to be theoretical, what is worthy of this name and what is not?'; for Arendt, indignation, and the style in which it is expressed, enter into the proper exploration of phenomena on the path to understanding.[20] Arendt's use of the word 'phenomenon' is interesting: common to both Arendt and Levinas, two of the key thinkers in this book, was an experience of studying under Martin Heidegger, who decisively altered the course of the philosophical discipline of phenomenology inaugurated by Edmund Husserl by emphasizing the lived experience of human beings, rather than the delimitation of philosophy to formal categories of logical, empirical, idealist or rationalist truth-claims. This emphasis upon lived experience constitutes a highly original aspect of the work of both Arendt and Levinas within political theory and philosophy, respectively, that while retaining the rigour of thoughtful argumentation does not step aside from the moral necessity of indignation, and indeed emphasizes the ways in which indignation *insists*.

The in-dignation animating the present argument is directed against those forms of political practice which deny dignity. Infamously difficult to theoretically elaborate, what is meant by *dignitas*, the worthiness or worth of the human being, is defined throughout in Arendtian–Levinasian terms, grounded in the actualization of human potentiality by being able to appear and belong amongst other human beings; and the active responsibility for the protection of the often precarious and vulnerable nature of human life, especially as experienced in exile.[21] The requirement for such an actualization is articulated as a conception of human subjectivity which is always-already cast as responsibility amongst plural human beings, who require the security of placedness (that is, being-in-place as constitutive of human life) and belonging. This argument is primarily informed by the understanding of unchosen human plurality as thought by Hannah Arendt, and ethics-as-responsibility as articulated by Emmanuel Levinas, and the possibilities that these thinkers provide for a reworking of the political understood as respect for the right to asylum. The thought of Arendt and Levinas will be brought into proximity with that of Jacques Derrida, Judith Butler, Andrew Benjamin, Theodor Adorno, Walter Benjamin, and others; but in particular, the nexus of Levinasian ethical responsibility joined with the implications of Hannah Arendt's thinking of unchosen human plurality should be understood as the fulcrum point of the entire argument.[22]

Asylum, from the Greek *asylon hieron*, meaning an inviolable haven or refuge, a place where seizure of persons is forbidden (*a* – without, *sulon* – right of seizure), originally referred to the status of religious sanctuaries in antiquity as sites of protection from persecution. However, protection was not guaranteed - David Scott FitzGerald observes that in fifth century BCE Athens, guards were placed at the entrance to the Acropolis, to prevent suppliants from entering – the denial of asylum being as old as the concept of asylum itself.[23] While a comprehensive genealogy is not feasible here, as a problem for political reflection in the Occidental tradition, asylum dates from at least the birth of democracy in Athens, even if it was treated by the tragedians such as Aeschylus and Sophocles more than it was by actual political philosophers such as Plato and Aristotle, who are all but silent on the question of refuge. Asylum emerges as an overt political theme during the Enlightenment, especially in relation to the French revolutionaries who held this right to be inviolable for the politically persecuted. Kant's famous essay on 'Perpetual Peace' stipulates as a condition of a peaceful cosmopolitan world order, the recognition of the shared possession in common of the Earth's surface by all human beings (although he refers to a right to visitation rather than the right to belong).[24] During the period of the early to mid-twentieth century and following both world wars, asylum was codified in international law as a matter of human rights – not only the right to seek asylum, but the corresponding duty of states not to refoul persons seeking asylum back to danger, and the obligation to assess their claims for refugee status. In this context, Arendt's famous notion of the 'right to have rights' has become increasingly important in thinking through the plight of the stateless, of which more below. Modern theoretical approaches to asylum typically emphasise a liberal or social contract version of rights, or a recourse to legalism, the attempt to institute a rules-based approach to international affairs, including the legal protection of human rights. Another line of thought would posit the need for 'open borders', which would remove, along with border controls, any obstacle for those wanting to cross a political frontier. Finally, much recent theory has focused upon the theme of 'hospitality', of the negotiation of the needs of the host and the guest, and the limits, if any, to hospitality (Derrida has written provocatively of the Law of 'unconditional' hospitality, which deconstructs the laws of actual existing hospitality in an endless negotiation). However, many of these modes of thinking asylum occur within the limits of the rights of a host political community to make determinations as to who it admits to its territory, with the lodestone of political theory being the willed, autonomous, free self-determination of a self-chosen people. The problem of asylum is often couched in the following terms: 'What do we owe to refugees'?[25] While it is true that the question of asylum implies a 'we' that could grant it, this form of argumentation will be opposed to the extent that it assumes a form of the 'we' that must consciously will a decision or make a choice about what is 'owed', within the existing paradigm of Westphalian sovereignty constructed upon the liberal, autonomous theory of the subject. Conversely, a relational, responsible approach would recognize the anoriginal relationality of human subjectivity where obligations are always-already 'owed' to others who were never chosen, who already belong to a different, plural 'we'. Nor is the argument simply a form of what Didier Fassin has termed 'humanitarian reason': Fassin is right to warn that 'in the contemporary world, the discourse of affects and values offers a high political return'.[26] As Fassin analyses in his book, humanitarianism as a political affect, and even when constituted as political acts, usually excludes the right to asylum from its considerations. That is, actions by states of the Global North may appear 'humanitarian', but are simultaneously exclusionary: as David Scott FitzGerald writes in *Refuge Beyond Reach:* 'Camps funded by the rich countries of the Global North are key building blocks in both the architecture of protection, which provides shelter for refugees, and the architecture of repulsion, which cages them far from the Global North'.[27] It is as though asylum for some reason represents a greater commitment, or perceived threat, than political communities (especially states of the Global North, the predominant targets of the criticisms within this book) are willing to accept. This resistance will be examined and critiqued throughout, in its relations to various phantasms whose ethereal forms are those of numbers, of economics, of threats and purported limits. The hunting down of these ghosts will often be paramount in what follows.

Hannah Arendt indicates a way out of the predicament. Given her emphasis upon the 'miracle' of natality, which enables human action and the possibility of new beginnings, it seems appropriate to credit Arendt with an entirely new paradigm of thought within political theory. One might go so far as to claim what she never would, that the *novum* of political thought she has provided for is Copernican in scale, in altering the very essence of how the political can be understood. As will be explored below, Arendt's call for a 'new law on earth', a 'new political principle', and a 'new guarantee of human dignity' takes the concept of the political beyond the friend–enemy distinction of Carl Schmitt, or the nationalist or sovereigntist categories of inside–outside, the delimited nature of a political community where the *demos* is already constituted. Rather, she articulates a vision of politics as *belonging*, where to be is to be able to *appear* amongst others and be recognized as an equal and distinct person, to exercise the faculties of action and speech in concert with other human beings. While it will be argued that Arendt herself did not fully explore the implications of her own work, and indeed seemed at times to resist the normative basis which that work arguably provided for political thought, it is nevertheless thanks to Arendt that the new direction can be pursued. She has definitively provided for the *possibility* of a new concept of the political, which it is the task of her readers to establish; much work on this has already been done, and the present book seeks to further these efforts. This requires a measure of thinking with Arendt against Arendt, and indeed some un-Arendtian claims will be advanced using Arendtian concepts. Ambiguity and difficulties are manifest in examining her texts, and even if Arendt has revolutionized political thought, she will often express her thinking in comportment with traditional lines of enquiry that limit the radical possibilities of her conclusions. (For example, her overt Aristotelianism, which accepts the virtues of moderation and of necessary limits to the size of a political community, two postulates which will both be radically challenged.) In an affirmative vein, two lines of thought in her œuvre are particularly important here. First, that of human *plurality* – 'that men, not Man, live on the earth and inhabit the world',[28] that is, that human beings are plural at both the individual and group level (the latter understood as a plurality of *peoples*, as racial, ethnic, religious, or other collective forms of humanity), a plurality which must be actively preserved. Second, the much-commented notion of the '*right to have rights*', the idea that the defence of human rights ultimately requires recognition by and membership of a political community. These can be called Copernican in the enormity of their implications, in that politics thus changes from a focus upon the life-world of the existing membership of a political community, to the possibility of being oriented from the beginning by respect for outsiders, who are permitted to enter and become members. The centre of gravity is decisively shifted, and a new locus of the political emerges, where the plurality of all human beings comes to lie at the centre of political life.[29] Again, in many places the argument that follows will depart from Arendt's own conclusions or emphases, and indeed take strong critical issue with many of her positions, but from within an arena of thought inaugurated by Arendt herself. There is nothing to be gained, in thinking asylum, from a retreat to a concept of the political that would be pre-Arendtian; and even her apparent errors or contestable arguments are in general highly fecund for thought, and represent an invitation to the kind of critical thinking as an exercise of responsibility, and which produces the possibility of judgement, that she consistently affirmed.

To state the argument directly: the politics of asylum is not reducible to choice. The constitution of the membership of a political community is not simply a matter of rational (or indeed fearful) decisions consciously willed by a self-selected community attending to its own interests, and the fate of the refugee should not be left to the sovereign power that alone may determine the 'exception'. The profound limitation of liberal theory, in seeking to constrain and direct Leviathan in the direction of the good, is to accept that there is a choice at all, that it is simply a matter of choosing to accept international human rights law that then becomes binding upon the state. Liberalism has completely failed in this task, across decades – on the one hand, failed to establish this as a universal, cosmopolitical law, and on the other, largely failed to respect that law even in those states where it is recognized. Thus, it is necessary to insist: the political subjectivity of the individual and the constitution of a community are always-already called into question by the ethical demands manifested amidst unchosen human plurality. That is to say, following Arendt, that, when it comes to asylum, human beings do not get to choose with whom they share the earth, or (perhaps going further than Arendt) 'their' political communities with; and following Levinas and contrary to liberal accounts of the subject, that human beings are always-already called to responsibility for those unchosen others, before any rational choice has been made, that ethics is prior to politics, even if the ethical must necessarily enter into processes of political calculation, weighing, and decision – that is, the move from ethics to justice. What results from this articulation of 'unwilled proximity and unchosen cohabitation' as the mediating conditions of political life is, to borrow Judith Butler's formulation, the conclusion that the ethics of just cohabitation is the proper work of politics, an imperative to preserve human plurality, 'the obligation not to destroy any part of the human population or to make lives unlivable': what is here termed an *ethos of responsibility*.[30]

If politics attends only to what it chooses to attend to, then it is not dealing in reality, but rather in the unreflective immediacy of what is most readily apparent, obvious, or self-interested, and yet remains haunted by the others it neglects; it thus becomes ontologically unserious, even spurious. Those things which are clear in the light of day do not constitute ultimate events of being (Levinas). Politics, as shall be argued in the concluding chapter or 'Coda', must take all of its ghosts very seriously, the ghosts of those it did not save, is not saving, and will not save. It must attend to all those who cannot fully 'appear' in Arendt's sense,[31] that is, to be able to live and act amongst their fellow human beings in a public setting, those cast into exile, phantoms haunting the exterior of the walls of the polis. To be sure, the ghosts can be denied, the unchosen can remain excluded, the call of responsibility can be ignored; but then the claim is that such 'political' actors who behave this way are no longer operating within the realm of the political, but are practising anti-politics, a charge not simply levelled at authoritarian or totalitarian regimes, but at every liberal-democracy in the world today. Similarly, this charge must be levelled at all theorists who defend the political right to self-determination of closed societies, of social contract theory, in ways that constitute ungracious, calculating limits to and denial of asylum, or the tacit or explicit endorsement of the right to self-determination in the face of asylum claimants (who must, in this context, be provisionally distinguished from other migrants, a bracketing which poses an enormous set of questions in itself) knowing what they do of history and the lethality that attends such denial, as well as its contribution to political instability. In a word – one that Arendt insisted was a political concept, a 'category of public life' – the articulation and the practice of the *dis-graceful*.[32]

At that time of previous disasters – 'the wholly enlightened earth is radiant with triumphant calamity' – Theodor Adorno and Max Horkheimer argued in

The Dialectic of Enlightenment that thought should reflect upon its own failure.[33] What is the role of thinking in the current refugee 'crisis'? (The word is apt, given the scale and nature of the problem and its likely future dimensions, but worthy of suspicious quote marks, given the way that the crisis seems to receive this appellation only when it is states of the Global North that are brought into acute proximity with it.) The refugee demands to be thought, and for that thought to provide meaningful criteria of judgement for action. Elias Canetti gave a lecture during the period of the Second World War, in which he quoted an unknown poet: 'It is all over now. If I were really a poet, I could have prevented the war'.[34] Such a sentiment jars with realist considerations; it could appear quixotic to think that poetry or thinking truly matters amidst the pressing horrors of the real. However, the real of politics (in its actual existing manifestations, rather than the Lacanian Real that is irreducible to the symbolic order) is itself informed, and perhaps in part formed, by *concepts* of the political; and the present argument is that the concept of the political that is required to face the present and future crisis of mass displacement has yet to be fully articulated. Despite an enormous and vital literature on the politics of asylum, on hospitality and welcoming, on refugees and human rights, on borders and climate migration, rarely if ever is it maintained that *the right to asylum is central to the meaning of the political as such.*

An endless source of disputation between philosophy and politics is the problem of how their conjunction is to be understood, and what might follow from such understanding in terms of praxis. Does that philosophy which, since Plato, aims at the 'good', constitute a violent imposition of principle upon the expression of freely held opinions amongst plural beings engaging in the activity of politics? The evocation of such a concern is usually attended by a reminder of Plato's unsuccessful dalliance in real-world politics with the tyrant of Syracuse, and Heidegger's unforgivable Nazism, apparently dispositive examples of the dangers of philosophical absolutes in the uncertain realm of human affairs (even though both of these thinkers completely failed to influence their master, and their commitments, while raising questions about their philosophy, led nowhere in terms of praxis). Politics, according to Arendt, is coterminous with freedom. For Arendt, the activity of thought, leading to the formation of *doxa*, freely held and expressed opinions amongst plural beings in the polis, is that which guarantees the continuance of the possibility of political action, and is thus hostile to the imposition of absolute norms.

Here, a position on this millennia-old debate must be made explicit. Asylum should be (to borrow a term Arendt also used to describe this right) considered 'sacrosanct' – inviolate, an absolute good.[35] It is a form of the good that trumps politics as the space of freedom (just as human rights are considered to act as 'trumps' over other considerations). The obverse of the concerns about the absolutism of philosophical claims to the good over the free space of politics as a potential form of violence, is the actualization of violence in multiple forms wrought by political decisions, upon those who are constantly denied asylum. Usually little more than exhortations that states might do better are offered in excuse. The lacuna in this debate – one that seems to rarely if ever be mentioned – is that the evidence that the surrender of self-determination in the context of asylum will lead to the destruction of the political realm, is totally lacking – no more than vague supposition, or the subject of fascist tracts (such as the execrable *Camp of the Saints*, where one wonders whether the writing is worse than the politics, an abyssal question not worth tarrying over). The counter-evidence, of the death and suffering that follow from the denial of asylum, is overwhelming, as will be explored throughout. One disaster (the destruction of the free political realm by an influx of refugees stemming from a misguided fidelity to principle) is end-lessly anticipated and never arrives, the other disaster (the destruction of the lives of refugees) continues without cessation and is no more than lamented. Certainly, one can and should disdain philosopher-kings, but the crimes of democracies are much more troubling and much more real, and standing over both should be a guarantee of human dignity, a guarantee called for by Arendt that nonetheless departs from her own parsing of this term.

Political theory and political philosophy, following the controversial work of theorist Carl Schmitt, will often have recourse to a distinction between 'the political' and 'politics', where 'the political' pertains to an interpreta-tion of politics in its conceptuality, its essence, interpretation or meaning, whereas 'politics' refers to the 'sphere of state and power'.[36] Schmitt also distinguishes between the political and the state, making it possible to theo-rize the former independent of the latter.[37] While both distinctions are present in the argument, they are also undermined to the extent that how one thinks the political may have decisive consequences for the lived experience of politics, including that practised in sovereign states but also beyond them, were such thinking to be actualized. Is a new concept of the political possible, beyond liberalism and beyond the influence of the will to moderation taught by Aristotle, beyond the utopianism of open borders or the distant withering of the state, which would, regardless of the form of the political community, posit active responsibility for persons seeking asylum as the *realization* of politics? This is precisely what will be argued in what follows, a political concept that it is possible to manifest in praxis as an *ethos* of responsibil-ity. The articulation of such an *ethos* represents a move beyond the standard traditions of varied human societies that they owe some kind of voluntarist, secondary, or derivative cultural duty of hospitality or refuge, to claim that the right to asylum is proper to the political in its essence, to the very meaning of *ethos* and the self-understanding of any political community. That is to say, that respect for asylum is not some kind of optional addendum, something political societies can choose or not to adopt and uphold, but rather something implicit in human subjectivity and political life, even if it has so often been denied.

Further, the question of limits and numbers will be opposed as a false problem often ranged against the realization of the right to asylum. On the one hand, if human dignity or worth – here conceived as actualized through placedness and belonging – is that which is beyond price, as Kant maintained, then the election to duty of responding to the needs of vulnerable others can in no wise be a matter of prudential calculation. Kant argued that 'imperatives of prudence, strictly speaking, cannot command at all'; and 'in the kingdom of ends everything has either a price or a dignity . . . whatever is above all price, and therefore admits of no equivalent, has a dignity'.[38] In this, Derrida's reflections upon 'unconditional hospitality' are relevant, as will be discussed further on; both Levinas and Derrida, despite other significant philosophical differences, can be seen as aligned with Kant around the question of the infinite or unconditioned, the implication of which is that one's duty can never be absolutely fulfilled. In the interplay of the conditional and the unconditioned, the unconditioned (here understood in Levinasian terms as as the infinite call of the other to have their dignity respected) provides a criterion of judgement that is irreducible to calculation.[39] However conversely, one can argue that, some extreme circumstances aside (which essentially never materialize), there is almost no limit to the asylum capacity of any major state that already numbers in the millions (there are concrete historical and contemporary examples of states absorbing enormous numbers in short periods, and no state has ever collapsed or been seriously threatened from the mass movement of refugees), and that globally there is simply no problem of numbers. The problem is one of politics and governance (as Arendt already knew when amongst the very first theoretical respondents to mass statelessness in her reflections in *The Origins of Totalitarianism*) which is at present stalled and sclerotic, with proffered solutions seemingly hopelessly unrealizable, and hence the need for a rearticulated concept of the political.[40] Consequently, regardless of the position one takes regarding the calculability of numbers in relation to stateless persons – its moral or practical irrelevance as a consideration – it is not a legitimate objection to be made against the concept of the political here mooted.

Asked once about his political convictions in an interview, Levinas replied: 'Listen, I am a democrat. What more would you like me to say?'[41] The elementary nature of this response echoes a broad consensus amongst political theorists; outside of authoritarian regimes, there are surely few people who would deny that governments should rule via consent of the governed. While it might be possible to conceive of undemocratic societies that sufficiently respect human rights, it is difficult to point to one in actuality, as Seyla Benhabib has noted: 'The absence of full democratic equality in these societies [she gives the example of Saudi Arabia] results in imperfect legitimacy and the less than commendable realization of justice.'[42] And yet paradoxically, one often observes a rupture between that which is just and that which is democratic. This problem is staged in Aeschylus's tragedy *The Suppliants*, where the demands of the suppliant women for refuge in the name of the transcendent justice of Zeus, protector-god of strangers, come into conflict with the King's insistence on first consulting his people before granting asylum.[43] It is interesting to note the claim by Paul Cartledge that the decision of the Argive citizenry that grants asylum to the 'Danaids' (the suppliant maidens who flee from Egypt to Argos to avoid forced marriage, forerunners of women today who flee crimes such as sexual and domestic violence and trafficking) constitutes the first recorded mention of deliberation by a democratic assembly. In this sense, democracy and the question of asylum have been bound up together from the beginning.[44] Yet this outcome was not assured; Aeschylus presents the difficulty in classical Greek tragedy-as-dialectics fashion, as two competing claims to justice – that of the God of Suppliants (Zeus *Hikesios*) and Strangers (Zeus *Xenios*) versus the right to self-determination and popular sovereignty of a polity that might risk its destruction by granting asylum, an example of the ambiguity that Simon Critchley argues is inherent to Greek tragedy.[45] In the present argument, this dialectic and the notion of ambiguity around asylum is rejected – there is no destruction risked and nothing to fear from the granting of asylum. By way of illustration, an analogous gesture is that of the 'violence' Bertolt Brecht does to the dialectics of Sophocles's *Antigone* by severing the knot of complexity and siding only with Antigone, presenting Creon as a fascist tyrant.[46] Brecht has Antigone respond to the ambiguous, dialectical worry, voiced by 'Kreon': 'And what if Thebes fell, through our conflict, to be devoured by the invaders?' Antigone's reply: 'The men in power always threaten us with the fall of the state', echoing the plaints of modern politicians who recommend appeasement of the political right through exclusion of refugees in order to preserve social cohesion.[47] But can one think of a society that has failed or even been seriously harmed by absorbing too many suppliants, or as having been attacked as a consequence of doing so? And even if the latter point were maintained, wouldn't such capitulationism risk even greater danger – 'then they came for the Jews', as Martin Niemöller's famous poem goes – where does the logic of appeasement end? What is remarkable in *The Suppliants* is the willingness of the Argive citizenry to uphold the justice of Zeus as the protection of those seeking asylum, to the extent of taking up arms in martial defence of the Danaids, an exorbitant assumption of responsibility. Equally remarkable, in his appeal to the democratic assembly, King Pelasgus refers to the 'twofold claim of guests and citizens' – not the competing claims of guest versus citizen, but that the suppliants themselves have a two-fold claim, *as guests and as citizens*. That is, the suppliants *are already citizens*, a reference to the Argive origins of Io: the woman desired by Zeus, consequently transformed into a cow by the jealous goddess Hera, and who fled from Argos to Egypt pursued by Hera's tormenting fly, yet who Zeus still manages to mate with, leading ultimately to the birth of the suppliant maidens who are now returning to their origins. The stranger is thus already kin; but what if one alters the claim slightly for contemporary purposes, that the foreign suppliant is already a citizen based simply upon shared humanity (which would imply a right of 'cosmopolitan citizenship', as articulated by Seyla Benhabib)?[48] While we moderns know that all human beings are 'kin', in sharing a common genetic ancestry, Hannah Arendt was right to eschew biologism and claims about human 'nature', and rather emphasized the human 'condition' of plurality, the preservation of which becomes the justification for inclusion. This is the case even if, as will be argued, her claims beg a normative question that she does not adequately address, which is why a turn to the thought of Levinas in conjunction with Arendt is required (as has been effectively explored by Judith Butler and Anya Topolski).[49]

It is not a matter of dialectical ambiguity, of the justice of the gods versus political self-determination, or universal liberal rights versus democracy, but rather a matter of committing or not committing an ontological crime against the givenness of unchosen human plurality. As Arendt observed, a democracy is capable of anything, even of taking the democratic decision to liquidate a people; consequently, in fulfilling demands of justice, it can be maintained that asylum should not be left simply to the whims of democratic will, and that the right to asylum need not be theoretically delimited to its relationship to the democratic.[50] There is a rather consistent tendency of democracies – particularly those of the prosperous Global North – to proffer either limited asylum to outsiders or even to shut them out completely. Thus while one might prefer the legitimacy that democratic decisions confer (in council or representative or direct form, however this is decided, which cannot be explored here), it is necessary to entertain Slavoj Žižek's provocation that the right to asylum should not be bound *a priori* by democratic procedures.[51] A novel concept of the political with asylum at its core implies that democracies must be bound by considerations of justice and an external criterion of judgement – as Robespierre observed, the magistrate should be subject to the people, but the people themselves should be subject to justice.[52] Neither does the chiasmatic relationship between liberalism and democracy offer reassurance on this front – leaving aside the other historical crimes of 'actual existing' liberalism (whose 'black book', when one day written, will dwarf that of communism in its relation to the horrors of colonialism and capitalism), when it comes to the politics of asylum in particular there is ample evidence that a liberal approach has proven to be insufficient; and even in idealized terms (a universal right of movement and non-interference with autonomy) it is, along with the notion of 'open borders', not yet an active solicitude and responsibility for others.[53] To respond to the other in distress is not simply to leave the border open so that they might enter, but to venture out to assist them to do so.

Moriz Scheyer, a survivor of the Shoah, wrote in his memoir of his time in hiding (simply titled *Asylum*) of the 'monstrous' indifference of Western states to the plight of the Jewish people, knowingly or unknowingly echoing a term employed by thinkers as different as Kant and Nietzsche to describe the sovereign state (Nietzsche: 'the coldest of all cold monsters').[54] As Richard Kearney explains, the etymological root of monstrousness, *monstrare*, means both to show and to warn.[55] The monster as the unknown, the foreigner, the stranger: this type of fearful thinking infects even ostensibly serious theorists in the context of asylum, that there is something to worry about when considering who it is that is arriving from the sea, from the dark, from the over-there; even the supposed limits of hospitality and the potential dangers constituted by the arrivant are treated as serious matters for consideration.[56] Here, the stakes are inverted; that which must be revealed and warned against is the monstrousness of a certain way of considering the politics of asylum, especially by sovereign states. Vulnerable supplicants are more or less never a matter for this kind of fearful concern; that is, analogies between asylum seekers arriving in a political community with the dangers of unknown strangers arriving on one's household doorstep are utterly dyssynchronous and irresponsibly misleading – *the household as the false synecdoche of the state*. The sovereign state as it currently exists in various iterations must be considered in the current crisis, as that for the most part is the political reality with which stateless persons must contend, and thus to ignore Westphalian sovereignty or to talk too idly about open borders would also violate politics understood as an *ethos* of responsibility. However, the concept of the political here pursued should by no means be understood as limited to Westphalian states. In the double gesture of taking the state seriously and looking also beyond it can be seen a necessary two-track notion of political praxis: firstly, the negotiation of immediate demands and ineluctable context; and secondly, the horizon of possibility towards which one wants to advance, the role of political imagination and the refusal to submit to that which is presently the case. One can neither bypass the state, given the dominant role it plays in the determination of recognizing the right to asylum, nor remain limited by it.

The question of asylum is here deliberately foregrounded in order to understand the role that it plays in politics; indeed, one could argue that asylum needs to be distinguished from other economic and political considerations, in that certain considerations of human belonging and the consequences of exclusion would pertain regardless of the contemporaneous hegemony of given economic and political systems. Additionally, it is true that the distinction between migration and seeking asylum is not always clear, that the reasons people leave their homelands can be diverse. The Refugee Convention, in referring to a refugee as someone who has a 'well-founded fear of persecution', circumscribes the ambit of its authority under the somewhat indeterminate descriptors of 'fear' and 'persecution', which do not necessarily capture all those who might be protected by refugee status.[57] Can persecution be redefined in broader systemic terms to include, for example, the loss of crops from climate change that is largely the fault of the Global North? Understanding what fear, persecution, refugee, and related terms mean, the work these terms do and how they might be changed or reoriented (perhaps conditions of emergency or urgency are preferable terms to persecution, or useful addendums) requires careful work of deconstruction qua a careful attention to language and its meaning. The production of refugee populations by neo-imperialist meddling abroad, the displacing effects of rapacious capitalism, either directly in capital flight or exploitation, or in the truly global sense of the impacts of climate change, are without doubt essential elements of understanding the current mass displacement crisis. Yet the focus here is less on causes than on *responses* in the ongoing context of asylum being required by tens of millions of people. The imperative at work in the argument is the need to absorb the lessons of the past for the present and future for the asylum that is required at any given moment as a matter of urgency; therefore, the present argument is not simply subsumed under the communist 'hypothesis', nor does it conflate asylum populations with other migrant populations under a generalized global 'nomadic proletariat' (Alain Badiou), nor does it await the resolutions of causative factors that produce refugee populations, nor does it simply press upon liberal states the pleading request to just be a little more decent, nor does it place its faith in the workings of legalism to establish a just international order. In this sense, while asylum can be seen as a last resort, which means other remedies have not been realized and human beings have been forced to take the terrible decision to flee – there is a certain irresponsibility to the positing of arguments that because such flight is distressing we should focus on other remedies, which may or may not eventuate. Resolvable or not, the exigencies that drive people into exile can be all be addressed at journey's end with the proffering of welcome to those in need. What matters most is the *response*: *respondere*, responsibility as a responding-to the other, the articulation of the Levinasian *me voici* – 'here I am!', the giving of an affirmative answer – the response of the responsible subject to the cry of distress.

But does not a problem arise around the concept of responsibility? This term has been traditionally understood in the history of philosophy as tied to the autonomy of the subject, who consciously wills, reflects, and makes decisions, and chooses one path or another to take. Such was the conception of responsibility shared by many thinkers from Aristotle to Kant; yet as François Raffoul elaborates, the post-Nietzschean turn in philosophy shifts the emphasis of responsibility from accountability to *answerability*.[58] It is not only that the autonomous subject is accountable, though decisions must indeed be taken and thinking, willing, and judging engaged, but also that they are answerable to an-other, to the call that comes from another. Responsibility is literally a responding-to, a response that is anterior to decision and choice. It remains the case that the subject can turn away from the call, refuse to make a decision, or decide unjustly, but the choice whether or not to respond, even in the negative, has already been compelled by another, as a non-negotiable response of the responsible subject. Ethical demands, and the permanent possibility of acting upon them, are primary; hence Levinas's arresting claim: 'The other is maintained and confirmed in his [sic] heterogeneity as soon as one calls upon him, be it only to say to him that one cannot speak to him, to classify him as sick, to announce to him his death sentence; at the same time as grasped, wounded, outraged, he is "respected"'.[59] Politics on this account is thus shifted from the dominant paradigm of a willing subject entering voluntarily into an agreement or social contract with other willing participants, to an account of ontology which is faithful to a relational world experienced as answerability, where ethics precedes ontology or is in anoriginal relation with it.[60] In the work of Levinas, the move from the infinite demand of ethics to justice still requires calculation, weighing and deciding, but it is a weighing of relative responsibilities between competing obligations rather than a matter of whether to take responsibility or not; that is, it results in a delimitation of freedom by responsibility. As will be seen below and in what follows, it is a matter of establishing a *guarantee* of the dignity of refugees as non-members within the free space of politics, an antinomic problem that requires careful exploration. In that sense, the nature of any *just* decision or choice is already predetermined as that which comports with the avoidance of ontological crime, in not denying the ability of plural human beings to exist and be recognized; other factors, such as economics, social cohesion, preservation of culture, and so on would be second-order considerations in relation to this pre-eminent imperative.

Intended here is the articulation of a more generalized concept of the political, not tied to a particular extant theoretical or institutional form of politics. Since Aristotle the idea that the human being is a *zoon politikon*, a political animal, has been recognized, that is, that it is proper to the species-being of the human animal that they are polis-dwellers, living amongst others in shared communities. This is a thought that has been developed by Hannah Arendt in relation to those who fall outside of political communities, in positing the 'right to have rights' as necessary for stateless persons in order to be fully human, that is, to appear amongst others and exercise the capacity for speech and action, in order to actualize one's potentiality. More recently, this line of thought has been developed and extended by Andrew Benjamin, whose philosophical anthropology stresses that what is proper to the human being is to be-in-common and be-in-place, where justice requires the exercise of judgement in the living out of a common life that recognizes the universal claim of human beings to belong.[61] But the recognition of the nature of human placedness and intersubjective life as being concomitant with the right to asylum – that this view directly implies that respect for asylum must become the matter of politics, its work and its goal – is a step that Arendt in particular did not explicitly take (the famous 'right to have rights', as will be explored, was not for her a normative claim per se but rather the articulation of a paradox). For Arendt there is a value of political activity qua activity in itself, as the realization of human freedom as participation in governance, and consequently the actualization of human potentiality. The delimitation of any specific normative content of politics, already evident in her (in)famous bracketing of the 'social question' as a corruption of political freedom in *On Revolution*, results in a fundamental lacuna of her account of the urgency of respect for the rights of human beings seeking asylum. There is a certain ambiguity in her work around this point – Arendt certainly thought that all human beings have a right to belong to a political community and thus enter a space of appearance where they can be judged on their actions and words, and she also made use of and appealed to normative concepts such as justice, but she was not a systematic thinker (the right to have rights disappears from her work after *Origins*) and, as will be seen, certain paradoxes and contradictions are present in her work which remain for her readers to contend with. It is this missing move from an Arendtian-inspired politico-philosophical anthropology of that which is proper to human beings, to the fulfilment of her own aporetic call for a right to have rights, and a reorientation of the *ethos* of the political as primarily concerned with asylum, that is of decisive importance.

A NEW LAW ON EARTH: COMPETING VISIONS

In the Summer of 1950, Hannah Arendt and Carl Schmitt are writing a Preface and Foreword, respectively, for their new books. These introductory remarks stage, without them knowing it, a polemic concerning competing *nomoi* of the earth.[62] For Schmitt, the *nomos* (law) of the earth has to do with the carving up of the earth in bounded territories by those who appropriate them; Arendt sees Schmitt as an odd supporter of *blut und boden*, who privileges soil rather than blood.[63] By contrast, in the first preface to *The Origins of Totalitarianism*, Arendt argues that 'human dignity needs a new *guarantee* which can be found only in a new political principle, *in a new law on earth*, whose validity this time must comprehend the whole of humanity while its power must remain strictly limited, rooted in and controlled by newly defined territorial entities'[64] (emphasis added). Schmitt publishes *Nomos of the Earth* in 1950, *Origins* is published a year later in 1951; while Arendt's comment is likely not an oblique response to Schmitt, given they were writing around the same time, it has been established that subsequently she carefully read and critiqued Schmitt's book (the marginalia of her copy are now available).[65] Thus, a new *nomos* of the earth was sought at precisely the same time by two German political theorists with conflicting views, who had also experienced the Second World War very differently – Arendt as a Jewish refugee who had defied the Nazi regime and actively worked to aid other refugees in Paris, and was sent to the Gurs detention camp before escaping and emigrating to the United States; and Schmitt, who went from being a prominent supporter and legal defender of the Nazi regime (including its racist Nuremberg Laws), to later being marginalized. (In self-serving fashion, he would compare his experience of inner exile in Germany to the captive state of 'Benito Cereno' in Melville's short story about the slave ship captain forced to play along with the mutinous slaves controlling the ship.)[66]

In the foreword to *Nomos of the Earth*, Schmitt, in an extraordinary phrase, reproaches the hostile reader who 'ignores the asylum I offer', and concludes with a dedication to peace-makers, to whom, he writes, belongs the world; but Schmittian peace is the peace of conquerors, of those who have usurped the earth for themselves.[67] His emphasis on land appropriation (which, he argues, is how Aristotle defines *nomos*, which leads Schmitt to deny its translation as 'law')[68] resonates with Locke's *Second Treatise of Government*, where the mixing of labour with land is what justifies possession, yet where such mixing was not extended to the practices of Indigenous peoples, despite their sophisticated methods of land management[69] (and as is well known, Locke had investments in a company that owned slaves; such are the foundation stones of the canon of political philosophy).[70] As Achille Mbembe writes in *The Critique of Black Reason*, 'In this case, then, law was a method for creating a juridical foundation for a certain idea of humanity that upheld distinctions between the race of conquerors and the other of slaves. Only the race of conquerors could legitimately attribute the quality of being human to itself'.[71] To be clear, Schmitt is not unaware of the problematic nature of this; however, it is not an emphasis of his analysis. Schmitt, like Hobbes and Machiavelli before him, wrote during times of political crisis and uncertainty and searched for a concept of the political that would provide a degree of order under the aegis of the will to power and domination.[72] While Arendt and Schmitt agree on the meaning of *nomos* – meaning both *nemein* as *nehmen*, to appropriate, and *nemein* as *teilen*, to divide, Schmitt sees appropriation as prior to division, whereas Arendt sees division as the constitutional moment of founding, that is, the paramount importance in politics of promising, occurring amongst plural beings, which Schmitt neglects. Arendt complains in her notes that promising as contract or constitution formation amongst human beings is absent from Schmitt's account.[73] Whereas Schmitt's emphasis on appropriation means the establishment of an inside and an outside, a friend and an enemy, Arendt is attentive to the givenness of human plurality – that one shares the earth with others whom one did not choose.[74] There is arguably an implicit normative dimension to Arendt's account of politics, which emphasizes freedom and plurality as intersubjectivity as the basis of founding political communities. Although it is interesting to note that both Arendt and Schmitt were critical of the Universal Declaration of Human Rights from not dissimilar positions: Schmitt arguing that claiming to represent humanity leads to the reduction of enemies to non-human status and multiplies conflict (Arendt felt this was just an apologia for the Nazis); Arendt thought that humanity as a concept risked becoming a dangerous ideology, in that the logic of the idea of humanity, in seeking a totalizing remit for political action could lead to 'monstrous immorality'.[75] In *The Human Condition* she discusses law as *lex*, the Roman term for law distinct from *nomos* that emphasizes 'the formal relationship between people rather than the wall that separates them from others') that would also be just.[76] Whereas *nomos* is the stability of placedness necessary for political community, *lex* allows for the contestation of the boundaries of political life through work and action, of plural human beings engaging their capacity for natality, for the introduction of the new into human affairs. Thus, the co-signer of the Nuremberg Laws proffers a conceptual 'asylum' based on exclusion, formed from the order that comes from violent appropriation, the European tradition of land grabbing that justified colonialism and the establishment of political communities that could exclude those beyond the boundaries, whereas Arendt refuses a return to colonial domination and nationalism and calls for a 'new law on earth' that will guarantee human dignity. In other words, the stakes of this unmanifested gigantomachy are of decisive significance for addressing the politics of asylum: Schmitt marks out a position that reflects with felicity current political realities of exclusion, including amongst liberal-democracies that were themselves often founded on the pillaging of other human communities and their territory, while Arendt provides for the possibility of a different politics. The new law on earth that she seeks is a response to the events of the Shoah but more broadly to totalitarianism as an anti-politics – to that which denies human dignity, spontaneity, and the realization of natality in action amongst plural beings. The upshot being that if asylum is denied, then these capacities of the human are rendered unrealizable, and in this context societies can no longer claim to be operating within the sphere of the political. Reading across her texts, one finds in the unfinished *The Life of the Mind* the following claim, which repeats a point from *The Human Condition*: 'Not Man but men inhabit this planet' (HC p. 7: 'men, not Man, live on the earth and inhabit the world'). But then she adds, in a similar phraseology to Schmitt but with an opposed emphasis: 'Plurality is the law of the earth'.[77] The *guarantee* that she seeks – a word that will be very important throughout and which needs to be kept in sight – relates to the recognition of and respect for the givenness, the unchosen nature, of human plurality as the law of the earth.

For Arendt, *nomos* establishes a space of appearance, but is tempered by *lex*, the law of human interaction that can be realized amongst plural human beings who can share a space of appearance and even contest the *nomos*, the basis of their foundation in a polis.[78] The root meaning of polis is the ring wall.[79] Politics pertains to bounded communities. This automatically raises the question of interpreting the meaning of politics for those outside the walls, of negotiating between the right of a political community to determine its members and the right to seek asylum. The Schmittian gap between politics and the state becomes very important on this point, but thought at the antipodes of Schmitt's own emphases, where rather than the friend–enemy, insider–outsider distinction, a broader concept of the political allows for modalities of inclusion of unchosen plurality rather than the binary of inclusion and exclusion. Arendt famously referred to a 'right to have rights', that is, a right to belong to a political community which could guarantee the fulfilment of all other rights. However, she did not see this as much more than a paradox – the right that one realizes is needed when the possibility of its realization has been lost. She also accepted Aristotle's idea that a political community cannot grow too large without becoming unworkable (though one could perhaps charitably interpret this in relation to her preference for smaller council democracies rather than mass states, the latter of which runs the risk of a 'despotism of a person or of majority rule'),[80] and regrettably refers to people the state renders stateless as 'barbarians' in *Origins*.[81] Further, Arendt's faith in the founding agreements of political societies can be seen as problematic, if, as Arendt herself has made clear and has been brilliantly elaborated by Judith Butler, the precondition of organized political life is *unchosen* plurality. One can add that the basis of political foundations such as the American Revolution, which Arendt so lauded, is built upon the dispossession of Indigenous populations and the 'primitive accumulation' that enables the founding of settler-colonial societies, as well as the legacies of slavery and colonial exploitation that enriched liberal-democratic societies around the world.[82] Both Arendt's account and those of many liberal theorists often fail to emphasize this context, even where their proposals concerning refugees appear ostensibly generous.

However, the ambiguity in Arendt's own position is productive rather than stymying, in that it presents an opening for a rethinking of the limits of political communities. What is proposed here is an argument concerning the way in which *nomos* becomes realized as *ethos* – from law as division-appropriation to the form of life proper to a particular community in its mode of being-together. For the purposes of introducing the argument of the book, what matters is how *ethos*, as the interrelatedness of human subjects and place, can be reconfigured in the direction of a new concept of politics concerning asylum. Here, Levinas figures prominently. Levinas is of course renowned as a thinker of ethics, which is itself etymologically derived from *ethos*, the meaning of which relates to place. While Levinas is a thinker of ethical subjectivity, which he defined as welcoming the other and hospitality, he is also a thinker of place, and a critic of the Schmittian-type usurpation of place at the expense of others. Repeatedly in his texts and interviews he quotes Pascal (the quotation also serves as one of the epigraphs to *Otherwise Than Being*): '"That is my place in the sun." That is how the usurpation of the whole world began'.[83] Arendt's critique of Schmitt is put in very similar terms by Levinas, apropos of Heidegger,[84] in *Totality and Infinity*: 'Heidegger, with the whole of Western history, takes the relation with the Other as enacted in the destiny of sedentary peoples, the possessors and builders of the earth. Possession is preeminently the form in which the other becomes the same, by becoming mine.'[85] But subjectivity and place are put into question by the other person, by the givenness of plurality – of diverse human beings who did not choose each other, who are already, to borrow a phrase from Luce Irigaray, sharing the world.[86] Thus, Arendt and Levinas come into decisive proximity around the politics of belonging. Judith Butler has written of this proximity in *Parting Ways*:

An obscure point of contact between Levinas and Arendt guides me here. Arendt was right when she argued that Eichmann thought he could choose with whom to cohabit the earth. In her view, cohabitation is not a choice, but a condition of our political life. We are bound to one another prior to contract and prior to any volitional act. The liberal framework according to which each of us enters into a contract knowingly and voluntarily does not take into account that we are already living on the earth with those we never chose and whose language is not the same as our own . . . This means that unwilled proximity and unchosen cohabitation are preconditions of our political existence, which is the basis of her [Arendt's] critique of the nation-state (and its presumption of a homogeneous nation), and implies the obligation to live on the earth and in a polity that establishes modes of equality for a necessarily heterogeneous population.[87]

The right to have rights, if understood as a normative claim and not simply as an aporia for thought, would involve the recognition of this unchosen state of common humanity, and thus a right of entry into a community and a right of belonging, in order to secure that which is proper to the flourishing of human beings. If it is necessary to appear amongst others in order to be fully human, and access to a political community is that which allows for this, therefore the right to have rights is paramount, and the realization of the political is bound up with a right to asylum. That is to say, that the proper work of politics is not only the preservation of the constitutive membership, but concomitantly is the recognition of the rights of vulnerable foreigners to belong. Otherwise, politics refuses its own exigency, which is to allow a space of appearance, amongst human beings whose subjectivity, according to Levinas, is originally manifested as responsibility and hospitality towards others, and whose plurality, according to Arendt, requires a sharing of the world with those we have not chosen. Political communities are thus in dereliction of their constitutive responsibility (in Levinasian as well as Arendtian terms) if they deny the ability of others to appear and to belong. As soon as this is denied, one is no longer in the sphere of politics but rather in anti-politics. The idea, developed by thinkers such as Arendt and Giorgio Agamben, of a lack of distinction between liberal-democracies and fascist societies concerning the reduction of stateless persons to a condition of superfluousness, means that politics requires reorientation if it is to remain within the domain of the actualization of the non-fascist life, that the denial of asylum no longer happen, at least not everywhere. That the Final Solution *'did not happen everywhere'* was the scant consolation Arendt saw in those events, and the minimum required 'for this planet to remain a fit place for human habitation'; the same lesson can be drawn from both the putting-to-death of the Final Solution (and the letting or making die of those who refused European Jewry asylum) and the deliberate letting-die of the denial of asylum, what Achille Mbembe has termed 'necropolitics' and which might also be termed tacit genocide,[88] which continues virtually everywhere.[89] (Denied asylum by every liberal-democracy, the matriarch of the refugee Jewish family portrayed in André Schwarz-Bart's harrowing novel *The Last of the Just*, which will feature throughout this book, exclaims: 'Are they then everywhere, the Nazis?')[90]

While Eichmann should of course be distinguished from the leaders of most modern states in the severity and exterminatory character of his actions, these very different actors are nevertheless comparable to the extent of being guilty of crimes against the givenness of human plurality, of imposing death sentences (or a life in misery). This is a thought that must be risked, for as Agamben writes apropos of the reduction of human populations to a biopolitical mass in the modern age, 'The idea of an inner solidarity between democracy and totalitarianism (which here we must, with every caution, advance)

. . . will allow us to orient ourselves in relation to the new realities . . . [and] will make it possible to clear the way for the new politics, which remains largely to be invented'.[91] Simon Critchley, in *The Problem With Levinas*, writes with reference to Conrad's *Heart of Darkness* that 'Civilisation requires expansion through force and the extermination of the brutes . . . then the distinction between liberalism and Hitlerlism collapses . . . What was Hitlerism? Hitlerism was the extension of the logic of colonialism within a different territory. The Germans wanted what the French and the British had, but the French and the British had already divided up the big chunks of the world.' Critchley concludes that 'What happened under the Third Reich is just a modification of the deep logic of colonialism'.[92] Critchley avers that this is a position beyond what Levinas would co-sign; however, Levinas seems to anticipate this line of thought in his essay 'Cities of Refuge', writing, in a way that indicates his shared concern with the 'systemic violence' examined by Slavoj Žižek, 'Are there not, somewhere in the world, wars and carnage which result from these advantages [of the West]?'[93] For Levinas, the modern state is akin to the 'involuntary manslaughterer' who would seek refuge in the ancient cities of refuge as portrayed in the Torah (Deuteronomy 4:41–44, Numbers 35). The responsibility for others is derived from the imperative not to be responsible for their deaths, either by causing their immiseration, or failing to take them in. Noam Chomsky observes in *Who Rules the World?* that colonial decisions such as the Sykes-Picot Agreement were the origin of the continuing instability in the Middle East that fuels the refugee 'crisis', linking it to more recent neocolonial adventurism in the destabilization of Libya and interventions by the United States in Central and South America.[94] As Natascha Uhlmann writes, 'a popular immigrant slogan perhaps says it best: *We are here because you were there*'.[95] The colonial, even Hitlerian, context of asylum politics is an essential component of understanding its causes, that is, as often driven by the rapaciousness and will-to-domination of states of the Global North. When a senior European Union figure recently referred to the EU as the 'world protagonist' of asylum, this claim should therefore be interpreted within that context.[96]

While the new concept of the political sought here may seem very similar to Arendt – a recapitulation of the right to have rights – there are some important differences to be marked. Firstly, the right to have rights requires interpretation, and much work has been done in this direction; this will be examined in chapter 2 in relation to a range of political theorists, including Seyla Benhabib, Peg Birmingham, Serena Parekh, Étienne Balibar, and others; the argument is that it is possible, and indeed necessary, *pace* some commentators, to see it as a normative claim that is linked to her call for a new law on earth.[97] Secondly, Arendt arguably did not consider asylum itself to be the realization of politics as it is presented here – she considered asylum to be that which secures access to the goods of politics, rather than being the concern of politics itself. As Arendt writes in *The Human Condition*, 'The calamities of action all arise from the human condition of plurality, which is the condition *sine qua non* for that space of appearance which is the public realm. Hence the attempt to do away with this plurality is always tantamount to the abolition of the public realm itself'.[98] Arendt's concern here is focused upon the preservation of the public realm and not the preservation of plurality as normative goal; a certain reordering of priority would render the right to asylum of uppermost importance, both for the preservation of the vulnerable outsider, but ultimately for the political community itself. Arendt recognizes the need (however unobtainably aporetic in her view) for the right to have rights in order to secure political participation, whereas the present argument is that political participation requires explicitly attending to the right to asylum. This is based upon an account of human subjectivity as oriented towards hospitality, as argued by Levinas, linked to Arendt's notion of unchosen plurality, resulting in a new account of political subjectivity and a new concept of the political which centres asylum as the realization of the active preservation of plural and precarious human life. In her view of political life and human subjectivity, Arendt is perhaps too close to Aristotle, and her thinking too bounded by his; the radicality of Levinasian responsibility alters the possibilities of a concept of the political beyond what Arendt would likely approve of. Nevertheless, the articulation of an *ethos* of responsibility which sees asylum as proper to the political as such relies on many of her arguments, in particular the right to have rights.

How can a state be convinced or compelled to respect the right to have rights? Without some movement on this, the call to ground rights in political membership will remain as impotent as Arendt (in agreeement with Edmund Burke) holds natural rights to be. A reply to this position might be: granted they are powerless, but so too is politics, and international law, and protest, and education, and critique as they pertain to asylum; the constant reproach of the state, writing articles, protesting, or taking them to court (then the government changes the law or abrogates a treaty, and so on) has not affected much change. Judith Shklar referred to the latter approach as 'legalism' – the attempt to instantiate respect for moral considerations (in this context, the right to asylum) via a rules-based legal system and adherence to international law.[99] These are essential, noble efforts that will and must continue, but whose limits in contending with political regimes that look askance at their obligations are continually manifest. Kant, writing in *The Conflict of the Faculties*, distinguishes between the work of the philosopher and that of the jurist: the task of the philosopher pertains to the application of the *a priori* principles of moral philosophy in order to test the laws of a society, whereas the jurist identifies that which is right with the given legal norms of the society.[100] To be sure, an emendation is required in this context – the human rights lawyer identifies 'right' with international and not only domestic law. However, these remain merely the laws that states are willing, or unwilling, to be bound by. Many important victories for upholding the rights of refugees (and those who seek to aid them) have been obtained in domestic courts, which has so often been a cause for hope in dark times. Yet it remains a Kafkaesque struggle – this exhausted analogy is unavoidably apposite – of the futile attempt to influence the will of an implacable, recalcitrant, and often unreachable sovereign via the laws that they simply hold in contempt or do not permit access to.[101]

It is that stubborn implacability that must be targeted and transformed, and the duty thus of that 'lower' faculty, philosophy, and especially political philosophy, to articulate another possibility, and provide criteria of judgement, 'that, having no commands to give, is free to evaluate everything'.[102] To be sure, Arendt was not unaware of this need for a new possibility – hence her call for a 'new law on earth' that would 'guarantee' human dignity, which as theorists such as Peg Birmingham and Andrew Benjamin have demonstrated, should be conceptually linked to the right to have rights.[103] With rare exceptions, states and their publics have for the most part to be dragged kicking and screaming in the direction of their moral obligations, and this has changed not at all in seventy years or more – from the Evian Conference in 1938 to the UN/Obama conferences in 2016, liberal states have decisively failed on these issues, evincing no more than an etiolated commitment to rights obligations, not to mention the descent into the nightmare in America that followed Obama's term, and the rising xenophobia and exclusion in Europe, Australia, and around the world. Not only state sovereignty, but nationalism is as strong as ever: As Benedict Anderson argues, 'The reality is quite plain: the "end of the era of nationalism", so long prophesied, is not remotely in sight. Indeed, nation-ness is the most universally legitimate value in the political life of our time'.[104] But despite these dispiriting realities, something must change. The right to have rights has not arrived, nor have 'newly defined territorial entities', and more of the same legalism, of mostly vain attempts to persuade inimical states to accept their duties, of a paltry ameliorationism rather than fundamental change, is unacceptable from the perspective of what is proper to human dignity qua safety and belonging. *Asylum cannot be only conceived of as a rights problem*, or even as a problem limited to the form of political organization (though both of these are relevant and important), *but as a problem with a more fundamental relationship to the political as such.* What is the source of state resistance to asylum? What is the *ethos* that informs such resistance, the economic, racial, cultural phantasms that seek to justify it, the understanding of the political that guides it, the ethico-ontological suppositions beneath that understanding? Until these can be shifted, one may as well point a lance at the nearest windmill. Millions more will live out their lives in camps, or die at sea and at borders, on and on it goes, but so it must not necessarily go, to alter Vonnegut's phrase; there is the *possibility* that matters can be otherwise, that the world can be othered.[105] Hence the urgent need for a reworked concept of the political that places asylum at the heart of politics. Montesquieu wrote of the 'spirit' of the laws, the principles by which a political community operates; however, he did not think that there was any underlying set of norms that had definitive universal applicability, but rather looked to the way human reason plays out in different societies in different circumstances and epochs; yet he does identify virtues such as 'honour' and 'distinction' (in monarchies), 'equality' (in republics), and 'fear' (in tyrannies). Arendt was influenced by Montesquieu, arguing in her essay 'On the Nature of Totalitarianism' that these three forms of government can be seen as authentic because they spring from aspects of the human condition.[106] The justification for a centring of asylum at the heart of political life also centres on an aspect of the human condition – that of unchosen human plurality, which provides a normative *telos* for politics, and consequently implies the necessity of upholding the right to asylum.

In the fall from favour of natural rights, there is a prevailing view in political theory that there can be no fixed normative foundations for politics outside of those agreed to via democratic procedures and agonistic or deliberative spaces of political decision. In *Hatred of Democracy*, Jacques Rancière discusses the 'much-commented-on duality of man and citizen . . . [and that it is generally held] if two principles are required for politics instead of only one, it must be because of some deceit or vice'. Burke and Arendt held that the Rights of 'Man' are powerless without civic instantiation, while the Rights of the Citizen '. . .are simply the rights of those who have rights, and hence a pure tautology'.[107] For Rancière, it is necessary that these names of the political be maintained in their heterogeneity, because 'political subjects exist in the interval between different names of subjects'.[108] Ultimately, rights are a political problem – here he is close to Arendt, in seeing a limitation in providing a normative grounding for human dignity, and seeking to understand rights strictly within the domain of the political: Rights '. . .were won through democratic action and are only ever guaranteed through such action. The "rights of man and of the citizen" are the rights of those who make them a reality'.[109] In a critique of Lyotard (but in terms highly reminiscent of a critique of Levinas), he dismisses the appeal to an ontological grounding of the suffering subject, preferring a 'heterogeneity of political dissensus' to 'a more radical heterogeneity' of the appeal that issues from Otherness.[110] Thus, he suggests: 'I think that we had rather leave the ontological destiny of the human animal aside if we want to understand who is the subject of the Rights of Man and to rethink politics today'.[111] In similar terms, Étienne Balibar, in

articulating his notion of 'equaliberty', writes: 'We may say that the identification of liberty and equality is the internal prerequisite of the universal
identification of man and citizen. A man is a citizen *if and only if* liberty and
equality become identified. Therefore a man is a citizen *inasmuch* as liberty
equals equality . . . the *basic right of man* . . . is *a right to politics*'.[112]

In couching their arguments in these terms, political theorists such as
Rancière and Balibar seek to avoid the pitfalls of normative claims grounded
in natural rights (without their being unaware of anthropological distinctions), and concepts of human 'nature', metaphysical claims about existence
or ontological descriptions of human life that are controversial; liberty and
equality are *political* qualities which can be readily and uncontroversially
identified and defended. But must these other types of claims be avoided? Are
the terms of political struggle the only ones in which to articulate political
responsibility? To require of some of the most powerless people in the world
– the stateless – that they struggle for equaliberty as the 'insurrectional' destabilization of the existing order, or for others to struggle for them, does not
go far enough in an account of responsibility.[113] What the present argument
suggests is that Arendtian plurality and Levinasian ethics provide an alternative and normative basis on which to approach these problems and articulate
the 'spirit' or 'principle' – the word *ethos* is preferred, given its etymological
relation to the intersubjective mode of being-in-place amongst others – in
which politics should be thought and acted out, without this representing a
problematic return to natural rights. States fail to act upon the law because
the animating principles of politics, the way in which it has been thought and
articulated for centuries, if not millennia, emphasize some principles and not
others. It is necessary to develop the conversation inaugurated by modern
thinkers such as Arendt around a new principle, a new law on earth, a new
meaning of the political that thinks through the implications of unchosen
plurality in its normative dimensions. Will this also be quixotic? Perhaps,
but then the wager of all thought that aims at the othering of the world may
find its ultimate refuge in Nietzsche's reassurance that it is those thoughts
that arrive as imperceptibly softly as the landing of the feet of doves, that
ultimately guide the whole world, for example, the quiet hope evinced by
Arendt in the Preface to *Origins* for the establishment of a new law on earth,
read ultimately by very few human beings other than humanities scholars,
which has permanently introduced at least the *possibility* of the realization of
that other world.

What Is an Ethos of Responsibility?

In order to establish the concept of the political that posits asylum as central the meaning of politics in the form of an '*ethos* of responsibility', a

number of arguments need to be elaborated. The radicality of the proposal is to invert the standard understanding of politics as that which pertains primarily to the promotion of self-interest of the constitutive members of a political society. A tradition of political philosophy exists that emphasizes mutual mistrust and a war of all against all, the will to order, strategy aimed at power and domination, where Thomas Hobbes, Niccolò Machiavelli, and Carl Schmitt would be amongst the proper names signifying this position. To this tradition is counterposed the thought of Hannah Arendt, Emmanuel Levinas, and Jacques Derrida. In particular, the implications of unchosen plurality, as thought by Arendt (and developed by Judith Butler), and in relation to the concept of responsibility as reconfigured by Levinas – anarchical, exorbitant, putting the other in first place, beyond the limits of reciprocity or moderation – enables the possibility of a reworked concept of the political which recognizes ethical responsibility, mediated via a process of justice, as the *ethos* of the political. The way in which ethics and ontology are understood and ground political theory in its dominant iterations up to the present is thus fundamentally challenged. Arendt wrote of the 'space of appearances' – of plural human beings appearing amongst each other – as being prior to the constitution of given political communities.[114] Connected to the thought of Arendt in this context is the notion of the 'anoriginal' relationality of human being-in-common (Andrew Benjamin). This is to be distinguished from that which individual *Dasein* encounters in the state of *geworfenheit*, thrownness into a world where *mitsein*, being with others, is already organized into and experienced in the form of political communities; the givenness of this mediating condition does not alter that from which such communities will always have been formed, which is the state of unchosen human plurality. Benjamin observes Arendt's agreement with this position: 'Arendt accepts, with justification, the identification of the being of being human with being-in-place, evidence for which is in part provided by a reformulation of Kant in which humans become "earthbound creatures"'.[115] In the context of asylum, thus even when there is an appeal to the solicitude of an extant polity, the argument is that the conditions prior to the founding or constitution of a political community remain in place: the state of unchosenness. A politics that denies this is denying an aspect of the human condition, but if the purpose of politics is human flourishing and the realization of human dignity, then to deny the realization of an aspect of the human condition in its flourishing is to deny politics itself.

In this way we can understand Derrida's claim that ethics is hospitality, but in a way that moves past 'hospitality' to *ethos* as *belonging* achieved through asylum, as the very realization of political life. A more generous 'politics of hospitality', mediated by extant traditions of welcoming and bounded by quotidian and moderate-mediocre notions of political decisionism, is not the present aim, but rather, a reconfiguration of politics itself as primarily oriented by respect for the right to asylum – if it is a matter of hospitality, then it is a hospitality transformed into a right to *belong* that is inscribed at the very heart of politics. The Derridian negotiation of conditional and unconditional hospitality, while provocative, arguably risks re-inscribing the liberal-democratic paradox or the dialectic of sovereign insider and excluded outsider (hence Derrida's paper entitled 'Hostipitality', noting the etymological root common to both host/hospitality and hostility), even if it urges it in a more generous direction, and thus a recapitulation of statist politics. Indeed, while hospitality is employed to describe Levinasian *subjectivity* in chapter 1, the thesis of this book is that hospitality as a *political* concept, related to asylum, is limiting, misleading, and even dangerous. The call for a 'guarantee' in the sphere of politics, for all its apparent violence to political freedom and despite originating in Arendt's work, would seem to contradict both Arendt and Derrida's accounts of responsibility, where the nature of politics as freedom (Arendt) and the undecidability implicit in negotiating given contexts (Derrida) mean that fixed guarantees cannot be given. While Derrida's challenge of an 'unconditional hospitality' remains important as a means of putting into question the claim to limits to asylum that are sometimes made by existing political communities, unconditional hospitality does little more than shadow real-world conditional hospitality as its other possibility, and this is a limitation that must be transcended by a guarantee; thus while hospitality plays a role in what follows, it must be insisted that asylum is not only a matter of hospitality, but of belonging.

What does an '*ethos* of responsibility' mean? Breaking down this syntagm into its constituent parts, firstly it is necessary to clarify the meaning of *ethos*. For Aristotle, *ethos* is tied to a place of dwelling, that is, an ontological foundation to the discussion of *ethos* that he pursues as it pertains to rhetoric, to appearing amongst other human beings (for example, in the Areopagus) and persuading them according to virtues derived from common life in the polis.[116] Heidegger addresses the meaning of *ethos* in his 'Letter on Humanism', where he defines it as the abode or dwelling-place, 'the open region in which man dwells'.[117] Correcting the modern translation of Heraclitus' fragment 119 – 'A man's character is his *daimon*', from *ethos anthropoi daimon* – *ethos* refers to dwelling rather than character, where the *daimon* is the relationship of the human to the gods who draw near to the human dwelling-place. Heidegger explicates this with regard to a story of strangers who visit Heraclitus, who invites them in: here too 'the gods come to presence', where the presencing of god refers to those who are unfamiliar.[118] The claim would thus be that the dwelling-place of human beings is oriented towards the reception of others who are unknown. This, however, is not for Heidegger an ethical claim in the normative sense of a prescriptive duty, but rather an aspect of 'fundamental ontology', one of increasing importance: earlier in the 'Letter' he writes that 'Homelessness is coming to be the destiny of the world'.[119] The 'world', as a construction of human beings, is distinguished from the physical earth; the world is a site of inter-human dwelling.[120] Homelessness is to be understood not as an absence of nationalism (despite Heidegger's political failures) but as an estrangement from the history of Being. Consequently, the recuperation of *ethos* as it relates to dwelling, is not constrained to nationalistic considerations but rather can be understood as an openness to others, as a proper understanding of the history of the fundamental ontology of Dasein as a being-in-relation.

A similar interpretation is pursued by Derrida, who argues that the meaning of *ethos* is bound up with that of hospitality. A striking definition of both *ethos* and hospitality, (which originally provoked) the work pursued here, is provided by Jacques Derrida:

> Hospitality is culture itself and not simply one ethic amongst others. Insofar as it has to do with the ethos, that is, the residence, one's home, the familiar place of dwelling, inasmuch as it is the manner of being there, the manner in which we relate to ourselves and to others, to others as our own or as foreigners, ethics is hospitality; ethics is so thoroughly coextensive with the experience of hospitality.[121]

Derrida thus provocatively delimits any thinking of the ethical to its interpretation qua hospitality. To suggest that ethics is coterminous with hospitality is to suggest that all ethical questions, in the political realm, are in some way bound up with the reception of others.

Secondly, responsibility, in its etymology, is formed from the Latin *respondere*, where *re-* is again, *spondere*, to pledge; in Old French, *Respondre* is to answer or to promise in return. Responsibility thus has the character of a repeated answer or promise, which, as noted above, is here interpreted as the Levinasian 'me voici!' ('here I am!'), the responding call to the vulnerable cry, whether voiced or silent, of the other. This is to be distinguished from responsibility delimited to accounting for one's actions, for the responsibility owed for an act committed; while not irrelevant, such an account posits a subject as a self-willing, rational, voluntary agent who acts as sovereign over their decision to respond, whereas according to Levinas, responsibility is not chosen, or accepted, by an imperious subject, but is rather imposed upon them – hence his use of dramatic-sounding terms such as 'persecution' and 'hostage' to describe the status of the responsible subject.[122] As François Raffoul writes in *The Origins of Responsibility*, distinguishing between standard accounts of responsibility in traditional philosophy (Kant and others) from more recent Continental work, 'The phenomenological sense of responsibility might be closer to a problematic of answerability than one of accountability'.[123] Levinas notes in the section of *Otherwise Than Being* on 'Substitution' that 'The self is a sub-jectum', that is, it is 'thrown under', beneath something (for Levinas, beneath the transcendence of the other who comes as though from a height), subjectivity as the delimitation of free choice: 'Responsibility for the other, this way of answering without a prior commitment, is human fraternity itself, and it is prior to freedom.'[124] The human subject, including the political subject, is conceived as substituting for the other in taking responsibility for them, a responsibility prior to any willed choice. This responsibility, however, enters into the realm of the demands of negotiating justice with the advent of the Third – where there is more than one other to contend with and choices do have to be made; however, the condition of such choices is set within a context of initial unchosenness, not a choice of whether to take responsibility but the necessity of choosing how responsibility is to be exercised). The *zoon politikon*, the human animal that lives amongst other human animals in placed, relational belonging, is also always-already called to responsibility for others. This is opposed to the liberal construction of the human subject as autonomous, self-willing, and entering into voluntary contract; rather the human being is relational and responsible, in addition to being free otherwise than as construed in liberalism, a 'difficult freedom' (Levinas's phrase) of responsibility.

Consequently, combining these terms, an *ethos* of responsibility refers to the manner of relating to others in the place of one's residence, in the form of answering to or responding to them. But what does this mean, how is one to understand this definition of political ethics? How is unchosenness to be interpreted as the basis of both political subjectivity, and also the social ontology or 'human condition' of political life? Finally, how can this *ethos* address and alter the nature of political responses to the plight of refugees and asylum seekers? Such are the questions this book seeks to answer.

STRUCTURE OF THE ARGUMENT

The book proceeds in the following way: elaboration of theoretical argument – a combination principally of political theory and philosophy – followed by illustration with historical case studies from the Shoah concerning refugees, ending with relevant implications for contemporary refugee politics. It is intended that in this way the stakes of the theoretical matter can be made manifest for readers, in the interplay of theory and practice, where the distinction between these terms is not rigorously maintained but rather deconstructed. Derrida pursued this problematic in relation to Marx's famous eleventh thesis on the philosophy of Feuerbach (that whereas philosophers had only interpreted the world, the point is to change it), pointing out that a thesis is proper to the working of philosophy, even if its thetic, dogmatic character in stipulating a demand or *telos* for action represents a move beyond mere inquiry, the question being whether a demand for praxis really escapes or exceeds the order of theorizing.[125] Derrida links this to Kant's third question in the *Critique of Pure Reason* – 'What may I hope?' – that, according to Derrida, engages the interplay of theory with practice, even if Kant and Marx understood practice in different ways.[126] As Donna Haraway argues, theoretical intervention into a set of problems brings with it the possibility of and responsibility for the othering of those problems into new directions, that is, the inherent performativity of the theoretical method being utilized.[127] Thus, for example, in chapter 2, following the articulation of Arendt's ideas concerning the right to have rights, this is analysed via an interpretation of a historical case study of both political action and asylum which she privileged as exemplary: the refuge given to Jewish people in Denmark during the Nazi occupation. It will be demonstrated that Arendt's reading of this history, while containing valuable insights, is ultimately flawed in failing to consider the limitations of the asylum that was granted; in truth, Denmark had closed its borders, and failed to properly evince an *ethos* of responsibility where asylum would be, in her words, 'considered sacrosanct'. Largely, Denmark saved Jewish Danes *because they were Danes*, and excluded many Jewish refugees from other states – with lethal consequences.[128] Arendt's judgement of this history via her theory of political action leads to a misunderstanding of political practice; if lessons are to be drawn from history, then the way in which theory alters its reception is not exogenous to practice. Following this, in chapter 3 I argue for the utility of Levinas for thinking the political by contrasting his understanding of justice with that of Aristotle; the claim is that Levinas allows for an exorbitant, excessive sense of justice (derived from his ethics in which, I argue, supererogatory obligation carries over into and is instantiated as justice) which is precisely what is at times required to safeguard the human dignity of refugees. This is illustrated by a second excursus in reference to the history of the Kindertransport, which saved ten thousand Jewish children – commendable, to be sure, but far too limited given the potentially much greater numbers of people, children and adults, that could have been saved. In chapter 4, I examine Derrida's thinking of unconditional hospitality as applicable to the politics of asylum. Derrida's claim that 'ethics is hospitality' was an original catalyst for my research – *what does that mean?* – and, even if limited in the ways I indicated above, is helpful in establishing an *ethos* of responsibility, oriented by the right to asylum, as a novel concept of the political. This work is situated in relation to France's self-identification of a land of asylum, and an analysis of a period when that identity was most challenged, during the reception of a large group of Jewish refugees in the 1930s, where the record of protection was decidedly mixed, as well as in relation to more recent asylum challenges in France.

The book concludes with a 'Coda', that is, an additional movement in the work which stands apart from the argumentation of the chapters that precede it, but which should be understood as informing the moral impetus of the whole. The Coda is a meditation on the politics of 'hauntology' (Derrida's neologism concerning the spectral nature of the ontological) and missing persons – the disappeared – and argues that the ultimate exigency and moral force of the *ethos* of responsibility is to be found not only in the needs of the living but also in the recollection of those who could have been saved but were not, and those yet to come, not even born, who are already dead because no one will save them.[129] This includes a discussion of what Walter Benjamin called the 'tradition of the oppressed', which has been pluralized in the Coda as 'traditions', referring to the ways in which different experiences of oppression might illuminate each other (without being conflated as all equivalent or easily comparable experiences, or on the other hand, without historical trauma being used as justification for further oppression of others), and which evinces an ethics of listening to and solidarity with the voices of the marginalized, such that they are not simply passive objects of pity or concern. The meaning of the present as found in remembrance of the past was a consistent and poignant theme in Benjamin's writings and is relevant in this context. In many ways this is as much a book on the Shoah as it is on contemporary refugees, in the hope that understanding and absorbing the lessons of the history of the former might aid in the construction of a more just politics for the latter. As discussed above in relation to asylum and the consequences of failing to provide it, the Benjaminian tradition of the oppressed names a continuous catastrophe as seen by his Angel of History, despite the unique and singular nature of each historical calamity, that is, a form of universal history. However, aside from the obvious moral relevance, a theoretical consideration underpins this choice: Hegel's oft-repeated remark that the wings of Minerva spread only with the falling of the dusk perhaps indicates that one can draw lessons from the historical past more clearly than from the flux of the present, yet precisely such lessons enable judgements that pertain to the present. These lessons indicate that there is nothing to decide when it comes to safeguarding the lives of the vulnerable. Deliberately intended here is a 'violent' argument that refuses the liberal-democratic 'paradox' (Chantal Mouffe's term) and contravenes Arendt's own definition of politics as freedom – usually considered in the context of the hopeless, meandering 'tension' between self-determination and recognizing international obligations that has accomplished virtually nothing for the stateless in the past century – in pursuit rather of the 'guarantee of human dignity' that Arendt sought, the argument being that such historical

lessons render the justification of this guarantee, which nullifies self-determination in the delimited context of the right to asylum, dispositive.

The argument also draws largely upon the work of European thinkers, and
many of the principal thinkers utilized here were themselves victims of the
events of the Shoah. However, if anything, rather than granting a privilege to
European matters thereby, the argument is rather a bill of indictment against
European and other Western states, constituted as a robust theoretical critique
of their grotesque political failures. Alongside them, one can add apropos
of contemporary asylum politics several of the Gulf States such as Saudi
Arabia, as well as, for example, China, Japan, and South Korea, all of whom
have abysmal records on refugee intake, as well as the appalling treatment
of families at the U.S. Border and the failure of the Dubs Amendment in the
United Kingdom and the criminal mistreatment of asylum seekers in offshore
detention by Australia which has been held to be in violation of the Torture
Convention. By contrast, numerous states of the Global South, by choice or
by necessity, proffer hospitality to most of the world's dispossessed, from
Lebanon to Uganda to Bangladesh and beyond.[130] (It could be argued that
states in the developing world that border conflict zones have no choice but to
receive large numbers of refugees; however, Joseph Carens has importantly
noted that even relatively poorer states of the Global South have armies that
could keep people out by force if they chose, but it seems for the most part
that they do not so choose.)[131] At the same time, it is important not to silence
the voices and concerns of so many in need of assistance, now and into the
future, nor to speak for them, and hence multiple contemporary voices are
included here: 'nothing about us without us', except where the voices have
been silenced and a deliberate work of recollection is required so that they do
not disappear twice, the second time into the oblivion of forgetting.

The indignant voices of survivors of the Shoah concerning the asylum that
could have been actualized but was not, runs through the book as the sounding of the fire alarm that, despite being unheeded, continues to resound today,
for those who may or may not face extermination but face desperate straits
regardless. As Butler observes, the history of the Shoah should be consulted
(without the 'then' standing in for the 'now' which would risk blinding us to
contemporary concerns) 'in order to conduct the comparative and reflective
work that would allow us to derive principles of human conduct that would
make good on the promise not to reiterate in any way the crimes of that historical time'.[132] Butler is greatly influenced by Edward Said in making such
comparisons – her controversial book *Parting Ways*, hugely influential for
the present argument, concerned the possibility of the Jewish and Palestinian
peoples recognizing each other as sharing a history of exile. I am using her
quote in a deliberately universal context concerning refugee politics, but
it should be noted that Butler is arguing in part against the misuse of the

memory of the Shoah as a justification for the oppression of Palestinians – following Arendt's observation on the same issue, that the solution to one refugee problem is not the creation of another,[133] and calling for (following explicitly in Said's wake) a shared understanding between two historically dispossessed peoples that could form the basis of a new ethical cohabitation of Israel–Palestine. Thus, her above comment on the memory of the Shoah is also pertinent when placed alongside Said's eloquent summation in *After the Last Sky*:

> It is inadequate only to affirm that a people was dispossessed, oppressed or slaughtered, denied its rights and its political existence, without at the same time doing what Fanon did during the Algerian war, affiliating those horrors with the similar afflictions of other people . . . This does not mean a loss in historical specificity, but rather it guards against the possibility that a lesson learned about oppression in one place will be forgotten or violated in another place or time.[134]

The claim of the argument pursued here is that such lessons and comparative work are of universal import, and must inform a new and urgent concept of the political centred on the right to asylum. The spectres of the already disappeared, those now in exile and those still to be born who will also ultimately disappear, bring the stakes of this demand into stark relief. Walter Benjamin, forced to flee for his life by the Nazis, distinguished in his writing between ordinary life and just life, arguing that it was unacceptable to tolerate forms of unjust life: 'It is false and ignoble to say that existence is superior to just existence, if existence is simply meant to mean bare life.'[135] If the *very meaning of politics as such* can be reconfigured, perhaps the lighted fuse he warned of can be cut, and even the scale of displacement portended by the looming climate crisis can be rerouted from the desperate straits of masses of bare life in immiseration, to forms of actualization of the just life. The normative significance of a concept of the political that identifies asylum as fundamental to the meaning of politics is manifest: in multifarious ways, the right to asylum can stand in for humanitarian politics tout court (another way of understanding Derrida's formulation that ethics equals hospitality). In providing the vulnerable with their place in the sun, in the sense of Levinas's reformulation of Pascal where the egoism of the subject in its usurpation of a part of the earth is suspended, this enables the other to simply *be* and *belong*, to obtain a refuge for life in its precarity and to be recognized as a human bearer of dignity. It is a terrible thing to have to flee one's home, and not something to be valorized or romanticized; but as a matter of politics, whether those seeking asylum are fleeing genocide, or war, or ethnocide, or ethnic cleansing, or famine, or torture, or domestic violence, or sexual or gendered violence, or homophobic or transphobic violence, or indefinite compulsory military service, or crushing poverty, or a lack of medical care, or climate impacts and weather disasters, or human trafficking, or the effects of neocolonial destabilization and systemic injustice, or politico-ideological or religious oppression, or labour exploitation, or child exploitation – and whatever else one wants to add to a Dante-esque catalogue of horrors – *all* can be met by an asylum *response*, where being-in-relation and being-in-place amongst the unchosen givenness of plural humanity comes together in the actualization of politics as belonging. Politics equals asylum.

NOTES

1. Judith Butler, *Parting Ways: Jewishness and the Critique of Zionism* (New York, NY: Columbia University Press, 2012), p. 176.

2. Martin Heidegger, 'Nietzsche's Word: God is Dead', in *Off the Beaten Track*, eds. Julian Young and Kenneth Haynes (Cambridge: Cambridge University Press, 2002), p. 163.

3. Different terms will be employed throughout the book: refugees, stateless persons, people seeking asylum, migrants. These are categories that are distinguishable both theoretically and in law. For the most part I will refer to refugees; however, usage will vary as all of these categories, migrants aside (and the refugee–migrant distinction is increasingly and rightly called into question), fall under the rubric of what is sometimes referred to as the total global 'population of concern', and the divisions between them are not fixed, in that a person seeking asylum may become recognized as a refugee, a stateless person may or may not be a refugee, and so on. Millions of people who are internally displaced within their own state are not technically classified as refugees simply because they have not crossed an international border; nevertheless, they belong amongst the numbers of the globally displaced.

4. Studies estimate the numbers of people migrating due to climate change between 25 million and 1 billion by 2050, with 200 million the generally accepted figure. See the IOM report at https://www.ipcc.ch/apps/njlite/srex/njlite_download.php?id=5866, accessed 21 January 2020. For an overview of climate change and its likely impacts from a political theory perspective, including scientific context, see Joel Wainwright and Geoff Mann, *Climate Leviathan: A Political Theory of our Planetary Future* (London and New York, NY: Verso, 2018). For human rights law related to climate refugees, see the excellent work of Jane McAdam, in books such as *Climate Change, Forced Migration and International Law* (Oxford: Oxford University Press, 2012).

5. Maurice Blanchot, *The Writing of Disaster*, trans. Ann Smock (Lincoln, OR and London: University of Nebraska Press, 1995), pp. 28 and 3.

6. Friedrich Nietzsche, *On the Genealogy of Morals: A Polemic*, trans. Michael A. Scarpitti, intro. Robert C. Holub (London: Penguin, 2013), p. 15.

7. The fire alarm is a metaphor for warning about looming disaster used by Walter Benjamin in his collection of reflections entitled 'One Way Street'. See Walter

Benjamin, *One Way Street and Other Writings*, trans. J. A. Underwood, intro. Amit Chaudhuri (London: Penguin, 2009), p. 87. See also Michael Löwy, *Fire Alarm: Reading Walter Benjamin's 'On the Concept of History'* (London and New York, NY: Verso, 2016), p. 9.

8. David Scott FitzGerald, *Refuge Beyond Reach: How Rich Democracies Repel Asylum Seekers* (Oxford: Oxford University Press, 2019), p. 3.

9. See Reece Jones, *Violent Borders: Refugees and the Right to Move* (London and New York, NY: Verso, 2016).

10. Wendy Brown, 'Resisting Left Melancholia', in *Loss: The Politics of Mourning*, eds. David L. Eng and David Kazanjian (Berkeley, CA and Los Angeles, CA: University of California Press, 2003), pp. 458–65.

11. Emmanuel Levinas, *Proper Names*, trans. Michael B. Smith (Stanford, CA: Stanford University Press, 1996), p. 3. On the theme of presentiment in Levinas, see the text 'Signature' in *Difficult Freedom*, and the introductory note to *On Escape*, where he writes of his 'forebodings' concerning the looming consequences of Nazism, which was not apparent to all in 1935; similarly in 1934 in 'Reflections on the Philosophy of Hitlerism' Levinas already thought that what was at stake in the confrontation with Nazism was no mere political dispute but rather 'the very humanity of man' [*sic*].

12. The etymology of the term 'Holocaust' is linked to sacrificial burning, and thus its use carries the problematic resonance of understanding these events as some kind of sacrificial ritual, whereas 'Shoah' means more simply calamity or catastrophe in Hebrew. See Richard Evans, *In Hitler's Shadow* (New York, NY: Pantheon, 1989), p. 142.

13. Samuel Moyn, *Human Rights and the Uses of History*, 2nd edition (London and New York, NY: Verso, 2017), chapter seven.

14. Moyn, *Human Rights and the Uses of History*, p. 113.

15. This claim concerning the consequences of asylum in this particular historical epoch, must be distinguished from problematic claims that the Jewish people in some sense stand in for humanity tout court, in moral or symbolic terms. The point is that in the history of the Shoah, it is particularly clear that extermination was very often the consequence of exclusion and the closing of borders.

16. Löwy, *Fire Alarm*, p. 57.

17. Löwy, *Fire Alarm*, p. 62.

18. Hannah Arendt, 'A Reply to Eric Voegelin', in *Essays In Understanding 1930 1954: Formation, Exile and Totalitarianism*, ed. Jerome Kohn (New York, NY: Schocken, 1994), p. 404.

19. Arendt, 'A Reply to Eric Voegelin', pp. 403–4.

20. Jacques Derrida, *Archive Fever: A Freudian Impression*, trans. Eric Prenowitz (Chicago, IL: University of Chicago Press, 1996), p. 5.

21. This is elaborated with particular reference to the work of Andrew Benjamin, discussed in chapter 1. References to human dignity often raise the question of the dignity of non-human animals, and indeed a common question to Levinas scholars is whether his concept of the 'Face' applies to such animals. These questions are beyond the scope of the present work, which foregrounds the question of asylum for human animals, though in my view it is possible to extend Levinasian ethics to think through the

ethics of the treatment of non-human animals, even if it is an interpretation of his work that Levinas did not emphasize. Perhaps a more novel question for the present context might be: can one think, or dream, of a politics of asylum for non-human animals? Could such a zoopolitics of asylum be linked, for example, to rescue of mistreated animals from farms or to the disruption of the shipping of livestock across the seas to their slaughter? Given the ongoing planetary scale of animal cruelty and industrial slaughter of animals in the billions, the moral argument for refuge from harm is surely somewhat analogous, though what such a politics would look like in practice remains to be imagined.

22. I would like to acknowledge my debt to two thinkers who have done the most work on the relatively under-theorized nexus of Arendt–Levinas: Judith Butler, especially in *Parting Ways*, and Anya Topolski, *Arendt, Levinas, and Politics of Relationality* (London: Rowman & Littlefield International, 2015). I have taken up some other thinkers in addition to Arendt and Levinas and thus present a different constellation of thought than Butler or Topolski; nevertheless, their reflections have been invaluable to me. Topolski articulates a 'politics of relationality' which, similar to my own approach, combines Arendtian plurality with Levinasian alterity; however, due to some minor differences in our positions, as well as my having a more narrowly conceived project pertaining to the politics of asylum, I have not utilized that term. The difference is primarily one of emphasis – I am much closer to Butler in focusing upon the implications of 'unchosen plurality'. It is the delimitation of freedom in the political sphere – contrary to Arendt's definition of politics of freedom, and the challenge that poses to liberal-democratic as well as other political communities – that I am most concerned with in this chapter and the next.

23. FitzGerald, *Refuge Beyond Reach*, p. 1.

24. Immanuel Kant, 'Toward Perpetual Peace: A Philosophical Sketch', in *Towards Perpetual Peace and Other Writings on Politics, Peace and History*, ed. Pauline Kleingeld, trans. David L. Colclasure (New Haven, CT and London: Yale University Press, 2006), p. 82.

25. Hence the title of David Owen's new book, *What Do We Owe to Refugees?* (2020). This phrase is also to be found almost verbatim in Serena Parekh's book *Refugees and the Ethics of Forced Displacement* (New York, NY and London: Routledge, 2017), pp. 1 and 67 (and is thus indicative of a consistency in phrasing this problematic within political theory). I discuss Parekh's work (to which I am in general highly sympathetic) in chapter 1.

26. Didier Fassin, *Humanitarian Reason: A Moral History of the Present*, trans. Rachel Gomme (Berkley, CA, Los Angeles, CA, and London: University of California Press, 2012), p. 3.

27. FitzGerald, *Refuge Beyond Reach*, p. 7.

28. Hannah Arendt, *The Human Condition*, 2nd edition (Chicago, IL and London: University of Chicago Press, 1998), p. 7.

29. For a discussion of what can be seen as Copernican versus Ptolemaic changes to thought (revolutionary versus reformist), see the New Preface to Zizek, Sublime Object of Ideology, pp. vii–viii.

30. Butler, *Parting Ways*, p. 24.

31. Arendt, *The Human Condition*, p. 50.

32. Hannah Arendt, 'Stefan Zweig: Jews in the World of Yesterday', in *The Jewish Writings*, eds. Jermoe Kohn and Ron H. Feldman (New York, NY: Schocken, 2007), p. 317. 'Disgrace and honour are political concepts, categories of public life'.

33. Max Horkheimer and Theodor Adorno, *Dialectic of Enlightenment: Philosophical Fragments*, ed. Gunzelin Schmid Noerr, trans. Edmund Jephcott (Stanford, CA: Stanford University Press, 2002), p. 1.

34. Elias Canetti, *Der Beruf des Dichters* (München: Hanser Verlag, 1976), p. 1. I owe this quotation to Professor Dennis Schmidt, from a paper he gave at the annual Heidegger conference at Australian Catholic University in Melbourne in 2019.

35. Arendt used this term in relation to asylum in her speech upon acceptance of the Sonning Prize in 1975, shortly before her death. See discussion in chapter 2.

36. Márton Szabó, 'Politics versus the Political: Interpreting 'das Politische' in Carl Schmitt', *Distinktion: Journal of Social Theory*, Vol. 7, No. 1, 2006, p. 28.

37. Gopal Balakrishnan, *The Enemy: An Intellectual Portrait of Carl Schmitt* (London and New York, NY: Verso, 2002), pp. 102–4.

38. Immanuel Kant, *Grounding for the Metaphysics of Morals with On a Supposed Right to Lie because of Philanthropic Concerns*, trans. James W. Ellington, 3rd edition (Indianapolis, IN and Cambridge: Hackett Publishing Company, Inc., 1993), pp. 28 and 40.

39. Andrew Benjamin, *Virtue in Being: Towards an Ethics of the Unconditioned* (New York, NY: State University of New York Press, 2016), p. 37.

40. Hannah Arendt, *The Origins of Totalitarianism* (San Diego, CA, New York, NY, and London: Harvest Book of Harcourt Inc., 1976), pp. 293–94: 'This, moreover, had next to nothing to do with any material problem of overpopulation; it was a problem not of space but of political organization.' However, as noted in the Introduction and in subsequent chapters, Arendt was also capable of a certain prevarication on the question of numbers.

41. Emmanuel Levinas, *Is it Righteous to Be? Interviews with Emmanuel Levinas*, ed. Jill Robbins (Stanford, CA: Stanford University Press, 2001), 195.

42. Seyla Benhabib, 'Defending a Cosmopolitanism without Illusions. Reply to My Critics', *Critical Review of International Social and Political Philosophy*, Vol. 17, No. 6, 2014, p. 704.

43. 'The Suppliants', in Aeschylus, *Prometheus Bound and Other Plays*, trans. Philip Vellacott (London: Penguin, 1961), p. 65.

44. Paul Cartledge, '"Deep Plays": Theatre as Process in Athenian Civic Life', in *The Cambridge Companion to Greek Tragedy*, ed. P. E. Easterling (Cambridge: Cambridge University Press, 1997), p. 20. I owe this reference to Simon Critchley's discussion in chapter 11 of his book *Tragedy, the Greeks and Us* (New York, NY: Pantheon Books, 2019), p. 56.

45. Critchley, *Tragedy, the Greeks and Us*, p. 58.

46. Bertolt Brecht, *Sophocle's Antigone in a Version by Bertolt Brecht*, trans. Judith Malina (New York, NY: Applause Theatre Book Publishers, 1984).

47. Brecht, *Sophocle's Antigone in a Version by Bertolt Brecht*, p. 32.

48. Seyla Benhabib, *The Rights of Others* (Cambridge: Cambridge University Press, 2004).

49. I part company from Topolski on the question of Levinas's 'ethical politics'; Topolski prefers what she calls a political ethics, which remains within the orbit of Arendtian 'post-foundationalism' and refuses the Levinasian progression from ethics to the third and justice. Post-foundationalism means the refusal of the ethical as prior to the political and the acting of that out in justice in the move to the third, but such a move is either implicit in Arendt (it is sometimes uncertain), or arguably *should* be, if her defence of human plurality, as articulated by Butler, is to have any norma-tive meaning in line with her call for a 'guarantee' of human dignity. See Topolski, *Arendt, Levinas, and Politics of Relationality*, p. 36 and passim.

50. Arendt, *The Origins of Totalitarianism*, p. 299.

51. Slavoj Žižek, *Against the Double Blackmail: Refugees, Terror and Other Troubles with the Neighbours* (London: Allen Lane, 2016), p. 11.

52. Maximilien Robespierre, *Slavoj Žižek presents Robespierre: Virtue and Terror* (London and New York, NY: Verso, 2007), p. 110.

53. The failures of liberalism in relation to the politics of asylum will be dis-cussed throughout the book but especially in chapter 1. For a broader account of the failings of liberalism, see Domenico Losurdo, *Liberalism: A Counter-History* (London and New York, NY: Verso, 2014).

54. Moriz Scheyer, *Asylum: A Survivor's Flight from Nazi-Occupied Vienna through Wartime France*, trans. P. N. Singer (New York, NY, Boston, MA, and London: Little, Brown and Company, 2016), p. 124. Nietzsche's use of this term is found in Friedrich Nietzsche, *Thus Spoke Zarathustra: A Book for Everyone and No One*, trans. R. J. Hollingdale (London: Penguin, 1969), p. 75. Kant's reference to the state as a 'monster' that may swallow its neighbours is found in Immanuel Kant, *Religion within the Limits of Reason Alone*, trans. Theodor M. Green and Hoyt H. Hudson (New York, NY: Harper and Row, 1960), pp. 28–29.

55. Richard Kearney, *Strangers Gods and Monsters: Interpreting Otherness* (Oxon: Routledge, 2003), p. 5.

56. Slavoj Žižek, in deliberate counterpoint to Levinas, emphasizes the 'mon-strosity' of the unknown other in the context of the 'neighbour', and has been criti-cized for his remarks about a clash of civilizations when non-European refugees arrive in Europe. In dialectical fashion, Žižek will claim that this monstrosity of the other is not a reason to exclude them, but the rhetorics of monstrousness and the focus on a Samuel Huntington-type clash of cultures seem at minimum problematic. Levinas has also been guilty of terrible myopia concerning non-European cultures, referring in one paper to 'Asiatic hordes' and problematically suggesting that Palestinians can be considered the enemy for Israelis (although the latter remark is more complex and nuanced than the former; it occurs in the context of his breaking his silence on Israel, a silence one could argue implied criticisms, in order to explicitly criticize the Sabra and Shatila massacres). For Žižek, see Slavoj Žižek, Eric L. Santner, and Kenner Reinhard, *The Neighbor: Three Inquiries in Political Theology* (Chicago, IL and London: University of Chicago Press, 2005), p. 162. For a discussion of Levinas's poor remarks (which are serious and should not be ignored, even by his partisans – Judith Butler is usefully explicit about this in her reading of him, even if at times she overstates the case), see Howard Caygill, *Levinas and the Political* (Oxon,

London, and New York, NY: Routledge, 2002), pp. 1 and 182–85. That is leaving to the side actual racists like Jean Raspail and his terrible book *The Camp of the Saints* (Petoskey, MI: Social Contract Press, 1987), which can be dismissed for all time with the following observation: his book posits a great fear that France will be overrun with a million migrants (from India, for some reason, the departure point and the arrival point seem rather random); in fact the number jumps around in the book, sometimes 800,000 (p. 4), sometimes a million ('for God's sake, a million immigrants!' – p. 76), testimony to the terrified irrationality of the argument; not only is this kind of fearful inconsistency, terrible writing (objectively and leaving the content to the side on this point, the authorial voice intrudes awkwardly into the text throughout – it is simply *badly written*) Germany's successful absorption of just such a number of people in a single year is the final nail in the coffin of such arguments when it comes to Europe, a fact already established in manifold places in the Global South, where huge populations of displaced persons are hosted without threatening the collapse of the state. This pathological fear of numbers as the phantasm of scarcity and social collapse is directly addressed, with reference to Derrida and the tradition of hospitality in France, in chapter 4.

57. For an interesting discussion of the term 'fear' in the context of forced displacement, see John Washington, *The Dispossessed: A Story of Asylum at the US-Mexican Border and Beyond* (London and New York, NY: Verso, 2020).

58. François Raffoul, *The Origins of Responsibility* (Bloomington, IN and Indianapolis, IN: Indiana University Press, 2010), pp. 17–18 and passim.

59. Emmanuel Levinas, *Totality and Infinity: An Essay on Exteriority*, trans. Alphonso Lingis (Pittsburgh, PA: Duquesne University Press, 2007), p. 69.

60. As will be explored in chapter 1, this is a minor point of difference between Levinas and Andrew Benjamin, but for both thinkers, ontology devoid of ethics is in no way originary. Whether ethics is prior to ontology or is anoriginally bound up with it may ultimately not be of major consequence; what is decisive in the work of these thinkers is the shift in the relationship of ethics to ontology, in that the former is no longer relegated to a secondary, derivative, or merely assertoric status.

61. This philosophical anthropology has been developed by Andrew Benjamin across multiple works, including the already mentioned *Virtue in Being* as well as *Place, Commonality and Judgment: Continental Philosophy and the Ancient Greeks* (London and New York, NY: Continuum, 2012); *Working With Walter Benjamin: Recovering a Political Philosophy* (Edinburgh: Edinburgh University Press, 2013); and *Towards a Relational Ontology: Philosophy's Other Possibility* (New York, NY: SUNY Press, 2015).

62. I thank Andrew Benjamin for bringing this connection to my attention.

63. Anna Jurkevics, 'Hannah Arendt Reads Carl Schmitt's The Nomos of the Earth: A Dialogue on Law and Geopolitics from the Margins', *European Journal of Political Theory*, Vol. 16, No. 3, 2017, p. 349.

64. Arendt, *The Origins of Totalitarianism*, p. ix.

65. See Jurkevics, 'Hannah Arendt Reads Carl Schmitt's The Nomos of the Earth', footnote 2, p. 362; she speculates that Arendt read Schmitt's book in 1952 owing to the citations in her notebooks.

66. The mutinous slaves can be interpreted as the Nazis themselves having commandeered the state with Schmitt as their supposedly unwilling hostage; an interesting, if less plausible reading, is Schmitt's resentment at being held captive by American occupiers and being interrogated by a Jewish American army officer, after the war. For a discussion of this self-pitying analogy of Schmitt's, see the Foreword by Tracey B. Strong to Carl Schmitt, *Political Theology: Four Chapters on the Concept of Sovereignty*, trans. George Schwab (Chicago, IL: University of Chicago Press, 2005), pp. viii–x and xxxiii.

67. Carl Schmitt, *The Nomos of the Earth*, trans. G. L. Ulmen (New York, NY: Telos Press Publishing, 2006), pp. 37 and 39.

68. Schmitt, *The Nomos of the Earth*, p. 68: 'In this Aristotle passage [of the *Politics*], *nomos* can clearly be seen as an original distribution of land'; p. 69: 'Thus, the original meaning of *nomos* – its origin in land-appropriation – still is recognizable'. See p. 70 for Schmitt's denial that *nomos* means law.

69. On the sophistication of Indigenous land management, see, for example, Bill Gamage, *The Biggest Estate on Earth: How Aborigines Made Australia* (Sydney: Allen & Unwin, 2011).

70. Losurdo, *Liberalism: A Counter-History*, pp. 4 and 15.

71. Achille Mbembe, *Critique of Black Reason*, trans. Laurent Dubois (Durham, NC and London: Duke University Press, 2017), p. 79.

72. See Richard Cohen, 'The Power of Carl Schmitt: Fascism, Dualism and Justice', *Religions*, Vol. 10, No. 7, 2019, p. 2.

73. Jurkevics, 'Hannah Arendt Reads Carl Schmitt's Nomos of the Earth', p. 350.

74. Jurkevics, 'Hannah Arendt Reads Carl Schmitt's Nomos of the Earth', p. 349.

75. See the discussion in Liisi Keedus, '"Human and Nothing but Human": How Schmittian is Hannah Arendt's Critique of Human Rights and International Law?', *History of European Ideas*, Vol. 37, No. 2, 2011, pp. 190–96.

76. Jurkevics, 'Hannah Arendt Reads Carl Schmitt's Nomos of the Earth', p. 350. For Arendt's understanding of *nomos*, see Arendt, *The Human Condition*, note 62 on p. 63.

77. Hannah Arendt (New York, NY: Harcourt, 1977), p. 19.

78. Jurkevics, 'Hannah Arendt Reads Carl Schmitt's Nomos of the Earth', p. 358.

79. Arendt, *The Human Condition*, p. 64.

80. Arendt, *The Human Condition*, p. 43. The clear allusion to the 'Greeks' in this passage seems to be to Aristotle's discussion of the limits of the polis in the *Politics*, though perhaps she also has in mind the absurdly specific number of 5,040 citizens mentioned in Plato's *The Laws*, and in any event is endorsing the principle of moderation (in her words, it is 'one of the political virtues par excellence' – Arendt, *The Human Condition*, p. 191). The vagaries of such notions of moderation as they affect the politics of asylum are interrogated in chapter 3 in a disputation staged between Levinas and Aristotle over the limits of political justice.

81. Arendt, *The Origins of Totalitarianism*, p. 302.

82. The argument here is that modern liberal-democratic societies and capitalist systems are built upon brutal exploitation which thus, in a different register to the main argument of this book, puts in question the moral right of such exploitative societies to

maintain their sovereignty against the needs of others. For a few examples, see Susan Buck-Morss, 'Envisioning Capital: Political Economy on Display', *Critical Inquiry*, Vol. 22, No. 2, Winter 1995, p. 444; the section of Karl Marx's *Capital* on 'primitive accumulation'; Adam Hochschild's devastating expose of Belgian conquest in the Congo in *King Leopold's Ghost*, which also recalls of course Joseph Conrad's *Heart of Darkness*. The point is – though it is not the seminal thrust of the overall argument – that the right to self-determination of such societies such that they would exclude the vulnerable (in addition to the destruction of Indigenous life-worlds), based as they are on such practices of self-constitution (Buck-Morss argues that such exploitative economics precedes the constitution of the political realm), is highly dubious; this is what political theorists and politicians may find themselves implicitly defending when they defend the right to self-determination in relation to excluding outsiders.

83. Pascals' Pensées, 112 – quoted in Emmanuel Levinas, *Otherwise Than Being or Beyond Essence*, trans. Alphonso Lingis (Pittsburgh, PA: Duquesne University Press, 2008), p. vii.

84. The connection between Schmitt and Heidegger is intriguing – in many ways they seem to enjoy the same ineluctable yet controversial influence in their disciplines, political theory, and philosophy, respectively. Both joined the party in the same month, and both, while having been early supporters of the regime, found themselves out of favour with the regime by the mid to late 1930s.

85. Levinas, *Totality and Infinity*, p. 46. One should note here the potential utility of the discourses of both Arendt and Levinas for the critique of colonialism and the defence of Indigenous rights.

86. Luce Irigaray, *Sharing the World* (London and New York, NY: Continuum, 2008).

87. Butler, *Parting Ways*, pp. 23–24.

88. https://timesofmalta.com/articles/view/tacit-genocides-and-the-curse-of-a-p unitive-morality.638438, retrieved 19 January 2020.

89. Hannah Arendt, *Eichmann in Jerusalem: A Report on the Banality of Evil*, intro. Amos Elon (New York, NY and London: Penguin, 2006), p. 233. For Mbembe's concept of necropolitics, see Achille Mbembe, *Necropolitics*, trans. Steve Corcoran (Durham, NC and London: Duke University Press, 2019).

90. André Schwarz-Bart, *The Last of the Just* (London: Penguin, 1977), p. 278. To Schwarz-Bart belongs the very first and the very last words of this book, my testament to him and to the impact his great novel had on me, a gesture also of *listening* to the voices of indignation of the victims themselves. Every member of Schwarz-Bart's family was murdered in the Shoah.

91. Giorgio Agamben, *Homo Sacer: Sovereign Power and Bare Life*, trans. Daniel Heller-Roazen (Stanford, CA: Stanford University Press, 1998), pp. 10–11.

92. Simon Critchley, *The Problem with Levinas* (Oxford: Oxford University Press, 2015), pp. 41–42.

93. Emmanuel Levinas, *Beyond the Verse*, trans. Gary D. Mole (London: Continuum, 2007), p. 39.

94. Noam Chomsky, *Who Rules the World?* (New York, NY: Henry Holt and Company, 2016), pp. 251–252.

95. Natascha Elena Uhlmann, *Abolish ICE* (New York, NY: OR Books, 2019), p. 7.

96. See https://euobserver.com/migration/145900, retrieved 31 January 2020.

97. For a view of the right to have rights as lacking the normative dimension which I view as plausible, see the essay by Samuel Moyn in Stephanie DeGooyer, Alastair Hunt, Lida Maxwell, and Samuel Moyn, *The Right To Have Rights*, Afterword Astra Taylor (London and New York, NY: Verso, 2018).

98. Arendt, *The Human Condition*, p. 220.

99. Judith N. Shklar, *Legalism: Laws, Morals and Political Trials* (Cambridge, MA and London: Harvard University Press, 1986).

100. Immanuel Kant, *The Conflict of Faculties*, trans. Mary J. Gregor (New York, NY: Abaris Books, 1979), p. xviii.

101. For a discussion of Kafka as depicting the plight of refugees, see the Conclusion (as discussed in Chapter Two) to Ayten Gündoğdu, *Rightlessness in an Age of Rights: Hannah Arendt and the Contemporary Struggles of Migrants* (Oxford: Oxford University Press, 2015). One might see in this a reflection of the struggles of Indigenous peoples, who are often caught by the paradox of seeking justice in the juridico-political systems that represent the oppressive colonizing power. (I thank Suzy Kilmister for drawing my attention to this point.) Given that in many settler-colonial societies, asylum seekers and Indigenous peoples are amongst the most vulnerable people in those societies, this points to the possibility of the recognition of common struggle, which has indeed been movingly evinced at times, for example, via the issuing of Aboriginal passports to asylum seekers as an act of solidarity. A similar solidarity was proffered by an Aboriginal delegation led by William Cooper which marched to the German consulate in Melbourne in 1938 to protest Germany's treatment of the Jewish people. This solidarity amongst oppressed groups is discussed in the 'Coda' that concludes this book.

102. Immanuel Kant, 'The Philosophy Faculty Versus the Faculty of Law', in *The Conflict of the Faculties* (New York, NY: Abaris Books, 1979), p. 27.

103. See Peg Birmingham, *Hannah Arendt and Human Rights: The Predicament of Common Responsibility* (Bloomington, IN and Indianapolis, IN: Indiana University Press, 2006), p. 4; and Andrew Benjamin, 'The Problem of Authority in Arendt and Aristotle', *Philosophy Today*, Vol. 60, No. 2, Spring 2016, pp. 253–76. In Birmingham's excellent book on Arendt, the emphasis is much more on natality rather than plurality; I share her views, but have chosen to emphasize 'unchosen plurality' via the Butlerian reading of Arendt as the 'unchosen' aspect constitutes a fundamental move in my argument, to wit that responsibility is not consciously willed but is something which we are always-already called to, which is even imposed upon us (hence the concatenation of Arendt with Levinas).

104. Benedict Anderson, *Imagined Communities: Reflections on the Origins and Spread of Nationalism* (London and New York, NY: Verso, 2016), p. 3.

105. This 'othering' of the world is described by (Andrew) Benjamin as a 'counter-measure', the 'left-handed blow' of which Walter Benjamin writes that instantiates the weak messianic power that others the world, that establishes an opening Andrew

Benjamin describes as a 'caesura of allowing'. See Andrew Benjamin, *Working with Walter Benjamin: Recovering a Political Philosophy* (Edinburgh: University of Edinburgh Press, 2013).

106. Arendt, *Essays In Understanding*, pp. 335–38.

107. Jacques Rancière, *Hatred of Democracy* (London and New York, NY: Verso, 2007), p. 58.

108. Rancière, *Hatred of Democracy*, p. 59.

109. Rancière, *Hatred of Democracy*, p. 74.

110. Jacques Rancière, 'Who is the Subject of the Rights of Man?', *South Atlantic Quarterly*, Vol. 103, No. 2/3, Spring/Summer 2004, p. 308.

111. Rancière, 'Who is the Subject of the Rights of Man?', p. 307.

112. Étienne Balibar, 'Man and Citizen: Who's Who?', *The Journal of Political Philosophy*, Vol. 2, No. 2, 1994, p. 105.

113. Étienne Balibar, *Equaliberty*, trans. James Ingram (Durham, NC and London: Duke University Press, 2014), p. viii.

114. Arendt, *The Human Condition*, p. 199.

115. Benjamin, 'The Problem of Authority', p. 260.

116. See Michael J. Hyde, ed., *The Ethos of Rhetoric* (Columbia, SC: University of South Carolina Press, 2004), pp. 2–4. Hyde's book discusses the debates about how *ethos* should be understood in Aristotle, and how it is deployed in his different texts.

117. Martin Heidegger, 'Letter on Humanism', in *Basic Writings*, ed. David Farrell Krell (London and New York, NY: Routledge, 1993), p. 174.

118. Heidegger, 'Letter on Humanism', pp. 175–76.

119. Heidegger, 'Letter on Humanism', p. 165.

120. Martin Heidegger, 'The Origin of the Work of Art', in *Basic Writings* (London and New York, NY: Routledge, 1993), esp. pp. 108–12.

121. Jacques Derrida, *On Cosmopolitanism and Forgiveness*, trans. Mark Dooley and Michael Huges (London and New York, NY: Routledge, 2001), pp. 16–17.

122. Raffoul, *The Origins of Responsibility*, pp. 8–9. For the subject as hostage, see, for example, Levinas, *Otherwise Than Being*, p. 112.

123. Raffoul, *The Origins of Responsibility*, p. 18.

124. Levinas, *Otherwise Than Being*, p. 116.

125. This is in part a pedagogical gesture; I have found in my teaching that theory is often best illuminated for students when it is concretized into historical or contemporary examples. For a more in-depth discussion of this relationship, see Derrida's seminars in Jacques Derrida, *Theory and Practice*, trans. David Wills (Chicago, IL: University of Chicago Press, 2019).

126. Derrida, *Theory and Practice*, p. 25.

127. See Zoe O'Reilly, *The In-Between Spaces of Asylum and Migration: A Participatory Visual Approach* (London: Palgrave MacMillan, 2020), p. 101.

128. Underscoring this point that the Jewish Danes were saved qua Danes, and not as Jewish refugees (although there were a small number of those who were saved also) is the title of a major work on this rescue operation, *Countrymen* (New York, NY: Alfred E. Knopf, 2013) by Bo Lidegaard.

129. Jacques Derrida, *Specters of Marx: The State of the Debt, the Work of Mourning & The New International*, trans. Peggy Kamuf (New York, NY and London: Routledge, 1994).

130. The annual UNHCR 'Global Trends' report can be accessed online for precise figures, which comprehensively demonstrates that the vast number of displaced persons in the world are hosted in the Global South.

131. See Joseph H. Carens, *The Ethics of Immigration* (Oxford: Oxford University Press, 2013), p. 220.

132. Butler, *Parting Ways*, p. 201.

133. Arendt, *Origins of Totalitarianism*, p. 290.

134. Edward Said, *After the Last Sky* (London: Faber & Faber, 1986), p. 44. I owe this quotation to Judith Butler's essay on Edward Said and Martin Buber. See Judith Butler, 'Versions of Binationalism in Said and Buber', in *Martin Buber: His Intellectual and Scholarly Legacy*, ed. Sam Shonkoff (Leiden and Boston, MA: Brill, 2018).

135. Walter Benjamin, 'On the Critique of Violence', in *One-Way Street and Other Writings* (London: Penguin, 2009), p. 26.

Chapter 1

A New Guarantee

This book will present subjectivity as welcoming the Other, as hospitality; in it the idea of infinity is consummated.

– Emmanuel Levinas, *Totality and Infinity*[1]

Plurality is the law of the earth.

– Hannah Arendt, *The Life of the Mind*[2]

INTRODUCTION

Climate change, refugees, human trafficking, international terrorism, drug cartels, pandemics, and other transnational issues, have demonstrated beyond any doubt that the 'imagined communities' of nation-states are not fit for purpose in addressing problems that transcend the limits prescribed by the Westphalian conception of sovereignty. These are globally shared concerns, with the potential to impact all of humanity. If cohabitation, the lived experience of plurality, is the law of the earth, then political communities, to the extent that they are concerned with the actualization of the just life, as opposed to mere life (following Walter Benjamin's distinction), must be concerned with asylum in a way that doesn't limit their response to the rights of their own citizenry, and the defence of their sovereign borders. To deny this is to deny the very rationale of politics as providing a 'world' of human construction lived in common upon the earth, the space of appearance (quoting Arendt) 'where I appear to others as others appear to me, where men [*sic*] exist not merely like other living or inanimate things but make their appearance explicitly . . . to men the reality of the world is guaranteed by the presence of others'.[3]

This chapter examines Hannah Arendt's call for a 'new guarantee' of human dignity, to be found in a 'new law on earth', and a 'new political principle', that would safeguard the rights of the stateless and ensure their right to protection and to belong to an organized political community.[4] Where the argument parts company from Arendt is in the necessity of this occurring within 'newly defined territorial entities', which, however desirable, cannot be awaited, given the ongoing crisis of mass statelessness.[5] It may be that a move beyond nationalism and sovereign states to bi-national or post-national states, or a move beyond the state form, or a shift from an emphasis upon sovereignty to more open modes of cohabitation, would serve to fulfil the new law on earth; but the new law should not depend upon such uncertain eventualities. The *ethos* of responsibility relevant to the guarantee would be that which pertains to any political community which recognizes that the givenness of unchosen human plurality *is* the law, the *nomos*, of the earth. Further, the claim is that the upholding of this law via the *active preservation* of human plurality is normatively dispositive, an imperative (though not of reciprocal universality bound to an autonomous will in Kant's sense, but rather derived from an account of human dignity otherwise construed in Arendtian–Levinasian terms), unconditional and absolute, admitting of no exceptions. No political actor may claim that parts of humanity do not deserve to belong, either on the earth tout court (a genocidal position) or simply to organized political communities, including those already extant (where exclusion may be tantamount to a genocidal position, or at least necropolitical, a tacit putting-to-death or allowing to die). If politics is recognized as that which is concerned with actively preserving human plurality, then to stray from this law of the earth is to violate the political as such. Justice in this context means recognizing the responsibility to ensure the ability of human beings to appear among each other and actualize their potentiality in mutual belonging and cohabitation (with both the challenges and security that such cohabitation involves).

Consequently, the *telos* of the political is the active preservation of plurality, the realization of which necessarily entails absolute respect for the right to asylum. In this sense, asylum as the realization of politics is proper to the identity of all political communities – without exception. Asylum is bound up with the fundamental meaning of politics – the provision of a space of appearances where plural human beings can appear amongst each other and exercise their innate capacity for natality, to take action and initiative, in Arendt's sense, or in the words of Machiavelli, to introduce a new order of things. In the 'Letter on Humanism' (which Arendt thought highly of), Heidegger, eschewing the simplistic formulations of existentialism, expounds upon the nature of human beings qua *humanitas*, as bound up with an *ethos* related to dwelling as the space of welcome where the 'unfamiliar one' may draw near, as discussed in the Introduction. Heidegger argues that 'this thinking is not ethics in the first instance, because it is ontology'.[6] Heidegger will go on to suggest that *humanitas* lies ultimately beyond both ethics and ontology, yet it is nevertheless tied to *ethos*.[7] While this move beyond ethics and ontology may represent an important resistance to metaphysical seizure of concepts such as the human (hence his reference to *humanitas* rather than humanism, a thinking of what is proper to human beings that is not yet an -ism), it is necessary to stipulate, as a philosophical anthropology, the ethical and ontological significance to human beings of being able to appear amongst each other and have their dignity respected. Andrew Benjamin, as discussed further on in the chapter, refers to the 'anoriginal' relationship of ethics and ontology in humanity's being-in-place and being-in-common, and Emmanuel Levinas will write of the ethical priority of giving place (and giving way if necessary) to the other. Despite Heidegger's essay providing a clearing for the thinking of *humanitas*, it does not necessarily help in explicating a normative political understanding or praxis (as Heidegger acknowledges), and Levinas is right to reproach Heidegger for a failure to emphasize ethical matters – especially given the latter's political commitments to Nazism. Levinas's entire post-war philosophical project can be seen as a disputation with Heidegger on the implications of his philosophy, given that commitment. The denial of belonging within the human 'world' (a world of human construction, as opposed to the physical earth) is a crime against *humanitas*, the *ethos* of that which is proper to the being of being-human, a denial which Germany Jewry faced at the very time that Heidegger chose to cooperate with the Nazis. The human being as *zoon politikon*, a political animal, as well as a placed being (that is, who requires a place to inhabit), who lives in common with others, requires the establishment and guarantee of a common world in order for their humanity to be fully realized. The fulfilment of this can be achieved via an *ethos* of responsibility which is manifest in respect for the right to asylum. In this sense, the new guarantee of a new law on earth is a law not just of the earth but of the *world*, that human beings build and share together.

A *guarantee* is a strong claim, one that, semantically as well as etymologically (of which more below), goes beyond an offer, a gracious welcome, a promise or a contract – it is an unbreakable commitment or absolute assurance. The difficult task of establishing the above arguments concerning the active preservation of plurality qua *nomos* of the earth as a 'guarantee' is the work of what follows. Despite this difficulty, the manifest failure of political communities, especially sovereign states, to improve conditions for stateless persons both historically and in contemporary experience necessitates the positing of a stronger claim concerning the meaning of 'the political', which might serve to reorient 'politics' as it is realized in the world - that is, no mere semantics. If politics is defined as freedom (according to Arendt), then it might ostensibly be viewed as opposed to the absolutism suggested by the notion of a guarantee. Arendt herself deployed the term guarantee more or less as a synonym for promising, as will be discussed further on in the chapter; however, the potential disjuncture between these terms opens up a dynamic field of inquiry into the realization of guarantees within politics, and the possible construction of a concept of the political around such a guarantee. Even if the promise and the guarantee are to be regarded as coterminous in Arendt's thinking, it may be possible and indeed necessary to disjoin them. Arendt, in *On Violence*, insisted upon rigour in the deployment of political terminology: 'It is, I think, a rather sad reflection on the present state of political science that our terminology does not distinguish among such key words as "power", "strength", "force", "authority", and finally, "violence" – all of which refer to distinct, different phenomena and would hardly exist unless they did.'[8] Here, a similar thought is ventured apropos of the difference between the nature of a promise and the nature of a guarantee. The promise (*pro* – 'forward', *mittere* – 'send'), to put forward or send forth, is an assurance made about future action, but in politics, a promise may be conditional upon the possibility of its realization or circumstances; a guarantee would be that which pertains regardless of circumstance. That is, a promise is arguably a less stringent and therefore more palatable stipulation available to political thinkers and decision-makers; political theorists, Arendt amongst them, are wary of the violent absolutism of a guarantee divorced from or going beyond the notion of promise, as the undoing of the freely decided nature of political action and the possible destruction of the political realm. One might think in this connection of Heinrich Von Kleist's novella *Michael Kohlhaas*, where the wronged Kohlhaas' frustrated and absolutist quest for justice, beginning in the mistreatment visited upon his horse by a nobleman, ends with him all but burning down the state in pursuit of redress. In her *Denktagebuch* (thought journal) dated September 1951 (i.e. about a year after she writes the Preface to *Origins* which calls for a new guarantee of human dignity), Arendt writes the following:

> By applying the absolute – justice, for example, or the 'ideal' in general . . . to an end, one first makes unjust, bestial actions possible, because the 'ideal', justice itself, no longer exists as a yardstick, but has become an achievable, producible end within the world. In other words, the realization of philosophy abolishes philosophy, the realization of the 'absolute' indeed abolishes the absolute from the world. And so finally the ostensible realization of man simply abolishes men.[9]

To seek a guarantee ('the absolute') of a particular just outcome means the potential undoing of any possibility of action of space of freedom whatsoever – at least, such would be the concern evinced in this passage by Arendt. In the context of the politics of asylum, this concern about absolutes imposing upon the freedom of political communities would translate into issues such as the delimitation of self-determination, the disruption of social cohesion, the supposed threat of terrorists or other undesirables such as criminal gangs, limits to absorptive capacity, economic downturn, and the primary obligation to one's own citizens, were societies to guarantee the right to asylum for all who claim it. But the obverse of this concern is the rolling disaster of statelessness. Borrowing Kafka's remark about hope, this disaster 'has been given – but not to us', that is, not to those who already live in safe conditions. The disaster has already happened, to the Jewish people in the Shoah (including Arendt herself, forced to flee as a refugee and who spent time in a concentration camp), to the Palestinians in *al-Naqba*, the Romani in the Shoah and their ongoing persecution and expulsions, the *Meds Yeghern* (explicitly, the *genocide*) of the Armenians, the mass slaughter and displacement of the Syrians, the Rohingya, the Tamils, the Uighurs, the Eritreans, the Sudanese, Central Americans, to name but a few in a long list of history's exiles, a 'universal' history of oppression to which I will return in the Coda that concludes the book. The abolition of 'men' that Arendt feared has already happened, is happening, and will continue to happen. What is the evidence that a change of asylum approach would produce a collapse of political stability, or the realization of any of these counter-fears? Is it not in fact the case that the protection of vulnerable human life can actually *increase* political stability (as will be argued further on in this chapter)? Is the motivating concern of theorists, to preserve those few human societies where a degree of political freedom has been established? But are not these societies also the societies of conquest and rapaciousness, often built upon slavery and colonialism (as Judith Butler observes in *The Force of Non-Violence*, that states are formed from racial violence) – in which case, should they even have an open-ended moral claim to maintain themselves in their present form?[10] The exploration of these concerns is the central task in the elaboration of an *ethos* of responsibility that recognizes plurality as the law of the earth, and asylum as attendant to plurality's preservation and thus the realization of politics. Margaret Canovan argues that 'however committed she herself [Arendt] might be to the ideas of equal worth and equal human rights, she certainly did not suppose that this was something that could be demonstrated or deduced from human plurality'.[11] The argument that follows will directly oppose Arendt's/Canovan's view and articulate a reading of Arendt's own concepts that goes beyond her own account of them, particularly with reference to the work of Judith Butler. The concern Arendt had for absolutes in politics will be countered with the concern that politics delimited to a space of freedom that avoids the use of normative banisters has decisively failed to produce a just politics for exiled humanity. It is not a question of seeking to remove freedom and the possibility of action – the kind of danger she imputes to the passion for justice shared by figures from Robespierre to Marx – but to side with these figures in the insistence that normative claims to justice be the central work of politics. In this context, relating to asylum, this

results in putting freedom into question, where it requires justification in the face
of demands of ethical responsibility, then translated into just political acts that
will safeguard the givenness of human plurality. Indeed, the etymological root
of 'guarantee' refers to protection, defence, giving security.[12] This is distinct
from the mere 'sending-forward' of a promise.

But how can the centring of asylum as a guarantee at the heart of the
political be asserted, in the face of an entire tradition of political philosophy
which sees asylum as a supplementary addendum to the life of a political
community? Joseph Carens, a liberal theorist noted for his generous writings
on the rights of refugees and a famous exponent of open borders, nevertheless
defines asylum as a 'secondary, derivative duty' – a remarkable phraseology,
which encapsulates the limits of liberal and social-contract thought.[13] For even
when asylum is construed as a generous tradition of hospitality, in liberal and
social-contract theory it is secondary to the self-determination of bounded
political societies and the responsibility to their own members, whose own
preservation and escape from the state of nature are seen as paramount. Or if
not an addendum, then a right of cosmopolitan citizenship (Seyla Benhabib)[14]
or visitation (Immanuel Kant)[15] or an ongoing, agonistic 'paradox' between
liberal universalist claims and the workings of a democracy which requires
the identification of a demos (Chantal Mouffe), none of which posit the right
to asylum as central to the meaning of the political as such. Mouffe: 'To
discard the illusion of a possible reconciliation of ethics and politics and to
come to terms with the never-ending interrogation of the political by the ethical, this is indeed the only way of acknowledging the democratic paradox'.[16]
Benhabib calls for 'first-admittance rights' for refugees, while also arguing
for the necessity of democratic legitimacy in determining citizenship: 'it is
inconceivable that democratic legitimacy can be sustained without some
clear demarcation of those in the name of whom the laws have been enacted
from those upon whom the laws are not binding'.[17] While Benhabib calls for
porous borders and a laudable, morally compassionate approach to refugees,
she is unwilling to move past the agonistic logic of democratic deliberation
in its interplay with universal demands, which poses a significant problem
given the record of democracies to date on asylum (yet the generosity of her
position should also be noted). Serena Parekh has also done important work
on Arendt and on refugees, wrestling with the problem of 'encampment', the
real-world problem of stateless persons being kept in long-term camps rather
than being allowed to enter into sovereign states.[18] While I have considerable
sympathy for Parekh's argument, in seeking to address the lived reality of
the plight of the vulnerable, the emphasis upon encampment, there is the risk
that the fundamental challenge to business as usual that I argue is required
will be marginalized; similarly in her analysis of Arendt's work, as in much
of the wider commentary on Arendt, Parekh remains faithful to Arendt's own

emphases and trajectory of thought, whereas the present work seeks to challenge that thought more radically.[19]

One might think that a socialist-internationalist response could conceive of asylum as the project of politics, in a universalizing solidarity beyond the constraints of nations and borders, and this may be true on a theoretical level; however, there is no shortage of historical rejoinders concerning the problematic interactions of socialist or communist states.[20] To be sure, as I observe in chapter 4 in an examination of the history of asylum in France, refugees have often fared much better under socialist governments than under right-wing governments, a common (though not consistent) trajectory that should be noted. Marx was also correct to insist in 'On the Jewish Question' that true emancipation requires more than formal, political rights, but requires material emancipation also, that rights are 'not enough', in Samuel Moyn's phrase; thus Marxism is indeed the 'unsurpassable horizon' that Sartre took it to be, in a world dominated by capitalist societies and their crimes that very often contribute to or produce refugee flows. However, the concept of the political pursued here, which centres asylum at the heart of politics, represents a somewhat competing position to historical materialism, in subjecting all societies, Marxist and non-Marxist alike, to judgement based upon their comportment with the imperative to safeguard human plurality as such (both actually existing liberalism and communism/socialism are subject to critical scrutiny from this perspective).

Nor does a position of 'open borders' yet meet the standard of an *ethos* of responsibility concerning the right to asylum, in that simply opening or even eliminating one's borders does not constitute an active solicitude on the part of political communities to outsiders. It may be necessary to do more than erase or demilitarize a border, but rather to actively venture beyond it to aid those in distress. This would also be the obverse of what states currently implement in the form of massive funding to maintain detention centres outside of the Global North, in places such as in Libya, designed to prevent people seeking asylum from arriving in Europe, or the 3 billion dollars paid by the EU to Turkey to prevent refugees from travelling onwards to Europe. As illustrative of an active *ethos* of responsibility, one might think of the initiative of Raoul Wallenberg to save Hungarian Jewry in the Second World War, or the Italian Navy's (now defunct) 'Mare Nostrum' programme which rescued migrants from the Mediterranean, or the activists of 'No More Deaths' in Arizona, who leave food, water, and supplies in the desert and provide first aid for refugees crossing the border; these examples are discussed further in subsequent chapters. Having open borders may also fail to privilege asylum in conditions of manifest urgency, when it would be arguably necessary to distinguish potential refugees from other less urgent modes of migration. Hence (returning to the question of economic emancipation) Alain Badiou's conflation of migrants with refugees under the rubric of the global 'nomadic proletariat', while accurate in its depiction of much exclusion as pertaining to the North–South divide, risks undermining the necessary privileging of those in most danger.[21] The Shoah, for example, generated refugees who were often themselves prosperous Europeans; not all asylum situations can be reductively explained by the horrors of capitalism, and thus a necessary distinction between asylum and other migration flows should be conceptually and legally maintained (while also deconstructed and interrogated), even if, in my view, the dignified treatment and protection of both migrants and refugees should be guaranteed.[22] The limits of what Judith Shklar called 'legalism' are also manifest in the inability of international law to compel state behaviour, despite certain modest achievements and occasional constraints or break-throughs achieved through going to court to protect the rights of refugees and those who assist them.[23] An *ethos* of responsibility requires a *political response*, even if, as an ethical question, such a response is not a matter of choice (Levinasian responsibility is not chosen or willed but rather imposed, and Arendtian plurality is similarly unchosen). Of course, the decision to help can always be refused, but such refusal can be *judged* as anti-political, and that is the point at issue – to shift the very ground on which these matters are considered and judged, to unsettle common assumptions concerning what does and does not constitute politics.

The 'guarantee' of human dignity sought by Arendt is brought into prox-imity with the possibility of an ethical politics that the thinking of Levinas provides, especially via the profound reading of these two thinkers articu-lated by Judith Butler in *Parting Ways*. To repeat the key claim from the Introduction, the combination of Levinasian ethical responsibility as provid-ing a new account of the (political) subject, with the Butlerian interpreta-tion of Arendtian plurality as fundamentally unchosen (and thus radically challenging the standard account of politics as freely chosen social contracts pertaining to closed societies), means that a new politics, realized via an *ethos* of responsibility, can be articulated that would recognize respect for the right to asylum as proper to the work of politics. This is further elaborated with reference to the philosophical anthropology of Andrew Benjamin, who has effectively argued that what is proper to the being of being-human relates to placedness and being-in-common. That is, in order to be fully realized in one's potentiality as a human being, it is necessary to *belong* – a thought similar to (and influenced by) Arendt's notion of the right to have rights, and the need for each human being to inhabit a space of appearance where they can be recognized and are able to act amongst other plural human beings. While Jacques Derrida is also a key thinker of the overall work, he does not play a role in the establishment of the argument in this section of the book; here the purpose is to establish the theoretical groundwork of the new concept of the political. While Derrida can also be aligned with this position via his provocation that 'ethics is hospitality', and that the *ethos* of a place of dwelling is thus always-already concerned with hospitality, of greater importance later in the book is Derrida's thinking of unconditional hospitality as a means of challenging the scope of welcome to asylum seekers, in refuting the claims made by theorists and politicians alike of necessary limits to such proffering of asylum. Derrida is also of decisive significance in the 'Coda' that ends the book where his thinking of 'hauntology' informs the arguments which have preceded it; to wit, that the new concept of politics pursued here must be considered in relation to the memory of the disappeared, as an active politics of mourning and remembrance, where melancholia does not portend a lapse into inaction but becomes the very exigency of ethical responsibility. Here, the focus is on Arendt, Levinas, Butler, and (Andrew) Benjamin (who I will distinguish from Walter Benjamin across the book where necessary so as to avoid confusion, as both are important throughout) to establish the claim, counter to standard accounts of politics, that respect for asylum and the right to belong is central to the meaning and realization of politics.

Arendt and the Antinomy of the Guarantee

Hannah Arendt was both theoretically and personally confronted with the horrors of totalitarianism, an 'anti-politics', which sought to reduce human beings to superfluity. This was accomplished by denying the possibility to exercise the innate condition of natality and the freedom provided by human beings able to interact amongst each other and initiate new beginnings in a mutually guaranteed space of appearances. For Arendt, it was of decisive importance that the possibility of political action be maintained. Consequently, not only was she opposed to totalitarianism, but attendant to this she was very suspicious of the intrusion of normative claims into political theory – not that she opposed them wholly, but preferred to think 'without banisters', and to engage in the open-ended activity of thinking, the two-in-one dialogue with oneself that could lead to the birth of conscience and furnish the possibility of judgement. As is well known, she expressed a preference for the American Revolution over the French Revolution due in part to the latter's inclusion of the 'social question' – that is, the material needs of the poor – as a political matter, which she thought should be a matter of policy but not of politics, as it threatened to undo the fragile space of freedom that enables political action. 'The Revolution, when it turned from the foundation of freedom to the liberation of man from suffering, broke down the barriers of endurance and liberated, as it were, the devastating forces of misfortune and misery instead . . . every attempt to solve the social question with political means leads into terror', and 'whose end is impotence, whose principle is rage, and whose conscious aim is not freedom but life and happiness'.[24] For Arendt, there is a good that inheres in politics *in se* – the activity and the space of politics, subject to the strictures of the activity of thinking and judging – which is put at risk by justice posited in the form of absolutist claims. This was also her objection to Marx, who for Arendt ended the 'authority' of the tradition of political philosophy by seeking to realize concrete claims of justice – Marx being, as she wrote to Karl Jaspers, 'someone whom a passion for justice has seized by the scruff of the neck' – and someone who aimed at undoing the space of political freedom in the realization of justice claims as the aim of politics, that was simply to be enacted and thus in consequence, the state would 'wither away'.[25]

Some theorists see in Arendt's thinking of the political a worrying aestheticization of political activity for its own sake. Hanna Pitkin, referring to Arendt's scepticism concerning the 'social question' in *On Revolution*, comments in biting terms:

> Thus it seems that for Arendt, because political action cannot solve economic problems, and because misery can become active only in destructive ways, it is best for the poor and laborers to be kept out of the public sphere. Like women, they belong in the household . . . On this account, the exclusion 'of everything merely necessary or useful' from political life means simply the exclusion of the exploited by the exploiters, who can afford not to discuss economics [or one might add to Pitkin, discuss them in ways that enrich the upper class], and to devote themselves to 'higher things', because they live off the work of others . . . put two questions to Arendt: What keeps these citizens together as a body? And what is it that they talk about together, in their endless palaver in the *agora*?[26]

The same concern might be raised concerning asylum as a question of political justice. Despite her well-known articulation of a 'right to have rights', it is not something Arendt calls for or insists upon. Nowhere in *The Human Condition*, for example (and aside from *Origins*, rarely in her other writings), is there any kind of sustained demand concerning the centrality of the right to asylum to the activity of politics. To be clear, the claim is not that Arendt was unconcerned with the plight of the stateless – the extensive section on the 'Rights of Man' in *Origins* obviously precludes such a conclusion, and she would hardly have inspired an entire cottage industry of publishing on her thoughts on the subject were that the case. There are also essays such as 'We Refugees' where she makes refugees her explicit focus, and of course she was herself stateless for a long period. The argument is rather that, curiously (given this experience), she does not centre the right to asylum as a primary normative task of politics, that is, she does not follow through on her own demand for a new guarantee of a new law on earth concerning human dignity for the stateless. Her view is restrained by her prioritization of politics over philosophical normative claims; and it may be that she linked the guarantee strictly to the need for 'newly defined territorial entities', which, given their state of unrealizability (then and now), made her despair of realizing the guarantee. And yet she recognized the *need* for the guarantee regardless. How can this seeming contradiction be reconciled?

A great deal of research has been conducted by political theorists on Arendt's notion of the right to have rights and her thinking about statelessness, most prominently by Peg Birmingham, Judith Butler, Seyla Benhabib, Serena Parekh, Anya Topolski, Ayten Gündoğdu, Étienne Balibar, and Jacques Rancière, amongst others. Rather than repeating or restating this important work other than where necessary (Butler and Birmingham aside, who feature prominently), in order to continue the elaboration of a concept of the political centred on the right to asylum, I will further pursue the argument concerning 'unchosen' plurality (Butler's extension of Arendt's term) as a normative foundation for the guarantee that Arendt seeks, a guarantee of decisive importance in cutting through the impasse surrounding the politics of asylum. It will be argued that respect for plurality – 'the law of the earth' and '*conditio per quam*' of politics – is the normative grounding of the guarantee of human dignity Arendt called for. As a matter of asylum and the right to have rights, the clear implication is that such respect is fundamental to the work of politics.

It is important to note that the motif of 'guarantee' is one that runs throughout Arendt's writings, from very early texts such as *The Origins of Totalitarianism* (1951), to *The Human Condition* (1958), to *On Violence* (1970). In *The Human Condition*, Arendt argues that promising (along with forgiving) is the force which keeps human beings together, realized in a social contract.[27] Yet the word guarantee recurs in this book as part of her articulation of the constitution of political life: 'To men the reality of the world is guaranteed by the presence of others.'[28] The space of appearances that precedes and founds the public realm represents a liberation from the monadic isolation of the private sphere: the polis is 'the guarantee against the futility of individual life',[29] a space 'physically secured by the wall around the city and physiognomically guaranteed by its laws – lest the succeeding generations change its identity beyond recognition – is a kind of organized remembrance'.[30] The political space secured within the city walls is secured by the mutual promises plural human beings make to each other, which Arendt refers to as a 'guarantee',[31] that is, in the context of promising Arendt will refer to the guarantee produced by plural human beings 'inhabiting together with others a world whose reality is guaranteed for each by the presence of all'.[32] In *On Violence*: 'The political realm of human affairs whose essential quality is guaranteed by man's faculty of action.'[33] In these same pages of *On Violence* she also refers to the notion of guarantee in a discussion of liberalism and Marxism, where she credits the notion to Marxism, however expresses doubts the consequences about such guarantees given the events of the twentieth century – she had intended to write a follow-up to *Origins* entitled 'Totalitarian Elements in Marxism', but never finished the project.[34]

The reason this use of the term 'guarantee' is striking is that Arendt is well known as a thinker who thought 'without banisters', that is, without any particular normative guard rails around her thought. She privileged thinking as an activity for its own sake – acutely aware of the dangers wrought by the novel forms of anti-politics (totalitarianism) in the twentieth century, she was wary of any attempt to set up an absolute within the realm of politics. For her, this was precisely the realm within which absolutes should be resisted, as they represent the forestalling and predetermination of human action, and therefore a contravention of the human capacity for natality and spontaneous initiative. Nevertheless, there are places in Arendt's writings when something like a 'banister', that is a normative claim or imperative, seems to be ventured. The call for a new guarantee of human dignity, a new law on earth, and a new political principle, is one such claim. Similarly, the claim that plurality is the 'law of the earth' seems like another, although her own intentions on this point are uncertain. It is possible to interpretively link these two moments in her writings, one emerging very early in *Origins*, where she insists upon the need for the new law; and in her very final book, *The Life of the Mind*, where she seems to answer her own demand (without making that answering explicit) by defining plurality itself as the law of the earth. Indeed, for Arendt if it is important to not make strong normative claims, it is often derived from the need to preserve the possibilities that adhere in human plurality, in the space of appearance amongst plural human beings that enables the possibility of action; but in this sense, surely human plurality itself becomes a norm? But is it only a post-foundational, political norm, or does it have an ethico-ontological justification?

The language of guarantee in Arendt's writings emerges as a response to the irruption within politics of the unprecedented phenomenon of totalitarianism; indeed, the call for a 'new guarantee' of human dignity rooted in a 'new law on earth' occurs in the preface to a book called *The Origins of Totalitarianism*. It is as though world history demands a response from the world of thought, from political philosophy, of a different order than that of the promise. One might compare this to Adorno's stipulation that 'Hitler has imposed a new categorical imperative on human beings in their state of unfreedom: to arrange their thoughts and actions in such a way that Auschwitz should never be repeated, that nothing of the sort should ever happen again'.[35] With the advent of the totalitarian, and the horrific events of the Shoah, a new evil of terrifying, planetary dimensions has emerged into human affairs which aims at, portends or accomplishes the destruction of entire sections of humanity, and which provokes a corresponding protective response of equal measure, without that measure becoming what it opposes. Totalitarianism in Arendt's sense is violent – anti-politics – not only in its direct physical brutality, but in that it represents coercion outside of the sphere of power, the latter understood as the ability and legitimacy of plural human beings freely taking action together. However, how can a 'guarantee' within the order of politics not be violent in the same sense? Even if the guarantee aims at the protection of precarious life and is thus opposed to the physical violence of totalitarianism, isn't it also a form of violence directed towards, or within, politics? There is indeed a mirroring of absolutism at play in this not-so-symbolic Manichaeism; however, the difference lies in the *telos* at work in each – in totalitarianism, the reduction of the human being to superfluousness; in the new law on earth, the active preservation of unchosen plurality. That is, the positing of a normative good or end (*telos*) for politics, beyond the activity of politics itself, is the explicit meaning of a guarantee, and it is just such an end that Arendt (in her critiques of Marx and Robespierre, for example) refuses.

It may be that on this point, a difficulty emerges in reading too closely a thinker who often wrote in response to events, eschewed systematic thinking, and who did not intend for great emphasis to be placed upon terms like 'guarantee' (or indeed, the 'right to have rights'). If a guarantee is understood simply as a form of promising, then it fits comfortably within the schema established rigorously by Arendt, where the possibility for action amongst plural beings, rooted in the ontological fact of natality, avoids the charge of violence and remains within the sphere of mutually promised and agreed political power. But a guarantee and a promise *might* be distinguished, while still retaining 'family resemblance' in Wittgenstein's sense, and thus open questions within the realm of the political concerning the actualization of just life, where a guarantee begins to appear 'violent' in its irreconcilability with the Arendtian conception of power. A guarantee is an absolute assurance that something will be realized, and seems an ostensibly stronger claim than a promise, even if it has the apparent form of a promise. Under a guarantee, the claim is that there is no possibility that the promised outcome will not be realized, whereas a promise does not seem as stringent a claim. It may appear that the distinction is merely semantic or rhetorical, and that the words are interchangeable; however, if the distinction is maintained with a degree of rigour, then it also may be the case that a deconstructive fissure emerges in the writings of Arendt, where her own discourse threatens to undo itself. This is not due to incoherence on her part, but rather because of the inherent instability of the dual nobility of her effort to at once secure the space of political freedom, while simultaneously reconciling it with plurality as a 'law of the earth' which requires a 'guarantee' for its security. Hence the 'antinomy' of the guarantee, the call for the realization of that which cannot be realized within politics conceived as a realm of freedom. This would represent a deconstructive reading of Arendt, in that in an 'eccentric centre' of Arendt's work, this call or desire for a guarantee lies at the foundations of the rest of what she develops in her account of politics, with the potential to undermine the edifice of that account.[36] Given her own equation of the guarantee with the promise, it is necessary to proceed with the caution of the Derridian 'perhaps' and not be too quick to certitude on this point. But nor should this possibility be ignored.

Arendt equated politics directly with freedom, but a freedom that is a product not of the will but borne of the condition of natality, comprising *initium* and givenness, the power to undertake new actions amongst the givenness of human relations.[37] In the final sentence of *Origins* she writes: 'This beginning is guaranteed by each new birth; it is indeed every man.'[38] Freedom amongst plural beings is opposed to sovereignty, where the latter is understood as a form of power dependent on violence, and therefore not power as a manifestation of action.[39] Human beings possess the 'twofold gift of freedom and action' that enables them to build a shared world that ensures continuity, 'guaranteed' by the fact of natality, and the 'virtuosity' of action which leads Arendt into something of an aestheticization of politics.[40] Whereas according to Arendt philosophy has long excluded freedom from its considerations, the realm of politics is for Arendt coterminous with freedom, which requires a political guarantee to be realized.[41] Such freedom is thus manifested in acts of founding.[42]

Thomas Keenan has argued that political freedom must always run the risk of its opposite in order to be operative at all, in that it requires foundations which themselves undermine freedom, and thus neither freedom or foundation is ever properly secured, putting into doubt the utility that Arendt sees in acts of promising.[43] For the political theorist the opposite to freedom is compulsion, which conjures the spectre of the totalitarian, or the authoritarianism of the Platonic guardian, the destruction of the space of appearances. But this space is already destroyed to the extent that some are excluded from it. That is indeed the implication of the 'right to have rights'; however, it is possible there is an alternative to freedom that would not be authoritarian or totalitarian, but a normative claim based upon responsibility that can either be respected or not. There is freedom in the ability to avoid responsibility, but there is not freedom in the type of decision that is morally justifiable. In that sense, freedom and choice in political decisionism are anticipated and predetermined. In *The Human Condition* she writes: 'Under the conditions of a common world, reality is not guaranteed primarily by the "common nature" of all men who constitute it, but rather by the fact that, differences of opinion and the resulting variety of perspectives notwithstanding, everybody is always concerned with the same object.'[44] However, Arendt accepted the Aristotelian argument concerning the necessary limitation of the size of the polis and was ambiguous around the question of numbers. She articulated the right to have rights without necessarily calling for it; and how can the common thing at issue be the right to asylum of those who are not yet admitted to a political community? As many critics have observed, there does seem to be a normative lacuna in Arendt's work where she does not follow through the possible implications or imperatives that her own work seems to demand.[45]

As Peg Birmingham has explained, Arendt argues in *The Human Condition* for political spaces as protection against violence, but also argues that political spaces can do violence to that which they cannot change or act upon (thus Arendt is aware of this problem concerning 'the common thing' of politics).[46] Arendt links this to the experience of Europeans encountering African 'others' whom they feared and did not understand, and failed to respect the givenness of human existence, what she called, apropos of refugees, 'the disturbing miracle of the given'.[47] Similarly she writes in *Origins* of 'the dark background of mere givenness' which 'breaks into the political scene as the alien which in its all too obvious difference reminds us of the limitations of human activity' – the context of the passage being strange, apparently evincing sympathy with those cast into this 'dark' state of exclusion, but this also being the section where she refers to the 'threat' posed by the stateless to 'our political life'.[48]

Consequently, a difficulty has to be marked in relation to the *antinomy of the guarantee* in Arendt's thought. While there is an explicit call for a new guarantee in the Preface to *Origins*, much of her work constitutes an overt disavowal of the possibility of such guarantees in political life. In *Origins* she observed that the guarantee must be provided by 'humanity itself', that is, via a work of politics amongst plural beings.[49] Thus, for example, the importance she places on relational acts like forgiving and promising as being able to form or re-form bonds of human community, acts which in no way constitute guarantees in the strict sense, dependent as they are upon the willed decisions of participants not bound a priori by any particular normative rule of the political. Consequently, an antinomy emerges in requiring of politics that which she has apparently determined cannot be provided. A further difficulty concerns the debates in the literature over whether, as mentioned previously, Arendt provides for any normative foundation for her outlook on politics. Apropos of the right to have rights, which are here being interpretively linked to her call for a guarantee of human dignity in a new law on earth, Seyla Benhabib summarizes the problem effectively:

In both cases, an anthropological normative universal is being invoked. In virtue of our humanity alone, Arendt is arguing, we are beings entitled to be treated in certain ways, and when such treatment is not accorded to us, then both wrongs and crimes are committed against us. Of course, Arendt was thinking along Kantian lines that we are 'moral persons', and that our humanity and our moral personality coexist. Yet these are not the terms that she will use; nor will she, like Kant, seek to ground the mutual obligation we owe one another in our capacity for acting in accordance with the principles of reason. Even her formula the 'right to have rights' is frustratingly ambiguous: if we have a right to have rights, who could have removed it from us? If we do not already all have such a right, how can we acquire it? Furthermore, what is meant by 'a right' in this formula: a legally recognized and guaranteed claim by the lawgiver? Or a moral claim that we, qua members of a human group, address to our fellow human beings, to be recognized as their equals? Clearly, it is the second, moral, meaning of the term *rights* that Arendt has in mind. But she is not concerned to offer a justification here. She was not a foundationalist thinker and she stayed away from strategies of normative justification. Her belated reflections on Kant's doctrine of judgement reveal, however, the extent to which she was and remained a moral universalist and modernist.[50]

For Arendt, political responsibility was exercised not through the application of ethical norms, but rather through the use of thinking and judgement. Indeed much of her work following the Eichmann trial was a disputation with Eichmann concerning his misuse of Kant, given that he scandalously claimed to have been following the Categorical Imperative, a completely confused understanding of Kant that conflated moral law with the will of the leader, rather than his own responsibility to reflect upon his actions. In relation to refugees, her preference for the activity of thinking and judging over adherence to concrete norms was connected to her scepticism concerning natural rights which had failed to guarantee the rights of the stateless. What has emerged in modernity is a political state of exception, where statelessness or apolity represents, in Giorgio Agamben's phrase, 'a space devoid of law, a zone of anomie'.[51] Stateless persons find themselves in a situation where, lacking citizenship rights and with only weak enforcement of international law, they are often unable to secure their human rights. They have (Agamben again) 'put the originary fiction of modern sovereignty in crisis. Bringing to light the difference between birth and nation, the refugee causes the secret presupposition of the political domain – bare life – to appear for an instant within that domain'.[52] The collapse of moral standards may quickly follow, as Arendt writes in 'We Refugees': 'Man is a social animal and life is not easy for him when social ties are cut off . . . Very few individuals have the strength to conserve their own integrity if their social, political and legal status is completely confused.'[53] The risk she identifies is 'that we expose ourselves to the fate of human beings who, unprotected by any specific law or political convention, are nothing but human beings'.[54]

On this account, there is something else which needs to emerge within the political, in order to guarantee human dignity. Yet dignity is not reducible to physical life; for Arendt it emerges in a political context, a view shared by Jean Améry, a writer who lived through the horror of Auschwitz: 'It is certainly true that dignity can be bestowed only by society . . . and the merely individual, subjective claim ("I am a human being and as such I have my dignity, no matter what you may do or say!") is an empty academic game, or madness'.[55] Améry and Arendt are in total agreement on this point – Améry wrote that 'Yes, the SS could carry on just as they did: there are no natural rights, and moral categories come and go like the fashions'.[56] One could link this to Arendt's observation that sets of morals as *mores*, customs, are as interchangeable as table manners.[57] For Arendt, the protection of the stateless is not achieved via an appeal to natural rights, but rather a political principle: 'We became aware of the existence of a right to have rights'.[58] But what exactly does it mean to have a right to have rights? What is the conception of personhood, or subjectivity, or the grounding that she posits for her claim in seeking to guaranteeing human dignity? What kind of a political configuration or principle does she in fact recommend? Gündoğdu summarizes Arendt's approach:

> Finally, Arendt follows the Socratic example when she concludes her inquiry aporetically and refuses to resolve the perplexities of human rights by grounding them in a new normative foundation or by putting forward a new institutional model. Her analysis suggests that the task of critical inquiry is not to offer such a resolution but instead to carefully examine how these perplexities become manifest in human rights norms, institutions, and policies as well as how political actors navigate and renegotiate them in response to challenging problems of rightlessness.[59]

Thus, Arendt offers no 'new normative foundation' nor 'institutional model' to account for the guarantee she calls for – rather remaining within a 'Socratic' example which can continue to trouble and rethink the politics of human rights, what Gündoğdu calls an 'aporetic' approach (interestingly, Gündoğdu notes that the German version of this famous section of *Origins*, 'The Perplexities of the Rights of Man', refers to aporia – 'die Aporien der Menschenrechte').[60] For Arendt, normative claims within the political are just that – something realized within politics, the products of political activity, rather than their ground.[61] (This, as will be seen, is a key difference that separates her understanding of the political from that of Levinas, for whom there *is* an normative, or ethical, grounding of politics.) There is nothing in political community or political principles or political compacts that will guarantee justice, which is to say, the recognition of human dignity – and particularly for those not already members of the polity making the decision. As Paul Muldoon observes, 'As a product of human artifice, the public realm is for-ever exposed, not only to the vast reaches of the merely given which press in upon it, but to the possibility that individuals will decide to order their relations otherwise (i.e. not in accordance with principles of justice)'.[62] As to the right to have rights, nothing compels states to make agreements between them to care for stateless persons; the total responsibility taken, in the modern era of promise-making in relation to stateless persons through treaties and reciprocally binding agreements, can be rounded down to almost zero (recall from the Introduction that rates of resettlement in the past few decades have never exceeded 1%). Yet Arendt does recognize the need for everyone to be allowed to belong somewhere. *Why*, if there are no normative grounds that orient the political prior to its conduct? A division between the political con-struction and exercise of a right, and its philosophical justification, opens on this point. James Ingram, in a discussion of the 'Right to have Rights', dis-tinguishes between 'philosophical and political approaches to human rights', and observes that'human rights' defenders are now less troubled by rights' extra-political provenance or justification and focus more on the practical task of realizing them'. For Arendt, rights are a practice of mutual recognition in a political context, and not recognition of a dignity prior to human construction, or any 'ontological guarantee'.[63] What Arendt recognizes, as Étienne Balibar notes, is the right to have rights as a 'right to politics'.[64]

This view of political activity as the proper grounding of rights – what Balibar calls 'equaliberty', a term taken up by Gündoğdu – would seem to be an inadequate response to her own call, in its refusal of a certain concept of the normative. Anya Topolski is persuasive in arguing that Arendtian plurality requires supplementing with Levinasian alterity, to articulate what she calls a 'politics of relationality'.[65] For at the heart of the call for a right to have rights is a demand for justice – justice for stateless persons – which itself implies a recognition of human dignity. While Arendt may be sceptical about the efficacy of the Rights of 'Man' untethered from political instantiation (and rightly so), she cannot, in building her account, do without them, but is in fact secretly dependent upon a kind of normativity, which informs her own project.

Does not a guarantee such as she demands require a conception of human dignity to which political actors – states or others – can be held accountable? Without such a conception, does not the right to have rights risk a kind of circularity, guaranteed only by political promise-making attached to no deter-minate conception of the good, and thus referring only to itself? For Arendt the human good is found in the capacity for action, exercised in conditions of *plurality*, where agreements must be kept – yet as will be seen further on, if democratic action itself can involve decisions that contravene human dig-nity, it would seem that some extra-political principles need apply. There is a danger in this, if no right precedes the political, as Werner Hamacher and Ronald Mendoza-de Jesús note: 'If the "right to have rights" is understood exclusively in accordance with its "legal-formity" (Rechtsförmigkeit) and interpreted as a program for nothing other than rights, then with the loss of this right must be extinguished as well every claim to politics and every claim that goes beyond the form of the political or that deviates from it.'[66] Is there not in fact something like a normative foundation to be discovered, and even more – an *ethos* of responsibility, that can guide political *praxis* on this question, an extra-political criterion for forming judgements in relation to the political, which emerges from calamity, that is, the disaster that followed denationalization before and during the Second World War? One might agree with her that the Rights of 'Man' are insufficient, but perhaps this can be read dialectically both ways – that political promise-making left to itself is also inadequate (which will be explored further in chapter 2, in the case of Denmark and refugees in the Second World War). Alison Kesby rightly notes the limitations of a perspective that would emphasize the agency of precisely those agents who have the least power to change their situation.[67] The valorisation of political struggle – 'the rights of those who have not the rights that they have and have the rights that they have not', as Rancière paradoxically expresses it – may lead to an impasse to the extent that those rights are not recognized and responded to by those with political power.[68] This is a fundamental problem with political theorists who emphasize the necessity of struggle for rights as only a political struggle, lacking any normative foundation or justification other than the rights being those rights which can be won or recognized. An account of how the political should be understood is required that goes beyond these limits. Struggle is necessary – the Gramscian notion of hegemony and counter-hegemony, which finds strange but productive proximity with the anti-liberalism of Carl Schmitt – has been importantly highlighted by thinkers such as Chantal Mouffe, and such struggle is necessary, to articulate a politics of the good, even though I have critiqued Mouffe's notion of the liberal-democratic 'paradox'. In political terms, the struggle is for the hegemony of those who will respect the preservation of the plurality of humanity over those who will not, which will likely comport with a democratically socialist left. But the struggle cannot be confined to the struggles of the damned of the earth and their few good-hearted allies; an ethical response of established political communities is also of the utmost importance; it is this that is lacking, and it has rarely been emphasized in the history of political philosophy. It may be that in the post-structural, post-humanist, and post-Foucaultian currents of academia, the notion of such normative claims has fallen decisively from fashion, but the present arguments explicitly oppose this general trajectory of thinking (one might express it simply as Levinas versus Foucault, another largely unstaged gigantomachy).

Arendt's view would seem to remain bounded largely within the sphere of positive law, informed by the condition of plurality, which is itself not an ethical category, but an ontological description of humanity. But as Leo Strauss aptly puts it, positive law must appeal to something beyond itself:

> To reject natural right is tantamount to saying that all right is positive right, and this means that what is right is determined exclusively by the legislators and the courts of the various countries. Now it is obviously meaningful, and sometimes even necessary, to speak of 'unjust' laws or 'unjust' decisions. In passing such judgements, we imply that there is a standard of right and wrong independent of positive right and higher than positive right: a standard with reference we are able to judge our positive right.[69]

One can agree with Strauss's critique of positive law/rights, without retreating back into natural rights. If, as Arendt maintains, the Rights of 'Man' qua *natural* rights are no longer tenable, following the Enlightenment and the disenchantment of the world, and yet we cannot do without a sense of rights that go beyond positive rights – then the Rights of 'Man' require reformulation along different lines. This is the problem that Levinas takes up in rethinking ethical responsibility via phenomenology, to which I return further on.

In her book *Arendt, Levinas and a Politics of Relationality*, Anya Topolski observes that Arendt looked askance at the absolutism in Kant's philosophy: 'For Arendt, as argued in the *Human Condition*, the interhuman realm is one rooted in relationships in which no absoluteness or absolute truth is possible or desirable . . . Arendt reiterates [following the dangers of totalitarianism] that absolute guarantees, such as those promised by ideologies, and total certainty are not possible in the realm of human interactions without destroying those spaces'.[70] Topolski links this to what she calls Arendt's 'post-foundationalism', a refusal of foundationalism as an appeal to absoluteness: 'Foundationalism is an appeal to truth as absoluteness that refuses to be undermined and that aims to silence doxa, thereby preventing the plurality of the human realm from emerging and it has no place in the political realm for Arendt.'[71] Plurality functions as a post-foundational principle, in Montesquieu's sense, that is generative of action in a political community.[72] It is the maintenance of the space of action that Arendt is concerned with, and thus with politics as freedom, given the loss of the tradition of political 'authority' in the modern age. As she writes at the conclusion to her essay 'What is Authority?': 'For to live in a political realm with neither authority nor the concomitant awareness that the source of authority transcends power and those who are in power, means to be confronted anew . . . by the elementary problems of human living-together'.[73]

However, there seems to be a contradiction in this argument; foundationalism, absolutism are refused, but they are refused so that human plurality – as

we have seen, 'the law of the earth' for Arendt, necessitating a guarantee –
may emerge. Topolski shares Arendt's antinomic view of the notion of guarantee in politics, wrestling with it throughout her book; at times denying that
Arendt's political thinking provides any guarantees,[74] at others underscoring
Arendt's call for a new guarantee of human dignity.[75] But is not plurality as
the law of the earth an absolutist claim, with an undeniable moral dimension,
serving as a normative 'foundation'? The resolution to this problem depends
upon how the term plurality is interpreted, which requires further analysis in
relation to the work of Judith Butler.

Judith Butler on Arendt: The 'Unchosen' Plurality of Peoples

In the opening pages of the *Human Condition*, Arendt makes a striking claim
that plurality (where 'men and not Man, live on the earth and inhabit the
world') is 'not only the *conditio sine qua non*, but the *conditio per quam* – of
all political life'.[76] The latter phrase is intriguing; while a condition that is
sine qua non refers to a condition without which something cannot be operable, a *conditio per quam* – 'condition by means of which' – is a condition
that *fulfils* something, that causes some specified effect. That is to say that
political life, understood as action, is fulfilled as an effect by the condition of
plurality; it is not only the condition or precondition of politics, but the very
realization of politics.

But what does Arendt really mean by plurality? In part this can be understood as referring to plural individuals who live amongst each other – the
inter homines esse, where to live and to be amongst men were for the Romans
synonyms, as she observes.[77] Even more precisely, however, Arendt defines
plurality in relation to equality and distinction:

> Human plurality, the basic condition of both action and speech, has the twofold
> character of equality and distinction. If men were not equal, they could neither
> understand each other and those who came before them nor plan for the future
> and foresee the needs of those who will come after them. If men were not dis-
> tinct, each human being distinguished from any other who is, was, or will ever
> be, they would need neither speech nor action to make themselves understood.[78]

For Arendt, the 'meaning of politics is freedom'.[79] Specifically, 'political freedom means the right to be a participant, or it means nothing'.[80]
Recognizing the nature of the equality and distinction (which are human qualities that she distinguishes from a more generalized 'otherness') allows for
the uniqueness of each human being to become manifest in politics. Indeed,
in the opening sentence of the essay 'Introduction *Into* Politics', Arendt
writes that 'Politics is based upon the fact of human plurality'.[81] The *fact*,

rather than the moral demand issuing from plurality itself: 'Politics arises
between men, and so quite *outside* of *man*. There is therefore no real political
substance. Politics arises in what lies *between men* and is established as relationships.'[82] At times, politics, action, and freedom seem to be interchangeable terms for Arendt; however as discussed in the previous section, Arendt
does not make of plurality a concrete normative claim, which would have
implications for specific political duties in relation to asylum as the respect
for plurality as the *telos* of the political. Consequently, despite the intriguing
possibilities that seem to be opened up by a thinking of plurality as *conditio
per quam*, Arendt did not take the next step, which is to say that asylum
therefore has a central meaning in politics, related to her own call for a new
law on earth and a new political principle, and the right to have rights. She
remains bound to an understanding of politics from Aristotle through Cicero,
Machiavelli, and Montesquieu that sees politics as related to action between
the members of an extant community and the obligations they owe to each
other.[83] In examining statelessness, she recognized the centrality of plurality
but only saw the right to have rights as an aporia. She did not explicitly join
the dots from this rights call to the 'new law on earth' through to the implications of plurality; indeed she recapitulates a problematic Aristotelianism in
worrying about the size of the polis, and even when she prioritizes Athenians
over Athens – that it is not the city walls but the people that matter – it is a
valorization of political life as an activity and end in itself that she seems to
privilege.[84] There is arguably a further move which Arendt could have made:
to recognize that plurality as *conditio per quam* means a normative respect
for *unchosen humanity*, and thus by implication, that the right to asylum for
those cast outside of politics is the fulfilment of the *telos* of politics as plurality itself. That is to say, politics is all about the right to asylum, as the fulfilment of plurality as *conditio per quam*; that politics, even though she didn't
want it to tarry with 'social' questions (though she did distinguish between
the poor and the stateless, where the former are at least afforded some rights
as members of a state), must, in order to properly realize itself, be concerned
with asylum as part of its fundamental work. While Arendt does not think
that appeals to 'natural right' or 'humanity' are politically compelling (I agree
regarding natural rights, less regarding humanity more generally), her views
are based upon concepts of the political and the ethical that are contestable,
and it is entirely possible to envisage a politics that demonstrates the opposite
(the project of the present book).

The reading of plurality as beyond the action and lived experience of
individuals and applying to *peoples* has been taken up by Judith Butler in
relation to the Israel–Palestine conflict. Butler has written a highly important book, *Parting Ways: Jewishness and the Critique of Zionism*, which
is extremely close to the present argument in several ways. Butler's text

pertains specifically to Israel–Palestine, though possibly she intends that it can be construed as having a more universal scope. Here she is in close proximity with both Arendt and Levinas in taking Jewish experience in living amongst plural groups in the diaspora – cohabitation with the other – as constitutive of ethical and political life, yet especially in regard to Levinas in making a more universal claim for this condition and thus taking it beyond the confines of that which is proper to Jewishness (it is equally true of the diasporic conditions in which millions of Palestinians live). Taking from Levinas the thought that the relation to alterity interrupts identity in its very constitution ('alterity is constitutive of who one is'), she thinks this interruption in a political context.[85] (I will return to Levinas further on in the chapter.) As human beings constitute a given plurality of unchosen-ness, she argues that this should inform a new politics based upon 'the common rights of the refugee'.[86] Following on from Edward Said's arguments, Butler argues that the proximity of two peoples, the Jewish and Palestinian peoples, who share a history of exile, might make for a new *ethos* for politics in the region.[87] Butler counters the model of sovereignty as the assertion of nationalist power, with a model of cohabitation which emphasizes mutual belonging, the refusal of ethnocentric nationalism, and the dispersal of sovereignty.

I want to mark a potential difficulty on this point, which would require a lot more space to do justice properly. It is of significant importance to first nations peoples that their sovereignty be recognized, the struggle for which marks much of their history in the colonial and 'post' colonial period (quote marks as colonization cannot be said to be a process that has ended). Sovereignty as dispersal does not necessitate the erasure of sovereignty, but its deconstruction qua forms of violent appropriation and domination. Butler in *Parting Ways* wrestles with the way in which the Shoah forms the basis for some claims for the justification of the establishment of the State of Israel; given what had happened, a protective space and a new place or places of belonging were needed, a point that is unanswerable in its moral force. However, this undeniable imperative needs to be disaggregated from the claims to which it is attached (as Butler does carefully): Was a settler-colonial process that which was required for this realization of safety?[88] Thus to state the implications of the presently argued *ethos* of responsibility in formal, universal terms, it is indeed that which would apply to any society, including first nations peoples, that a duty of asylum be upheld (and such examples of solidarity in conditions of colonization have been instantiated, for example, by the symbolic issuance of Aboriginal passports to refugees kept in off-shore detention by Australia).[89] However, this would need to be rigorously distinguished from processes of settler-colonialism and unjust usurpation. (Following Levinas, one might think, strangely and at first blush disturbingly, that there are *just* forms of usurpation, that is, a moral rectitude in providing place and giving way in order to allow the other simply to exist and have their life preserved; early- to mid-twentieth century Palestine as a scene of asylum and cohabitation rather than conquest could have been a very different story, an-other history and an othering of history. I return to this difficult question in the Coda at the end of the book.)[90]

Attendant to this reading is the way in which Butler interprets Arendt's notion of 'plurality'. Butler performs an integrated reading of Arendt's texts, from *The Human Condition* to *Eichmann in Jerusalem*. Whereas for Arendt plurality is explained as 'equality and distinction' amongst plural individual human beings, Butler emphasizes the plurality of *peoples* – of ethnic, cultural, religious, racial, or political groups distinct from other peoples. This is the profound insight of the Butlerian reading, which links Arendt's thinking on plurality to her indictment of Eichmann. Beyond the obvious monstrosity of his crimes, the descriptive nature of the crime for Arendt was that he and his superiors arrogated to themselves the right to decide with whom to share the earth – that is, not with the Jewish or the Romani people – a crime against the *givenness* (a word Peg Birmingham emphasizes) or *unchosen* (Butler's emphasis) condition of human plurality, an ontological crime.[91] It thus becomes, in Butler's terms, an active duty, once one acknowledges the moral priority of preserving the unchosen and given condition of human plurality, to not violate it, which has obvious implications for the safeguarding of all precarious life, including those seeking asylum. Birmingham suggests that Arendt intends this in her indictment of Eichmann, as illustrative of the principle undergirding the 'right to have rights': 'Only a principle of humanity is able to provide the normative source for an imperative of common responsibility', and that in articulating this normative principle, 'Arendt remains a humanist'.[92] When Arendt reproaches Eichmann for his arrogance – 'As though you and your superiors had any right to determine who should and who should not inhabit the world' – she is making not only an ontological but an implicitly ethical, normative claim about the givenness of human plurality, without making it explicit or linking it back to her own call for a right to have rights and call for a new law on earth.[93] The tremendous originality and importance of Butler, Birmingham, and other commentators is to have made these necessary links. The moral implication is that the preservation of unchosen plurality becomes an *active* political duty, and not simply a precondition of the establishment of politics. No one has the right to determine who gets to share the earth, an observation which goes back to Christian Wolff (everyone has the right to belong) and Kant (the surface of the earth must necessarily be shared in common); but nor do they have the right to deny access to a human 'world', distinct from the earth, a place where being-in-common and being-in-place can be actualized, where the space of appearances between human beings can found new political beginnings. Not only the right to asylum but the right to *belong* must be guaranteed – Ayten Gündoğdu observes that several participants in the drafting of Article 14 of the UDHR wanted its wording to read 'the right to seek and *to be granted* asylum', 'but that the proposal was eventually rejected by the majority of state representatives due to concerns that it would put restrictions on sovereign power over immigration control'.[94] Not only is this concern a harmful conflation of asylum and migration, but represents a refusal of the active duty to preserve human plurality, and the descent, therefore, into crime.

What follows from this is the possibility of 'cohabitation', even for fraught disputes between peoples such as the Israel–Palestine conflict. To be sure, Arendt also thought in similar terms, as when, for example, at the end of 'The Jew as Pariah' she writes that 'only when a people lives and functions in consort with other peoples can it contribute to the establishment upon earth of a commonly conditioned and commonly controlled humanity';[95] and at the end of 'We Refugees', that 'the comity of European peoples went to pieces when, and because, it allowed its weakest member to be excluded and persecuted'.[96] As Butler makes clear, Arendt also opposed colonialist Zionism in favour of a federated model of cohabitation in a bi-national state.[97] Topolski points out that Arendt's notion of responsibility seeks a 'political guarantee that is post-foundational and intersubjective'.[98] Topolski, as with Birmingham, argues that plurality itself is the political principle that Arendt sought in *Origins*. However this reading of plurality is not shared with Arendt, nor agreed on by all Arendtian scholars; indeed, Seyla Benhabib has criticized Butler's use of this concept for straying from Arendt's own intentions in not referring to speech and action.[99] However, Benhabib, in remaining faithful to the political nature of Arendt's work, is not willing to recognize the normative guarantee for precarious life articulated by Butler.[100] Benhabib's counterclaim is that the value of thought and the potential for action amongst human beings, especially 'when the chips are down' in conditions of political lies and oppression, are of central importance, and thus we cannot abandon the terrain of the political in thinking through Arendt's concepts.[101] While this is a compelling claim, delimiting politics to such possibilities and negating the possibility of a 'guarantee' (which Benhabib accurately, in my view but possibly not in Butler's, identifies as an implication of Butler's reading of Arendt)[102] maintains politics within the space in which protection of precarious life can always be denied. Butler's argument represents a move beyond that which is posited in *The Rights of Others* by Benhabib, who calls for moral universalism and cosmopolitan federalism, while maintaining democratic norms. This does not 'guarantee' anything, neither the rights of the stateless nor indeed the political stability she is seeking to maintain. For one of the key claims of both Arendt and Butler is that political stability itself depends upon how the rights of non-citizens are addressed; the failure to achieve political equality for Palestinians is Butler's example. Benhabib, in her critique of Butler, very problematically elaborates a tragic symmetry between Israelis and Palestinians (another limitation of the deployment of tragedy-as-dialectics thinking in politics as a way of misleadingly positing an equivalence between opposed positions). She writes:

> They now face one another in an increasingly multipolar Middle East. Politics is often the site of the tragic. I mean 'tragedy' here in the sense developed by the young Hegel who saw tragedy, not as in the Greek plays to be a product of 'hamartia', of a certain kind of arrogance or blindness on the part of the hero or heroine, but rather as the clash of two rights, of two moral principles with equal claim upon our allegiance facing each other in struggle.[103]

Such a reading of the Israel–Palestine conflict fails to recognize the fundamental asymmetry of the conflict, and the continued brutalization of Palestinians and denial of their rights, including the right of return for refugees (concomitant to the positive upholding of the law of return for Jewish people). The failure to guarantee this right has been a continuing source of instability – Ilan Pappé argues that the refugee issue is the 'heart of the Palestine conflict'.[104] Benhabib refuses the term 'settler-colonial' to describe the project of constituting the state of Israel,[105] but not only is this term undeniably apposite, but increasingly the term apartheid is gaining relevance, given the checkpoints and cantonization of the West Bank (while also being distinguished in important particulars from South Africa), as thinkers such as Pappé and Noam Chomsky suggest.[106] The concern here about Benhabib's work, and her criticism of Butler, is that despite the generous nature of her calls for porous borders and the challenge to sovereignty, and the demand for the recognition of the rights of strangers, she is also in a sense recapitulating the 'paradox' of democracy versus universalism where the constitutive demos will always be able to form the exclusionary laws, that they usually do. In terms of her concrete political judgement, including the very fraught refugee question in Israel/Palestine, this seems even more concerning. Her commitment to Habermasian discourse ethics where norms are only valid when they can be agreed to by all under proper communicative conditions, while extended universally in a formal sense to all those capable of speech and action, in practice, is difficult to provide for those excluded from political membership. (This account of Benhabib's work, which is in other ways highly compelling, is of course no more than schematic and would require greater elaboration than can be pursued here.) The struggle of the voiceless for their voice, and those who would speak in their aid, is one thing; the responsibility of the established *demos* to recognize their inherent responsibility for the active preservation of plurality should not necessarily depend upon such struggle.

As long as a guarantee is denied and the tension between democracy and rights is maintained, people are going to die or be immiserated.

The insight of Butler's reading of Arendt – even if it moves past what Arendt would endorse – is that given that human plurality is unchosen, and often precarious, then this necessitates modes of cohabitation which limit political freedom and impose duties of active preservation of that plurality in its precariousness, leading to the fulfilment of rights and belonging. This fulfillment of rights may also increase the stability of the political community that liberal theorists worry will be undermined by the delimitation of self-determination.

To leave off the analysis of this disputation, there is a point of common agreement or at least affirmative proximity between Arendt, Butler, and Benhabib, which is a preference for a system of federated, democratic post-nationalist polities – what Benhabib calls 'cosmopolitan federalism',[107] Butler calls 'a postnational polity based on the common rights of the refugee'.[108] These can be linked to Arendt's call for a 'right to have rights' and 'newly defined territorial entities' as Peg Birmingham notes, Arendt called for post-national, federated political structures in her writings.[109] However, here I part company with all these thinkers to a degree. For an *ethos* of responsibility that recognizes plurality as the normative law of the earth to be effective, it must apply regardless of the political form. Such political entities as proposed by these thinkers are surely the best route to the upholding of this norm, but also cannot be awaited. The law of plurality must apply at all times as the *telos* of the political, a criterion of judgement for all politics, where asylum is necessarily one of the privileged scenes of its realization or abnegation. Plurality as the law of the earth holds as a universal concept of the political, its condition and its fulfilment, both *conditio sine qua non* and *conditio per quam*. Anything that calls itself politics must uphold this law in order to avoid the charge of anti-politics. Thus, thinking Arendt against Arendt – if plurality is truly to be the law of the earth, then politics cannot be delimited to or even necessarily defined as freedom. This, ultimately, is the provocative implication of Butler's reading of Arendt (I am not accusing Butler of negating freedom as a political value, but rather I note that she calls it into question) and which Benhabib disputes. Recall the epigraph to this book's Introduction, drawn from Butler's *Parting Ways*: 'But if we take seriously the inability to choose with whom we cohabit the earth, then there is a limit to choice, a kind of constitutive unfreedom that defines who we are and even, normatively, who we must be.' Freedom is constitutive of who 'we' are – in a situation of asylum, asked or proffered, there must be by definition a 'we' that can give asylum. Thus, a decisive point: political communities are constituted not simply by freedom, but also by the *unfreedom of responsibility* – 'hostage', to employ Levinas's term, to unchosen responsibility for the other person. To the extent that migration is distinguishable from asylum (a difficult question which cannot be answered here, but it would be plausible to argue that economic migrants count as 'persecuted', the legal definition of an asylum claimant, even if the violence is systemic and indirect), then responsibility is not necessarily engaged in that context; in the context of asylum, it is ineluctable. In that sense, it is necessary to speak of a guarantee as that which *should*, normatively, be upheld, a delimitation of freedom in order to secure human dignity. It will be rejoined that it is impossible to force any society to guarantee any such thing, that only political promises may secure any kind of commitment, which will always be fragile and contestable. But the guarantee is a matter of judgement, a moral law of the earth; all that falls beyond its ambit fall outside of the realm of legitimate politics, where the latter is defined as the active preservation of unchosen human plurality. The discourse of the promise is a tepid iteration of human security, easily broken, where such breaks are often justified in relation to the right of self-determination. The argumentative force of the guarantee of a new law on earth is that it will admit of no such justifications, and judgement is clear. To be sure, the struggle to secure such a guarantee remains just that – a political struggle. But the terrain of the struggle must move beyond the realm of promises made by independent actors, to a recognition of mutuality and relational coexistence that requires guarantees that reflect that already-existing relationality and the concomitant responsibility to preserve the plural humanity that constitutes it. A promise or agreement, freely willed, does not reflect the 'constitutive unfreedom' (Butler) of human relations, which are constituted precisely as a responsibility that is not chosen (Levinas). It is in the context of understanding this difference between ways of interpreting the nature of political life, that the move from the promise to the guarantee may be posited.

Such is the richness of Arendt's work, that multiple different emphases are possible. For example, Peg Birmingham puts much more stress on natality than plurality, although they should be seen as fundamentally related; one of the principles that emerges from natality – that of givenness – is closely related to the notion of plurality, that is, the given nature of unchosen plurality, of human beings who are in the world as though 'given' without being 'chosen'.[110] Nevertheless, Butler's reading of plurality as a plurality of *peoples* remains a powerful reinterpretation of Arendt's work, even if it strays from the overt intentions promulgated by Arendt. In the Introduction, Butler's argument was cited to the effect that, contra Eichmann, cohabitation (amongst unchosen plural human beings, both individuals and peoples) is the precondition of politics. She writes: 'This means that unwilled proximity and unchosen cohabitation are the preconditions of our political existence, which is the basis of her [Arendt's] critique of the nation-state (and its presumption of a homogenous nation) and implies the obligation to live on the earth and in a polity that establishes modes of equality for a necessarily heterogeneous population.'[111]

The new concept of the political here mooted emphasizes that which Butler for the most part only intimates, which is to insist on the universality of Butler's own argument, thought in relation to the discussion of plurality above, that this model of recognizing mutual exile and non-belonging, is constitutive of all political communities (and not just a potential model for Israel–Palestine). Butler, borrowing from Edward Said as well as Arendt, Levinas, Primo Levi, and more, argues that dispersion is a condition of possibility for thinking justice.[112] For Butler, relationality displaces ontology; this relation to alterity that is irreversible and defining is 'constitutive of identity, which is to say that the relation to alterity interrupts identity, and this interruption is the condition of ethical relationality'.[113]

This claim undermines the liberal conception of politics as voluntary contractualism amongst individuals, but rather emphasizes that human lived experience is always lived in conditions of relationality, that indeed the individual is only possible in such conditions. The importance of this as an orientation for a concept of the political is manifest: rather than trying to always compel or persuade liberal societies to accept liberal universalism in the respect for human rights, unchosen plurality as the *conditio per quam* means that the very work of politics itself is the preservation and realization of plurality, and that thus respect for the right to asylum is, as it were, baked into the cake. It is then not a matter of the Mouffian 'paradox' between liberalism and democracy, where one goes with a begging bowl constantly to liberal-democracies and pleads with them to admit foreigners in the name of liberal universalism or basic decency while simultaneously admitting the ultimate right of democracies to determine their own members. Rather, it is that the constitution of a political community amongst plural beings requires the admission of those without which such admission would mean the erasure of a dimension of unchosen plurality. Butler writes:

> In *Frames of War* I suggested that we are already in the hands of the other before we make any decision about with whom we choose to live. This way of being bound to one another is precisely not a social bond that is entered into through volition and deliberation; it precedes contact, is mired in interdependency, and is often effaced by those forms of social contract that presume and instate an ontology of volitional individuals.[114]

Butler's claim – and the reason it becomes possible to speak of a guarantee within the sphere of politics, without this form of absolutism being an illegitimate violence but remaining within the political – is that human precariousness means that human beings require each other for their mutual safety, that they depend upon each other. In her book *The Force of Non-Violence*, Butler presents a critique of the version of the 'state of nature' that would posit the human being as originarily individual – 'Dependency is, as it were, written out of the picture of the original man'.[115] Tellingly, the liberal man, whom she discusses as embodied in the figure of Robinson Crusoe, was *never a child*, but from the beginning was autonomous: 'He sprang, lucky guy, from the imaginations of liberal theorists as a full adult, without relations'.[116] What is false, in the liberal and republican social-contract vision of politics, is the elision of the inescapable network of human mutuality, vulnerability, and dependence. Returning to the beginning of this chapter, it is now clear from a host of challenges that strict autonomy and sovereign boundaries are no longer capable of meeting global crises, crises which are a literal threat to the survival of human plurality in its diversity. If plurality is the law of the earth, then its preservation must be guaranteed. Butler calls for the radical equality of grievability – that all lives *should be* treated as equally worthy of being mourned, even if they are not at present. 'The phantasmagoria of racism', in addition to other phantasms – of nationality, class, gender, sexuality, religion – often determines who is worthy of grievability, which enters into the failure to take responsibility for those lives that are considered ungrievable.[117] Butler: 'The historic-racial schema that makes it possible to claim, "This is or was a life", or, "These are or were lives", is intimately bound up with the possibility of necessary modes of valuing life; memorialization, safeguarding, recognition, and the preservation of life'; regarding those who die at sea, Butler adds that 'the metric of grievability is built into these decisions in such a way that migrant populations are ungrievable from the start'.[118]

To be sure, exclusion can still be effected and almost always is, but much political thought is too quick to legitimate the liberal-democratic paradoxical nexus, without a proper interrogation of the ethico-ontological preconditions from which the work of politics emerges. If subjectivity begins not in ontological self-possession and willed, conscious self-regard but as welcoming the other and hospitality; and if unchosen plurality, rather than choice exercised through contracts, is the condition of political life, where relationality and mutual dependence is the experience of life as lived on the earth, then a whole new perspective on the proper status of the right to asylum within political life emerges:

> If Arendt is right, then it is not only that we may not choose with whom to cohabit, but that we must *actively preserve* the unchosen character of inclusive and plural cohabitation: we not only live with those we never chose and to whom we may feel no sense of social belonging, but we are also obligated to preserve their lives and the plurality of which they form a part. In this sense, concrete political norms and ethical prescriptions emerge from the unchosen character of these modes of cohabitation.[119] [emphasis added]

This latter prescription of active preservation is of the utmost importance for the meaning of the *ethos* of responsibility as a new concept of the political. It is not simply that plurality serves as the precondition or condition of politics, but it is the realization – the *conditio per quam* – of politics, that which it aims to fulfil or realize, its *telos*. Plurality is the *telos* of the political, just as it is the *nomos* of the earth. Consequently, the fulfilment of the right to asylum is bound up with the realization of politics; thus, it can be argued that asylum is not secondary but primary, it is at the heart of politics, and as the realization and preservation of plurality, politics thus equates, ultimately, to the right of asylum.

The other major thinker in *Parting Ways*, as well as in the development of the present *ethos* of responsibility (hence the tremendously close proximity to and admiration for Butler's book evinced here), is Emmanuel Levinas. Before proceeding to further elaborate how Butler brings Arendt and Levinas together, in order to develop the argument further, some exploration of the work of Levinas is required.

Levinas and Ethical Subjectivity: Hospitality, Responsibility, and the Night of Being

Human rights in the modern period, including the right to asylum, emerged from and remain heavily influenced by the political philosophy of liberalism. Yet the politics of asylum as practised by liberal societies before and during the Second World War, as well as during more recent history, has manifestly failed to safeguard the lives of vulnerable refugees. If a brutal dictatorship fails to protect people, there is not much to question and judgement can be easily applied; what really becomes questionable is why ostensibly 'liberal' societies, that is, those that purport to uphold universal liberal values such as the rights of every individual to freedom from harm, fail to do so. Two quotations from Levinas are apposite in this context, where he observes that National Socialism

> overwhelmed a world built on the foundation of liberal principles. For better or worse, it was on this foundation of liberalism that the existence of the Jewish people rested and depended. Then came the events that tore from anti-Semitism its apocalyptic secret, revealing the extreme, demanding, and dangerous destiny of humankind.[120]

Given this dependence upon liberalism that was for the most part betrayed, Levinas puts its role in determining the limits of politics into profound question: 'We must ask ourselves if liberalism is all we need to achieve an authentic dignity for the human subject.'[121] Apropos of asylum, this is a refrain that runs throughout literature and memoir concerning the Shoah: Moriz Scheyer (mentioned previously), a survivor, writes in his memoir *Asylum* of his indignation concerning the indifference of states: 'To this day I cannot rid myself of a feeling of bitterness, when I think of the endless forest of red tape that was put in our way by most states at that time, as we begged for visas. With a little good will, it would have been possible to save everyone'.[122] Similar bitterness is expressed by André Schwarz-Bart: 'everything under the skull-cap of the heavens that called itself a democracy was paying Germany back in her own coin and condemning her, by way of punishment for her anti-Semitism, to keep her Jews. The punishment was brilliant, for it was applied at the precise moment when Nazism, outraged or suffocating with Yiddishness, opened Hamburg to Yiddish emigration. Flooding into the port in tens of thousands, the German-Jews hammered painfully against democracy's order of the day: no visa'.[123] As American journalist Dorothy Thompson wrote at the time, 'It is a fantastic commentary on the inhumanity of our times that for thousands and thousands of people a piece of paper with a stamp on it is the difference between life and death'.[124]

The task to be established is the construction of a new concept of the political that would understand asylum to be proper to the work of politics, and not a derivative duty, or conflated with migration under open borders, or restrained by the impotencies of democratic decisionism or international law. Rarely if ever have political theorists been challenged by an alternative account of politics that centres the place of asylum rather than marginalizing it; such a challenge is vital if the politics of asylum is to be reoriented in a way that instantiates forms of just life, as opposed to mere life, or even exile and death. The first part of this argument has been outlined in relation to the implications of Arendtian plurality; the second part relates to the political implications of Levinas's ethical philosophy. As noted, both Judith Butler and Anya Topolski have done similar readings that bring together Arendt and Levinas in their writings. In seeking to extend their work, a particular emphasis to be given here is the notion of hospitality as it figures in Levinas's philosophy, as well as taking into account recent developments in Levinasian scholarship. The argument is that Levinas provides an account of human subjectivity that makes of political subjects, agents that are always-already called to be responsible for other human beings. Second, the thinking of Levinas, especially in *Totality and Infinity*, provides for a reworked understanding of ontology that fundamentally alters the relationship of morality to politics beyond that normally evinced in political theory (including by Arendt). The implications of this recasting of political subjectivity as responsible, or 'hospitable' – 'subjectivity . . . as hospitality' (see epigraph at beginning of this chapter) and ontology as connected to the ethical, are then examined in relation to the consequences for a theory and practice of politics concerning asylum.

In the extraordinary Preface to *Totality and Infinity* (hereafter *TI*), Levinas contests the view of politics that would dismiss morality as *näiveté*. In a tradition from Hobbes to Machiavelli to Schmitt, and taking in the teleology of Hegel, politics would have mostly constituted an impersonal resort to war and domination, where the dignity of individuals finds its meaning only in the totality of history, in the oblique movement of Spirit towards freedom. To the extent that it has been more than this – the self-determination of liberal-democratic societies, for example – politics has still for the most part remained within the orbit of self-interest and self-protection, of the primary obligation to one's own members and the twin dynamics of sovereignty consisting of protection-obedience (Hobbes) and the friend–enemy distinction (Schmitt). The 'mocking gaze of the political man' (Levinas) has cast aspersions on any kind of primary obligation to non-members.[125] The modern history of the politics of asylum is dispositive on this point.

In order to oppose this tradition and establish a new concept of the political – that the right to asylum constitutes the very realization of the political – a reworked understanding of the ethical and the political is required, that takes up the radicalization of both ethics and ontology that has been established by Levinas, yet perhaps not sufficiently absorbed by political theorists and philosophers who treat the political. In particular, the reworked understanding of responsibility provided by Levinas is of vital importance in what follows. Maurice Blanchot provides an excellent summation of Levinasian responsibility in *The Writing of the Disaster*:

> Responsibility: a banal word, a notion moralistically assigned to us as a (political) duty. We ought to try and understand the word as it has been opened up and renewed by Levinas so that it has come to signify (beyond the realm of meaning) the responsibility of an other philosophy (which, however, remains in many respects eternal philosophy). Responsible: this word generally qualifies – in a prosaic, bourgeois manner – a mature, lucid, conscientious man, who acts with circumspection, who takes into account all elements of a given situation, calculates and decides . . . But now responsibility – my responsibility for the other, for everyone, without reciprocity – is displaced. No longer does it belong to consciousness . . . *My* responsibility for the Other presupposes an overturning such that it can only be marked by a change in the status of 'me', a change in time and perhaps in language.[126]

A philosophy at once eternal, and an-other philosophy: eternal in that it is faithful to that philosophy which seeks a 'good' beyond being, and other in that it turns aside from understanding this good and responsibility as products of reason. An-other philosophy which liberates political responsibility from the 'bourgeois' prudential calculus, where the subject is displaced and reoriented (the changed 'me'), from self-concern and an emphasis on imperious sovereignty, to the possibility of an anarchic responsibility for others. Responsibility took on increasing importance for Levinas; the presence of this word increases almost tenfold from *TI* to *Otherwise Than Being*, although it is also a theme of the earlier work.

When they are listed alongside each other, the innovations that Levinas introduces into the realm of ethical philosophy are striking in their number and originality: the Face, the saying and the said, the 'me voici', the interpretation of insomnia, ipseity as ethical subjectivity, the subject as oriented to hospitality, the subject as 'hostage' to the other, the advent of the third as the birth of justice, a metaphysical ontology that is thoroughly ethical (*TI*), the move beyond metaphysical language to an emphasis upon responsibility (*Otherwise Than Being*), to name but a few. The relations between these concepts and his various texts (which evolve in their concerns and focal points while also maintaining a consistency of argumentation, 'the same wave returning to the same shore' as Derrida described Levinas's work) as well as the body of interpretation, and further complications such as the mutual imbrication, explicit or implicit, of his philosophical and Talmudic studies, make quick summaries impossible. However, despite their different significations, these innovations can be broadly categorized as all representing fundamental challenges to the ways in which ethics is normally thought. As a thinking that emerges from the phenomenological tradition, Levinas builds upon but also departs from the approaches of Husserl and Heidegger in giving primacy to the ethical – his fundamental claim is that ethics is 'first philosophy', prior to rather than supplementary to ontology. Ethics as first philosophy concerns the relation of the human subject to alterity, to the epiphany of the infinite; as in Descartes, where the I thinks more than it can think (the infinite), the subject is exposed from the beginning, before it is even constituted and settled into place, by the epiphany of the other person, an experience which Levinas names 'Face'. The Face (*visage*) is not the assemblance of features of the front of the head, but rather the way in which the vulnerability of the other person is made manifest, and calls for a response: Levinas, also a Talmudic scholar, borrows Biblical language in expressing this call as the 'thou shalt not kill'. Subjectivity is thus primarily oriented to the other, that is, experienced as a modality of hospitality. (This is a reading of Levinas that Derrida emphasizes in *Adieu* – 'Although the word is neither frequently used nor emphasized within it, *Totality and Infinity* bequeaths to us an immense treatise of *hospitality* . . . the face always lends itself to a welcome'.)[127] However, the infinite responsibility, which one can have for a singular other, is challenged by the advent of the third (an advent that has always-already taken place – the third does not name a temporal disjuncture but rather an account of intersubjectivity), where decisions will have to be made between competing obligations. This represents the move in Levinas from ethics to justice, and thus to the sphere of politics.

In this sphere, the usual matters of politics, of decision, of weighing and calculating, are still pertinent. However, there is an important shift in politics accomplished by Levinas's ethics, which will be discussed further in chapter 3, but to summarize for present purposes, the move from ethics to justice does not undermine the anarchic nature of responsibility in Levinasian ethics. Responsibilities are still infinite and can never be wholly satisfied; which is to say, that the move from ethics to justice in Levinas does not represent a lapse into Aristotelianism, but rather the maintenance of an exorbitant sense of responsibility.

As Diane Perpich observes, in standard ethical philosophy, responsibility is often related to the proximity of the agent to the other in need.[128] For Levinas, however, this weighting is undermined: 'peace to the near and the far off', as he quotes from scripture; responsibility does not end with only those who are closest. Whereas some accounts of ethics emphasize reciprocity, Levinas is at pains to emphasize the non-reciprocal, asymmetric nature of the ethical demand, where all duties are incumbent on me, all rights due to the other, and where the responsibility of the other for me is not my concern. Instead of responsibility as autonomy, as the decisions willed by a conscious, free agent, responsibility in Levinas becomes an answerability to an obligation that is received prior to being made aware of it; as Alphonso Lingis writes in the translator's introduction to *Otherwise Than Being*, responsibility 'is already in act. To elucidate responsibility is to bring to light a bond in which one is already held, where there is still a demand to be answered'.[129] Responsibility, as noted above, is infinite rather than exhaustible; it is also not contained within 'reasonable limits', but is persecutory and open-ended, where the subject is held 'hostage' to the ethical demand produced by the other person.[130] According to Levinas, ethical responsibility calls freedom into question: indeed, in *TI* he defines ethics this way: 'We name this calling into question of my spontaneity by the presence of the Other ethics'.[131] Freedom is subject to 'investiture', that is, invested as goodness, consisting 'in an infinite movement of freedom putting itself ever more into question'.[132]

It is evident that a reconfigured sense of responsibility and its relation to freedom is made available by the thought of Levinas. However, how is this to be related to the mooted new concept of the political, on the one hand, and the effectuation of changes within the realm of lived political experience, on the other?

While Levinas is indeed not a political theorist sensu stricto, this does not mean he did not think the political. The very first lines of *TI*, indeed the entire opening section, situate Levinas's discourse precisely in relation to politics. Consequently, as a thinker of politics and of hospitality, Levinas is of paramount importance in thinking through the politics of asylum. In articulating eschatological peace, Levinas does not claim that there is no violence, or no possibility of violence, or that war and violence do not dominate, that realism holds sway. The point is that they do not exhaust the meaning of what is proper to human existence, which, in its exposure to the infinite, is always-already oriented towards hospitality to the other. This has little if anything to do with the politics of decency or of benevolence, that or the disavowal of conflict via a pietistic politics of ethics, as Chantal Mouffe imputes to him.[133] It has to do with a reoriented understanding of subjectivity and the relationship of ethics to ontology.

To assert the imperious ontology of the dominating subject denies the undeniable transcendence of the other, revealed in the Face, which is constitutive of subjectivity. As soon as this is acknowledged, then the 'ultimate events' of being are no longer those reducible to consciousness or rational thought, and the permanent possibility of eschatological peace is revealed as that which lies beyond totality. Such was the revolution effected by Levinas in phenomenology: to move it beyond *phanein*, that which shines or appears, to reveal the 'night' of the structures of being that are not disclosed to consciousness, but which orient and inform it. But politics does not treat of this understanding of subjectivity, of ethics as prior to and constitutive of ontological beings. The failure to treat the infinite or unconditioned – dismissed as religion – is the failure to undertake a serious assessment of that which underpins political life – the experience of the human beings who participate in such life, and their anterior constitution by the ethical relation. The sense of responsibility that is thus articulated by the work of Levinas has barely been noticed or taken seriously by political theorists and political philosophers. But why this tremendous unseriousness about so serious a matter? Why this resting of an entire tradition of political thought on erroneous ontological presuppositions? Why is transcendence, the idea of the infinite, in the Descartian–Levinasian sense, not a part of the schema of understanding what subjectivity means, that subsequently informs the nature of politics?

This need for a reworked understanding of the relationship between ethics and ontology that would inform concepts of the political puts *TI* in focus. According to a post-Derridian reception of Levinas, *TI* has been viewed as a kind of early draft for *Otherwise Than Being*, with the earlier work being too problematically implicated in metaphysical language that does not escape the realm of ontology, which, subsequent to Derrida's critique in 'Violence and Metaphysics', is corrected and reworked in *Otherwise Than Being*. Yet this view has been significantly challenged in recent scholarship, most notably in a wonderful reading by Raoul Moati in *Levinas and the Night of Being: A Guide to Totality and Infinity* (hereafter *LNB*). Moati's reading demonstrates that the projects of these books are distinct, and that the understanding of ontology and metaphysics provided by TI reveals a world shared in common by 'nocturnal events', that is, events which are not revealed by the light of consciousness but which are constitutive of the ontological as such; an ontology which is 'ethical through and through'.[134]

Such an ontological ethics is distinct from the fundamental ontology of Heidegger (where ethics is subsequent to the unveiling of being and the thrownness of Dasein) or of Sartre (where ethics, as he notes at the end of *Being and Nothingness*, cannot be derived from ontology). *LNB* takes up Levinas as an ontological thinker who nevertheless goes beyond Heidegger in describing 'nocturnal' events, that is, prior to unveiling, as that which give ontological/ethical meaning to the human, that are not reducible to thrownness, but are manifested as the sociality engendered by language, the holding of the world in common. Moati writes of a 'de-totalised communism', that is, a key lesson of *TI* is that the world is that which is always-already shared amongst plural beings.[135] Key to the emphasis of this reading is that events disclosed by the 'daytime' of consciousness do not exhaust the meaning of human experience: as Levinas writes in *TI*, 'Hence intentionality, where thought remains an *adequation* [a reference to Husserl] with the object, does not define consciousness at its fundamental level. All knowing qua intentionality already presupposes the idea of infinity, which is preeminently *non-adequation*'.[136] Consequently, 'Consciousness [consists in] overflowing this play of lights . . . No prior disclosure illuminates the production of these essentially nocturnal events'.[137]

A particularly interesting element of Moati's analysis is the exploration of Levinas's discussion of 'eschatology', which is a prominent feature of *TI* that is not emphasized in *Otherwise Than Being*. The use of the term eschatology is the type of religious terminology that has a tendency to irk secular academics and lead to lazy dismissals of Levinas as sneaking religion into the secular. But what does Levinas mean by eschatology? It is not, to be sure, the literal end-times of religious prophecy, the final moments of human earthly destiny; rather, eschatology 'designates an experience in which being is produced as transcendence', through language, which '"breaks with the totality of wars and empires in which one does not speak"'.[138] Language is the primary mode of the revelation of the 'Face' (*visage*), which reveals the Other in their transcendence and thus 'undoes every totalizing form which would aim to attribute a sense to it through its inscription in an objective system of signification'.[139] However, traditional philosophy prefers rational epistemology as a grounding for knowledge, and even in phenomenology, the emphasis on intentionality recapitulates the diurnal privilege within philosophy – those things that appear in the light of consciousness. What *TI* thus provides is a move beyond the diurnal, beyond the surface evidence of human interactions – so often bound up with war and conquest – to the nocturnal, that which is occurring beyond the light: 'The existence of a *nocturnal deployment of being* means that all that is not revealed by the regime of objective evidence – the idea of infinity above all – can no longer be relegated to the level of opinion, consecrated to the universal domination of totalization and history over human beings'.[140] In other words – and this is the key point when considering these matters for a reworked concept of the political – an emphasis upon ethics, human commonality and sociality, can no longer be 'relegated to the sphere of opinion', the freely willed decisions of the autonomous subject operating from a position of self-mastery who would dismiss moral claims as mere assertion. The revelation of (the idea of) infinity in human subjectivity reveals the world beyond the imperious self, an ipseity that is found precisely in its relation to the Other, an ethics that is bound up with the ontological itself. Ethical subjectivity is not the projected opinion of bleeding hearts, but the structure of subjectivity as such. On this point, Moati notes that Levinas situates his discourse deliberately in a post-Nietzschean landscape, beyond the illusions of religious piety and moral assertion. If morality has sought to escape reality by lying about it, the task which Levinas has to accomplish is to demonstrate the reality of moral demands – hence Descartes and infinity, the 'night of being' and nocturnal events that ultimately reveal world shared in common, a 'communism' beneath the totality of being where the latter is understood as the potential for divisive war of all against all. Moati also criticizes the Derridian reading of *TI* in 'Violence and Metaphysics', which has held such dominant sway over Levinas reception, arguing that Derrida and Levinas part company concerning intentionality and eschatology, a complex argument that needs to be read in full to be appreciated, but which rehabilitates the Levinasian position by demonstrating the disagreement between Derrida and Levinas, as opposed to the simple error of the latter. For Derrida, history is interrupted by otherness *within* history (and hence the correctness of Husserlian transcendental philosophy), whereas for Levinas the infinite is eschatological in that it *suspends* the flow of history,[141] and thus the real of history needs to be considered by that which lies beyond the light of intellection as revealing a world shared in common: 'The categorical error of the ontology of knowledge lies in the confusion that consists in attempting to deduce what undergirds and constitutes events from the visibility of the light of those events themselves.'[142]

Understanding subjectivity as hospitality and welcoming the other represents a fundmaental challenge to more dominant accounts of political subjectivity which, blinded by the light of the merely apparent, end up committing a category error concerning the real. Thus, when we turn to a discussion of a reworked concept of the political around the right to asylum, a truly 'realist' assessment will be to note the given nature of ethical subjectivity that is constitutive of those subjects that engage in politics, who may engage in hostility, but who also retain the permanent possibility of hospitality to the other who has called to them from the beginning. This is vitally important in the elaboration of an *ethos* of responsibility, because in terms of understanding the political, a proper understanding of the onto-logical claims or suppositions upon which political concepts rest will be of decisive importance. Moati writes, 'In deducing the ontological productivity of metaphysical events, *Totality and Infinity* leads to a – nocturnal – enlarge-ment of ontology and thus announces the advent, within being, of the human sociality beyond war and empire'.[143] The permanent possibility of welcom-ing the other – a welcome constitutive of subjectivity – is constitutive also of *political* subjects who enter into plural dialogue and dissent concerning political decision-making. If an orientation to hospitality is part of sub-jectivity, then the decisions of such subjects concerning political asylum, once free from the warping of a false ontological understanding, can be understood beyond the limits of the immediately comprehensible. As David Steiner writes – and this is a decisive summation for the overall argument pursued here – 'Levinas' account supplies, as it were, the *missing history* of the pre-socialized self: the political animal is itself a consequence of the ethical call of the other's visage that summons me to an autonomy already cast as responsibility'.[144]

The non-identity to itself of the subject is as true at the monadic individual level as it is at the social and political level: 'what is proper to a culture is to not be identical to itself', as Derrida wrote in *The Other Heading*, and thus what is proper to a responsible society is to be engaged in 'advancing itself in an exemplary way toward what it is not'.[145] Here the recourse to Arendt via Butler's reinterpretation with reference to Levinas is decisive. In *Parting Ways*, Butler emphasizes that the implication of unchosen plurality and Levinasian responsibility is that obligation is a pre-contractual matter;[146] the 'we' of a political community is never only free but already obligated:

> For whoever 'we' are, we are also those who were never chosen, who emerge on this earth without everyone's consent, and who belong, from the start, to a wider population and a sustainable earth. And this condition, paradoxically, yields the radical potential for new modes of sociality and politics beyond the avid and wretched bonds of a pernicious colonialism that calls itself democracy.[147]

The reference to colonialism is to Israel–Palestine, but is more broadly appli-cable, not only in relation to settler-colonial societies, but to the history of Europe and other imperial powers who have carved up the world in the name of their sovereign power. This is an outdated model of self-determination that is now dramatically at odds with the urgent need to safeguard a 'sustainable

earth', in the looming climate crisis (including a significant refugee dimension
which cannot be dissociated from climate change in a mutuality of disaster)
that will not respect state borders in its impacts. Arendt opposed a certain logic
of sovereignty with that of freedom, but her assessment of freedom is altered
in Butler's argument. Butler will even refer to the 'violence' in the thought
of Levinas – ostensibly paradoxical for a preeminent thinker of the ethical
– 'It is this foreclosure of freedom and will through the command that is its
"violent" operation, understood variously as persecutory and accusatory'.[148]
Why does this constitute violence? For Levinas, without being held hostage
there is no responsibility; this is because the other is not simply exterior to
the subject, but is constitutive of subjectivity as such, that impacts it prior to
the subject being able to will or exercise freedom.[149] 'According to Levinas,
we affirm the unfreedom at the heart of our relations with others, and only by
ceding in this way do we come to understand responsibility.'[150] Freedom for
Levinas is a 'difficult' experience – the free self can fix the limits of responsibility only 'in the name of that original responsibility', which is anterior to
freedom.[151] It should be noted that Arendt distinguished freedom from willing,
even though she recognized that willing is related to the exercise of freedom.
Yet Arendt's concept of responsibility is by no means the same as Levinas,
but relates to the activity of thinking which leads to the ability to form judgements but is made possible because freedom qua politics can be actualized.[152]
What emerges in Butler's reading is a repositioning of Arendtian themes in
a new Levinasian direction, where it is not a matter of emphasizing freedom
but rather responsibility as 'unfreedom'. If there is a constitutive normative
unfreedom in unchosen plurality, then the meaning of politics is not simply
freedom, as Arendt explicitly defined it in her essay 'What Is Freedom?'.[153]
Here a return to the thematic of violence is required. In *On Violence*, Arendt
directly opposes power to violence, arguing that the manifestation of violence
is the failure of power: 'Power and violence are opposites; where the one rules
absolutely, the other is absent. Violence appears where power is in jeopardy,
but left to its own courses it ends in power's disappearance.'[154] There is a resonance here with Walter Benjamin's much-analysed essay 'Towards a Critique
of Violence', with the distinction between law-making and law-preserving
violence on the one hand, and 'divine' violence on the other.[155] What Arendt
means by 'power' would seem to be resonant with 'divine' violence in the
othering of forms of official violence in the manifestation of novel forms of
action by plural human beings acting in concert.

    In *The Human Condition*, Arendt argues that attempts to define human
nature usually end in an attempt to construct a deity, the God of Plato (leaving talk of human nature aside, there is certainly a linkage of transcendence to
Plato in Levinas).[156] But then how does Arendt address transcendence? What
is the normative content of the plurality she defends? If it's just given as an

ontological condition then what would be wrong with messing with plurality, reducing it? There must be something there, in human plural human beings, that is worth defending, surely beyond their 'meaningful speech'. It is on this point that the Levinasian account of subjectivity complements, and perhaps completes, the Arendtian picture of plurality.[157] Anya Topolski argues that there is an ethical lacuna (a failure to think alterity) in Arendt, and a political lacuna (a failure to think plurality) in Levinas, and that plurality and alterity can be brought together under the banner of 'relationality', built upon four 'background elements' that these thinkers have in common: the Shoah, phenomenology, Heidegger, and the Judaic.[158] Key to this idea of relationality, according to Topolski, is a shared sense of responsibility.[159] However, Arendt is not animated by the same conception of responsibility as Levinas. Arendt's thinking of responsibility is related to Kantian notions of judgement and the activity of thinking, whereas for Levinas responsibility is a response – *me voici* (or *hineni* in the Jewish tradition) – to the Face of the other person. Nevertheless, there are points of commonality and complementarity in their work; hence the importance of the work that Butler and Topolski accomplish in thinking these two in conjunction. Butler's extends this work explicitly into the realm of thinking the 'common rights of the refugee', and her argument in particular is extremely close to what is intended here by an *ethos* of responsibility.

Arendt charged that philosophy was not concerned with freedom, thus if politics is coterminous with freedom on her account – that is, the guarantee of a space of appearances where the 'miracle' of natality can be realized in action – does that mean that the normative implications of unchosen plurality and Levinasian responsibility are forms of Platonism, of attempting to impose upon free spaces ideals of the good?[160] Levinas will acknowledge in *TI* that the implication of his metaphysical account of ethics in that work means 'we thus encounter, in our own way, the Platonic idea of the Good beyond Being'.[161] But his account of the ethical, along with Arendt's own thinking of plurality as reinterpreted by Butler, represents a phenomenologico-philosophical account of the preconditions of political life, which the latter – if posited as self-constituting ex nihilo, as merely the effect of agreements, contracts, voluntary willed association – fails to take into account. Arendt did acknowledge that appearing, speaking, and acting precede the constitution of government.[162] In this sense, she is aligned with Levinas in the human conditions that are prior to but constitutive of political life; however, she did not address the normative implications of ethical alterity – when she refers to *alteritas* in *The Human Condition*, she distinguishes it from human distinctness, the latter being a feature of plurality, the former being a kind of mere generalized non-human otherness.[163]

Arendt noted the 'pragmatic soundness' of Edmund Burke's condemnation of natural rights, as powerless to prevent the immiseration of stateless persons. And yet if politics is dependent upon promising, then the security of political agreements is no stronger than the willingness of parties to agree to honour their commitments. The promises of liberalism at the time of the Second World War evaporated, as both Arendt and Levinas bitterly noted. In this sense, political promise-making is as unreliable as natural rights. A move beyond both liberalism and natural rights is required, that will not restate the fallacies of natural rights, but will also answer the 'elemental' 'philosophy of Hitlerism', with an 'alternative elemental philosophy' (Critchley) that attends to the human condition without falling into biologism and racism, that proceeds on a universal basis, that will 'guarantee' without succumbing to the totalization of political life. From Levinas's 'Reflections on the Philosophy of Hitlerism' to Arendt's call for a new guarantee, the mutual search for this basis, qua *guarantee*, is evident: as Topolski writes, 'While there are certainly many fundamental differences between their projects, which is why we cannot simply reduce alterity to plurality, I believe that Levinas's ethics as first philosophy, like Arendt's rethinking of the political, seeks a new post-foundational guarantee of human dignity rooted in difference'.[164] However, Topolski is unclear about Levinas's commitment to the notion of guarantee, arguing in one place that he accepts that there are no guarantees, and a bit further on quoting Levinas from his essay 'The Rights of Man and the Rights of the Other', to the effect that recognizing the phenomenology of the 'rights of man' has an 'immutable significance and stability, better than *guaranteed* by the state'[165] (emphasis added). What is striking in Levinas's claim is that it is precisely opposite to Arendt, not in the defence of natural rights – his work is a move beyond natural rights in the articulation of humanity via phenomenology – but in establishing the basis of human dignity outside of political life, an 'immutable' and universal claim that will always hold and provide a criterion of judgement for the political at all times:

> The order of politics (post-ethical or pre-ethical) that inaugurates the 'social contract' is neither the sufficient condition nor the necessary outcome of ethics. In its ethical position, the *I* is distinct both from the citizen born of the city and from the individual who precedes all order in his natural egotism, but from whom political philosophy, since Hobbes, has tried to derive – or succeeded in deriving – the social or political order of the city.[166]

Thus, Levinas extends the possibilities of thinking political life beyond the order of what Arendt allows for, in an ethical direction, where there is something beyond the social contracts of political philosophy, *a good at which politics must aim*: '"Thou shalt not kill" – that means then "Thou shalt cause thy neighbour to live"', an active preservation of the lives of others as a political duty.[167] However, here a limitation must be marked. Neither Arendt nor Levinas ever explicitly developed a politico-philosophical anthropology that might fully account for the necessary interrelation between ethics and ontology, being that which is proper to the being of human beings, and the actualization of the ethical, or the just, forms of realization of the good or 'virtuous' life. As has been seen, Judith Butler has developed a reading of politics that combines Arendt and Levinas in important ways, a task developed by Anya Topolski in combining plurality and alterity into a politics of 'relationality'. Yet this may be further extended and deepened with reference to the work of Andrew Benjamin, a contemporary philosopher who has recently pursued the task of constructing a philosophical anthropology that can furnish criteria of judgement for thinking the nature of place and belonging, including for stateless persons, in a way that is never fully elaborated by either Arendt or Levinas. An examination of his work follows.

ANDREW BENJAMIN: PLACEDNESS AND BEING-IN-COMMON

Subjectivity is hospitality, and subjectivity is lived out in conditions of plurality – of multiple subjects sharing a world. And yet with so many people on earth lacking a world (employing Heidegger's distinction between earth and world), that is, a place of common belonging, Hannah Arendt's idea of the 'right to have rights' has garnered enormous attention in recent times; greater analysis of this right will be undertaken in the following chapter. But before preceding to the analysis of the right to have rights, it must be established: why does a human being need such a right? And can this right be thought of as itself a primary goal of politics? What is the relationship of this right to the new law on earth concerning plurality, and how does this fit with having a place to be and a right to live in common with others?

Here the work of Andrew Benjamin becomes of decisive importance. Benjamin has developed across multiple texts a 'philosophical anthropology' where he outlines an account of that which is proper to the being of being-human, which can provide criteria of judgement for the political, including questions of asylum.[168] Of particular importance in thinking Arendt alongside Benjamin is that both are explicitly thinkers of *plurality*. Benjamin has in the past three decades developed a thinking of plurality from his 1993 book *The Plural Event*, to 2015's *Towards a Relational Ontology*. In the latter he writes that 'the truth of relationality brings a form of plurality into play, and therefore what is true of relationality, correspondingly, could not be given by any one form of singularity in which that singularity would have been taken as primary'.[169] In 'anoriginal' relationality as a form of plurality ('the anoriginal plurality of the event',[170] the plural nature of all that occurs between human beings), the political implication is clear – Benjamin's work can be thought alongside the preceding reflections, where the world is always-already shared in common (Levinas and the 'night' of being), amongst unchosen plural humanity (Arendt–Butler). This would also constitute a further riposte to political liberalism, in that the latter posits, erroneously, the autonomous, monadic subject that then enters into contracts with others, neglecting the anoriginal nature of relationality, the 'communism' (Moati's provocative term) underlying human identity, the plural event of being-in-common.

In *Place, Commonality and Judgement*, Benjamin questions whether there are not 'conditions of possibility' of thinking measure that 'allows for forms of interruption' This is linked to *place* as the site of contestability of *nomos* and *diké*, law and justice. The polis, the city or state, is the place in which the negotiation between law and justice is enacted: 'The ineliminability of alterity and thus the need to think the possibility of a conception of alterity that involves reconciliation to irreconcilability is that which is staged by the city wall.'[171]

This reference to the 'ineliminability of alterity' underscores the Levinasian–Arendtian nexus of unchosen plurality as the permanent condition of human cohabitation, and the experience of the human subject as formed by its encounter with the other which calls to it, engaging its responsibility. But to these thinkers, Benjamin adds the emphases of place and commonality. For example, the Arendtian emphasis upon the 'space of appearances' is not a thinking of placedness in the same way, but rather an account of human inter-subjectivity. She distinguishes 'Athenians' from 'Athens' as the proper locus of the polis, whereas Benjamin emphasizes the necessity of a physical place to inhabit, as well as to belong in the Arendtian sense – a thought not opposed to Arendt's, but which complements and extends it. As Benjamin articulates, that which is proper to the being of human beings is to be in-place and to be in-common;[172] he argues that Arendt did accept such a view, even if less directly: 'Arendt accepts, with justification, the identification of the being of being-human with *being-in-place*, evidence for which is in part provided by a reformulation of Kant in which humans become "earthbound creatures"'.[173] Benjamin writes 'that central to the primordiality of both *nomos* and *diké* is an original sense of place. Human being is placed. As such human being is always *being-in-place*'.[174] For Benjamin, in similar fashion to Levinas, there is an anoriginal relation between ethics and ontology, that is, that difference lies at the origin of human life and human community.[175] 'Rather than uncovering ways of connecting the ontological and the ethical, what their already existent relation identifies is the presence of what will henceforth be described as *virtue in being*'.[176] The contingency of being human gives rise to the oscillation between conditioned and unconditioned, which 'underscores the necessity for judgment'.[177] Such being-in-common is not only an ontological but an ethical status: 'The substantive point is that the presence of the anoriginal understood as irreducibility is a claim that defines the being of being human . . . There is no need to account for how the ontological could come to attain or acquire an ethical dimension. The position would be that they are always already related.'[178] This is very close to Levinas, who conceives of ethics as prior to ontology – whether prior or coterminous, the point remains that for these thinkers the ethics does not arrive as an optional addendum after the fact of the cold reality of the ontological, but is always-already present.[179] Levinas too is a thinker of place, in the persistent calling into question of ones' being as the potential usurpation of the right of the other to be – hence his persistent quotation of Pascal, that my place in the sun is the beginning of the usurpation of the entire earth.[180] It is also very close to Arendt in being at the antipodes of Carl Schmitt, in that placedness does not refer to the violent appropriation of a territory, but rather the ontological requirement of every human being to reside somewhere, in place and in common with others, a claim that is ethical and ontological at once, without requiring appropriation, dispossession, or domination but rather aims at actualization of forms of the just life.

This leads to the establishment of what Benjamin calls a 'relational ontology' where the necessity of being-in-common with others, or what Arendt similarly refers to as the space of appearance amongst plural human beings, is the essential characteristic of human existence as such.

There is a rich fund of concepts operative in the Benjaminian philosophical anthropology – being-in-place, being-in-common, virtue in being, the anoriginal relation of ethics and ontology qua relational ontology, place as linked to judgement, and the '*caesura* of allowing' – an interruption of measure that allows for forms of countermeasure, in (Walter) Benjamins's sense, that opens the gateway to justice: as Andrew Benjamin writes, 'the counter-measure, is provided by the potentiality for the "just life" that inheres in 'mere life'.[181] It is difficult to treat all of these concepts here; however, one particular emphasis might be marked in relation to *law*, a key theme in the present elaboration of the *ethos* of responsibility. The link between Benjamin and Arendt is interesting in the insistence upon a reference to the 'law' – from a new 'law on earth' in Arendt, to the 'law' in Benjamin as the striving at work in the interplay between the conditioned and the unconditioned, as well as (quoted above) the centrality of place to *nomos*. In defining what he means by law, Benjamin writes: 'As a result of the possibility of the unconditioned within the structure of law, finite being would then be understood as *being before-the-law* where the latter is the constancy of an opening to justice'.[182] Law figures as the constant exposure of the finite or conditioned, to the infinite or unconditioned, which opens the possibility of justice, a before-the-law which leads to the realization of justice, rather than its opposite as in Kafka's nightmarish tales. In reference to Kant's notion of radical evil, Benjamin argues: 'What this means of course is that the calculable has undone the incalculable. Evil is another name for actions that work on the fragility of the unconditioned's presence and thus the attendant possibility to undo it. In Arendtian terms, this is the continual threat of violence. The essential point, however, is that evil can be judged.'[183] Evil here pertains to the undoing of the unconditioned, or what one might also refer to in Levinasian terms as the infinite demand issuing from the other, where the ethical nature of a decision is not reducible to calculation.

This line of thought will be of the utmost importance in the chapters that follow, in that the problem of numbers as a delimitation of the possibilities of proffering asylum will be critically analysed. Benjamin agrees with Arendt in seeing the undoing of the political space of appearances as 'violent', that is, opposed to power constituted as the plurality of peoples who may undertake action together. To the extent that the right of people to enter into such spaces is denied, this reading of violence seems dispositive. However, as has been argued throughout, it may be necessary to be violent to those forms of self-determination that would themselves delimit the access to the space of appearances, which as seen in relation to Arendt's Aristotelianism, she was not immune to. Hence the important addition of the notion of the interplay of the conditioned with the unconditioned as an order of law above legality. The elimination of worldliness and the production of mere life, as opposed to just life, is effectuated by violence, where the conditioned and the merely calculable dominate or defeat the possibility of the actualization of the unconditional demand. It is this, which can be defined in Kant/Benjamin's terms as a form of *evil*, that the law which Benjamin articulates guards against by articulating possibilities of judgement. In other words, Arendt's new law on earth must be thought in relation to the Benjaminian law concerning the relation between the conditioned and the unconditioned, where the necessity of human beings to live as being-in-place and being-in-common with each other is produced as the unconditional demand within the mediating conditional context of political life.

This new perspective then provides an orientation for the forming of political judgements; as Benjamin argues, one should recognize and respect the modesty of philosophy (and one can add, political theory) in informing rather than forming political life, 'to mark the limit of the philosophical'.[184] Yet the relational ontology that recognizes the anoriginal relation of ethics and ontology in reference to place and commonality, furnishes clear criteria for judgement concerning the position of the stateless person – to be denied placedness or the ability to live amongst others is a crime against the realization of their very humanity. It is not a matter of new philosopher-kings who will *impose* the right to asylum(!), but the articulation of a new understanding of the political and the means to form judgements on that basis that might move the politics of asylum beyond its current death-producing sclerosis. On the question of judgement, Benjamin, Arendt, and Butler come into fascinating proximity. For Benjamin and Arendt, as avowed Kantians, judgement is the necessary form in which thinking must crystalize. In a close reading of Arendt's verdict on the Eichmann trial, Butler discerns in this text of multiple voices (the different voices of Arendt, and the judges) that judgement itself is a plural undertaking, an activity that goes on between plural beings.[185] For Benjamin, the polis, the political community is the locus of justice where judgements can be formed. Judgement itself is to be informed by the human being as a being-in-place and a being-in-common, where commonality constituted of unchosen plurality amongst subjects who in becoming subjects are oriented towards hospitality.[186] However, it must be emphasized that Benjamin does not articulate his work in the language of guarantee; here the *ethos* of responsibility must be distinguished from Benjamin's work, while being articulated in affirmative relation to it.

CONCLUSION

Politics, as it pertains to asylum, when reconsidered in the preceding ways, undergoes a shift in emphasis from the optional, contestable configuration of the liberal-democratic 'paradox' and is transformed into a *guarantee* of the safeguarding of the human dignity and wellbeing of stateless persons. The term 'guarantee' plays an interesting role in the thought of both Levinas and Arendt – as discussed, Arendt calls for a 'new guarantee of human dignity' in the Preface to *Origins of Totalitarianism*, which scholars have linked to her analysis of the 'right to have rights'. As noted above, Levinas similarly sought a respect for the rights of others 'better than guaranteed by the state'.[187] Such is the true violence of their arguments, where violence is opposed to power defined as the free exercise of action, in the undoing of the right of communities to determine their own members, the undoing of tragic dialectics or liberal-democratic paradoxes around asylum.

Even if they are violent in that sense, the implication of these arguments is that an anti-thanatoic concept of the political can emerge that provides essential criteria of judgement, criteria opposed both to the much graver violence of the death-producing practices of the Nazi state, and the violent death-producing or death-allowing practices of modern (including liberal) sovereign states.[188] In the Epilogue to *Eichmann in Jerusalem*, Arendt argues that 'the unprecedented, once it has appeared, maybe become a precedent for the future . . . If genocide is an actual possibility of the future, then no people on earth . . . can feel reasonably sure of its continued existence without the help and protection of international law'.[189] In this the universality of the demand for the protection of human plurality that runs throughout Arendt's work is manifest as that which is relevant to the safety of all. Yet in *Origins* she also recognized the limitations of international law in the formal, legal sense, hence her desire for a new law on earth that would serve as a new political 'principle'. In place of a model of politics focused around sovereignty and the distinction between citizens and foreigners, Arendt (and reading Arendt, Butler) provides for the possibility of a politics built around cohabitation and respect for plurality as the *telos* of the political, realized via respect for the right to asylum. Butler shares Arendt's concerns about mutual protection – in *Precarious Life*, she writes: 'One insight that injury affords is that there are others out there on whom my life depends, people I do not know and may never know. This fundamental dependency on anonymous others is not a condition that I can will away. No security measure will foreclose this dependency; no violent act of sovereignty will rid the world of this fact'.[190] A move beyond sovereignty as security is required: 'I would suggest, however, that both our political and ethical responsibilities are rooted in the recognition that radical forms of self-sufficiency and unbridled sovereignty are, by definition, disrupted by the larger global processes of which they are a part, that no final control can be secured, and that final control is not, cannot be, an ultimate value.'[191]

Attendant to this is the Levinasian conception of subjectivity which is constituted as hospitality and responsibility. These alternatives of political life and political subjectivity are vitally important, because politics as currently practised means inevitable death and immiseration for some people. Hobbesian fear of strangers is not the only, or necessarily even meaningful, way of understanding intersubjectivity, nor the reciprocal arrangements of Aristotle – to mention but two dominant proper names in this domain – hence the foundational challenge to political philosophy represented by the thought of Arendt and Levinas. It may be that fear of foreigners will always exist, that people sometimes feel like strangers in their 'own' societies. But that's as should be in a world of unchosen plurality: as Adorno observed, 'it is part of morality not to be at home in one's home'.[192] In the delimited context of the right to asylum, states and political communities generally should not even have the right to determine who exercises that right – this means, as I have argued elsewhere, that the right to have rights means a right to enter and have one's case heard, a right not just tolerated but actively facilitated by the political community.[193] And more than open borders or respecting the right to asylum are required – rather an overt solicitude, an *ethos* of responsibility, which is to say the *active preservation*, to borrow Butler's formulation, of human plurality. Of course, many liberal theorists would argue that they respect the right to asylum and to resettlement, but crucially, not in the context of defining asylum as the proper work of politics, which ends up casting the whole game back into the lamentations of the failure of states to make better judgements. The guarantee, while opposed to absolute political freedom in stipulating duties of responsibility, is nevertheless not an authoritarianism or totalitarianism – cheap objections should be dispensed with early – in that it is evinced from the entirely defensible, in my view dispositive, moral demand that stateless persons have a right to be protected and to belong, developed from an account of a rigorous philosophical anthropology linking Arendt to Levinas, Butler, Benjamin, and others. Those who argue that this poses a threat to organized political life (which has at times included Arendt) have yet to furnish the evidence of this, have certainly *never*, to my knowledge, furnished it *convincingly*; it is a vague fear concerning the limits of politics, as troublingly vague as Aristotle himself in setting such limits in *The Politics* (more on this in chapter 3). The analysis of such arguments and their debunking, as well as the demonstration of their moral bankruptcy, will be the work of the chapters that follow.

Political freedom – of association, or the right to self-determination exercised as the trinity of state, people, and territory (Arendt) – is not an absolute good if its continuance depends upon the filling of graveyards, graveyards in the earth, in the sea, in the sky, and this, as will be seen, is no hyperbole. In order for responsibility to become manifest, what is required is an undoing of the 'paradox' of the liberal-democratic chiasmus, replaced with a *guarantee*, for all the violence of that notion to the space of politics as freedom – strictly in the context of asylum, a new guarantee of human dignity. Once more: plurality is the *nomos* of the earth, and thus normatively the *telos* of the political as such, in ensuring that all human beings may appear amongst others and find a place to belong and to act. In order to guarantee this *qua* the *active* preservation of the dignity of all human beings, in a world of bounded communities where responsibility and cohabitation are understood as primary and not derivative, the right to asylum becomes central to politics, the condition of its realization. Thus, respect for asylum becomes coterminous with the essence of politics as such.

NOTES

1. Emmanuel Levinas, *Totality and Infinity: An Essay on Exteriority*, intro. Richard Cohen and trans. Alphonso Lingis (Pittsburgh, PA: Duquesne University Press, 2007), p. 27.

2. Arendt, *The Life of the Mind*, p. 19.

3. Arendt, *The Human Condition*, pp. 198–99.

4. Arendt, *The Origins of Totalitarianism*, p. ix.

5. Arendt, *The Origins of Totalitarianism*, p. ix.

6. Heidegger, 'Letter on Humanism', p. 176.

7. Heidegger, 'Letter on Humanism', p. 176.

8. Hannah Arendt, *On Violence* (London: Allen Lane The Penguin Press, 1970), p. 43.

9. Hannah Arendt, *The Promise of Politics*, ed. Jerome Kohn (New York, NY: Schocken Books, 2005), p. 3.

10. Judith Butler, *The Force of Non-Violence* (London and New York, NY: Verso, 2020), p. 3. In this more recent book (recent in comparison to the privilege I accord in my reading of Butler to 2012's *Parting Ways*) there is a pivot to a close reading of psychoanalytic texts, which produces a shift in Butler's emphases, such that the unavoidable nature of hostility as the obverse of love must be contended with in political life, a move beyond Levinasian responsibility and certainly beyond what Levinas would endorse (he eschewed psychoanalysis entirely). On the question of the subject as hostile or hospitable, it might be illuminating to read Butler's book in relation to both Levinas and, for example, Pierre-Saint Amand's influential book *The Laws of Hostility*. My own view is that Levinasian responsibility provides an account of human subjectivity where the binary of love and hate as evinced in certain psychoanalytic postulates is, if not overcome or defeated, importantly challenged; there is an event of contact beyond that parsed in the conscious or unconscious mind, a demand placed upon the subject by another, the 'epiphany' of the other that is at once an external event and constitutive of the ipseity (selfhood) of the subject, a call to responsibility that is not reducible to psychoanalytic explanation.

11. Margaret Canovan, *Hannah Arendt: A Reinterpretation of Her Political Thought* (Cambridge: Cambridge University Press, 1995), pp. 198–99.

12. See https://www.etymonline.com/word/guarantee, retrieved 25 August 2020.

13. Carens, *The Ethics of Immigration*, p. 221. The limits of a book-length discussion of my own argument mean that a full engagement with alternative positions must be pursued elsewhere. However, I want to mark my respect for many of Caren's positions; not only is he known as an advocate of open borders, but in the chapter on refugees in *The Ethics of Immigration* his instincts are on the whole very generous, compassionate, and open. He even stipulates a criterion of judgement which I am also employing throughout this book – when we think about the politics of asylum, we must consider what our approaches would have resulted in for European Jewry at the time of Nazism (p. 194). However, the above cited limitation in relation to the tension of self-determination with universal liberal obligations finds Carens ending his chapter with the lament that it would be a considerable achievement just to get states to accept their obligations. The reason asylum is a 'secondary' duty, according to him, is because the primary duty to an individual is owed by their state. While I share his lament, it is this logic that the implications of plurality as the law of the earth moves beyond, where cohabitation is a shared, primary, anoriginal relation and duty to uphold. He also tarries with concerns about 'absorptive capacity' (but how to define this?) and 'reasonable limits' (while also saying that the limit is 'almost never' reached).

14. Benhabib, *The Rights of Others*.

15. Kant, 'Toward Perpetual Peace', p. 82.

16. Chantal Mouffe, *The Democratic Paradox* (London and New York, NY: Verso, 2009), p. 140.

17. Benhabib, *The Rights of Others*, p. 220.

18. Parekh, *Refugees and the Ethics of Forced Displacement*.

19. Serena Parekh, *Hannah Arendt and the Challenge of Modernity: A Phenomenology of Human Rights* (New York, NY and London: Routledge, 2008). As Parekh writes, 'In the spirit of Arendt's phenomenological method, the goal of the book is not to develop a normative theory, but to clarify and bring to light the complexities and contradictions in the concept of human rights within modernity' (p. 6). I think Parekh is correct to emphasize the phenomenological character of Arendt's quest for understanding as a move beyond natural rights; however, we part company on the quest for a normative theory; I agree more with thinkers like Birmingham and Butler who see just such a theory as latent in Arendt's work, if not developed or even agreed to by Arendt herself.

20. For an example of intra-socialist state disputation, see Grant Evans and Kelvin Rowley, *Red Brotherhood at War: Vietnam, Cambodia and Laos Since 1975* (London and New York, NY: Verso, 1990). The book 'explains why communist victory did not usher in a period of peace based on proletarian internationalism'. Similarly, Benedict Anderson's highly influential *Imagined Communities* begins with a meditation on the phenomenon of '*large-scale conventional war* waged by one revolutionary Marxist regime against another' (Vietnam versus Cambodia), as well as China's attack on Vietnam, and Soviet interventions in Eastern Europe. The role of nationalism in the success of twentieth-century revolutions potentially undermines confidence that the success of socialism will necessarily give rise to the kind of internationalism that will make respect for asylum and non-nationals a fait accompli. See Anderson, *Imagined Communities*, pp. 1–2. However it should also be noted that nascent socialist/communist revolutions are usually immediately attacked and undermined by the forces of capital and hegemonic states, which should form at least part of the context in analysing the difficulties and failures of such revolutions. Thanks to Valentin Cartillier for the reminder on this point.

21. The phrase 'nomadic proletariat' is employed in a number of Badiou's texts; for an explicit discussion of this theme, see his *Migrants and Militants* (Polity, 2020).

22. Dignity should be guaranteed for both migrants and refugees, but the legal as well as the rhetorico-political impact of the term refugee argues for its retention as a distinct category. An example: In 2014, with a surge of children from Central America arriving in the United States, Obama treated it as a migration issue rather than a refugee crisis, and thus instead of travelling to the border and embracing the children as a humanitarian cause, created (to his eternal shame) a 'priority docket' for the rapid deportation of these 'migrant' children. See Valeria Luiselli, *Tell Me How It Ends: An Essay in Forty Questions* (London: 4th Estate, 2017). I return to this excellent book in the Coda.

23. For the original text by Shklar on legalism, see Shklar, *Legalism*. Seyla Benhabib has written on Shklar's work in her book *Exile, Statelessness and Migration*, discussed further on in this chapter. For a discussion of legalism from a

non-Western perspective or what is called Third World Approaches to International Law, see the work of B. S. Chimni.

24. Hannah Arendt, *On Revolution*, intro. Jonathan Schell (London: Penguin, 2006), pp. 102–3.

25. Arendt originally set out to redeem Marx in Jasper's eyes, but came to regard Marx as a 'pain in the neck'. See Jerome Kohn's discussion in the Introduction to Arendt, *The Promise of Politics*, p. xv.

26. Hanna Pitkin, 'Justice: On Relating Private and Public', *Political Theory*, Vol. 9, No. 3, August 1981, pp. 335–36.

27. Arendt, *The Human Condition*, pp. 244–45.

28. Arendt, *The Human Condition*, p. 199.

29. Arendt, *The Human Condition*, p. 56.

30. Arendt, *The Human Condition*, p. 198.

31. Arendt, *The Origins of Totalitarianism*, pp. 477–79. On pages 478–79 Arendt links promising, as new beginning, to the guarantee. On page 477 she refers to the 'mutual' guarantee in a common world.

32. Arendt, *The Human Condition*, p. 244.

33. Arendt, *On Violence*, p. 82.

34. Arendt, *The Promise of Politics*, p. vii.

35. Theodor W. Adorno, *Can One Live After Auschwitz?: A Philosophical Reader*, ed. Rolf Tiedemann (Stanford, CA: Stanford University Press, 2003), p. xiv. Thanks to Andrew Benjamin for bringing this comparison to my attention.

36. In *Memoires for Paul de Man*, Derrida writes: 'The very condition of a deconstruction may be at work, in the work, within the system to be deconstructed; it may already be located there, already at work, not at the center but in an ex-centric center, in a corner whose eccentricity assures the solid concentration of the system, participating in the construction of what it at the same time threatens to deconstruct.' Jacques Derrida, *Memoires for Paul de Man: Revised Edition*, trans. Cecile Lindsay, Jonathan Culler, Eduardo Cadava, and Peggy Kamuf (New York, NY: Columbia University Press, 1989), p. 73.

37. Hannah Arendt, *Between Past and Future: Eight Exercises in Political Thought*, intro. Jerome Kohn (London: Penguin, 2006), p. 150. See also the discussion in Peg Birmingham, *Hannah Arendt & Human Rights: The Predicament of Common Responsibility* (Bloomington, IN and Indianapolis, IN: Indiana University Press, 2006), especially Chapter Two.

38. Arendt, *The Origins of Totalitarianism*, p. 479.

39. Arendt, *Between Past and Future*, p. 163.

40. Arendt, *Between Past and Future*, pp. 169 and 153.

41. Arendt, *Between Past and Future*, p. 247.

42. Arendt, *Between Past and Future*, p. 166.

43. Alan Keenan, 'Promises Promises: The Abyss of Freedom and the Loss of the Political in the Work of Hannah Arendt', *Political Theory*, Vol. 2, No. 2, May 1994, pp. 298–99 and passim.

44. Arendt, *The Human Condition*, pp. 57–58.

45. Birmingham, *Hannah Arendt & Human Rights*, pp. 1–2.

46. Birmingham, *Hannah Arendt & Human Rights*, p. 74.

47. Birmingham, *Hannah Arendt & Human Rights*, p. 74.

48. Arendt, *The Origins of Totalitarianism*, pp. 301–2.

49. Arendt, *The Origins of Totalitarianism*, p. 298.

50. Seyla Benhabib, *The Reluctant Modernism of Hannah Arendt* (New York, NY: Rowman & Littlefield, 1996), p. 185. Benhabib's phrase 'anthropological normative universal' is derived from her interpretation of Arendt, *The Human Condition*, where the idea of human *plurality* and its articulation provide an anthropology that can be seen as a normative foundation of the political. This notion of a (philosophical) anthropology will be further pursued in this chapter in relation to the work of Andrew Benjamin.

51. Giorgio Agamben, *State of Exception* (Chicago, IL: University of Chicago Press, 2005), p. 50.

52. Agamben, *Homo Sacer*, p. 131.

53. Hannah Arendt, 'We Refugees', in *The Jewish Writings*, eds. Jerome Kohn and Ron H. Feldman (New York, NY: Schocken, 2007), p. 271.

54. Arendt, 'We Refugees', p. 273.

55. Jean Améry, *At the Mind's Limits: Contemplations by a Survivor on Auschwitz and its Realities*, trans. Sidney and Stella P. Rosenfeld (Bloomington, IN: Indiana University Press, 1980), p. 89.

56. Améry, *At the Mind's Limits*, p. 11.

57. Hannah Arendt, 'Personal Responsibility Under Dictatorship', in *Responsibility and Judgment*, ed. Jerome Kohn (New York, NY: Schocken Books, 2003), p. 43.

58. Arendt, *The Origins of Totalitarianism*, p. 296.

59. Gündoğdu, *Rightlessness in an Age of Rights*, p. 14.

60. Gündoğdu, *Rightlessness in an Age of Rights*, p. 28.

61. See the discussion on this point by Paul Muldoon, 'The Injustice of Territoriality', *Critical Review of International Social and Political Philosophy*, Vol. 15, No. 5, December 2012, p. 639 and passim.

62. Muldoon, 'The Injustice of Territoriality', p. 641.

63. James Ingram, 'What is a "Right to Have Rights"? Three Images of the Politics of Human Rights', *American Political Science Review*, Vol. 102, No. 4, November 2008, pp. 402 and 410.

64. Étienne Balibar, *Masses, Classes, Ideas* (London and New York, NY: Routledge, 1994), p. 212.

65. Topolski, *Arendt, Levinas and a Politics of Relationality*.

66. Werner Hamacher and Ronald Mendoza-de Jesus, 'On the Right to Have Rights: Human Rights; Marx and Arendt', *CR: The New Centennial Review*, Vol. 14, No. 2, Law and Violence Issue, Fall 2014, pp. 169–214.

67. Alison Kesby, *The Right to Have Rights: Citizenship, Humanity and International Law* (Oxford: Oxford University Press, 2012), pp. 132–33.

68. Jacques Rancière, *Hatred of Democracy* (London and New York, NY: Verso, 2014), p. 61.

69. Leo Strauss, *Natural Right and History* (Chicago, IL: University of Chicago Press, 1965), p. 2.

70. Topolski, *Arendt, Levinas and a Politics of Relationality*, p. 79.
71. Topolski, *Arendt, Levinas and a Politics of Relationality*, p. 79.
72. Topolski, *Arendt, Levinas and a Politics of Relationality*, p. 68.
73. 'What is Authority?', in Arendt, *Between Past and Future*, p. 141.
74. Topolski, *Arendt, Levinas and a Politics of Relationality*, p. 88.
75. Topolski, *Arendt, Levinas and a Politics of Relationality*, pp. 100 and 140.
76. Arendt, *The Human Condition*, p. 7.
77. Arendt, *The Human Condition*, pp. 7–8.
78. Arendt, *The Human Condition*, pp. 175–76.
79. 'Introduction *Into* Politics', in Arendt, *The Promise of Politics*, p. 108.
80. Arendt, *On Revolution*, p. 221.
81. 'Introduction *Into* Politics', in Arendt, *The Promise of Politics*, p. 93.
82. 'Introduction *Into* Politics', in Arendt, *The Promise of Politics*, p. 95.
83. I owe this concatenation and many valuable reflections on Arendt to Paul Muldoon.
84. Arendt, *The Human Condition*, p. 195.
85. Butler, *Parting Ways*, p. 120.
86. Butler, *Parting Ways*, p. 16.
87. Butler, *Parting Ways*, p. 16.
88. Butler, *Parting Ways*, pp. 25–26.
89. https://www.abc.net.au/news/2019-07-17/refugees-on-manus-island-to-recieve-aboriginal-passports/11310214, retrieved 21 February 2020.
90. My thanks to Melbourne-based scholar and artist Rachel Joy for valuable insight into these matters.
91. Birmingham, *Hannah Arendt & Human Rights*, p. 73.
92. Birmingham, *Hannah Arendt & Human Rights*, p. 8.
93. Arendt, *Eichmann in Jerusalem*, p. 279.
94. Gündoğdu, *Rightlessness in an Age of Rights*, p. 19.
95. 'The Jew as Pariah: A Hidden Tradition', in *The Jewish Writings*, p. 297.
96. Arendt, 'We Refugees', p. 274.
97. Butler, *Parting Ways*, pp. 101 and 119.
98. Topolski, *Arendt, Levinas and a Politics of Relationality*, p. 97.
99. Seyla Benhabib, *Exile, Statelessness and Migration: Playing Chess with History from Hannah Arendt to Isaiah Berlin* (Princeton, NJ and Oxford: Princeton University Press, 2018), pp. 91–93.
100. Benhabib, *Exile, Statelessness and Migration*, p. 94.
101. Benhabib, *Exile, Statelessness and Migration*, p. 94.
102. Benhabib, *Exile, Statelessness and Migration*, p. 95.
103. Benhabib, *Exile, Statelessness and Migration*, p. 96.
104. Ilan Pappé, *Ten Myths About Israel* (London and New York, NY: Verso, 2017), p. 104.
105. Benhabib, *Exile, Statelessness and Migration*, p. 82.
106. Noam Chomsky and Ilan Pappé, *On Palestine* (London: Penguin Books, 2015), pp. 72–76.
107. Benhabib, *The Rights of Others*, p. 221.

108. Butler, *Parting Ways*, p. 16.

109. See the Conclusion to Birmingham, *Hannah Arendt & Human Rights*.

110. Birmingham, *Hannah Arendt & Human Rights*, especially Chapter One.

111. Butler, *Parting Ways*, p. 24.

112. Butler, *Parting Ways*, p. 5.

113. Butler, *Parting Ways*, p. 5.

114. Butler, *Parting Ways*, pp. 129–30.

115. Butler, *The Force of Non-Violence*, p. 37.

116. Butler, *The Force of Non-Violence*, p. 38.

117. The reference to phantasm is derived from Melanie Klein's psychoanalytic work on 'phantasy', which denotes an 'unconscious set of relations to objects . . . a scene with multiple actors disposed by vectors of desire and aggression'. Butler, *The Force of Non-Violence*, pp. 34–35.

118. Butler, *The Force of Non-Violence*, pp. 116 and 121.

119. Butler, *Parting Ways*, p. 151.

120. Quoted in Alain Finkielkraut, *In the Name of Humanity* (New York, NY: Columbia University Press, 2000), p. 35. One might think on this point of the tragic confidence that Hermann Cohen displayed in seeing the safest option for Germany Jewry being to remain where they were, safely assimilated into German society. Arendt comments on the tragedy of this view (and briefly quotes Cohen in a footnote, p. 112) in her essay 'Antisemitism' – see *The Jewish Writings*, pp. 46–121.

121. Emmanuel Levinas, Prefatory Note, 'Reflections on the Philosophy of Hitlerism', trans. Sean Hand, *Critical Inquiry*, Vol. 17, Autumn 1990, p. 63. This article first appeared in 1934 and is often regarded as a remarkably prescient piece on the fundamental implications of Nazism – see Giorgio Agamben's remarks in *Homo Sacer*, pp. 151–53.

122. Moris Scheyer, *Asylum: A Survivor's Flight from Nazi-Occupied Vienna Through Wartime France* (New York, NY: Little, Brown and Company, 2016), p. 12.

123. Schwarz-Bart, *The Last of the Just*, p. 277.

124. Quoted as the epigraph in Michael Dobbs, *The Unwanted: America, Auschwitz and a Village Caught In Between* (New York, NY: Alfred A. Knopf, 2019).

125. Levinas, *Totality and Infinity*, p. 22.

126. Maurice Blanchot, *The Writing of the Disaster*, trans. Anne Smock (Lincoln, NE and London: University of Nebraska Press, 1995), p. 25.

127. Jacques Derrida, *Adieu to Emmanuel Levinas*, trans. Pascale-Anne Brault and Michael Naas (Stanford, CA: Stanford University Press, 1999), p. 21.

128. Diane Perpich, *The Ethics of Emmanuel Levinas* (Stanford, CA: Stanford University Press, 2008), p. 82.

129. Emmanuel Levinas, *Otherwise Than Being or Beyond Esssence*, trans. Alphonso Lingis and foreword Richard Cohen (Pittsburgh, PA: Duquesne University Press, 2008), p. xix.

130. Perpich, *The Ethics of Emmanuel Levinas*, p. 89.

131. Levinas, *Totality and Infinity*, p. 43.

132. Perpich, *The Ethics of Emmanuel Levinas*, pp. 91 and 88.

133. Mouffe, *The Democratic Paradox*, pp. 129–30.

134. Raoul Moati, *Levinas and the Night of Being: A Guide to Totality and Infinity*, trans. Daniel Wyche and foreword Jocelyn Benoist (New York, NY: Fordham University Press, 2017), p. xii.

135. The terminology here rather invites a discussion of a potential 'left Levinas', which I am writing of elsewhere. Sometimes written off as a liberal given his enthusiasm for French Republicanism and his reticence around political commentary, he lamented in multiple interviews the demise of the emancipatory promise that the Soviet Union had represented, and various elements in his writings also indicate sympathy with left politics.

136. Levinas, *Totality and Infinity*, p. 27.

137. Levinas, *Totality and Infinity*, pp. 27–28.

138. Moati, *Levinas and the Night of Being*, pp. 6–7.

139. Moati, *Levinas and the Night of Being*, p. 7.

140. Moati, *Levinas and the Night of Being*, p. 11.

141. Moati, *Levinas and the Night of Being*, Conclusion but especially pp. 185–87. In the conclusion the theme of time will be more prominent, where the thinking of Levinas will be brought into proximity with that of Walter Benjamin and Jacques Derrida, amongst others.

142. Moati, *Levinas and the Night of Being*, p. 189.

143. Moati, *Levinas and the Night of Being*, p. 190.

144. David Steiner, 'Levinas' Ethical interruption of Ethical Reciprocity', *Salmagundi*, Vol. 130/131, Spring–Summer 2001, p. 124.

145. Jacques Derrida, *The Other Heading: Reflections on Today's Europe*, trans. Pascale-Anne Brault and Michael B. Naas (Bloomington, IN and Indianapolis, IN: Indiana University Press, 1992), pp. 9 and 29.

146. Butler, *Parting Ways*, p. 23.

147. Butler, *Parting Ways*, p. 24.

148. Butler, *Parting Ways*, p. 59.

149. Butler, *Parting Ways*, pp. 59–60.

150. Butler, *Parting Ways*, p. 43.

151. Emmanuel Levinas, 'From the Rise of Nihilism to the Carnal Jew', in *Difficult Freedom: Essays on Judaism*, trans. Seán Hand (Baltimore, MD: John Hopkins University Press, 1997), p. 225.

152. See the essays in Arendt, *Responsibility and Judgment*.

153. Arendt, *Between Past and Future*, p. 145.

154. Arendt, *On Violence*, p. 56.

155. Walter Benjamin, 'Critique of Violence', in *Selected Writings 1913–1926*, eds. Marcus Bullock and Michael W. Jennings (Cambridge and London: The Belknap Press of Harvard University Press, 2002), pp. 236–52.

156. Arendt, *The Human Condition*, p. 11.

157. I share this conclusion with Anya Topolski. See Topolski, *Arendt, Levinas and a Politics of Relationality*.

158. Topolski, *Arendt, Levinas and a Politics of Relationality*, p. 180.

159. Topolski, *Arendt, Levinas and a Politics of Relationality*, p. 225.

160. Arendt, *Between Past and Future*, p. 144.

161. Levinas, *Totality and Infinity*, p. 293.

162. Arendt, *The Human Condition*, pp. 198–99.

163. Arendt, *The Human Condition*, p. 176. See also Topolski, *Arendt, Levinas and a Politics of Relationality*, pp. 62 and 105. It would be possible to pursue a thinking of *alteritas* qua generalized otherness versus human distinction in terms of the deconstruction of the human and non-human animal distinction, in both Arendt and Levinas, for example, in reference to Derrida's work and the burgeoning literature on this topic, however this cannot be pursued here.

164. Topolski, *Arendt, Levinas and a Politics of Relationality*, p. 105.

165. Topolski, *Arendt, Levinas and a Politics of Relationality*, pp. 154 and 160.

166. Topolski, *Arendt, Levinas and a Politics of Relationality*, pp. 160–61.

167. Emmanuel Levinas, *Alterity and Transcendence*, trans. Michael B. Smith (New York, NY: Columbia University Press, 1999), p. 127.

168. The development of this philosophical anthropology includes but is not limited to the volumes *Place, Commonality and Judgment, Working with Walter Benjamin, Towards a Relational Ontology*, and *Virtue in Being: Towards an Ethics of the Unconditioned*, as well as numerous journal articles.

169. Benjamin, *Towards a Relational Ontology*, p. 1.

170. Andrew Benjamin, *The Plural Event: Descartes, Hegel, Heidegger* (London and New York, NY: Routledge, 1993), p. 9.

171. Andrew Benjamin, *Place Commonality and Judgment: Continental Philosophy and the Ancient Greeks* (London and New York, NY: Continuum, 2012), p. 73.

172. There is rich potential to bring Benjamin's work on place and relationality into dialogue with emerging research on the role of place in Indigenous philosophy, such as in the important work of Mary Graham. For Graham's work on place, see, for example, Mary Graham, Morgan Brigg, and Polly Walker, 'Conflict Murri Way: Managing Through Place and Relatedness', in *Mediating Across Difference: Oceanic and Asian Approaches to Conflict Resolution* (Honolulu, HI: University of Hawai'i Press, 2011), pp. 75–99.

173. Benjamin, 'The Problem of Authority', p. 260.

174. Benjamin, *Place, Commonality and Judgment*, p. 4.

175. Benjamin, *Virtue in Being*, pp. 1–2. Benjamin distinguishes difference from differance, to which it is related but which in his version allows for a reworking of ontology precluded by the Derridian version, in that Derrida's privileging of impossibility precludes the possibility of 'judgment [which] depends on an opening staged by the relation between the unconditioned and the conditioned' (pp. 142–43). Benjamin suggests that 'what escapes Derrida . . . is the possibility of the *othering* of the ontological: that is, a rethinking of the question of being as philosophy's other possibility, in other words, a thinking guided by a relational ontology, thus one in which *being-in-relation* and *being-in-place* play central roles' (p. 131).

176. Benjamin, *Virtue in Being*, p. 1.

177. Benjamin, *Virtue in Being*, p. 5.

178. Benjamin, *Virtue in Being*, p. 4.

179. Benjamin, *Virtue in Being*, p. 7. The difference between Benjamin's position and that of Levinas is to be fully elaborated, but can perhaps be understood as the difference between ethics and ontology in being in anoriginal relation (Benjamin) – that is, coterminous, arriving on the scene together as it were – and ethics being prior to ontology (Levinas), but which nevertheless is constitutive of the ontological subject. For the purposes of the present argument, in their efficacy this seems like a distinction without much difference; however, I intend to clarify this difference in future work on these thinkers.

180. This quotation is one of the epigraphs to Levinas, *Otherwise Than Being*, p. vii.

181. Benjamin, *Working With Walter Benjamin*, p. 8.

182. Andrew Benjamin, 'God and the Truth of Human Being', *Journal for Continental Philosophy of Religion*, Vol. 1, 2019, p. 146.

183. Benjamin, *Virtue in Being*, p. 117.

184. Benjamin, *Virtue in Being*, p. 14.

185. Butler, *Parting Ways*, p. 168. In the essay 'Some Questions of Moral Philosophy', collected in *Responsibility and Judgment*, Arendt writes: 'The validity of such judgments would be neither objective and universal nor subjective, depending on personal whim, but intersubjective or representative' (p. 141).

186. Benjamin, *Place, Commonality and Judgment*, p. 50.

187. Emmanuel Levinas, *Outside the Subject*, trans. Michael B. Smith (Stanford, CA: Stanford University Press, 1993), p. 125. See Also Topolski, *Arendt, Levinas and a Politics of Relationality*, p. 160.

188. Agamben, *Homo Sacer*.

189. Arendt, *Eichmann in Jerusalem*, p. 273.

190. Judith Butler, *Precarious Life: The Powers of Mourning and Violence* (London and New York, NY: Verso, 2004), p. xii.

191. Butler, *Precarious Life*, p. xiii.

192. Theodor Adorno, *Minima Moralia: Reflections from Damaged Life* (London and New York, NY: Verso, 2005), p. 39.

193. Asher Hirsch and Nathan Bell, 'The Right to have Rights as a Right to Enter: Addressing a Lacuna in the International Refugee Protection Regime', *Human Rights Review*, Vol. 18, No. 4, December 2017, pp. 417–37.

Chapter 2

Limitations of the 'Right to Have Rights'

The Case of Denmark

And many of us drowned just off the beaches.
  The long night passed, the sky began to clear.
  If they but knew, we said, they'd come and seek us.
  That they did know, we still were unaware.

                                          – Bertolt Brecht[1]

INTRODUCTION

This short poem in Bertolt Brecht's *War Primer* captures with devastating economy a principal concern relating to the continuing plight of a large population of stateless persons: how to ensure that their human rights are recognized and upheld by sovereign states? The dimensions of the global refugee crisis have led to considerable attention being paid by theorists to Hannah Arendt's strange and ingenious syntagm that consists of a doubling of terms: the right to have rights.[2] This rights claim relates to asylum, that is, the right of stateless persons to enter into political communities where political membership means respect for their human rights can be guaranteed.[3] Yet the continuing failure of states to affirm this right – a right of recognition, entry, and belonging – raises the problem of how the right to have rights should be understood, what this concept has to teach us about the politics of asylum, and whether there are meaningful possibilities for the upholding of this right by political actors.[4]

   It is unclear that Arendt intended for this idea to serve as a way of measuring adequate rights protection. Rather it seems to serve in her writing as an aporia (i.e. an irresolvable problem, a no-way-out) for thought: 'We became

105

aware of the existence of a right to have rights (and that means to live in a framework where one is judged by one's actions and opinions) and a right to belong to some kind of organized community, only when millions of people emerged who had lost and could not regain these rights because of the new global political situation.'[5] That is, if the sovereign state is the primary political form currently able to uphold human rights, then those who fall outside of its boundaries no longer have rights, which thus become little more than empty talk in that context. However, she also writes that given 'humanity has in effect assumed the role formerly ascribed to nature or history', this means that 'the right to have rights, or the right of every individual to belong to humanity, should be guaranteed by humanity itself', while evincing an uncertainty that this is possible.[6] This latter claim, as argued in the previous chapter, might be interpreted in relation to her writings on plurality – that 'humanity' or human 'plurality' is the 'law of the earth' (*Life of the Mind*), what she also calls an 'inescapable fact' (*The Origins of Totalitarianism – hereafter OT*).[7] Consequently, the concept of the right to have rights in Arendt appears fundamentally ambiguous – at once an aporia and a normative rule, an impasse but also an ought-claim or imperative (as she writes, something that in this context of humanity playing such a role in politics in place of nature or history 'should be guaranteed'). While she intends a political guarantee amongst plural beings who provide each other with that guarantee via mutual promising, this becomes limiting if not dangerous in situations where such coming together of persons is not possible, where some are excluded in advance.

In this chapter I take up the ambiguity inherent in the right to have rights, reading it both ways, as both aporia and as a normative claim (the latter is often the dominant way in which it is interpreted, as will be seen below; certainly it makes sense to read Arendt this way, given her commitment to the just treatment of stateless persons). The argument is that in examining Arendt's thinking about this right, it is instructive to bring it into proximity with another Arendtian theme: the historical example of Denmark in the Second World War, which saved most of its Jewish population from extermination by the Nazis, but which also excluded a great many Jewish refugees from entry into its territory, who might otherwise have been rescued. My claim is that reading Arendt's reflections on the right to have rights alongside her writings on the Denmark may provide greater illumination of both. Arendt does not link her analysis of Denmark to the right to have rights, nor does this linkage seem to have been made in the secondary literature. Indeed, it should be noted that the right to have rights does not figure prominently in Arendt's own work – she mentions it only a couple of times, seemingly in passing, and does not take it up in subsequent texts.[8] The importance attached to this concept as something of a rallying cry for human rights, is a consequence of its critical reception in the wake of Arendt.

In several places in her writings, Arendt lauds the Danish actions as exemplary of political action and the granting of asylum, but this is problematic in that precisely this example represents a failure of her own recognition of the need for a right to have rights, if one understands this as the willing acceptance of refugees into a political community. This is not a contradiction of the aporetic claim – Arendt is consistent in recognizing the need for the right at the moment the potential for its actualization fails – but a contradiction of the normative claim in relation to this history, which represents this very failure, thus underscoring the limitation of Arendt's conception of politics. The argument is that Arendt's understanding of political action, which as will be seen, guides her reception of the Danish case, leads her to miss the essential issue: that Denmark in fact deliberately denied access to its territory to Jewish refugees and thus to the subsequent, and very successful, protective actions concerning the Jewish people already within Danish borders. This denial constitutes a violation of the right to have rights, understood as a right to be admitted to the territory and enter into the political life of a polity, in order that the human rights of the stateless be upheld. In short, Denmark is held up by Arendt as an example of a state that mounted successful resistance to the Nazis during the Shoah (in that it saved most of its Jewish citizens), but when it comes to Jewish *refugees, it is an example of precisely what went wrong*. Analysis of those events in Denmark thus is not simply of historical importance, but is also of decisive consequence for the theory and practice of asylum, with reference to Arendt's views but also going beyond them.

Now as then, states remain reticent about proffering asylum to stateless persons, and state sovereignty remains the geopolitical framework that refugees have to negotiate.[9] This situation persists in the absence of a reordered international system of, in Arendt's phrase, 'newly defined territorial entities',[10] or a world of open borders, or of enforceable international law that can compel states to admit refugees to their territory. Consequently, it is necessary to articulate the obstacles to the granting of such asylum, and the fulfilment of the right to have rights, precisely within the context of the Westphalian system of state sovereignty. For despite the stipulation in international law of a right to seek asylum, recognition of which is required of all signatories to the *Convention Relating to the Status of Refugees* (which builds upon Article 14 of the *Universal Declaration of Human Rights*), in practice many states have adopted a regime of *non-entrée* measures designed to prevent people seeking asylum from claiming refugee status at all.[11] Two alternatives to this – the call for new forms of political communities, on the one hand, and the ability of refugees and their advocates to press their demands in political struggle, on the other – both risk falling into a hopeless struggle against the legal dictates of sovereign states as already constituted.

In counterpoint to the Danish example, the contemporaneous actions of Sweden towards refugees during the war will be examined, as a means of illustrating the sense of responsibility for outsiders that is lacking in the Danish example. (Although the history here is complex, and the Danish case remains laudable in the highly effective rescue effected for Danish Jewry; it is the failure to save non-Danish Jewry and other refugees that is problematic.) That politics might be rethought and reordered as a comportment of justice and active responsibility-taking towards refugees, even within the existing geopolitical system of state sovereignty, is a vitally important consideration in achieving the fulfilment of the right to have rights. The claim is that this right does have normative force, rather than simply functioning aporetically, but that Arendt failed to conceive of the right to asylum as the proper work and realization of the political as such. For her, the right to have rights secures access to the space of political action, but there is a necessarily complementary relationship here, in that the content of political action itself must be oriented towards asylum in order to fulfil respect for the 'law' (*nomos*) of the earth, plurality, as the *telos* of the political (rather than politics simply concerning freedom and action amongst plural beings). Politics requires a normative orientation, one that is, to borrow her terms from *The Human Condition*, a *conditio per quam* in addition to a *conditio sine qua non*, where the condition of the political and its fulfilment are coterminous. Without such an orientation aimed at a 'new guarantee' of human dignity, the right to have rights is rendered meaningless. Both the strengths and limitations of Arendt's views are thus evinced in a manner that serves to reconfigure the meaning and import of the right to have rights, and – despite some moments of disagreement – to reinforce the continuing urgency of her concept for elaborating a just politics of asylum.

UNDERSTANDING THE RIGHT TO HAVE RIGHTS

Events before, during, and after the Second World War led to the creation of an enormous population of stateless persons, the most significant phenomena of statelessness in modernity up to that point, though now surpassed in scale by the present global refugee 'crisis'. Given their similar scope, and origins in humanitarian calamity (while different in kind), it may be the case that lessons drawn from that earlier period can meaningfully address present events.[12] Hannah Arendt was one of the first political theorists to examine the plight of stateless persons, as she belonged to the generation that experienced unprecedented dislocation and exile, and proffered a number of fascinating insights. In *OT*, she writes:

> Not the loss of specific rights, then, but the loss of a community willing and able to guarantee any rights whatsoever, has been the calamity which has befallen ever-increasing numbers of people. Man, it turns out, can lose all so-called

Rights of Man without losing his essential quality as man, his human dignity. Only the loss of a polity itself expels him from humanity.[13]

As discussed in the previous chapter, in the Preface to *OT* she argues that 'human dignity needs a new guarantee which can be found only in a new political principle, in a new law on earth, whose validity this time must comprehend the whole of humanity whilst its power must remain strictly limited, rooted in and controlled by newly defined territorial entities'.[14] Thus, the guarantee of human dignity, if linked to the right to have rights, can be understood as that which will be ensured by 'newly defined territorial entities'. For Arendt, natural rights have been exposed as powerless to preserve the rights of human beings once they are stateless: 'The world found nothing sacred in the abstract nakedness of being human.'[15]

It's important to note that Arendt herself did not put a lot of stock in the expression 'right to have rights'. It is mentioned just briefly in *OT* and never before or after it; it was not for her a rallying cry, and she 'invests no confidence in the phrase'.[16] Her point was that rights are not inalienable but rather contestable, and need to be fought for in a political space where plural beings can appear amongst each other. For Arendt, action and speech are the activities proper to plural human beings, which enables them to undertake new political initiatives: 'If action as beginning corresponds to the fact of birth, if it is the actualization of the human condition of natality, then speech corresponds to the fact of distinctness and is the actualization of the human condition of plurality, that is, of living as a distinct and unique being among living equals.'[17] Consequently, she argued that the right to be admitted to the shared life of a political community is anterior to the achievement of other rights (hence the doubling of the term), but Arendt is less interested in proposing a solution than in articulating a perplexity, an aporia – that the need for the right to have rights is only recognized when the possibility of its fulfilment has already been denied.

And yet as noted above, the right to have rights also carries the sense of a normative claim. Even if Arendt did not intend the right to have rights to have the meaning of a hopeful, emancipatory call, nevertheless this concept, as Alistair Hunt observes, 'provides a resource for calling into question the exclusion of individuals from membership in a polity.'[18] It reminds us that the assertion of rights 'cannot necessarily rely upon support from existing institutions of a political community', and invites us to question existing laws and norms.[19] As Hunt puts it, 'a chief characteristic of the "right to have rights" is that it directs political communities to consider whether they really have already included as members all individuals with a legitimate claim to membership . . . In short, by naming the "right to have rights" as belonging to those who themselves do not belong, Arendt does the opposite of abandoning those who are expelled beyond the borders of political community. She places them at the center of politics.'[20]

As Arendt understood, a claim to a right must be recognized by a duty-bearer, in this case a sovereign state, and it can always go unrecognized.[21] More than seventy years on from the end of the Second World War, no such acknowledgement of a general right to have rights – specifically, a right to asylum and belonging, that is, a right to enter a territory and become a member of it – has gained significant traction in actual state practices (as opposed to the 'soft law' recognition of the right to asylum, which does exist); nor has an alternative model to the nation-state that would guarantee such a right emerged (even supra-state entities like the EU with internal freedom of movement do not admit of such a right for non-Europeans, with member states often implementing highly restrictive border control policies). Arendt is aware of this difficulty: 'It is by no means certain whether this [the recognition of a right to have rights] is possible. For, contrary to the best-intentioned humanitarian attempts to obtain new declarations of human rights from international organizations, it should be understood that this idea transcends the present sphere of international law which still operates in terms of reciprocal agreements and treaties between sovereign states; and, for the time being, a sphere that is above the nations does not exist. Furthermore, this dilemma would by no means be eliminated by the establishment of a "world government".'[22] Thus, it can be asked: How should the right to have rights be understood? I argue that this idea of rights needs to be reconsidered by a reorientation of Arendt's view of politics, where the faith that she places in action is somewhat misplaced. On the one hand, she lauds the actions of a country that deliberately excluded refugees; on the other, she sees a role for action amongst the powerless that risks a hopeless outcome.

Additionally, one issue of particular significance in what follows is that of *numbers* in relation to the politics of asylum, which runs like a guiding thread through much of Arendt's writing on the topic: she refers at two points in *OT* to 'ever-increasing numbers': 'the calamity which has befallen ever-increasing numbers of people', arguing that 'their ever-increasing numbers threaten our political life'.[23] It was the sheer scale of statelessness around the time of the Second World War that had collapsed the ability of states to proffer a right to asylum in the manner which they had previously engaged in, which was mutual promise-making and an allowance of exceptions, the tradition of the sovereign right of grace, rather than governance under international law.[24] While Arendt does not seem to allow that numbers are a real issue – 'This, moreover, had next to nothing to do with any material problem of overpopulation; it was a problem not of space but of political organization'[25] – she also evinces a certain prevarication, if one reads this alongside her highly Aristotelian remarks on political organization in *The Human Condition*: 'The

Greeks, whose city-state was the most individualistic and least conformable body politic known to us, were quite aware of the fact that the polis, with its emphasis on action and speech, could survive only if the number of citizens remained restricted.'[26] In *OT* she also mentions the difficulties that states 'swamped with refugees' faced with processes of repatriation and naturaliza-tion,[27] and ends the chapter by suggesting that 'the danger in the existence of such people [are that] . . . their ever-increasing numbers threaten our political life, our human artifice, the world which is the result of our common and co-ordinated effort . . . The danger is that a global, universally interrelated civilization may produce barbarians from its own midst by forcing millions of people into conditions which, despite all appearances, are the conditions of savages'.[28] 'Ever-increasing', 'swamped', 'danger', 'barbarians' - and yet there is no problem of overpopulation? What is striking in her formulation here is the seeming privilege she accords to politics over actual endangered life – the danger is to the former! Thus, her own view is ambiguous, which has led one commentator to argue that the case of Germany in the 1990s sug-gests that 'The right of asylum in Germany has proven Hannah Arendt right that the right of asylum collapses if the number of asylum seekers becomes too large'.[29] (This claim, however, would seem to be belied by the more recent experience of Germany which admitted close to one million refugees in 2015 alone, without any significant deleterious impacts, notwithstanding the ability of other states to absorb a much higher ratio of refugees.)[30] That Arendt's work lends itself to such claims in serious scholarship is highly problematic. It is thus of decisive importance to clarify what weight, if any, should be given to the question of numbers in the context of the geopolitics of asylum, as it represents a major potential stumbling block to the fulfilment of the guarantee she sought.

THE CASE OF DENMARK

One of the privileged examples for Arendt of both the possibilities of non-violence political action and a state's treatment of a vulnerable group is Denmark's protection of its Jewish population – both citizens and refugees – during the Second World War. In order to further illustrate the limita-tions of the right to have rights in Arendt's terms, a brief excursus on this example follows. While this case study will be critical of Arendt, it must be acknowledged that not everything presented here was information she could have known when she wrote her texts; more recent scholarship in Denmark has expanded and clarified the experience of Jewish people at the time, both residents and refugees, and now presents a more complex and somewhat less laudable picture. That the vast majority of Danish Jewry were saved remains an exemplary and inspiring story, but there are additional factors that need to be considered in evaluating these events in toto.

Arendt lauds this chapter of Danish history in *Eichmann in Jerusalem*: 'One is tempted to recommend the story as required reading in political science for all students who wish to learn something about the enormous power potential inherent in non-violent action and in resistance to an opponent possessing vastly superior means of violence.'[31] Whether this remark is so apposite in this case or as it applies more generally may be doubted, given Hitler's desire to hold up Denmark as an exemplar of the New German Europe, 'Neuropa', and an example of how client states would be treated, which may have restrained the violence of the German occupying forces.[32] Yet she was correct to the extent that Denmark – and working with Denmark, Sweden – managed to save almost all of its native Jewish population, as well as a number of stateless Jewish persons who had entered the state, from the fate of deportation to their deaths. Arendt described the Danish attitude thus (quoting Leni Yahil, an early authority on the subject): '"For the Danes . . . the Jewish question was a political and not a humanitarian question"'; Arendt contrasted this with the approach of the Italians when faced with the deportations, who evinced the 'almost automatic general humanity of an old and civilized people.'[33] As Elsebet Jegstrup writes, the Danes acted '*not* for humanitarian reasons, but in a political manner consistent with Hannah Arendt's notion of conscious action in the public realm . . . the Danish Jews were saved not in spite of themselves, as Hannah Arendt might suggest; rather they escaped the concentration camps precisely because they were Danes', that is, via decision-making amongst plural beings, who protected each other qua fellow members of the political community, and who were reacting to a disturbance to their political life.[34]

Concerning the relative treatment of native Danish Jewish people and Jewish refugees, Arendt observes: 'It was decisive in this whole matter that the Germans did not even succeed in introducing the vitally important distinction between native Danes of Jewish origin, of whom there were about sixty-four hundred, and the fourteen hundred German Jewish refugees who had found asylum in the country prior to the war and who now had been declared stateless by the German government.'[35] She comments on German incredulity at this protection of non-citizens, 'since it appeared so "illogical" for a government to protect people to whom it had categorically denied naturalization and even permission to work.'[36] For Arendt, 'This was one of the few cases in which statelessness turned out to be an asset, although it was of course not statelessness per se that saved the Jews but, on the contrary, the fact that the Danish government had decided to protect them.'[37] (As will be seen in Chapter Four, the distinction between Jewish citizens and Jewish refugees in France was a significant factor in determining rates of survival, where the lack of citizenship came at the cost of thousands of lives.) What is more, the cost of ferrying Jewish refugees to Sweden 'was paid largely by wealthy Danish citizens, and that was perhaps the most astounding feat of all, since this was a time when Jews were paying for their own deportation [in other countries]'.[38] Arendt expanded on these reflections in a talk given in Denmark upon receiving the Sonning Prize in 1975, the year of her death, and thus indicative of a consistency of outlook that she maintained many years after the Eichmann trial:

> This episode of your history offers a highly instructive example of the great power potential inherent in nonviolent action and in resistance to an opponent possessing vastly superior means of violence. And since the most spectacular victory in this battle concerns the defeat of the 'Final Solution' and the salvation of nearly all the Jews on Danish soil, regardless of their origin, whether they were Danish citizens or stateless refugees from Germany, it seems indeed only natural that Jews who are survivors of the catastrophe should feel themselves related to this country in a very special way.[39]

Arendt specified why she regarded this episode as so instructive:

> There are two things which I found particularly impressive in this story. There is *first* the fact that prior to the war Denmark had treated its refugees by no means nicely; like other nation-states it refused them naturalization and permission to work. Despite the absence of anti-Semitism, Jews as foreigners were not welcome, but the right to asylum, nowhere else respected, apparently was considered sacrosanct. For when the Nazis demanded first only stateless persons for deportation, that is, German refugees whom they had deprived of their nationality, the Danes explained that because these refugees were no longer German citizens the Nazis could not claim them without Danish assent. And second, while there were a few countries in Nazi-occupied Europe which succeeded by hook or by crook in saving most of their Jews, I think the Danes were the only ones who dared speak out on the subject to their masters. And the result was that under the pressure of public opinion, and threatened neither by armed resistance nor by guerilla tactics, the German officials in the country changed their minds; they were no longer reliable, they were overpowered by what they had most disdained, mere words, spoken freely and publicly. This had happened nowhere else.[40]

There are some concerns to be raised in this context. Firstly, the vagaries of contrasting the Danish political attitude versus the Italian 'general humanity of an old and civilized people' (What does 'general humanity' mean here?) rather dilutes one's ability to understand which approach is preferable. Is it a matter of 'whatever works'? Secondly, and most decisively for the present argument, Denmark, along with other Scandinavian states, maintained an exclusionary policy with regards to refugees before and during the war, thus preventing many thousands of Jewish refugees from Germany and Central/ Eastern Europe from being saved. Bo Lidegaard, the author of *Countrymen*, a detailed study of the Danish rescue, observes: 'From 1937, when persecution of the Jews in Germany was intensified, Denmark, like most of Germany's other neighbors, tightened its procedures as Jewish refugees were stopped at the border.'[41] When the Evian conference was convened in 1938 to address the Jewish refugee issue, 'All agreed that something urgently had to be done – and that preferably this something should be done by anybody but themselves', including Denmark, whose representative assured the Danish public 'that he had not left room for one single Jewish refugee to cross the Danish border.'[42] (Denmark was not alone in such attitudes: the Australian representative at Evian infamously declared that 'as we have no real racial problem, we are not desirous of importing one'.)[43] Lidegaard comments:

> Still, *the problem was conceived as one of numbers*. There were more than a million Jews in Germany and Austria. How many of these unfortunates could and should Denmark receive? *The apathy toward the disaster only grew with the numbers*, and Denmark, like other countries, turned its back on the problem and reinforced immigration controls at the border.[44] (Emphasis added)

It must be said that there are considerable lacunae in Arendt's remarks, and not simply an inevitable consequence of those who couldn't have known more at the time. Perhaps as a guest in Denmark on receiving the Sonning Prize, her remarks were politely restrained; however, she does not refrain from criticism either, and the tenor of her remarks is consistent with those in the Eichmann book on the same topic. Arendt was a contemporary of those responsible for the infamous Evian conference, and was she not aware of the failure to achieve meaningful action for Jewish refugees at that conference, including by Denmark? Absent from her discourse is a recognition that Denmark had actively excluded Jewish refugees from entering its territory after 1935.[45] Not only did Denmark not treat its refugees 'nicely' and 'refused them naturalization and permission to work', but for the most part it refused them a *right of entry*, of admission to its territory; that is to say, Denmark refused to admit significant numbers of refugees that might otherwise have been saved from persecution and death, and thus had hardly considered the 'right to asylum' to be 'sacrosanct' as she suggested. Recent scholarship by Greg Burgess on the struggles of refugees in the 1930s confirms the picture of Denmark as one link in a concatenation of European states 'where the borders were all but closed'.[46] Burgess confirms Arendt's account of Danish attitudes to refugees with respect to their right to work – Denmark had indicated that it 'would make no concessions for refugees' in this regard.[47] Even more horribly, some Jewish refugees were not only denied entry, but were turned over to the custody of the Gestapo.[48]

As already noted, Danish bravery in speaking their minds to the Nazis needs to be understood in the context of Hitler's desire to uphold Denmark as an exemplar of the Neuropa to come, a point Arendt neglects; Raul Hilberg, in his magnum opus *The Destruction of the European Jews* (which Arendt depends upon frequently in her Eichmann book), observes that even though it was occupied, Denmark was respected as a neutral state until as late in the war as 1943.[49] Scandinavian countries had successfully integrated their Jewish populations over the centuries; however, they had also gone to some lengths to exclude Jewish people, and thus there was a relatively small but well-assimilated extant Jewish population. Given the resistance to German plans, it was decided by senior Nazis to delay deportation action at the Wannsee Conference in 1942.[50] However, while the efficacy of Danish resistance speaks to Arendt's argument to an extent, there is nevertheless a problem with Arendt wanting to see her conception of meaningful political action demonstrated in the Denmark example. The privilege that Arendt grants to public speech, to human beings interacting in a shared space of appearance, leads her astray when she ascribes to this element of plural human activity a share in the success over the German occupiers. Public outcry and attendant governmental action were hardly decisive in this context: the Danish government outlawed all assistance to Jewish refugees from Danish Jewish people in 1941, which had been their primary means of support in the absence of basic civil rights and access to employment.[51]

Another fact of which Arendt was unaware,[52] which has emerged from recent scholarship, is that some Jewish refugees were expelled from Denmark during the period 1940–1943 – twenty-one people in total, including families, most of whom were killed in the death camps, whose deportation had not been 'ordered or demanded by the occupiers'.[53] As with other states occupied by the Nazis, there were collaborators amongst the Danes, an awkward fact when recounting the nobility of the Danish example. Some Danish companies employed Jewish slave-labour, and Denmark 'exported agricultural products that helped feed the German army'.[54] (Tellingly, the playwright Bertolt Brecht, quoted above, was moved to write *Mother Courage and Her Children* – which suggests bitingly that war is commerce by other means – explicitly 'as a warning to the Danes that they could not hope to sit on the sidelines and profit with impunity if their aggressive neighbour, Nazi Germany, went to war'. Brecht, who was himself a political exile from the Nazis in Denmark prior to the war, commented: 'I wrote the play quite expressly for Scandinavia'.)[55] There were Danes who were guilty of war crimes, such as a Danish SS doctor who experimented on homosexuals in Buchenwald,[56] and there were Danish volunteers in the Waffen-SS.[57]

I do not mean to suggest by the preceding arguments that the efforts of the Danes to save the Jewish people already in their territory were not laudable, or that it was not for the most part a resounding success – it was a tremendous achievement, albeit limited to those already within Denmark following an initial exclusion of foreign Jewish refugees. Nor do I think that Arendt, in theoretical terms, is wrong tout court to emphasize the importance of political action amongst plural beings, nor the need for a right to have rights that would safeguard the rights of the stateless. To deny entry to their territory is to be sure a violation of Arendt's idea of the right to have rights; in that strict sense, she missed nothing. But she misapplies, or does not apply at all, her own concepts in relation to this particular historical case study, most especially as concerns the Danish failure to provide asylum to refugees; this is especially curious if one understands the right to have rights, as noted above, as a provocation to states to consider whether they have fully included all individuals with a claim to membership. That is to say, that it is by Arendt's own lights that the Danish example is most questionable, and thus one can rightly be shocked at the perplexing and somewhat uninformed commendation she bestows upon Denmark.

It is important to understand the exclusion of refugees in the Danish example, because it speaks to a key limitation of the right to have rights: how to get states or other polities to agree to admit refugees in the first instance. Arendt, in her remarks and her laudation of this history, picks up the story after the exclusion has already taken place, and does not seem to be aware of it. It is not that Arendt is wrong in describing the need for a right to have rights, but that her articulation of it, leaning as it does on her thinking of political action, leads her to misinterpret events, especially in a context where no meaningful political action in terms of agitating for their rights can be accomplished by the powerless – that is, the stateless – as is so often the case. What is limited is her determination to locate the response to these issues as necessarily rooted in political action. Solutions for refugees who are excluded are not always amenable to solution by collective action, such that they become members of the polity that they are excluded from; they may simply remain excluded, with life-threatening consequences. The intractability of the refugee crisis, in its current dimensions and throughout the twentieth and into the twenty-first century – the ongoing plight of the Palestinian diaspora is a case in point – means that depending upon those lacking political power to secure their own place at the table with sovereign power and be recognized seems at minimum problematic. Thus, one must also engage with the converse difficulty of getting states to agree to admit those who need protection, and an account of why they have such a responsibility (the work of chapter 1). Political contestation concerning the stateless pertains in part to the self-understanding of the polity as such. The source of the guarantee of human dignity, in the absence of other options (the ability of refugees to press the demands themselves, or other schemas such as cities of asylum or 'newly defined territorial entities' which remain for the most part utopian and unrealized), must necessarily issue from within the established political community itself – it requires an *ethos* of responsibility where asylum figures as the very realization of the political as such.

Thus, to restate some of the limitations of calling for a right to have rights: first, Arendt seems misled by her own confidence in the importance of politics as an experience of shared political life in a space of appearances, while simultaneously failing to make explicit the safeguarding of humanity a normative goal of the political; second, the absence of any kind of what she described as 'newly defined territorial entities' to arise that would supersede the role of individual sovereign states undermines her own call for a new guarantee of human dignity that would be secured by recourse to a 'right to have rights'; and third, the problem of numbers, which plays an ambivalent role in her own discourse, especially important as it serves as a leitmotif of exclusion in the politics of asylum around the world, including in the Danish case study at issue. These are theoretical problems with her account: the remaining problems are her misreading of the historical facts, but the misreading is in part also guided by theory – in simple terms, she often makes historical facts fit her theories. In her essay on Bertolt Brecht in *Men in Dark Times*, Arendt asks whether Brecht, in his fidelity to the Soviet Union (including its Stalinist period), did not know what he was doing in his evident misjudgements.[58] Yet the same must be said of Arendt in relation to this episode of the history of Denmark, which Brecht, who had spent time in Denmark as a refugee (a status he defined as being that of a 'messenger of ill-tidings') in fact understood with much more insight, hence the warning issued to the Danes in *Mother Courage*.[59] The dominant interpretation of these events – given the influence Arendt's name (rightly) carries – requires emendation.

A pattern may be discerned in the gap between people who are saved qua members of a polity, and people who are not saved because they are not members; as Arendt observes, 'As in practically all other countries, the deportations from Holland started with stateless Jews, who in this instance consisted almost entirely of refugees from Germany, whom the prewar Dutch government had officially declared to be "undesirable"'.[60] This was also the case in France, where Jewish refugees fared far worse than Jewish French nationals.[61] Granting them membership under the rubric of the right to have rights might ameliorate this; however, political realities indicate that most of the time, states are unwilling to take on this responsibility, and cannot be compelled by unenforceable international law to do so. The right to have rights is arbitrary if states do not actively respect it, which mostly they don't. This was true in the 1930s (Evian) as it remains true in the present, when in 2016 two summits on refugees in New York failed to agree on meaningful figures for resettlement of stateless persons.[62] The right to have rights has not arrived.

Thus, the right to have rights require *moral force*. An explanation of responsibility is required, one that establishes clear *criterion for judgement* of political behaviour, that is, an *ethos of responsibility*, wherein the work of the political as such is understood as bound up with respect for the right to asylum. The right to have rights cannot be fulfilled unless the normative content of political action is oriented towards the preservation of plurality as its *telos*. This normative imperative is what is perhaps lacking in Arendt's concept of natalist politics amongst plural human beings, and thus undermining of the right to have rights. This has been analysed by Arendtian scholars in powerful ways: as noted previously, Seyla Benhabib has critiqued the lack of normative justification found in the right to have rights (a concept of the human subject such that the right is not simply tautological); Peg Birmingham locates the 'predicament of responsibility' in Arendt's views of natality and action; Judith Butler has emphasized unchosen plurality as the foundation of a new politics based upon 'the common rights of the refugee'.[63] This latter view, as discussed in Chapter One, comes closest to the argument made here, that politics must recognize asylum as its fundamental work, that 'active preservation' of human plurality is a political duty.

Further, such an understanding of politics would recognize that in a time of crisis, when *large numbers* of people are in urgent need of protection, it is necessary, in ethico-political terms, to invoke a protective politics of disproportion, of breaking the bounds of measure, in order to safeguard human dignity – to recognize, as in the case of Denmark, those who could have been saved but were not. That is to say, that the right to have rights needs to be supplemented by a political principle of gracious welcome, borne of the recognition of a world of unchosen plurality where political communities, despite being bounded, do not choose who they share the earth with. (As previously discussed, Butler is original and convincing in emphasizing this charge of Arendt's against Eichmann in the context of asylum; while not overtly genocidal, the exclusion of people resulting in their death can plausibly be described as *tacit* genocide). The political promises, laws, and agreements that might follow from a right to have rights, require grounding in an *ethos* of responsibility that will orient them, and subject them to judgement to the extent that they do not comport with the guarantee of human dignity, where the very essence of the political is justice, including for non-members of existing societies. That is the fundamental implication of plurality as the 'law of the earth', the 'new law on earth' required to safeguard human dignity.

An *ethos* of responsibility would also recognize the violence that borders themselves are responsible for, creating, as Reece Jones puts it, 'the economic and jurisdictional discontinuities that have come to be seen as its hallmarks', owing to their role in preserving 'privilege and opportunity for some by restricting access to resources and movement of others'.[64] Thousands of people die attempting to cross the borders of sovereign states each year; the International Organization for Migration estimates that 40,000 people died attempting to cross a border between 2005 and 2014.[65] Thus, the right to establish a border should be seen as entailing the corresponding duty of the state to ensure the rights and dignity of those who encounter those borders, that is, to construct and enforce a border is always-already to assume the responsibility that follows from it (or why respect the right of a state to a border?). Importantly, this must be recognised as a *primary duty* and not a 'secondary, derivative duty' (Carens), comporting with the insight that the preservation of human plurality is the *telos* of politics. Further, there may at times be some value to a border – refugees often seek the protection that is afforded by a border – such that the *ethos* of responsibility is not necessarily coterminous with a 'case for open borders', even though this *ethos* represents the articulation of a cosmopolitan, internationalist solidarity amongst all human beings.

SWEDEN AND RAOUL WALLENBERG: TOWARDS AN ETHOS OF RESPONSIBILITY

In order to illustrate how the right to have rights might be fulfilled, it is useful to consider a contemporaneous example to that of Denmark – the actions of Sweden before, during, and after the war. Their initiatives represent an admixture of admirable conduct, pragmatism, and self-interest, but which are nevertheless somewhat illustrative of the *ethos* of responsibility that is required in the context of life-saving asylum practices.

Like Denmark, Sweden did not have an exemplary record when it comes to practices of asylum at that time; as Steven Koblik writes, 'Prior to the war Sweden ignored, or even actively rejected, the possibilities of taking in significant numbers of Jewish refugees. Only after 1942 did Sweden seriously begin to seek ways to help Jews. It was late – very late.'[66] Nevertheless, public outrage did begin to mount at the treatment of Jewish refugees, including the deportation of Norwegian Jewish people and the impending threat to Danish Jewry.[67] Koblik mentions a number of factors that led to Sweden's more activist stance towards refugees: the existing values of the Swedish state, the desire to help fellow Scandinavians (Jewish people had been naturalized in Sweden for centuries, which may make them a different case to other refugee groups, as seen in present-day Swedish asylum politics), a means of justifying Swedish neutrality in the war to the Allied powers, and the abhorrence of the

Swedish people towards the Final Solution.[68] The Swedes were encouraged by the evidence provided by the Danish experience that suggested the Nazis would not necessarily press the programme of the Final Solution in all cases. By the time Sweden was ready to act decisively, a significant proportion of European Jewry had already been destroyed, with the exception of a remaining population of about 800,000 Jewish citizens in Hungary.[69]

In assessing Sweden's efforts to save European Jewry during the war, a significant amount of attention has focused upon the role of Raoul Wallenberg, the extraordinary individual who issued Swedish visas to Hungarian Jewry at great personal risk; but in truth it was also a collective effort. The result was that significant numbers of Jewish refugees from the neighbouring states of Norway and Denmark – both of which were occupied by the Nazis – were accepted by neutral Sweden, as well as some 45,000 Jewish people from Hungary.[70] Koblik notes that 'the Hungarians indicated a willingness to respect virtually any document that purported to be a foreign passport or *statement of responsibility*'[71] (emphasis added). Arendt comments on the effects of this Swedish attitude: once in Sweden, 'The non-Danish Jews were better off than ever before, they all received permission to work'.[72] This directly contrasts with the attitude of the Danes, which Arendt herself commented upon in her Lessing Prize speech (as mentioned previously).

Thus, the authorities of Sweden, with significant public support, issued thousands of protection visas – statements of *responsibility* – to Hungarian Jewish people. This extraordinary gesture goes to the heart of the meaning of an *ethos* of responsibility. The remarkable answer of the Swedes to the question, who are we as a people?, at a certain historical moment was: we are those who are responsible for the Jewish people of Hungary. This gratuitous, exorbitant responsibility concerning a population in no way directly related to the political life or self-interest of Sweden (aside perhaps from some reputational positioning vis-á-vis the Allies) resulted in the saving of tens of thousands of lives. In the absence of a change in the global order of sovereignty or the enforceability of international law to meaningfully safeguard the rights of refugees, this *ethos* must be upheld by states in order that the right to have rights be fulfilled.

The Swedish example is particularly pertinent in relation to Denmark, given its contemporaneity and geographical proximity, faced with similar challenges. However, other examples, illustrative of an *ethos* of responsibility, might be mentioned, amongst those states of the Global North whose record is normally so poor (in contradistinction, as already mentioned, to states of the Global South). For example, the Kindertransport, where the United Kingdom took in ten thousand Jewish children after Kristallnacht, evinces an *ethos* of responsibility (more on this in the following chapter). Or one might consider the responsibility-sharing amongst multiple states in accepting thousands of refugees from Vietnam during the 1970s, including states such as Australia (which now pursues punitive policies of offshore detention for refugees).[73] Also, the now-defunct programme of the Italian Navy 'Mare Nostrum', wherein thousands of people seeking asylum by boat on the Mediterranean were rescued. Mare Nostrum is Latin for 'Our Sea': Our Sea, and therefore our responsibility, an inversion of this motto as an imperialist creed of domination into its opposite, a willing solicitude. What is required in each case is that a polity – a town, region, city, or state, or international grouping of states – are 'willing and able' (Arendt's phrase quoted above) to assume responsibility for significant numbers of people not constitutive of their existing demos. Further, that this willingness proceeds from a recognition of the need to preserve human plurality and the need for everyone to be allowed to belong somewhere so that their rights be respected – that is, the fulfillment of the right to have rights in its normative dimension, beyond aporetics.

CONCLUSION

Yanis Varoufakis has observed that the Europe of today is a postmodern version of the Europe of the 1930s.[74] Neither Denmark nor Sweden have covered themselves in glory during the recent refugee 'crisis' in Europe, both opting for exclusionary policies, just as they did in the 1930s.[75] Denmark recently used legal interpretation to revoke protection status for a thousand Somali refugees, a posture typical of states of the Global North.[76] The vaunted image of Scandinavian states as apparently progressive social-democratic utopias begins to unravel when one examines their recent record on asylum. Yet as examined, both states also undertook positive actions towards Jewish refugees during a time of disaster. Thus, the lessons that the historical example of these two polities can provide – good and bad – remain important. Historical calamity has already shown the consequences that result where an *ethos* of responsibility was lacking; Arendt's reflections on the right to have rights were prompted precisely by the suffering of European Jewry (she was herself a refugee for many years), and remains relevant to other calamities today (more on this latter point in the Coda that concludes the book).

    From the standpoint of a just, compassionate politics, what is desirous in relation to the politics of asylum? That refugees be admitted to a place where they may belong, in the Arendtian sense, that is, to appear in a public space and be heard, and in so doing have their human dignity respected. Given this need of admittance, a number of ways of actualizing this are possible: (1) the global model of state sovereignty is fundamentally changed such that people fleeing disaster are not bound by existing state borders and can readily find refuge and acceptance; (2) international law becoming binding and enforce-able such that states can be compelled to admit the stateless (in defiance of state sovereignty); (3) states adopt an *ethos* wherein responsibility for others becomes part of the orienting principle of the life of the state and its members.

It is this third option that has been in focus here, in an emphasis upon *response*. To ask that politics be ordered on the basis of ethical responsibility may seem utopian, yet what alternatives are proffered by theorists at present? That the international regime of state sovereignty be reordered (which is highly unlikely – all signs point not to a relaxation but a strengthening of state borders and assertion of sovereignty)? Or that there be a world of open borders (which also will not happen any time soon, nor is this even dispositively desirable – there may well be compelling reasons why states should retain some rights of self-determination in relation to *migration*, but not asylum)? Or that international law acquire force (but who will force states to admit refugees, when so many states, and most of the most powerful ones, are determined to exclude)? Or a kind of tepid liberalism which restates the world as it is, (which confirms both the right of states to self-determination while making certain prudential allowances for a right to asylum). All these positions are tantamount to a position of irresponsibility, given the scale of statelessness and the terribly slow rates of resettlement. Here a return to the work of the previous chapter is necessary; Andrew Benjamin argues that 'evil' is defin-able as the violation of the incalculable by the calculable. The demand of the unconditioned – in the context of asylum, manifested as significant numbers of human beings requiring protection – where it is undone by calculation, by calculating in such a way that undoes the preservation of human plurality, the givenness of being-in-common – manifests a clear judgement. The riposte will normally be that politics requires self-determination, and that this tension or paradox must be maintained. The present claim (perhaps going further than Benjamin) is that strictly in the context of asylum, this is false, there is no evidence for any danger issuing from the delimitation of self-determination in this context, it is mere assertion. The dialectic is refused. The only clear evidence is all the people who are dead who could have been saved.

Michel de Montaigne, in a meditation upon judgement, argued that 'every action reveals us'.[77] *Ethos* relates to identity as much as action. It is not only a question of 'What are we to do?', 'What obligations do we owe?', but just as importantly, 'Who are we'? Not simply a virtue ethics counterposed to the deontology-utilitarian divide, this mode of self-examination would pertain to the activity of thought. Such a reflection would bring us back to Arendt, even in the course of a critique of Arendt, as she has so eloquently articulated the birth of conscience that comes from the exercise of our capacity for thought and judgement, the two-in-one that must answer to itself.[78] But should not the reflection of a political community upon itself aim at a determinate conception of the good, rather than whatever is simply decided by democratic agreement (as previously noted, Arendt recognized that a democracy might one day decide democratically to liquidate a people)?[79] Are 'we', however the 'we' is to be constituted, responsible for the Jewish people of Hungary, the Rohingyan people of Myanmar, the Tamil people of Sri Lanka? And if yes, why? Such a claim might seem arbitrary – unless it is argued that preservation of human plurality is an active duty of all human societies, indeed the very *telos* of politics; and that in consequence, upholding the right asylum is necessarily the realization of politics. The nature of this *telos* and the attendant necessity of asylum, in forming a new concept of the political, provide clear criteria of judgement of politics. Here is where a marked difference from Arendt is clear – there is a normative 'banister', to use her term, that must be invoked, and it is her own claim that plurality is the law of the earth.

Arendt once wrote a penetrating essay on Kafka, in which she linked the fate of Kafka's characters to the experience of European Jewry: 'But this world actually has come to pass. The generation of the forties and especially those who have the doubtful advantage of having lived under the most terrible regime history has so far produced know that the terror of Kafka adequately represents the true nature of the thing called bureaucracy – the replacing of government by administration and of laws by arbitrary decrees.'[80] An effective staging of the problem of admittance to the law and the upholding of rights can indeed be found in Kafka's novels. To the extent that law remains inaccessible, that is, guarded by a Castle or Court that makes the rules, the supplicant to the law must rely upon the good graces of these forces. The protagonist of *The Castle*, 'K', observes: 'I don't want gracious handouts from the Castle, but my *rights*' (emphasis added); and his struggle throughout the novel is to press those rights claims upon the remote forces of the Castle. However, K discovers, in Arendt's words, that 'everything natural and normal in life has been wrested out of men's hands by the prevalent regime of the village, to become a present endowed from without – or, as Kafka puts it, from "above".'[81] K, as Arendt observes, 'is a stranger who can never be brought into line because he belongs neither to the common people nor to its rulers. ("You are not of the Castle and you are not of the village, you are nothing at all".)'[82] K is rendered 'superfluous' and dependent upon others, by both the Castle and the villagers.[83] In the conclusion to her book *Rightlessness in an Age of Rights*, Ayten Gündoğdu observes that 'in the case of K., Arendt refuses the conclusion that his struggle for rights ultimately fails because it cannot achieve the goals it pursues. She highlights the significance of K.'s struggle, which sets an example for other villagers by demonstrating to them "both that human rights are worth fighting for and that the rule of the castle is not divine law and, consequently, can be attacked"'.[84] Gündoğdu argues that the merit of Arendt's approach is that it 'provides a different understanding of "politics", centered on the struggles of subjects whose rights are at stake, and not on the interventions of external actors . . . there is an ineluctable tension between human rights and the institutions established to guarantee them; this tension arises not only because institutions can turn against the very rights that they were supposed to uphold but also because human rights can be mobilized for the purpose of opposing new ones'.[85]

Here there is a fundamental problem, one that is, in my view, a symptomatic tendency of political theorists in thinking through these matters, in their remaining faithful to political struggle on the one hand and self-determination on the other, and being sceptical of normative claims that should orient political life when issuing from a source anterior to political life itself. Jeffery Isaac, author of a paper on Arendt's call for a new guarantee, can conceive of the realization of this guarantee only in Arendt's own terms:

> As she recognized, human rights are not a given of human nature; they are the always tenuous results of a politics that seeks to establish them, a vigorous politics intent on constituting relatively secure spaces of human freedom and dignity. And as she saw, the nation-state, far from being the vehicle of the self-determination of individuals and peoples, is in many ways an obstacle to the dignity that individuals and communities seek. Those interested in human rights, who wish to provide a new guarantee for human dignity, have no alternative but to take responsibility upon themselves, to act politically as members of elementary republics, locally and globally, on behalf of a dignity that is in perpetual jeopardy in the world in which we live.

As discussed in chapter 1, this is also a view shared by theorists such as Mouffe, Balibar, and Rancière, who emphasize the political nature of rights, and their achievement via struggle. Somehow, contempt for the impotence of natural rights – from Burke to Arendt to Rancière and more – is de rigeur; and yet the concomitant reality of the impotence of much political struggle is ignored. To have required of Jewish refugees that they press their demands in political struggle at the Danish border (where they were simply turned away, often to death), or to require it of those who languish presently in terrible conditions in, for example, Libya – that is, precisely those who have the least ability to enforce their demands – seems a terribly limited approach. To the extent that they are able to undertake such struggle, or that advocates act on their behalf, or that they can gain entry to a society in which to press their demands, this line of argument is of merit and these struggles must of course continue; and yet *non-entrée* policies are the order of the day all around the world. As Stephanie DeGooyer writes, 'There is no guarantee that a performative rights claim to rights will be validated, especially if the community that the claimant seeks entrance into is itself responsible for the loss of rights'.[86] Nothing will change, until a new concept of the political comes to the fore that challenges an entire tradition of self-determining bounded communities as expressed in political philosophy from Aristotle to Hobbes and up to the present, with a differing account of politics that places the right to asylum at the heart of political life as such, that identifies responsibility and relationality as foundational to politics. To repeat a key point, the evidence has not been furnished that a delimitation of self-determination in relation to asylum would produce societal disintegration, or the destruction of the possibility of politics; I know of no example. How have political theorists been excused such vagueness for so long? The caesura, the crack in the tradition, is inaugurated by the incredible work of Hannah Arendt, in her demand for a new guarantee of human dignity via a new law on earth, which she identified as plurality itself. And yet it sometimes seems – and Arendt was self-avowedly not a systematic thinker – that she did not follow through the logic of her own position. The emphasis on political struggle fails to mark the 'active preservation' (Butler) of unchosen human plurality as the very work of politics itself, of those societies already constituted, the 'we' that could *respond* to the vulnerable. K's struggle is worthy, *but K remains without*. The benevolence of states, especially developed states, concerning refugees is of course anything but trustworthy. And yet unless something changes in the mindset of the Castle residents, or the villagers wrest control away from them – that is, unless the leaders or citizens of the state can be recalled to an *ethos* of responsibility as the realization of politics – stateless persons will remain stuck between the messianic hopelessness of calls for a new arrangement of the international order, and their current plight in immiserated exile, and the right to have rights will remain the aporia it may always have been. Sadly, if one construes the 'villagers' as majoritarian democratic citizenry and the 'Castle' as their political leaders, there is often no difference of opinion between these forces ('mob above, mob below', to borrow a phrase from Nietzsche) on the necessity of exclusion. No doubt it will be rejoined that the reconceptualization of the political as an *ethos* of responsibility is as utopian as the fruitlessness of much political struggle. And yet, when has politics been challenged by such a different account of itself? That challenge began with Arendt; it remains to be fully elaborated and enacted by us, her readers, in the admixture of admiration and perplexity that is evinced by all the truly great writers of her stature whose contradictions, to paraphrase what she wrote of Marx, are as productive as their consistency.[87] I have argued that the right to have rights should best be understood as an ethical imperative which recognizes and upholds the duty to actively preserve human plurality, a duty that is coterminous with the law of the earth.

NOTES

1. Bertolt Brecht, *War Primer*, trans. John Willett (London and New York, NY: Verso Books, 2017), p. 58.

2. See DeGooyer et al., *The Right To Have Rights*.

3. Arendt, *The Origins of Totalitarianism*, pp. 296–97.

4. Hirsch and Bell, 'The Right to have Rights', pp. 417–37.

5. *OT*, pp. 296–97.

6. *OT*, p. 298.

7. *OT*, p. 298.

8. DeGooyer et al., *The Right To Have Rights*, p. 9.

9. Emma Larking, *Refugees and the Myth of Human Rights: Life Outside the Pale of Law* (Surrey: Ashgate and Burlington: Ashgate, 2014), p. 141.

10. *OT*, p. ix.

11. Matthew Gibney, 'A Thousand Little Guantanamos: Western States and Measures to Prevent the Arrival of Refugees', in *Displacement, Asylum, Migration: The Oxford Amnesty Lectures 2004*, ed. Kate E. Tunstall (Oxford: Oxford University Press, 2006), pp. 139–69.

12. See the UNHCR Global Trends report online, updated annually, for details of the scope of global displacement.

13. *OT*, pp. 296–97.

14. *OT*, p. ix.

15. *OT*, p. 299.

16. DeGooyer et al., *The Right To Have Rights*, p. 31.

17. Arendt, *The Human Condition*, p. 178.

18. DeGooyer et al., *The Right To Have Rights*, p. 93.

19. DeGooyer et al., *The Right To Have Rights*, p. 93.

20. DeGooyer et al., *The Right To Have Rights*, pp. 93–94.

21. DeGooyer et al., *The Right To Have Rights*, pp. 28–29.

22. *OT*, p. 298.

23. Arendt, *The Origins of Totalitarianism*, p. 302.

24. *OT*, p. 280.

25. *OT*, pp. 293–94.

26. Arendt, *The Human Condition*, p. 43.

27. *OT*, p. 283.

28. *OT*, p. 302.

29. Stefan Heuser, 'Is There a Right to have rights? The Case of the Right of Asylum', *Ethical Theory and Moral Practice*, Vol. 11, No. 1, Political Ethics and International Order, February 2008, p. 7.

30. Markus Gehrsitz, and Martin Ungerer, 'Jobs Crime and Votes: A Short-Run Evaluation of the Refugee Crisis in Germany', *ZEW Discussion Paper No. 16-086*, December 2016, https://papers.ssrn.com/sol3/papers.cfm?abstract_id=2887442, retrieved 1 February 2020. Other states such as the United States, many times larger and more powerful than Germany, could presumably do much more, even in a single year.

31. Arendt, *Eichmann in Jerusalem*, p. 171.

32. Lidegaard, *Countrymen*, pp. 20–21. Lidegaard's views are controversial – some historians hold that he has engaged in a 'white wash' of this chapter of Danish history; see the blog entry by Vilhjálmur Örn Vilhjálmsson, https://fornleifur.blog.is/blog/fornleifur/entry/1308693/, retrieved 1 February 2020.

33. Arendt, *Eichmann in Jerusalem*, p. 179. For more concerning the high rates of survival of Italian Jewry, see Susan Zuccotti, *The Italians and the Holocaust: Persecution, Rescue & Survival* (London: Peter Halban Publishers, 1987).

34. Elsebet Jegstrup, 'Spontaneous Action: The Rescue of the Danish Jews from Hannah Arendt's Perspective', *Humboldt Journal of Social Relations*, Vol. 13, No. 1, 1986, pp. 260 and 267. On this point see also the work of Jacques Rancière, for example, in *Hatred of Democracy*.

35. Arendt, *Eichmann in Jerusalem*, pp. 171–72.

36. Arendt, *Eichmann in Jerusalem*, p. 172.

37. Arendt, *Eichmann in Jerusalem*, p. 172.

38. Arendt, *Eichmann in Jerusalem*, p. 174.

39. Hannah Arendt, 'Prologue' [Sonning Prize Lecture], in *Responsibility and Judgment*, ed. Jerome Kohn (New York, NY: Schocken Books, 2003), p. 6.

40. Arendt, 'Prologue', p. 6.

41. Lidegaard, *Countrymen*, p. 12.

42. Lidegaard, *Countrymen*, p. 14.

43. Klauss Neumann, *Across the Seas: Australia's Response to Refugees – A History* (Collingwood: Black Inc., 2015), p. 35.

44. Lidegaard, *Countrymen*, p. 14.

45. Viljámur Vilhjálmsson and Bent Blüdnikow, 'Rescue, Expulsion and Collaboration: Denmark's Difficulties with its World War Two Past', *Jewish Political Studies Review*, Vol. 18, No. 3/4, Fall 2006, pp. 3–5.

46. Greg Burgess, *The League of Nations and the Refugees from Nazi Germany: James G. McDonald and Hitler's Victims* (London and New York, NY: Bloomsbury, 2016), p. 96.

47. Burgess, *The League of Nations*, p. 145.

48. Paul Levine, 'Sweden's Complicated Neutrality and the Rescue of Danish Jewry', in *The Routledge History of the Holocaust*, ed. J. C. Friedman (London and New York, NY: Routledge, 2011), p. 306.

49. Raul Hilberg, *The Destruction of the European Jews: Vol. 2*, 3rd edition (New Haven, CT and London: Yale University Press, 2003), p. 465.

50. Hilberg, *The Destruction of the European Jews*, p. 584.

51. Vilhjálmsson and Blüdnikow, 'Rescue, Expulsion and Collaboration', pp. 5–6.

52. Arendt relied heavily on the work of Leni Yahil, whose own work was limited by the archive sources available at that time. See Vilhjálmsson and Blüdnikow, 'Rescue, Expulsion and Collaboration', p. 6.

53. Vilhjálmsson and Blüdnikow, 'Rescue, Expulsion and Collaboration', p. 5.

54. Vilhjálmsson and Blüdnikow, 'Rescue, Expulsion and Collaboration', p. 9.

55. See Bertolt Brecht, *Mother Courage and Her Children*, trans. John Willet (London and New York, NY: Bloomsbury, 2016), p. xvii.

56. Vilhjálmsson and Blüdnikow, 'Rescue, Expulsion and Collaboration', pp. 8–9.

57. Claus Christensen, Niels Poulsen, and Peter Smith, 'The Danish Volunteers in the Waffen SS', in *Denmark and the Holocaust*, eds. Mette Jensen and Steven Jensen (Copenhagen: Institute for International Studies, Department of Holocaust and Genocide Studies, 2003).

58. Hannah Arendt, *Men In Dark Times* (San Diego, CA, London, and New York, NY: Harcourt Brace & Company, 1993), p. 210.

59. Arendt, *Men In Dark Times*, p. 226.

60. Arendt, *Eichmann in Jerusalem*, p. 167.

61. Arendt, *Eichmann in Jerusalem*, pp. 164–65.

62. https://www.amnesty.org/en/latest/news/2016/09/refugee-crisis-leaders-summit-fails-to-show-leadership/, retrieved 1 February 2020.

63. Butler, *Parting Ways*, p. 16.

64. Jones, *Violent Borders*, p. 5.

65. Jones, *Violent Borders*, p. 4.

66. Steven Koblik, 'Sweden's Attempts to Aid Jews, 1939–1945', *Scandinavian Studies*, Vol. 56, No. 2, Spring 1984, p. 110.

67. Koblik, 'Sweden's Attempts to Aid Jews, 1939–1945', pp. 95–96.

68. Koblik, 'Sweden's Attempts to Aid Jews, 1939–1945', p. 110.

69. Koblik, 'Sweden's Attempts to Aid Jews, 1939–1945', p. 98.

70. Koblik, 'Sweden's Attempts to Aid Jews, 1939–1945', p. 110.

71. Koblik, 'Sweden's Attempts to Aid Jews, 1939–1945', p. 101.

72. Arendt, *Eichmann in Jerusalem*, p. 174.

73. Claire Higgins, *Asylum by Boat* (Sydney: UNSW Press, 2017).

74. Yanis Varoufakis, 'How I Became an Erratic Marxist', *The Guardian* (Online), 18 May 2015, https://www.theguardian.com/news/2015/feb/18/yanis-varoufakis-how-i-became-an-erratic-marxist, retrieved 1 February 2020.

75. Sasha Abramsky, 'If Sweden and Denmark are So Progressive, Why Did they Close their Doors to Refugees?' *The Nation* (Online), 27 September 2016, https://www.thenation.com/article/if-sweden-and-denmark-are-so-progressive-why-did-they-close-their-doors-to-refugees/, retrieved 1 February 2020.

76. https://www.asyluminsight.com/maria-osullivan#.XjT_jWgzZPb, retrieved 1 February 2020.

77. Michel Montaigne, *Essays* (London: Penguin Books, 1958), p. 131.

78. 'Thinking and Moral Considerations', in *Responsibility and Judgment*, pp. 159–89.

79. *OT*, p. 299.

80. H. Arendt, 'Franz Kafka: A Reevaluation on the Twentieth Anniversary of his Death', in *Essays in Understanding 1930–1954*, ed. J. Kohn (New York, NY: Schocken Books, 1994), pp. 69–80.

81. Arendt, 'The Jew as Pariah', p. 293.

82. Arendt, 'The Jew as Pariah', p. 290.

83. Arendt, 'The Jew as Pariah', p. 291.

84. Gündoğdu, *Rightlessness in an Age of Rights*, p. 205.

85. Gündoğdu, *Rightlessness in an Age of Rights*, p. 210.

86. DeGooyer et al., *The Right To Have Rights*, pp. 29–30.

87. Arendt, *The Human Condition*, pp. 104–5.

Chapter 3

Political Justice

Levinas contra Aristotle, or the Problem with the Kindertransport

For the value of a thought is measured by its distance from the continuity of the familiar.[1]

– Theodor Adorno, *Minima Moralia*

. . .the exaltation of a logic *other* than that of Aristotle, of a thought other than civilized.[2]

– Emmanuel Levinas, 'Peace and Proximity'

INTRODUCTION: PROPER NAMES[3]

To recall a 'proper name', for Emmanuel Levinas, was the evocation of an encounter with a singular Other, an individual whose philosophical *saying* marks out a particular territory of meaning within philosophy. Not just those who define a meaning or set of meanings, however, but who also provide an ability to 'resist the dissolution of meaning and help us to speak'.[4] The names that Levinas lists in his book of that title *Proper Names* (*Noms propres*) are for the most part his intellectual contemporaries of the twentieth century.[5] This selection is made for good reason: in the Foreword to the book, Levinas, providing a catalogue of twentieth-century horrors that his generation faced. In response, Levinas rallies to his side those thinkers in whom he recognizes 'A non-indifference of one toward the other!',[6] who work to ensure that ethical meaning can be preserved against horror, and who recognize the seeming failure of an entire Occidental philosophical and cultural tradition to prevent those horrors. These names – amongst them Jacques Derrida, Paul Celan, Jean Wahl, Martin Buber – are largely thinkers with whom Levinas had positive affinities, whose work he was to some extent prepared to affirm or countersign, even while marking out important areas of difference and disagreement.

There is, however, another list of proper names associated with Levinas that could be collated, in a more agonistic vein. Indeed, for a philosopher so profoundly associated with kind-sounding words like 'peace' and 'ethics', it is remarkable to consider that Levinas has quite the 'rogues gallery' of villains, like a superhero, that is, other philosophers with whom he had serious disagreements. His thoughtful polemic against Heidegger – arguably characteristic of almost the entirety of Levinas's œuvre – is well known; given that Levinas is a thinker concerned with disrupting 'totality' (in this effort, heavily influenced by Franz Rosenzweig), Hegel can be seen as an implicit foe;[7] his ethics, in not privileging reason, is certainly a disputation of Kant;[8] minor disagreements with contemporaries like Martin Buber and Jacques Derrida occurred during his life;[9] as a thinker who affirmed, in his own unique register, the highly contested concept of 'humanism', one could add other figures who critique or rejected humanism, such as Louis Althusser and Michel Foucault, to this list;[10] and it would be possible for his readers to stage themselves a spectral, posthumous encounter between Levinas and interlocutors such as Alain Badiou and Slavoj Žižek, who often criticize Levinas in order to better establish some of their own claims.[11]

Each of these proper names represents the staging ground, the mise-en-scène of a profound philosophical issue which was of concern to Levinas. Yet in this chapter one name in particular will be isolated, which is one of *the* defining proper names of Western philosophy: Aristotle. It goes without saying that Aristotle ranks amongst the most influential philosophers of history; criticizing Aristotle is an extremely difficult, one might suggest hubristic task, given the enormity of this figure within philosophy and the practically unassimilable scope of the total critical literature – Derrida's remark that apropos of Levinas's large body of work, one can 'no longer glimpse its edges', applies exponentially to the legacy of Aristotle.[12] And yet, such a critique may be necessary, indeed unavoidable from the perspective of taking Levinas's texts seriously. Levinas himself did not make Aristotle an explicit, extended focus of critique – though if one consults the index of most of Levinas's books, references to Aristotle are to be found in most of them, and usually couched in a critical vein (some of his remarks on Aristotle are examined below).

The argument is simple: Levinas and Aristotle are radically opposed over the question of the meaning of justice. However, some difficulties are faced in establishing this claim; furthermore, the consequences for a philosophical conception of political justice, and how that might be understood in matters of praxis, are profound. In the conjuncture of unchosen plurality (Arendt) with ethical responsibility (Levinas) as forming the basis of a new concept of the political, this chapter will be concerned with exploring the implications of the latter. If the political subject is called to ethical responsibility prior to willing any decision, it must be asked what form such responsibility takes in political practice, that is, whether the move from ethics to justice radicalizes the nature of the latter term, or whether Levinasian justice, once it moves beyond the ethical, is just more Aristotle. Here, the claim is that justice as thought by Levinas is a decisive move beyond Aristotle, which, when thought in the context of asylum, evinces possibilities of going beyond the limits of moderantism, and the achievement of just outcomes for stateless persons.

At stake is the difference between the moderate and the excessive, where a thinking of the unconditioned or infinite comes to interrupt the conditional. Pragmatic approaches to the political have no ground of judgement for the actualization of the good life, understood as justice, because they have no external criteria of judgement outside the calculable; Aristotle recognized this problem but doesn't have a sufficiently robust answer to it. Conversely, in the ethics of Levinas, there is a recognition of an anarchic, infinite responsibility – 'an inexhaustible responsibility: for with the other our accounts are never settled'.[13] William Simmons illustrates the meaning of this effectively with reference to the scene towards the end of *Schindler's List*, where Oskar Schindler (played by Liam Neeson), despite having saved so many people, nevertheless reproaches himself for not having done more.[14] Such are also the stakes in the present argument; the horrors of the Shoah, which preoccupied Levinas and arguably inform the entirety of his post-war work, will provide the historical context and a case study intended to illustrate the implications of what follows.

The theoretical task is difficult, in part due to the following considerations. Firstly, there is the problem of the *nunc pro tunc* fallacy, of 'presentism' – the imposition of current opinions or judgements upon the past. To criticize Aristotle for his well-known justification of slavery by seeing it as an anti-humanist stance seems terribly redundant; similarly, the applicability of his conception of the political, generated from the exigencies of the life-world of the Athenian polis, may also seem highly circumscribed. As Alasdair MacIntyre observed in *After Virtue*, 'Aristotle takes himself not to be inventing an account of the virtues, but to be articulating an account that is implicit in the thought, utterance and action of an educated Athenian . . . for he holds that the city-state is the unique political form in which alone the virtues of human life can be genuinely and fully exhibited'.[15] Thus, to the extent that Aristotle's views on justice are shaped by a specific historico-political context, comparisons between these thinkers may seem ostensibly difficult to draw.

Secondly, the potential field of comparison is very large – one could engage their relative thinking on epistemology, on metaphysics, as well as on ethics, justice, and politics, and do so situated in a wider philosophical context where other proper names would become pertinent (e.g. the extent to which Heidegger can be seen as an Aristotelian, and how Levinas's critique of Heidegger thus is in some way an implicit critique of the latter).[16] Such a treatment would be beyond the scope of one chapter.

Yet despite these difficulties, such a comparison is necessary. In thinking through moderation as it relates to politics, an important question arises as to the legacy of Aristotle: to what extent do his writings and the influence of the philosophemes that fall under his proper name – such as conceiving of justice as moderation, which will be a key focus of the critique – continue to hold widespread currency in contemporary political thought? Adorno wryly comments on this in *Minima Moralia* when he writes of the enduring influence of 'the doctrine inculcated since Aristotle that moderation is the virtue appropriate to reasonable people'.[17] It is this concern about Aristotle's version of justice, and its possible effects, that will be explored in what follows.

It is even possible to put in question the strength of the objection concerning presentism, and to ask whether the world as Aristotle understood is so unrecognizably different to ours, such that the thinking of questions of political justice would be inapplicable depending on the epoch. Political violence of the kind discussed in Thucydides's *History of the Peloponnesian War* continues in similar forms in contemporary history, including the history that was so decisive for Levinas's own experiences, and which marked his philosophical work; as briefly referenced previously, Jean Amèry noted in *At the Mind's Limits*:

> Yes, the SS could carry on just as it did: there are no natural rights, and moral categories come and go like the fashions. A Germany existed that drove Jews and political opponents to their death, since it believed that only in this way could it become a full reality. And what of it? Greek civilization was built on slavery and an Athenian army had run wild on the Island of Melos as had the SS in Ukraine.[18]

Amèry's comments on the continuity of history as it rhymes, if not repeats (to cite Mark Twain's apocryphal phrase) suggests that the applicability of past thinking to the present and vice versa may not necessarily be ill-conceived, if the implications of political decisions can be equally horrific. And yet concomitant to this is a counter-thought of rupture: that, following the thinking of Levinas (and Adorno could be said to underscore the thinking of Levinas throughout what follows), it is necessary to put into question (and possibly, into the dock) the continued influence of the ancients and an entire tradition of Western philosophy, in the post-Auschwitz world where that tradition and culture failed to stop the horror. Here, Adorno's quote which I have selected for the epigraph above is apposite: it may be that radical departures are needed from the canonical tradition of philosophy, new thoughts which, to quote the poetic and moving ending of *Minima Moralia*, 'contemplate all things as they would present themselves from the standpoint of redemption. . . . Perspectives must be fashioned that displace and estrange the world, reveal it to be, with its rifts and crevices, as indigent and distorted as it will appear one day in the messianic light'.[19] If anything in philosophy is so 'familiar' that may require 'distancing', it is certainly the thought of Aristotle. This is not to lay the violence of Melos, or the SS, or other political calamities, at the feet of Aristotle; that would be an absurd proposition. It is rather about a distancing or displacing of canonical philosophical axioms, in order that urgent ethico-political questions be thought anew; it is to worry not that Aristotelian forms of justice will directly lead to the perpetration of horror, but to worry that it will fail to produce adequate responses to horror (and thus perhaps, indirectly exacerbate it).

Further, what may come into sharper relief through the staging of this encounter between Aristotle and Levinas is the familiar theme of an oscillation in Western thinking and politics between 'Athens' and 'Jerusalem' – proper names often taken to signify different perspectives which nevertheless find themselves imbricated in European culture and philosophy.[20] It may be that the more 'exorbitant' ethics, leading to an exorbitant justice, which is found in Levinas, finds its provenance in the Judaic tradition that was so important to him, which certainly influenced his philosophical thinking (even if he also took care to mark a differentiation between his Talmudic and philosophic writings). A thinking from that tradition may radicalize a more Hellenic preference for measure and moderation, with important consequences for matters of political praxis. This is another enormous set of questions that cannot be adequately addressed here, but should be understood as an important consideration informing the arguments that follow.

In order to illustrate the differences between Aristotle and Levinas, the stakes of this disputation of the meaning of justice will be applied to the plight of people seeking asylum and refugees. Aristotle is silent on the question of asylum – aside from worrying in the *Politics* about foreigners becoming too numerous for the polis to monitor them, discussed below. The notion of individual or human rights was of course unknown to him, and it may seem a fallacious presentism to seek it in his writings; but as noted in the introduction, the theme of asylum is present in Greek tragedies, which implicate the workings of politics deeply (e.g. in the *Suppliant Maidens* and *Oedipus at Colonus*), yet remain unthematized in his work.[21] His concerns are elsewhere. What implications might Aristotle's thinking of justice, as a form of virtue, and conceived as moderation, have for the way in which asylum politics is understood and practised? The further implication of this inquiry, although not explicit in this chapter, is a deepening of the possible resonances of Aristotle in Arendt's work. As discussed in previous chapters, Arendt was highly influenced by and close to Aristotle on many questions of politics; yet Hanna Pitkin suggests that Arendt and Aristotle part company on the question of justice as a political theme, which was more important for Aristotle than Arendt: 'The idea of justice, central for Aristotle, is conspicuously absent from Arendt's otherwise closely parallel account'.[22] If this is the case – given the limitations that will be discussed apropos of Aristotle – then it brings the possible difficulties with Arendt's work into starker relief.

How might Levinas offer a different, more radical, or even excessive orientation to the same considerations? After first examining the meanings of justice to be found in both thinkers, their thinking is applied to this question, and in particular, the historical case of the Kindertransport which will illustrate the distinction being drawn. Ten thousand Jewish children were saved under this scheme, itself an exemplary act in many ways, but perhaps bounded by a prudential, moderate vision of justice, itself inadequate when one realizes that the total number of Jewish children destroyed in the Holocaust was 1.5 million, along with thousands of Romani children and German children with disabilities, as well as children in Poland and the Soviet Union and from across Europe; the total Jewish Holocaust was six million, and the total victims of the Holocaust numbered around ten million.[23] Thus an exorbitant, welcome, on the part of the UK at the time, might have saved so many more from calamity. And while the responsibility was not solely on the UK – other states in or outside Europe might have played a similar role – nevertheless, the focus on a single state taking such responsibility will serve to illustrate another important point where Aristotle and Levinas part company: on the question of reciprocity. As I will explain further below, Aristotle sees a positive role for generous reciprocity in the functioning of a political community, whereas Levinas will repeatedly insist that ethics should not be generated from reciprocal considerations. To be sure, even for Levinas the move from ethics to justice as instantiated in the political requires some measure of reciprocity. However, the radical claim of Levinas is that the ethics which he proposes shapes the nature of justice itself, giving it an exorbitant, anarchical temper that takes it beyond Aristotelianism in the recognition of the potentially infinite nature of responsibility.

ARISTOTLE AND JUSTICE

As is well known, Aristotle's conception of the good is that of happiness, but a happiness, *eudaimonia*, understood as realized via the pursuit of a virtuous life. The happy person acts in accordance with virtue, and one of the qualities of the virtuous person is to be just. Justice, then, is related to Aristotle's conception of what is good both for the individual and the political community of which they are a part.

The meaning of justice is, to be sure, a dominant theme of philosophy going back to the pre-Socratics, and famously a major topic of Plato's *Republic*. A particularly influential account of the meaning of justice, however, is that given by Aristotle in his *Nicomachean Ethics* (hereafter *NE*). There are multiple interpretations of justice given in Book Five of the *NE*, from justice as respect for the law, to justice as complete virtue, as distributive or reciprocal, as corrective or equitable; the distinctions are not always clear, which may be due to the *NE* being a set of lecture notes rather than as a completed text which Aristotle had fully elaborated.[24] Yet across the different meanings of justice, there is a particular theme that I wish to isolate (while also being attentive to some other aspects): that of moderation. He wrote that justice is a 'sort of proportion',[25] and that 'Injustice, on the contrary, is concerned with what is unjust, that is, a disproportionate excess or deficiency of what is beneficial or harmful; so injustice is an excess and a deficiency, because it is concerned with excess and deficiency'.[26]

On this account justice itself is the avoidance of excess, a keeping within bounds of proportion, of measure, of moderation. To be just is not to go too far, nor to do too little – one might call it, a little tongue-in-cheek, the Goldilocks principle of justice. *Meden agan*, μηδὲν ἄγαν– nothing too much – was the inscription on the temple of Apollo at Delphi and was a leitmotif of the Athenian polis.[27] While it is difficult to quantify in any kind of absolute way – one can only infer its influence for the most part by reading between the lines of arguments – it is arguable that this concept of justice continues to dominate philosophical thinking through to the present day. Thus, the task of the present section is to understand just what is meant by justice in Aristotle, how it relates to virtue, and the implications for politics – particularly for questions of foreigners and the politics of asylum. As I will elaborate further on, my argument is that an integrated reading of Aristotle's reflections on justice with his reflections on politics, demonstrates a commitment to a bounded polis that seeks to delimit the number of foreign arrivants, based on considerations of numbers; thus, an Aristotelian conception of justice is problematic for those seeking a compassionate and more open approach by sovereign states to refugees where the question of numbers is at issue.

A part of the difficulty, and ambiguity, of establishing what Aristotle means by justice – and then thinking this specifically in relation to political justice – concerns the problems of integrating what he writes about justice with his writings on virtue (where justice is itself one of the virtues), and at the same time his writings on politics (and one could add metaphysics, rhetoric, and so on). A particularly important question in this context is: if justice is a virtue, does that mean that the just act does not have to do with the result, the thing in itself, but rather the character disposition of the actor? Is this the only way to measure political justice?

An important distinction here is between *mesotēs* and *meson* – between a mean state (*mesotēs*) and the mean (*meson*), neither excessive nor deficient, the virtue relative to the self.[28] Aristotle intends for us to understand virtue as a state of character, as opposed to a feeling or a capacity, as famously outlined in Book Two of the *NE*. However, a key question is whether establishing what is meant by a virtuous character can be accomplished by reference to the responses of the actor. Scholars disagree on this point, but will often acknowledge the inherent ambiguity in Aristotle's text.[29] Lesley Brown argues that Aristotle is wrongly understood as a precursor to modern theories of virtue ethics, in asserting the primacy of the virtuous character of the actor prior to engaging in acts – as Brown notes, Aristotle acknowledges that some just acts are committed by people who are themselves not yet just (i.e. just in that they are virtuous).[30] However, this is disputed by other scholars such as David Bostock, who writes that 'the best suggestion seems to be that it is not the virtuous action, on each occasion, that has something middling about it, but rather the general disposition from which it flows'.[31] It should also be noted that Aristotle does not delimit his thinking to moderation, but thought that moderation without liberality would be misery.[32]

Moderation for Aristotle requires *phronesis*, practical wisdom. *Phronesis* enables reciprocity between two persons who cannot know what is best for each other; practical wisdom is the knowledge of one's limits of understanding, both of oneself and of the other person.[33] Aristotle writes that justice is 'complete virtue; virtue, however, not without qualification but in relation to another person'.[34] This explains why Aristotle considers justice the greatest and most complete virtue (what he also refers to as 'general justice') because it refers to another person.[35] (In passing, an affinity can be noted here with Levinas's definition of justice in *Totality and Infinity*: 'the relation with the Other, that is, to justice' – a conception of justice that has to do primarily with a relation to another human being, rather than, for example, a formal definition of justice as simply fairness).[36]

Is justice, then, as a virtue, related to the disposition of character of the actor, or does it have to do with the nature of the act performed by the actor? In Book Five of the *NE*, Aristotle writes the following about justice: 'So the just is a sort of proportion. Being proportionate is not a property peculiar to abstract number, but belongs to number in general.'[37] This is explained by reference to geometric proportion, wherein a just distribution can be established.

And yet Aristotle was not ignorant of the problematic nature of referring to justice with reference to numbers; in the *Eudemian Ethics*, he criticizes unnamed opponents for doing just this:

> They ought in fact to demonstrate (the existence of) the good itself in the opposite way to that in which they do now. As things are, beginning with objects not agreed to possess the good, they demonstrate what are agreed to be goods; starting with numbers, (they prove) that justice is a good, and health, on the grounds that they are forms of order and numbers, good belonging to 20 numbers and monads because the one is the good-itself. They ought to start with agreed (goods), such as health, strength, and temperance, (in order to show) that the fine is present even more in unchanging things.[38]

As Stephen Menn observes: 'Aristotle thinks that the reduction of Forms to numbers and of philosophy to mathematics . . . means that our explanations in fact have nothing to do with goodness.'[39] But despite this awareness, Aristotle's own conception of justice seems to undermine this claim. In *A Democracy of Distinction*, Jill Frank argues that Aristotelian justice, while referring to mathematical formulae as illustrative of reciprocal justice, is nevertheless attentive to difference, which means justice is concerned with equality that 'accommodates distinction'.[40] It can be noted on this point that equality and distinction are the qualities that Arendt uses to describe human plurality. Consequently, Aristotelian justice can be described as the interplay of a calculative form of justice, of a measuring of an appropriate reciprocal response in a given context, that is nevertheless attentive to the equality amongst individuals and their distinctive characteristics, a conception of political life that Arendt favours in *The Human Condition*.

This picture becomes more problematic when these considerations are linked to what Aristotle says about justice and political communities, in both *NE* and the *Politics*. In *NE* in reference to justice as obeyance of the law, he writes: 'So, in one sense, we call anything just that tends to produce or to preserve happiness and its constituents for the community of a city';[41] in the *Politics* he writes 'In the state, the good aimed at is justice; and that means what is for the benefit of the whole community.'[42] Justice as lawfulness is here linked to *eudaimonia*, the happiness or good-fated-ness of polis-dwellers; and happiness, as defined in Book One of *NE*, relates not to simple pleasure or contentment but rather being in conformity with virtue: 'happiness is a certain kind of activity of the soul in accordance with complete virtue', and complete virtue pertains to justice.[43]

There would seem to be a function for justice in keeping political communities happy, and so doing by conforming to justice-as-virtue. However, it can be asked what this means when it comes to the relationship of a political community to foreigners who arrive to it? To repeat, Aristotle is silent on the question of political asylum (despite himself being for a time an exile, and his familiarity with themes of exile and hospitality from the Greek tragedies which he wrote about), but he does address the issue of foreigners in the *Politics*. In chapter 7, he writes that in considering the size of the state, 'one ought to look not at numbers but at capacity', which reads as an implicit critique of Plato's bizarrely specific ideal citizenry figure of 5,040 citizen farmers and their dependents in *The Laws*.[44] He continues, 'Even granting that we must have regard to numbers, we must not do so without discrimination: although we must allow for the necessary presence in states of many slaves and foreigners (residents or visitors), our real concern is only with those who form part of the state, i.e. with those elements of which a state properly consists.'[45] As previously noted, this is a concern that Arendt also shared.

Thus, there is a distinction drawn between numbers and capacity – that the number of people only matters to the extent that it affects the proper functioning of the polis: 'In order to give decisions on matters of justice . . . it is necessary that the citizens should know each other and know what kind of people they are'; if this is no longer the case, 'it becomes easy for foreigners, and aliens resident in the country, to become possessed of citizenship, because the excessive size of the population makes detection difficult'.[46] In the *NE* he quotes Hesiod approvingly: 'on the subject of hospitality, "Neither let many share thy board, nor none"', and observes that 'one cannot have a city with ten people and with 100,000 it would no longer be a city. Presumably there is no one correct number, but anything between certain limits'.[47]

In the move to political justice, then, numbers are indeed an explicit consideration because capacity, as Aristotle seems to acknowledge ('even granting that we must have regard to numbers. . .') cannot but be figured as an issue of numbers in this context, and he gives a numerical range within which moderation is to be achieved, without specifying the number. *Excess in relation to the number of foreigners entering a political community is precisely figured as a question of numbers – not as a disposition of character by polis-dwellers*. There is a capacity beyond which it would be necessary to limit the intake of outsiders, in order that the proper functioning of the state be maintained.[48]

In other words, what emerges in Aristotle's thinking about political justice, as it pertains to outsiders, is a consideration of justice, figured as a question of capacity, understood as numbers, which is both affirmed and denied in different places in his writings (affirmed in *NE*, denied in the *Eudemian Ethics*). The account of virtue-as-justice which provides the shared conception of *eudaimonia* which defines and informs the life of the polis pertains to the good of the members of that polis, and on that basis, delimits membership and eschews excess, including excess figured as capacity (which I argue, *must* necessarily mean a question of numbers), as the above-quoted remarks in the *Politics* bear out. Justice becomes tied to forms of knowledge – the ability to know the proper size or limits of the polis. Michelle Boulous Walker has pointed out that from Aristotle onwards, a decisive shift in philosophy occurs, from an emphasis upon the love of wisdom (the meaning of the word philosophy itself) to the desire for knowledge.[49] In the reflections upon the size of the polis can be seen the limitation of a reading of Aristotle that would delimit his thinking to a virtue not bounded by considerations of calculation or knowledge, wherein justice-as-virtue comports with that which is appropriate to the character of the actor. Reading across his texts, this is clearly not a consistent view.

Before turning to Levinas, some critical comments on the Aristotelian conception of justice will help make the distinctions between these thinkers clearer further on in the chapter. Firstly, as indicated (aware that I have only briefly touched on a vast field), there is a certain ambiguity and extant disagreement amongst Aristotelian scholars as to the meaning of virtue; there is also ambiguity about the meaning of justice in Aristotle and whether it should be understood as pertaining to the nature of acts (figured as calculation, including with reference to numbers) or as pertaining to dispositions of character.

Secondly, referring back to the issue raised concerning Aristotle's discourse and its reception down to the present: on one level there may be simply a rhetorical effect of the repeated recourse to moderation, measure, produce, geometric proportion, and so on – an ethics of temperance and calculation, whether understood properly or perhaps misused in modern political discourse and reasoning. Perhaps it is necessary to be attentive to this rhetoric of moderation and calculation, and to ask what justifies a 'moderate' position on political questions, and what results such a position would generate for political praxis. Aristotle's own vagueness on the numbers proper to the size of a political community is precisely echoed in the vague talk of limits propounded by modern politicians when discussing the politics of asylum – there is a number that is too much, we don't know what it is, but will assert the givenness of this logic nevertheless (a problem that will be pursued further in chapter 4). Whether this issues from Aristotle or not, the thought is identical, even if the motivation is perhaps less noble (a modern politician using an Aristotelian-sounding argument as a fig leaf for xenophobia, political pandering, or avoidance of responsibility).

Thirdly, a comment on the prudential *ethos* that informs the ethics of Aristotle – the need to for communities to be healthy and sustaining. As Roger Crisp observes in his introduction to the *NE*, 'nowhere in Aristotle is there a recommendation of any kind of genuine self-sacrifice'.[50] It may be that following from Levinas, what we understand by ethics, and also crucially, in the move from ethics to justice (more on this below), should preserve at least the possibility of sacrifice, and of going to excess, in order to safeguard the welfare of others. One thinks in this context of states like Jordan and Lebanon, Chad and Ethiopia, who host enormous populations of refugees, at a very high ratio to their own populations: one in four people in Lebanon is a refugee, a ratio that would make Western policy-maker's heads explode.[51] That is to say, that justice as understood by Levinas would not pertain to the maintenance of the extant political community alone, but have a different *telos* – that of responsibility for others, the active preservation of unchosen plurality. It would perhaps be possible to construct an Aristotelian argument about natural political justice that might do the work of a universal guarantee of human dignity, in modern parlance; though this is a complicated idea, if one understands *physis* to entail a human being that is already a being-in-place as a polis-dweller, and if this should be understood as pertaining only to members of organized political communities.[52] And while it is possible to establish such an account in neo-Aristotelian terms, such as in the work of Martha Nussbaum and her 'capabilities' approach where recognition of human dignity becomes possible, something is clearly lacking in these terms in that refugees continue to go unrecognized. As Hannah Levinson observes apropos of Nussbaum's approach:

> On Nussbaum's account, the 'moral concept of the human' drives us toward 'recognition', or moral acknowledgment and thus accession to capability-oriented rights claims. How, then, are refugees relegated to their statelessness by another conscious moral being, or set of conscious moral beings? How are they left languishing under the effete jurisdiction of international law, unprotected by the state, banished from her birthplace, former residence, and former community? If Nussbaum stands by her argument, these questions which pertain specifically to the situations and traumas of the refugee cannot be answered adequately by the capabilities approach as I read it. The normative ideal Nussbaum purports has not, and perhaps cannot, account for the treatment of the stateless, rightless bodies of refugees.[53]

Also important to consider is the role that reciprocity plays in Aristotle's thinking of justice. Aristotle distinguishes reciprocity from distributive or equitable forms of justice (as not all reciprocity can be equitable – he gives the example of an official having the right to employ violence, where it is not proper to extend to the citizen a right to strike back).[54] He does see a role for reciprocity, however, in getting citizens to requite good acts with good acts in a virtuous circle of reciprocity: 'This is why they erect a temple of the Graces in a conspicuous place, so that benefits might be repaid. This is the special characteristic of grace, because one ought both to perform a return service to someone who has been gracious, and another time to make the first move by being gracious oneself.'[55] Thus, a political community is well served, on this account, when its members requite good acts with good acts. This is important to note because as will be seen, it marks out another crucial point of difference with Levinas, who is at pains to deny the importance of reciprocity in his understanding of ethics (and, I will argue, the move from ethics to justice).

Finally, the differing senses of responsibility that lead into the working of justice between Aristotle and Levinas need to be marked. In the *Origins of Responsibility*, François Raffoul argues that Aristotle establishes the dominant interpretation of responsibility in the canon of Western political philosophy.[56] Raffoul distinguishes between responsibility as accountability versus responsibility as answerability, the former category includes Aristotle and Kant, and in the latter, following the genealogical work of Nietzsche, can be placed other names such as Heidegger, Derrida, and Levinas. For Aristotle, responsibility is bound up with voluntariness – close to but not identical with Kantian free will, in that for Aristotle, the voluntary is that which is outside of chance, fortune, or the determinism of nature.[57] Voluntariness, that is, involves choice, the conscious assumption of responsibility.[58] Evidently, this marks an important difference from Levinas in that the responsibility for others is not originally a matter of voluntariness but is rather imposed (the notion of 'unchosen' plurality also needs to be kept in mind in this context) by the ethical responsibility for the other that is experienced as persecution, trauma, being taken hostage, assignation of responsibility prior to the acceptance of being accountable, a response to a demand, an answerability.

LEVINAS AND JUSTICE

The argument in this section is that Levinas shifts the meaning of justice from an avoidance of excess, to the necessity of having to choose how one's responsibility is enacted with the advent of the third. In other words – and this is the truly radical moment in Levinas, that offers an entirely different way of thinking political justice – on his account, ethical excess survives the transmutation of ethics into justice, that is, responsibility for others becomes divided, but remains excessive.

As stated above, Levinas does not make of Aristotle an especial focus for critique; there are, however, critical references to be found in his work. Two interesting references to Aristotle occur early in his career. This from *On Escape*:

> Therefore, the need for escape . . . leads us into the heart of philosophy. It allows
> us to renew the ancient problem of being qua being. What is the structure of
> this pure being? Does it have the universality Aristotle conferred on it? Is it the
> ground and limit of our preoccupations, as certain modern philosophers would

have it? On the contrary, is it nothing else than the mark of a certain civilization, firmly established in the fait accompli of being and incapable of getting out of it. And in these conditions, is excendence possible, and how would it be accomplished? What is the ideal of happiness and human dignity that it promises?[59]

And from *Existence and Existents*:

> Western philosophy and civilization never gets out of 'numbers and beings', remaining conditioned by the secular world . . . the orekton of book 10 of Aristotle's Metaphysics is the supreme being, immobile, loved but never loving, terminus. The problem of the Good is formulated as a problem of ends.[60]

Here there are two references to Aristotle as associated with a society too bound up with the 'fait accompli' of beings, too preoccupied with numbers. That is, Aristotle is decisively implicated in the overall critique of the history of philosophy that Levinas pursues from an early stage of his career. Aristotle prefers ends to excendence (climbing out of or escaping out of), numbers and beings to transcendence and the otherwise-than-being, reciprocity to unilateralism, moderation to excess, and eudaimonia to sacrifice.

For Levinas, ethics – and following from ethics, justice – has little if anything to do with happiness, or reciprocity, or moderation. It is not bound to numbers or calculation, to moderation or reciprocity, or to the happiness of the responsible subject or their political community. As Diane Perpich observes, 'Never in the history of Western philosophy has there been an ethical responsibility so severe: a responsibility that increases with my every attempt to discharge it: that does not depend on choice or voluntary action; that is a responsibility not just for the other but for all of his responsibility as well'.[61] The very excessiveness of Levinas's ethics means that 'in this picture of responsible subjectivity, there seems to be no place for the complacencies of ordinary moral life, where obligations are met, duties attended to, and the ego has time afterward to attend to his own cares and concerns'.[62] Responsibility is excessive and infinite, the responsible subject is as if held hostage by the other whom they are responsible to (and not, as observed previously, a matter of voluntariness as it is for Aristotle). All of this is a long way from the account of justice which Aristotle gives, discussed above, which pertains to the wellbeing of the members of a political community. In order to clarify the differences, before proceeding in the next section to give a practical example of what these differences might look like in situation, I will elaborate some elements of Levinas's thought which I argue are opposed to that of Aristotle.

At a simple level, Aristotle's is a virtue ethics, whereas Levinas derives his ethics from the tradition of phenomenology and well as Judaic influences (a thinking of God as the infinite, which one also finds in Descartes). Aristotle's thinking of ethics is just that – a thinking, a working through of the source of eudaimonia in virtue and the description of its qualities. Whereas for Levinas, the ethical moment precedes its entering into the processes of intellection; ethics is manifest in the Face of the other, the advent of which is a pre-phenomenal event, that is, prior to the signification that makes the other manifest in thought; ethics, then, is not a product of reason, but is prior to it. As Michael Fagenblat observes, 'Levinas sought to restore a new sense of an unconditional ethical imperative that could not be dismissed as merely abstract, formal, ahistorical, inauthentic, and ontologically inadequate. He did this by developing a phenomenology of the moral imperative that was derived not from the fact of Reason but from the face of the Other'.[63] For Levinas, it is possible to be totally responsible for the other person, whose Face calls me into question and places a demand upon me to exercise such a responsibility. For Levinas, this ethical demand is excessive, even exorbitant – it is a delimiting of one's own self in the name of the other, a tearing of the bread from one's mouth to give to the other (more on the ethico-poetics of food below).

Levinas writes in a moving summary of the ethics of Vladimir Jankélévitch, which the context makes clear he is in full agreement with, that the ethical demand is

a spending without counting, a generosity, goodness, love, obligation toward others. A generosity without recompense, a love unconcerned with reciprocity; duty performed without the 'salary' of a good-conscience-for-a-duty-performed, without even the good conscience of being the bad-conscience-of-the-duty-not performed! All duties are incumbent upon me, all rights first due to others . . . It is an ethics without eudemonism.[64]

The reference to 'eudemonism' and the anti-moderate language would seem to confirm this ethical thinking as a form of anti-Aristotelianism, and indeed Levinas links this passage to a thinking of ethics from a Judaic context. To the extent that eudaimonia is to be understood as a good-fatedness that is linked to happiness, Levinas is unconcerned with the effect of happiness engendered by the ethical response – what matters is the response itself, 'a generosity without recompense'.

Ethics in the thinking of Levinas is excessive, a result of the transcendence of the other of which one is never freed – held hostage by the demand placed upon oneself by them. This responsibility is not a matter of measuring out appropriate duties: as Raoul Moati explains, for Levinas, 'to welcome the other in its excess is no longer to measure it'.[65] And yet as soon as there is more than one other other – that is to say, with the advent or arrival of the third – there may arise a need to start making choices between them. Levinas explains the point in *Ethics and Infinity:*

> How is it that there is justice? I answer that it is the fact of the multiplicity of men [*sic*] and the presence of someone else next to the Other, which condition the laws and establish justice. If I am alone with the Other, I owe him everything; but there is someone else . . . It is consequently necessary to weigh, to think, to judge, in comparing the incomparable. The interpersonal relation I establish with the Other, I must also establish with other men; there is thus a necessity to moderate this privilege of the Other; from whence comes justice. Justice, exercise through institutions, which are inevitable, must always be held in check by the initial interpersonal relation.[66]

Note the use of the word moderate here, which, the present argument suggests, represents a key difference between Levinas and Aristotle. The reference to moderation, for Levinas, is not an avoidance of excess, but the inability to no longer simply give everything to or be entirely responsible to a singular other, as there is now a third who also places a demand upon the subject. 'One must, then [with the advent of the Third] compare the incomparable. For me, this is the Greek moment in our civilisation . . . The importance of knowing, the importance of comparing, stems from them; everything *economic* is posed by them, and we then come to something other than love.'[67]

In other words, justice, on Levinas's account, retains the excessive quality found in ethics, rather than retreating into a moderation that would precisely delimit excess. As Richard Cohen writes, 'Justice, then, has a source and a guide: the moral transcendence of the other'.[68] The key passage which makes this point occurs towards the end of *Otherwise Than Being*. Levinas writes:

> In no way is justice a degradation of obsession, a degeneration of the for-the-other, a diminution, a limitation of anarchic responsibility, a neutralization of the glory of the Infinite, a degeneration that would be produced in the measure that for empirical reasons the initial duo would become a trio. But the contemporaneousness of the multiple is tied about the diachrony of two: justice remains justice only, in a society where there is no distinction between those close and those far off, but in which there also remains the impossibility of passing by the closest. The equality of all is borne by my inequality, the surplus of my duties over my rights. The forgetting of self moves justice.[69]

Justice, then, according to Levinas, is 'in no way' a 'limitation of anarchic responsibility'. The excess he attributes to ethics is retained in the move to justice following the advent of the third. And this is the fundamental point. Justice in Levinas is no longer bound to the moderate, but rather to the inevitable limitation of responsibility for a singular other by the presence of the third, where decisions will have to be made, and justice-as-politics begins.

One other phrase from this passage needs to be remarked: the reference to those near and far off, a quotation from Isaiah 57:19 which he refers to repeatedly throughout his work. Thought in the context of the politics of the asylum, this reference to a peace between both those near and distant might trouble or undermine the privilege granted only to those who are near, that is, to the extant constituents of a political society, the limit problem of the demos – who counts in and who counts out in the considerations of a political community? This could also be linked to Levinas's thinking of the 'frater-nité' element of the famous French motto and his reflections upon the Rights of 'Man'.[70] In Levinas there is a move to a sense of responsibility that goes beyond the most evident obligations of one's fellow citizens to a broader answerability beyond the state.

Another key point in considering the difference between Levinas and Aristotle concerns reciprocity. In the *NE*, Aristotle refers to the Temple of the Graces, which encourages the citizenry to requite good acts with good acts in a kind of virtuous circle of reciprocal generosity. However Levinas is actively opposed to limiting ethics to reciprocity, as emerges in his engagement with, and critique of, Martin Buber. His issue with Buber's 'I and Thou' is the sym-metry and equality that he sees in this relationship.[71] For Levinas, ethics is not delimited to the reciprocal, but is rather asymmetrical – the other comes from a dimension of a height, and commands me – and he is at pains to emphasize that the other's responsibility for me is not my concern.

If space permitted, these reflections could also be extended into other inter-esting areas between Levinas and Aristotle, such as their accounts of the expe-rience of eating and the use of dietary imperatives as illustrative of ethics. For Aristotle, excess would be doing that which damages one's own health, such as an excess of consumption of food; for Levinas, eating can be compared 'with loving, which occurs beyond economic activity and the world',[72] and belongs to the realm of permanent desire, but which also constitutes enjoyment – in this they may not be so far apart. Yet, Levinas will often refer to food to illus-trate the possibility of self-sacrifice as a meaning of the ethical and indeed the human interruption of being's persistence in being, which he will even link to hospitality: 'It is not a gift of the heart, but of the bread from one's mouth, of one's own mouthful of bread. It is the openness, not only of one's pocketbook, but of the doors of one's home, a "sharing of your bread with the famished", a "welcoming of the wretched into your house"' (Isaiah 58).[73] And while Aristotle will refer to beneficence towards others, it is not a logic of sacrifice of oneself, of giving to and even dying for the other.

In summary, justice for Levinas is anarchical and potentially excessive; as Howard Caygill writes of Levinas's ethics, a thought which is here extended to his views on justice, 'The experience of the other is one of excess and so does not figure in economy, or at least is not reducible to it'.[74] For Levinas, politics must be able to be judged against ethical demands[75] and is not bound to reciprocity: Diane Perpich observes, 'The relation to the other is an asymmetrical relationship that cannot be made reciprocal or symmetrical because the others' alterity is not a relative quality but rather the very content of her being'.[76] Such an asymmetrical relationship may lead to the possibility of sacrifice – even, 'hardly possible, but holiness demands it – to die for the other'.[77] One might see Levinas here as aligned with Brecht's version of Antigone in refusing the dialectic of a responsibility for the near that is opposed to a responsibility for the far off, for the insider against the outsider; rather anarchical responsibility means a weighing of competing demands where responsibility is assumed for all parties, but some calculation may still be required.

WHY MODERATION IS A VICE, OR THE
PROBLEM WITH THE KINDERTRANSPORT

In order to clarify the difference which separates Levinas from Aristotle concerning political justice, it will be considered in a context where implications for praxis might be made manifest: specifically, concerning the politics of asylum. In particular, the focus is upon the case of the 'Kindertransport' – the rescue transport of approximately ten thousand Jewish children from central Europe to safety in the United Kingdom in the late 1930s – and what I think is wrong with it.

It may strike the reader as indecent to suggest that something is 'wrong' with saving ten thousand children from calamity. But the failure is not contained within the nature of the act itself – the admirable refuge proffered to the vulnerable – but to its scope – ten thousand children,[78] when a total of around 1.5 million Jewish children ultimately perished in the Shoah.[79] Separating children from their parents also caused an enormous amount of trauma and grief, and the privileging of children above adults or above the total family unit is problematic: as Jennifer Craig-Norton has written, 'the fate of the parents has been buried in the narratives of rescue and salvation'.[80] There are multiple issues to be raised concerning the history of the Kindertransport – not only the family separation but the abuse and neglect that some children suffered, the inability to maintain cultural ties, as well as the question of the category of the child refugee as providing a stable identifier with which to ensure their protection. Carly McLaughlin has ably demonstrated how this category is contestable and even deniable, concerning the attempt to admit child refugees under the Dubs Amendment (where reactionary press suggested that 'they don't look like children').[81] McLaughlin writes, 'The foregrounding of children as innocent and vulnerable victims of the European border regime in the media and humanitarian campaigns have had little impact on the material and political reality of these children, who number in the tens of thousands'.[82] (This theme of the figure of the child as a focus of protection will be explored at length in the Coda that concludes the book.) Here the question is more simply one of scale; given this stark disparity between those saved and those killed, who might have been saved, the moral stakes of how one conceives of political justice are brought into stark relief. It is the size of the Ark that is in question.

Here is where the differences that distinguish Levinas from Aristotle become vitally important. It was noted above that a certain ambiguity regarding Aristotle and the figuring of excess and the size of political communities as a question of capacity, despite Aristotle's critique of reckoning virtue as a set of numbers. For the Aristotle of the *Politics*, as noted above, it is permissible to limit the intake of foreigners if their number becomes too large to manage. The emphasis on moderation and the avoidance of excess – if this pertains to the nature of acts and not just dispositions of character, as discussed above – would already prepare the way, both philosophically and rhetorically, for a delimitation of the limits of welcome to foreigners. And while it is true that in the *NE* Aristotle refers to 'magnificence' and large-scale generosity, how to reconcile this with the counsel against excess on the one hand, and the limitation of the size of the polis, on the other, in determining what an appropriate Aristotelian response to the plight of vulnerable suppliants should be, where the question of numbers becomes ineluctably engaged? It is difficult to establish exactly how we should see Aristotle's thinking of moderation, of numbers, of justice-as-virtue, and the political, in order to form political judgements on questions of this sort. But the question of the foreigner, their treatment and status, was not unknown in Aristotle's day; thus, the critique is not simply an unfair imposition of modern sentiments upon the past. The concern is how the philosophy of Aristotelian moderation may influence how these questions are taken up, from the perspective of seeking to safeguard the human dignity of large numbers of persons in need, which might challenge and strain the ability of a state to cope with their arrival and integration.

One could also be concerned about the Aristotelian emphasis on reciprocity as a safeguarding of just outcomes, in that good acts are involved in a reciprocal cycle of good acts committed by others; in terms of political asylum, this would manifest in a state refusing to take in refugees unless others agree to do the same, and eschewing unilateralism. In short, to the extent that an Aristotelian conception of the political lacks an element of self-limiting or even self-harming sacrifice, as noted above, which fails to give the other person priority and to accept that priority as the orienting focus of one's political responsibility, then outcomes like that noted above concerning the Jewish children of Europe in the time preceding and during the Shoah are possible and remain probable.

A radically different conception of political justice becomes possible when thinking Levinas in relation to politics (given that he is not himself ostensibly a political theorist, and treated political questions somewhat indirectly or at a level of abstraction that did not necessarily provide concrete suggestions for praxis). What would have been the consequences for the United Kingdom to have accepted 1.5 million child refugees, eschewing moderation or prudence, acting unilaterally without regard for reciprocity on the part of other states, for the safeguarding of those 'far off', taking the bread from their own mouths to give (or at least, to share) with the other, the possibility of sacrificing for the other, demanded by 'holiness'? Is this an impossible, 'pure' hospitality, to speak Derrida's language? But there are examples of this; as mentioned above, one thinks of all the non-Western states who put the West to shame in their hosting of the vast majority of stateless people in the world; from Jordan and Lebanon to Chad and Ethiopia to Bangladesh and Colombia. On a lower scale but still significant, the possibility of Western states acting in similarly exemplary fashion, as in the German decision to accept close to a million refugees in one year, or Italy's now defunct programme 'Mare Nostrum' which rescued thousands of people from the sea who otherwise might have less disappeared completely. Such a politics is not impossible, it is just mostly not done; most politics tacks towards Aristotelian moderation, if not outright mean-spiritedness and cruelty, and opts for what is wrongly thought to be best for the flourishing of the extant political community. Things are even going backwards on this point in Western states: one might argue that the Kindertransport was terribly inadequate, but within its limits it was still highly noble. More recently, the United Kingdom (Perfidious Albion!) was willing to take less than 500 Syrian children under the Dubs Amendment established by Lord Dubs, himself a child of the Kindertransport, who has received little support.[83] One should be attentive to the disappeared as the very meaning of political responsibility and justice: peace to those now gone who will never come back, peace to those *not yet born, who have already disappeared* because of 'moderate' considerations which they are inexorably moving towards.

CONCLUSION

In the *Dialectic of Enlightenment*, Horkheimer and Adorno reflect upon the dominance of numbers and calculation in philosophy from the time of Plato through to the age of Enlightenment: 'The mythologizing equation of Forms with numbers in Plato's last writings expressed the longing of all demythologising: number became enlightenment's canon. The same equations govern bourgeois justice and commodity exchange'.[84] They quote Francis Bacon on the relationship of number to justice: 'is there not a true coincidence between commutative and distributive justice, and arithmetical and geometrical proportion?'[85] That is to say, that 'bourgeois justice' is bound up with the mathematically calculable: 'Bourgeois society is ruled by equivalence. It makes dissimilar things comparable by reducing them to abstract qualities. For the Enlightenment, anything which cannot be resolved into numbers, and ultimately into one, is illusion; modern positivism consigns it to poetry'.[86] (One finds a resonance here with the Preface to *Totality and Infinity*, where Levinas questions of the apparent naivety of morality in comparison to the realism of war). What they identify is a certain pathology of the economic that dominates modernity, which Adorno in *Minima Moralia* will even link to the politics of asylum via an excoriation of bourgeois life: 'The caring hand that even now tends the little garden as if it had not long since become a "lot", but fearfully wards off the unknown intruder, is already that which denies the political refugee asylum.'[87] (Again, the house as the false synecdoche of the state.)

What is the import of Levinas's philosophy? It was written in the 'presentiment', the experience and the aftermath of the war, of Nazism and the Shoah. It calls for living and thinking in a state of 'insomnia' – a vital concept for Levinas – that is, a kind of moral wakefulness, a guarding against the reappearance of the worst, or the indifferent response to the vulnerable. It is no exaggeration to say that Nazism hangs over every word in the Levinasian corpus. His ethical philosophy is fundamentally a response to a politics; its import is essentially political. This moment in history has been described as humanity's 'zero hour' or 'midnight in the century', which was perhaps the moment when the 'Face' of the other was most thoroughly and systematically violated or destroyed, which was in part an economic process.[88] Hannah Arendt discussed the economic side of the extermination in *Eichmann in Jerusalem*: 'This "objective" attitude – talking about concentration camps in terms of "administration" and about extermination camps in terms of "economy" – was typical of the S.S. mentality, and something Eichmann, at the trial, was still very proud of'.[89] In a late interview, Levinas is asked about totality as it relates to a thinking of numbers:

Q: In this way we could come back against to the theme of 'totality'. When you earlier characterised thinking as an adding-up . . . that's how Jews were handled during the Third Reich, as numbers.

E.L: The final expression of an 'adding-up'. Adding up is a concrete figure in pure economic life, in purely economic conditions.[90]

This logic of adding-up adheres in the economic logic of states, which is to say, the dominant logic of states:

> This adding up of the sum total is the economic life, absolutely: precisely there, the face plays no role, human beings are terms, they come into an ensemble, adding themselves sup. The adding up of totality, is, concretely, economic life and the State; economic life is concrete in the State [. . .].[91]

Politics as an adding-up, on this account, runs a very great risk of inhumanity. What was true in the concentration and extermination camps – the reduction of human beings to a number – is also true in a similar, if mostly less severe way, in modern detention camps for people seeking asylum. For Levinas, to avoid inhumanity it is necessary to get beyond the logic of calculation in considering the plight of others:

> Humanity precisely as grace, in the passage from the one to the other: transcendence. Passage from the one to the other, without concern for reciprocity, pure gratuity, from the unique to the unique. That is also reason, or peace, or goodness. Reason as generosity above reason as calculation. This human generosity is certainly not a statistical given.[92]

Should political justice be delimited to the moderate? What are the implications of this for political praxis? If, for example, in the context of the politics of asylum, moderation demands that one not go too far, and instead have regard to the flourishing or even survival of the extant political community, and that therefore one not be excessive in the welcome proffered to the vulnerable other – is that acceptable as an ethical politics? And how much of all this is Aristotle's fault? 'Luridly the horror of the ending lights up the deception of the origin', Adorno writes in *Minima Moralia*; the tradition of Occidental thought is fatally implicated in the actualization of the worst, or at minimum, the failure to prevent the worst.[93]

As discussed above, it is somewhat undecidable (and debated in the critical literature) whether Aristotle is guilty of the things that Levinas (and myself) accuse him of – a thinking that 'never gets out of numbers and beings', that emphasizes moderation in deed (and not just in the comportment of the virtuous person) that may be itself deforming of political consequence. It is impossible to rigorously draw a straight line from the profound, if sometimes contradictory or unclear teachings of the *NE* and the *Politics*, to the pronouncements of ostensibly prudent (and mostly, Western) politicians giving fine reasons why there is only so much that can be done. Just recently, Emmanuel Macron repeated Michel Rocard's nonsensical hyperbolic line that France 'cannot welcome all the misery in the world' (as is someone had asked them to).[94] These attitudes obtain, and appeal to a sense of the moderate, the prudent, the cautious. Perhaps this is no more than a misuse of the legacy of the philosopheme of moderation; it may even be the antipodes of Aristotle. But it is nevertheless necessary to question whether it is the case, that Aristotle, and more specifically, the concept of justice as it permeates in multiform fashion throughout philosophical and political life, is responsible for harmful delimitations of political action as I have described above in relation to the Kindertransport. It may be that those who insist that moderation pertains to the virtuous actor and not the action are correct, in which case, prudential or mean-spirited attempts to not go to excess in times of moral urgency are not acts of fidelity but rather betrayals of the *ethos* that Aristotle promulgated. Perhaps. But can one be convinced of this, based upon the insistence in his writings on the need for measure as a leitmotif of justice itself (and not simply the virtuous actor), or the need to keep political communities from admitting too many foreigners? Also, this does not resolve the problem about a demand for reciprocity which one also finds in Aristotle, which is also directly contrary to the seminal thrust of Levinas's ethics: 'Here [in ethics] there is no "human commerce", not a simple swapping of responsibilities!'[95]

A wonderful illustration of the Levinasian excessive figuration of justice can be found in Martin Luther King Jr's profound 'Letter from Birmingham Jail'. In responding to the criticisms he faced from white pastors in Alabama – Why, King, are you stirring up this trouble and not being patient? – King critiques the attitudes of what he calls 'white moderates', who, he writes, 'are more devoted to "order" than to justice; who prefers a negative peace which is the absence of tension to a positive peace which is the presence of justice'.[96] In distinguishing justice from the law, King insists that justice is not moderate or prudential, but rather can or even should be disruptive and extreme; he embraces the word 'extremist' as it applies to a seeking of justice in the name of love, and calls for 'creative extremists' to fight for justice.[97] King even rejects the argument that such action is irresponsible in that it may provoke a backlash, and that he should take the counsel of white moderates and 'wait for "a more convenient season"'.[98] What matters (and here King sounds very much like Levinas) is not what happens to me, but what happens to the other person;[99] for King, it is irresponsible to refuse to disrupt a social order in order to preserve one's own harmony or the existing harmony of a political community, preferring or to the justice of responding to the needs of others. It is difficult to read Aristotle as in agreement with this, despite what his defenders might argue about how his account of virtue covers every ethical decision we might want to take, as proper to the virtue of that person; a reading of the *Politics*, as discussed above, makes clear that the flourishing of the extant political community is of primary concern for Aristotle.

In the context of the politics of asylum, this latter point is of paramount importance. Recently, former presidential candidate Hillary Clinton counselled European decision-makers to limit migration in order to avoid provoking the extreme right.[100] In this, she is not far from right wing ideologues like Jean Raspail, who in his book *The Camp of the Saints* depicts a France overwhelmed by a million migrants (a fear belied by Germany's recent and relatively painless absorption of a similar number of refugees).[101] What justifies this appeal to prudence, what polemically, we might call with Nietzsche *tepidity*: the 'tepid temperature which is the presupposition upon which every calculation of prudence or expediency is always based'?[102]

It might be possible to argue that those policy-makers who lived in the world before the Shoah could not have known the potential consequences of their failure to admit a great many more people. Even if one accepts this argument, despite the history of pogroms and massacres and genocides which predate the Shoah, it certainly cannot be maintained in a world where events have revealed that anything is possible. This knowledge is what makes the failure of efforts such as the Dubs Amendment so barbarous and inexcusable, as well as the exclusion of adults because they are not seen in the same vulnerable light, despite the enormous difficulties and dangers that attend their plight. Previously, it was noted that Arendt had referred to the stateless as 'barbarians'; however this could be counterposed with the concluding lines of Levinas's essay *On Escape*: 'Every civilization that accepts being – with the tragic despair it contains and the crimes it justifies – merits the name "barbarian".'[103] Referring back to chapter 1 and the Levinasian refiguring of ontology as ethical and oriented to responsibility, it is those 'civilizations' that neglect the 'night of being' which are the barbarians, hence the view expressed by Levinas at the beginning of the chapter, of the need for 'a logic *other* than that of Aristotle, of a thought other than civilized'. In the context of the historical disaster and the one unfolding in the present, 'Heavy is the responsibility for those who could have been saved' among civilized states.[104] Nothing has changed or been remembered and yet another, more devastating conclusion here is possible: things have gone backwards, and liberal societies are now in such massive dereliction of duty that even the category of the child refugee does not command minimal respect and protection. The life of the child refugee is precarious, to use Judith Butler's term, but so too is the category of child qua privileged protection category, where even children's lives are not considered sufficiently vulnerable to merit protection.[105]

Ten thousand children went on trains going West and were saved; other children went on other trains going East, and 1.5 million children would ultimately lose their lives in the Shoah. One direction or the other resulting from a political decision can mean a great deal – to borrow from Primo Levi's *The Periodic Table*, 'The differences may be small but can lead to radically diverse results, like railroad switches'.[106] It is necessary to remember that we don't live in the world as it would have been, we live in the *other* world, where the 1.5 million children were not saved, but rather only ten thousand. One example in an endless catalogue of horrors, in the Benjaminian pile of disasters that rises to the sky, but one that effectively makes the point about limits and numbers, and the dangers of moderation. To emphasize a pruden-tial consideration and say that it would have been impossible to take them in, required too great a sacrifice, is to posthumously condemn them to death once more, and to condemn to death or immiseration those tens of millions of people currently without membership in a political community that will guarantee their rights. They are denied, as Hannah Arendt termed it, their 'right to have rights', and hundreds of millions of others may follow as the effects of climate change escalate.[107] Prudence and moderation are morally suspect, even, in some circumstances, morally bankrupt. What Levinas – and King – invite us to do is to consider the possibility that justice can be radical and excessive, not prudent and moderate. 'The possibility of sacrifice as a meaning of the human adventure!'[108] – a responsibility that is infinite, and not bound to the calculative or the moderate, which, figured as political justice, looks a lot different to contemporary politics, including the politics of asy-lum, as the ships of state of the international community drift along in a state of moral torpor. Adorno, who put into question the influence of Aristotelian moderation on modern sensibilities, observed with Horkheimer that it may be necessary to 'scorn logic if it is against humanity'.[109] This is amongst the vital themes bequeathed to our understanding of the ethical by Levinas: 'And all I have done is to find a relation that is not an adding up.'[110]

NOTES

1. Adorno, *Minima Moralia*, p. 80.
2. Emmanuel Levinas, *Alterity and Transcendence*, trans. Michael B. Smith (London: The Athlone Press, 1999), p. 133.
3. My thanks to Professor Richard Cohen and Dr Jolanta Saldukaityte for welcoming me to their Levinas seminar in Paris in July 2018, where the reading of Levinas presented in this chapter was first conceived.
4. Levinas, *Proper Names*, p. 4.
5. As opposed to simply philosophical contemporaries – he includes poets and theologians, individuals who are not all sensu stricto philosophers. There are also some entries for non-twentieth-century thinkers such as Kierkegaard.
6. Levinas, *Proper Names*, p. 6.
7. There is no systematic critique of Hegel in Levinas, but there are references to Hegel throughout his texts; probably the closest to a systematic treatment occurs in the 'Death and Time' lectures collected in Emmanuel Levinas, *God, Death and*

Time, trans. Bettina Bergo, ed./annotated Jacqeus Rolland (Stanford, CA: Stanford University Press, 2000).

8. For a detailed comparison of Kant and Levinas, see Catherine Chalier, *What Ought I To Do? Morality in Kant and Levinas*, trans. Jane Marie Todd (Ithaca, NY and London: Cornell University Press, 2002).

9. Levinas, *Proper Names* includes essays devoted to both thinkers. For Levina's response to Derrida, at once affirmative and critical, see Emmanuel Levinas, 'Wholly Otherwise', in *Re-Reading Levinas*, eds. Robert Bernasconi and Simon Critchley (Bloomington, IN and Indianapolis, IN: Indiana University Press, 1991), pp. 3–10.

10. For an example of Levinas's embrace of humanism, including the very title of his book, see Emmanuel Levinas, *Humanism of the Other*, trans. Nidra Poller and Richard Cohen (Chicago, IL: University of Illinois Press, 2006).

11. See Žižek's essay in S. Slavoj Žižek, Eric L. Santner, and Kenneth Reinhard, *The Neighbor: Three Inquiries in Political Theology* (Chicago, IL: University of Chicago Press, 2013); Badiou discusses what he sees as the limitations of Levinas's ethics in Alain Badiou, *Ethics: An Essay on the Understanding of Evil* (London and New York, NY: Verso, 2012), especially chapter 2.

12. See Derrida's funeral address for Levinas, 'Adieu', in Derrida, *Adieu to Emmanuel Levinas*, p. 3.

13. Emmanuel Levinas, 'The Rights of Man and the Rights of the Other', in *Outside the Subject*, trans. Michael B. Smith (Stanford, CA: Stanford University Press, 1993), p. 149.

14. See William P. Simmons, 'The Third: Levinas's Theoretical Move from An-archical Ethics to the Realm of Justice and Politics', *Philosophy and Social Criticism*, Vol. 25, No. 6, 1999, p. 87.

15. Alasdair MacIntyre, *After Virtue: A Study in Moral Theory* (London and New York, NY: Bloomsbury, 2007), p. 173.

16. For more on this question, see Michael Fagenblat, *A Covenant of Creatures: Levinas's Philosophy of Judaism* (Stanford, CA: Stanford University Press, 2010), especially chapter 3.

17. Adorno, *Minima Moralia*, p. 130.

18. Améry, *At the Mind's Limits*, p. 11.

19. Adorno, *Minima Moralia*, p. 247.

20. Derrida made this the theme of his first essay on Levinas: 'Are we Jews? Are we Greeks? We live in the difference between the Jew and the Greek, which is perhaps the unity of what is called history'. See Jacques Derrida, 'Violence and Metaphysics: An Essay on the Thought of Emmanuel Levinas', in *Writing and Difference*, trans. and intro. Alan Bass (London: Routledge, 2001), pp. 97–192. Levinas himself often made similar remarks: 'Europe, then, is the Bible and the Greeks.' See Levinas, *Is it Righteous to Be?*, p. 137.

21. Fred D. Miller, *Nature, Justice and Rights in Aristotle's Politics* (Oxford: Oxford University Press, 1995), p. 89.

22. Pitkin, 'Justice', p. 339.

23. Mark Jonathan Harris and Deborah Oppenheimer, *Into the Arms of Strangers: Stories of the Kindertransport* (London: Bloomsbury Publishing, 2001), p. xii. See

also the US Holocaust Memorial Museum, https://encyclopedia.ushmm.org/content/e
n/article/children-during-the-holocaust, accessed 28 December 2019.

24. Aristotle, *Nicomachean Ethics*, ed. Roger Crisp (Cambridge: Cambridge
University Press, 2004), p. viii. All references to the *Nicomachean Ethics* are drawn
from this edition.

25. Aristotle, *Nicomachean Ethics*, 1131a, p. 86.

26. Aristotle, *Nicomachean Ethics*, 1134a, p. 92.

27. See, for example, 'Protagoras' in Plato, *Protagoras and Meno* (London:
Penguin, 2005), p. 51.

28. Lesley Brown, 'Why is Aristotle's Virtue of Character a Mean? Taking
Aristotle At His Word NE ii 6', in *The Cambridge Companion to Aristotle's
Nicomachean Ethics*, ed. Ronald Polanksy (New York, NY: Cambridge University
Press, 2014), pp. 64–65.

29. Brown, 'Why is Aristotle's Virtue of Character a Mean?', p. 78.

30. Brown, 'Why is Aristotle's Virtue of Character a Mean?', p. 78.

31. David Bostock, *Aristotle's Ethics* (Oxford: Clarendon Press, 2000), pp. 42–43.

32. Jill Frank, *A Democracy of Distinction: Aristotle and the Work of Politics*
(Chicago, IL and London: University of Chicago Press, 2005), p. 74.

33. Frank, *A Democracy of Distinction*, p. 94.

34. Aristotle, *Nicomachean Ethics*, 1129b, p. 83.

35. Aristotle, *Nicomachean Ethics*, p. xxi.

36. Emmanuel Levinas, *Totality and Infinity: An Essay on Exteriority*, trans.
Alphonso Lingis (Pittsburgh, PA: Duquesne University Press, 1969), p. 89.

37. Aristotle, *Nicomachean Ethics*, 1131a, p. 86.

38. Aristotle, *The Eudemian Ethics Books I–II–VIII*, trans. Michael Wood, 2nd
edition (Oxford: Clarendon Press, 2005), pp. 10, 1218a.

39. Stephen Menn, 'Aristotle's Theology', in *The Oxford Handbook of Aristotle*,
ed. Christopher Shields (Oxford: Oxford University Press, 2012), p. 429.

40. Frank, *A Democracy of Distinction*, p. 98.

41. Aristotle, *Nicomachean Ethics*, 1129b, p. 82.

42. Aristotle, *The Politics*, trans. T. A. Sinclair and Trevor J. Saunders (London:
Penguin Books, 1992), 1282b14, p. 207.

43. Aristotle, *Nicomachean Ethics*, 1120a, p. 20.

44. Aristotle, *The Politics*, 1325b33, pp. 402–3.

45. Aristotle, *The Politics*, 1325b33, p. 403.

46. Aristotle, *The Politics*, 1323b11, p. 405.

47. Aristotle, *Nicomachean Ethics*, 1170b, pp. 249–50.

48. I will not dwell here upon Aristotle's disparaging remarks about the inferior-
ity of foreigners relative to Athenians, except to note with interest that it has been
argued that Aristotle understands human nature as changeable and shaped by political
membership. My criticisms of Aristotle are not simply about how he sees foreigners,
but the implications for foreigners – specifically, those in need of asylum – of his con-
ceptualization of justice and politics. See Jill Frank, 'Citizens, Slaves and Foreigners:
Aristotle on Human Nature', *American Political Science Review*, Vol. 98, No. 1,
2004, pp. 91–104.

49. Michelle Boulous Walker, *Slow Philosophy: Reading Against the Institution* (London and New York, NY: Bloomsbury, 2017), p. 3.

50. Aristotle, *Nicomachean Ethics*, p. xi.

51. https://www.bbc.com/news/av/world-middle-east-35163273/lebanon-one-in-four-a-refugee, retrieved 15 February 2019.

52. On this question, see Benjamin, 'The Problem of Authority', p. 269.

53. Hannah Levinson, 'Refocusing the Refugee Regime: From Vagrancy to Value', *Res Cogitans*, Vol. 1, No. 1, Article 18. In her paper, Levinson turns to Judith Butler's thinking on precarity and a language of affect which can be appealed to in coalitional political pushes to achieve the recognition that is lacking. For Nussbaum's account, see Martha Nussbaum, 'Social Justice and Universalism: In Defense of an Aristotelian Account of Human Functioning', *Modern Philology*, Vol. 9, May 1993, pp. S46–S73.

54. Aristotle, *Nicomachean Ethics*, 1132b, p. 89.

55. Aristotle, *Nicomachean Ethics*, 1133a, p. 89.

56. Raffoul, *The Origins of Responsibility*, p. 39.

57. Raffoul, *The Origins of Responsibility*, p. 46.

58. Raffoul, *The Origins of Responsibility*, p. 44.

59. Emmanuel Levinas, *On Escape*, trans. Bettina Bergo and annotations Jacques Rolland (Stanford, CA: Stanford University Press, 2003), p. 56.

60. Emmanuel Levinas, *Existence and Existents*, trans. Alphonso Lingis (Pittsburgh, PA: Duquesne University Press, 2001), p. 29.

61. Perpich, *The Ethics of Emmanuel Levinas*, p. xiii.

62. Perpich, *The Ethics of Emmanuel Levinas*, p. xiii.

63. Fagenblat, *A Covenant of Creatures*, p. xix.

64. 'Vladimir Jankélévitch', in *Outside the Subject*, p. 87.

65. Moati, *Levinas and the Night of Being*, p. 16.

66. Emmanuel Levinas, *Ethics and Infinity: Conversations with Phillipe Nemo*, trans. Richard Cohen (Pittsburgh, PA: Duquesne University Press, 1985), pp. 89–90.

67. Robbins, *Is It Righteous to Be?*, p. 133.

68. Richard Cohen, 'Buber and Levinas – and Heidegger', in *Levinasian Meditations* (Pittsburgh, PA: Duquesne University Press, 2010), p. 92.

69. Levinas, *Otherwise Than Being*, p. 159.

70. See 'The Rights of Man and the Rights of the Other', in *Outside the Subject*, and the two essays on the Rights of Man in Levinas, *Alterity and Transcendence*.

71. See 'Dialogue with Martin Buber', in Levinas, *Proper Names*, p. 38.

72. Levinas, *Existence and Existents*, p. 35.

73. Levinas, *Otherwise Than Being*, p. 74.

74. Caygill, *Levinas and the Political*, p. 64.

75. Levinas, *Ethics and Infinity*, p. 80.

76. Perpich, *The Ethics of Emmanuel Levinas*, p. 35.

77. Robbins, *Is It Righteous To Be?*, p. 47.

78. Vera K. Fast, *Children's Exodus: A History of the Kindertransport 1938–1948* (London and New York, NY: IB Taurus, 2011), pp. 14–15.

79. https://encyclopedia.ushmm.org/content/en/article/children-during-the-holoc aust, retrieved 17 January 2019.

80. Jennifer Craig-Norton, 'Contesting the Kindertransport', *European Judaism*, Vol. 50, No. 2, Autumn 2017, p. 31.

81. Carly McLaughlin, '"They Don't Look Like Children": Child-Asylum Seekers, the Dubs Amendment and the Politics of Childhood', *Journal and Ethnic and Migration Studies*, Vol. 44, No. 11, 2018, pp. 1757–73.

82. McLaughlin, 'They Don't Look Like Children', p. 1765.

83. https://www.independent.co.uk/news/uk/home-news/dubs-child-refugees -home-office-immigration-home-office-supreme-court-a8566191.html, retrieved 17 January 19.

84. Horkheimer and Adorno, *Dialectic of Enlightenment*, p. 4.

85. Horkheimer and Adorno, *Dialectic of Enlightenment*, p. 4.

86. Horkheimer and Adorno, *Dialectic of Enlightenment*, pp. 4–5.

87. Adorno, *Minima Moralia*, p. 34.

88. 'Midnight in the Century' is the title of the novel by Victor Serge, written at the apotheosis of Hitlerian and Stalinist power.

89. Arendt, *Eichmann In Jerusalem*, pp. 68–69.

90. Robbins, *Is It Righteous To Be?*, p. 150.

91. Robbins, *Is it Righteous To Be?*, p. 142.

92. Robbins, *Is It Righteous To Be?*, p. 111.

93. Adorno, *Minima Moralia*, p. 226.

94. https://www.newstatesman.com/world/europe/2018/01/macron-s-v isit-calais-shines-light-his-theresa-may-immigration-policies, retrieved 17 January 2019.

95. Levinas, *God, Death and Time*, p. 175.

96. Martin Luther King, Jr., *Letter from Birmingham Jail* (London: Penguin, 2018), p. 13.

97. King, *Letter from Birmingham Jail*, pp. 19–20.

98. King, *Letter from Birmingham Jail*, p. 13.

99. King, *Letter from Birmingham Jail*, p. 40.

100. https://www.theguardian.com/world/2018/nov/22/hillary-clinton-europe-m ust-curb-immigration-stop-populists-trump-brexit, retrieved 17 January 2019.

101. It may be objected that infamous incidents such as the Cologne attacks have put Germans in greater danger by accepting refugees. But even taking such attacks into account, statistically Germans have not been subject to greater levels of crime. For an overview, see https://www.forbes.com/sites/freylindsay/2019/08/29/ref ugees-in-germany-did-not-bring-higher-risk-to-germans/#333af1c61101, retrieved 23 August 2020.

102. Nietzsche, *On the Genealogy of Morals*, p. 15.

103. Emmanuel Levinas, *On Escape*, trans. Bettina Bergo, annotations and intro. Jacques Rolland (Stanford, CA: Stanford University Press, 2003), p. 73.

104. Rachel Pistol, '"Heavy is the Responsibility for all the Lives That Might Have Been Saved in the Pre-War Years": British Perceptions of Refugees 1933– 1940', *European Judaism*, Vol. 50, No. 2, Autumn 2017, pp. 42–49.

105. See Butler, *Precarious Life*; and *Frames of War: When is Life Grievable?* (London and New York, NY: Verso, 2009). McLaughlin discusses Butler's work in the context of child protection in 'They don't look like children', pp. 1766–67.

106. Primo Levi, *The Periodic Table*, in *The Complete Works of Primo Levi Volume Two*, ed. Anna Goldstein (New York, NY and London: Liveright Publishing Corporation, 2015), p. 803.

107. The phrase originally appears in Arendt, *Origins of Totalitarianism*; for a recent in-depth discussion of this concept, see DeGooyer et al., *The Right To Have Rights*, published by Verso in 2018.

108. Robbins, *Is It Righteous To Be?*, p. 204.

109. Adorno and Horkheimer, *Dialectic of Enlightenment*, p. 180.

110. Robbins, *Is It Righteous To Be?*, p. 142.

Chapter 4

France Alone? Testing the Limits of Asylum

France is charged with representing the cause of humanity.[1]

– Ernest Lavisse

The [French Interior] minister sent urgent telegrams to the prefects of the northeastern border provinces instructing them to bar the entry of German Jewish children in particular.[2]

– Vicki Caron, on the actions of the French interior minister Albert Sarraut *after* Kristallnacht

INTRODUCTION

The Last of the Just by André Schwarz-Bart is a harrowing text, replete with suffering. It recounts the fictional odyssey of a Jewish family, the Levys, throughout European history, a family amongst whom each generation is born a 'Lamed-Vav', representatives of the Jewish mythic tradition of the thirty-six 'just men' who are alive at any given time. The 'just men' take the world's suffering upon themselves, often without knowing it, and without whom life for everyone else on earth would be intolerable.[3] The bleak title intimates that an end point has been reached – in a world capable of and responsible for Auschwitz, Schwarz-Bart implies that the idea that just persons can by their presence redeem the world, has become untenable; disaster has carried away with it the possibilities of justice, meaning, and comprehension. The descent to this ending is traced from the pogroms of earlier centuries up to the predicament of European Jewry in the mid-twentieth century, from the brutal

159

bullying by child fascists in school and in the street visited upon the title's child protagonist, Ernie Levy, through a series of exiles and calamities, to his adult denouement in the gas chamber. There is a particularly terrifying scene in the book when Ernie and his little brother flee through the streets of their German town, lost and trying to find their way to the relative shelter of the synagogue, with Nazis roaming the streets looking to harm any Jewish person they find.[4] Refuge is in short supply in this not-so-fictional world.

Yet Schwarz-Bart occasionally allows the reader a little room to breathe (very little!), introducing moments of hope which indicate how everything could have been otherwise; and while these moments are quickly snatched away, they are perhaps illustrative of the redemptive 'tiny fissure in the continuous catastrophe' that Walter Benjamin identified as the only possible form of hope.[5] Such a moment occurs in book six of *The Last of the Just*, where Ernie and his family escape from Germany and find refuge in Paris. Schwarz-Bart excoriates the Western democracies who failed to provide refuge for European Jewry when their very lives were at stake (he rehearses the ill-fated passage of the St. Louis, the infamous 'voyage of the damned' who were turned away at every port and had to return to Europe, where almost half of them were ultimately murdered),[6] yet for him, France is an exception, at least for a while. This caesura of allowing[7] lasts only three pages in a long book, but what hope resides in those pages!

> At least the Barbarians had not reached the balmy banks of the Seine, where the hours still passed so peacefully that the Levys were appalled. How could such oases exist? So God was tracing lines of demarcation upon the earth, decreeing: Here you will be hanged at any time of day, and there only at mealtimes; farther on your heads will be cut off, and elsewhere it will be France. . .?[8]

The patriarch of the family reproaches himself for ever having opted for Germany over France in the first place. The family delights in 'savouring the exquisite, downy warmth which reigned in the garden at all hours of the day, under the leafy bower that sheltered the old stone bench where the women knitted with both fingers and mouths, heaving a long, solemn, grateful Jewish sigh at a well-turned stitch or a well-turned phrase'.[9] They converse with their friends and fellow exiles, and for a brief period are able to relax. What the reader is presented with in these pages is an idyll, a dream of France, a France as it was many yesterdays ago, as it existed for a time, however briefly and insecurely, for some Jewish exiles as a welcoming refuge. It has been noted that during the 1930s, France was the preeminent country of asylum in the world, not only for European Jewish refugees fleeing persecution but also because it hosted a large number of Spanish Republicans who had fled following Franco's victory; in part it had little choice in sharing a border with Germany and Spain, but it also received Jewish refugees from other states.[10] It was France in 1791 which was the first European state in modernity (following Poland centuries earlier) to emancipate Jewish people politically in Europe from a secondary status by making them equal citizens. French historian Sophie Wahnich observes that this act of the French Revolution makes it symbolically the precise opposite to Nazism, in granting rather than depriving membership to Jewish people, a secular humanist universality of belonging opposed to ethno-nationalist particularism and exclusion, which nevertheless allows for groups to practice their own traditions.[11] (Marx also emphasized the importance of this latter point in his polemic against the assimilationist arguments of Bruno Bauer, in his 'On the Jewish Question'.)[12] This claim is also confirmed on the contemptible side of this equation by Goebbels, who trumpeted the success of the Nazis as representing the erasure of '1789' from history.[13] Elisabeth Weber refers to emancipated Jewry as 'the youngest children of the Republic', laying down the foundations of 'Franco-Judaism' and establishing almost a 'cult of the Revolution' to replace religious fidelity; 'in the words of the historian Théodore Reinach, the "second homeland, moral homeland" for "any Jew of today with a memory and a heart"'.[14] However, it should also be noted that the emancipation provoked a backlash and antisemitic reaction from some parts of France, leading to long debates and a delay in the granting of rights for all French Jewry.[15] Napoleon later pursued policies that were antisemitic in nature, convening an Assembly of Notables in 1806 to question Jewish leaders as to their practices being in conformity with the expectations of France.[16] Thus even during times of admirable advances, an ambivalence was evinced by French authorities concerning the Jewish 'question'. At the end of the nineteenth century, the Dreyfus affair brought this antisemitism into stark relief.

Nevertheless, the French Revolution had inaugurated a new era of the political in relation to what was termed *les droits de l'homme* – 'The Rights of Man'. The defence of the universal Rights of 'Man' was held to be an orienting principle, an *ethos*, and the foundation of law in the nascent Republic. This included a view that the right to refuge – given that the Republicans understood France to be in opposition to tyranny everywhere – formed an important element of the Rights of Man. Yet the same founding declaration refers to the rights of the 'Citizen', thus producing a potential tension or conflict between those rights held by dint of common humanity, and those as members of a polity. Does it make sense, however, to require of a political entity (be it a city or state or a region, etc.) that it take responsibility for those that do not form a part of its existing constitutive membership (the limit problem of the *demos*)? The remarkable answer of the French Revolution, especially in its idealistic apogee, the writing of the 1793 Constitution, was – yes.

However, as is true of many societies, there are distinct French traditions that, from a progressive point of view, are either laudable or contemptible. Primo Levi once wrote of 'the other soul of France, the one that sent Dreyfus to Guyana, accepted Hitler, and followed Pétain'.[17] Alain Badiou has repeatedly stressed that 'there is a second history of France', of 'dark and ruthless conservatism', which he has labelled 'transcendental Pétainism'.[18] Badiou distinguishes 'Pétainism' from fascism in as much as the latter has 'affirmative force', while the former 'presents the subjective abominations of fascism (fear, informing, contempt for others) without its [fascism's] vital spirit'.[19] That is, he posits a kind of zombie-fascism proper to France, just as dangerous as the real thing but undead in appearance, a reactionary bent that can lead to lethal consequences for those it fears, representing a nationalist, particularist drive to exclusion that is the opposite of Badiou's stipulated (and very Kantian-Arendtian) universal truth procedure, that 'there is only one world', from which solidarity with vulnerable people should follow.[20] In a wonderful piece of polemic in a debate against Alain Finkielkraut, Badiou nicely summarizes the distinction between these French worldviews, a version of 'choosing one's heritage' that brings his thought into proximity with that of Derrida:

> The heritage of France is a heritage that I am prepared to embrace when it's a matter of the French Revolution, the Commune, the universalism of the eighteenth century, or May '68. But it's a heritage I totally reject when it's a matter of the Restoration, the Versaillais [counter-revolutionary forces against the Paris Commune], colonialist and racist doctrines, Pétain, or Sarkozy. There's no such thing as 'a' French heritage. Rather, there is a constitutive division of that heritage between what's acceptable in terms of a minimal universalism and what should be rejected precisely because, in France, it has to do with the extreme ferocity of the possessing classes and with the monopolizing of the idea of 'national identity' by an oligarchy of careerists, politicians, military men, and media lackeys.[21]

The decision to devote an entire chapter to France's tradition of asylum is not because their modern asylum policies are laudable. In fact they can be judged contemptible, as evidenced by the treatment of those who found themselves in the Calais 'jungle', an ugly descriptor which nevertheless is indicative of the dehumanizing effects of this states' treatment of refugees, the attempt to reduce them to bare life in Agamben's sense. The historical record of France and asylum is also quite mixed; when one reads, for example, Vicki Caron's excellent book *Uneasy Asylum: France and the Jewish Refugee Crisis 1933–1942*, there is a constant oscillation between generosity and mean-spiritedness or fearful prudence; in 1933, at the outset of this period,

France's reputation as the *terre d'asile*, the land of asylum, is proudly upheld, yet this stance does not last.[22] Thus, Frantz Fanon's judgement that one should have done with a Europe that never stops talking about 'Man' but has no problem putting human beings to death is resonant in this context.[23] The same revolutionary France that considered itself a land of asylum was also a colonial power that brutally fought against the desire of Haitians to liberate themselves from slavery, and deliberately and indefinitely immiserated Haiti once it lost the struggle to the 'black Jacobins'.[24]

However, it may be that the more progressive tradition of France of which Badiou speaks, as embodied in the advances of the Revolution, and particularly its Jacobinist phase, is worth defending (the Terror, which is another debate entirely, I leave to the side).[25] The 1793 Jacobinist constitution was the first modern state constitution in the world to enshrine the right to asylum (although it was never implemented), as discussed further on.[26] Practices of asylum and hospitality stretch from antiquity to the present in a multitude of societies and have included formal welcoming traditions, ceremony, treaties, the notion of 'sanctuary' as tied to religious traditions, Islamic hospitality, Old Testament cities of refuge, the grace of kings, through to its modern state form as informed by international law. Powerful, hegemonic societies often promote themselves for their exceptionalism; Athens, during its period of hegemony following the defeat of the Persians, prided itself on magnanimity to suppliants, a generosity which needs to be understood in the context of its imperial behaviour (e.g. the slaughter on the island of Melos, where might simply equalled the right to exterminate).[27] In relation to the preceding above reflections on its colonial record, a similar theme may be tracked in the history of France. However, few societies have ever identified the right to asylum as fundamental to the identity of the political community and the *telos* of its existence; France seems to be an exception in this regard, despite the gap between this claim and the history of its actualization. What is at stake in this chapter is an exploration of a political community – the state of France – which perhaps comes closest in the history of organized political communities to the self-identification with the concept of the political argued for in this book, that of an *ethos* of responsibility which respects the right to asylum as proper to the identity of the polity as such. It is specifically an identity tied to respect for asylum, rather than a broader openness to migration, the latter an alternative tradition of openness that runs from Pericle's funeral oration (Athens as a city open to the world) to the words on the Statue of Liberty.

Derrida linked ethical responsibility-as-answerability explicitly to this process of sifting through the inheritance of the past:

> If our heritage assigns contradictory tasks to us . . . this is because it is a testimony to our finitude. Only a finite being inherits, and his finitude obliges him

[*sic*]. It obliges him to receive what is larger and older and more powerful and more durable than he. But the same finitude obliges one to choose, to prefer, to sacrifice, to exclude, to let go and leave behind. Precisely in order to respond to the call that preceded him, to answer it and to answer for it – in one's name as in the name of the other. The concept of responsibility has no sense at all outside of an experience of inheritance. Even before saying that one is responsible for a particular inheritance, it is necessary to know that responsibility in general ('answering for', 'answering to', 'answering in one's name') is first assigned to us, and that it is assigned to us through and through, as an inheritance.[28]

The title of this chapter alludes to its intention to counter a repeated, and strange, proclamation by French politicians that France cannot take in all the poor or stateless persons in the world. The problematic rhetoric and framing of this statement aside, in this chapter it is argued that the exact opposite is true: that were it required, France could and perhaps should do exactly that. What this claim brings into relief, building on the gigantomachy staged between Levinas and Aristotle in the preceding chapter, is the problem of limits, of saturation, of purported moderation and the avoidance of excess in these politician's claims.

As with the other chapters, here a certain history of the Shoah as it relates to asylum will be examined, this time in the context of the history of France in the 1930s and early 1940s. This will serve to illustrate the limitations of liberal-democratic responses to asylum, and the need for a new concept of the political, which will then be related to the contemporary politics of asylum. Vicki Caron, whose seminal work on this history will be vital throughout, observed that 'the period from 1933 through 1945 was in reality the last battle of the long civil war that began with the Revolution of 1789. The "Refugee Question", and ultimately the "Jewish Question", emerged as central themes of this battle, repeating a pattern established during one of this civil war's earlier skirmishes, the Dreyfus Affair'.[29] Yet not only the French civil war, but arguably a symbolic planetary struggle between two opposed revolutions was at stake – the French Revolution (especially in its Jacobinist phase as exemplified by the idealism of the 1793 Constitution) and the Nazi counter-revolutionary horror. Further at stake were both the French Republican tradition of asylum and 'the fate of liberalism in general' – Caron refers to Arendt's linking of the fate of Jewish people in Europe with that of liberalism, a point made also by Levinas, as noted in chapter 1.[30] The record of this time is decidedly mixed – the majority of French Jewry survived, but the majority of Jewish refugees in France were deported to their deaths (two-thirds of those deported were refugees, one-third French nationals)[31] – yet despite the severe consequences of this calamitous period, few lessons appear to have been learnt in modern France, where xenophobia and continuing poor treatment of persons seeking asylum continues into the present. The Republican tradition and liberalism in France, as a means of understanding and responding to asylum, remains fraught and problematic. A move beyond tradition and beyond liberalism is necessary, to an *ethos* of responsibility of the right to asylum as the primary work of politics. An examination of the tradition of asylum in France and the failures in this context will reinforce the need for the active preservation of unchosen plurality to be identified as the proper work of politics as such. As will be examined, not only moral horror in the form of the Shoah, but political calamity and collapse attends the failure to engage in such preservation of precarious life and the granting of a right to refuge and belonging. As in the previous two chapters, the problem of numbers as a limitation upon asylum will be explored, with reference to Derrida's work on 'unconditional hospitality', however not without posing some critical questions to Derrida about the framing of asylum in the context of what is called hospitality. To wit, hospitality posits a host and an implicit hostility of ownership and exclusion, whereas the implications of the 'active preservation' of unchosen plurality (Butler) and Arendt's call for a 'guarantee' of human dignity in a 'new law on earth', associated with the preservation of plurality, require a move beyond the negotiation of conditional and unconditional hospitality to a different conception of politics, where the delineation between host and guest is undermined, if not effaced, and it is not a question of hospitality but mutuality and belonging, of cohabitation. Hospitality as an emphasis in articulating the politics of asylum is holding the discourse back.

THE LAND OF ASYLUM

What is the political tradition of refuge in France? In the context of asylum, France cultivated an overt *ethos* of responsibility from the time of the Revolution, that is, it made an articulation and appeal to a politics of asylum, that other states might only take on as a pragmatic task, without formalizing their approach. Historian Peter McPhee observes: 'Before the Revolution, refugees had been accorded refuge of sanctuary "by the King's Grace". Now the universalism embedded in the Declaration generated a key transition to a generalized right of asylum.'[32] Following the Enlightenment period and the Revolution, asylum became a matter of political rights that were amongst the founding principles of the new society. Historian Greg Burgess, in his book *Refuge in the Land of Liberty*, tracks the history of asylum in France from the revolution of 1789 into the mid-twentieth century. He notes that Enlightenment ideals concerning natural rights entered into the realm of the political via the Declaration of the Rights of Man and Citizen in August 1789, which he links to statements by thinkers such as Hugo Grotius and (below) Christian Wolff:

> By nature the right belongs to an exile to dwell anywhere in the world. For exiles do not cease to be men because they are driven into exile . . . Therefore, since by nature all things are common . . . by nature the right belongs to an exile to live anywhere in the world.[33]

(Although derived from a natural rights claim and thus antithetical to Arendt's convictions, Wolff's rhetoric here concerning commonality and the right to reside anywhere in the world is resonant with Arendt's notion of the 'right to have rights', as well as a move prior to but already beyond Kant, who allowed only for a right of visitation rather than belonging in *Perpetual Peace*.) France, which saw itself in the vanguard of resistance to oppression (in combatting the monarchies of Europe and providing shelter to political dissidents), thus took as a founding principle the notion of itself as a *terre d'asile* – land of asylum – for oppressed peoples everywhere.[34] The leading figures of the French Revolution attempted to inscribe in the new Republic a set of universal principles, which, in Kant's phrase from his remarks on the Revolution in *The Conflict of the Faculties*, 'permits people to hope for progress towards the better'.[35] There is a deliberate attempt to put principle into practice, in the words of Robespierre: 'Morality used to be in philosophers' books; we have put it in the government of nations'.[36]

This discourse unfolds at a time of the apotheosis of eighteenth-century cosmopolitan universalism, when an international group of visitors to the National Assembly press for their right to participate in the 1790 anniversary celebration of the storming of the Bastille, making of the commemoration a universal celebration of liberation beyond the confines of France.[37] As Sudhir Hazareesingh has argued, in French thought from the Enlightenment on there has been a 'yearning towards universality'.[38] The revolutionaries intended the values of the Republic to apply to all humanity, and not just France, as Robespierre puts it: 'I have regarded it [the Declaration of the Rights of Man and of the Citizen] as a body of judicial axioms at once universal, unchangeable, and imprescriptible, intended to be applied to all mankind.'[39] The Revolution proceeded from a unity based in the opposition to external oppressors, and thus asylum is politicized: 'The family of French legislators is the homeland; it is the human race as a whole, less the tyrants and their accomplices'.[40] In consequence, 'The men of all countries are brothers, and different peoples should help each other to the best of their ability, like citizens of the same state.'[41] And these expansive sentiments were even codified, as in the 1793 Constitution, which states: 'They give asylum to foreigners who, in the name of liberty, are banished from their homelands';[42] it also gives a very wide-ranging definition of citizenship. Alain Badiou quotes that definition to the effect that 'whenever a man took in and raised an orphan, anywhere in the world, well, just by doing so he acquired French national-ity'.[43] Badiou's recollection is slightly off – citizenship is granted to those foreign-born persons who have resided in France for at least one year, and do one of a number of things: adopt an orphan, support an elderly person, and so on – but to support Badiou's point, the text ends the definition of citizen-ship by encompassing, 'Finally, every foreigner who is considered by the legislative body to be deserving of being treated humanely'.[44] This would, in formal terms, seem to represent a remarkable openness to all of humanity. The much-commented upon conjunction of 'man' and 'citizen' undermines the opposition between inside and outside, foreigner and citizen; just as (recall from the introduction) King Pelasgus in the Suppliant Maidens argued that the suppliants were guests and citizens, the French Revolution similarly erases the division between groups of human beings in establishing their common right to belong.

Burgess charts the varying fortunes of this idealism as it met with political and social challenges. For example in the 1930s, Burgess notes the comments of a British observer, that France was the nation par excellence of refuge in Western Europe, and that the French people cherished the ideal of the right of asylum for refugees.[45] Yet it is also true that during this period, both left and right political parties were divided as to how this shared principle of asy-lum should be exercised in practice.[46] And even around the time of the 1793 Constitution, Robespierre himself started to doubt the wisdom of providing refuge, as he suspected the presence of foreign saboteurs amongst those admitted to France.[47] Robespierre's universalism should also be understood in the context of its limitations – despite opposing slavery in the Assembly, for example, C. L. R. James in *Black Jacobins* noted that Robespierre was objecting to the word and not the thing, and was inconsistent, even if further left than the Girondins and other factions.[48] The Jacobins were also hostile to the religious practices of the Jewish community in their desire to move beyond organized religion, 'pursuing policies that appeared anti-Judaic at best, anti-semitic at worst'.[49]

How is the ostensible idealism of the Jacobinist phase of the French Revolution to be compared with other forms of politics? Sophie Wahnich writes that 'whereas democratic conflict is now supposed to be based on a politics made up of compromise, approximations and calculations, the Revolution dreamed of an absolute politics, illusory and utopian, resting on principles; whereas democratic justice is penal, and restricted by positive law, revolutionary justice is political, resting on social vengeance and the idealism of natural right'.[50] Wahnich discusses the objections of Arendt to the French Revolution, where in her book *On Revolution* she had objected to the 'social question' – the amelioration of poverty as a goal of politics, which privileged equality over liberty and thus delimited the possibilities for political action and inaugurated a politics of cruelty in the name of compassion.[51] But the natural rights claims underpinning revolutionary advances pointed to a universalism applicable beyond the agreements formed by action undertaken by willing participants. In addition to Arendt, theorists such as Étienne Balibar and Jacques Rancière have challenged the validity of natural rights, arguing that it is via political struggle and the granting of political rights that rights are to be properly guaranteed.[52] However, while natural rights may have rightly fallen from favour in political theory, there are nevertheless universal norms that can be posited as the basis of claims about the proper work of politics which are not dependent upon naturalism in its classical sense. Rather, they are claims about the human 'condition' and the phenomenology of the human subject (Arendt was right in this sense to distinguish the human condition from more problematic and contestable claims concerning ape account of human nature). As discussed in previous chapters, Judith Butler's innovative interpretation of the 'unchosen' nature of Arendtian human plurality, coupled with a sense of the responsible ethico-political subject derived from Levinas, generates an account of political norms that are universal and provide normative criteria of judgement (has plurality been actively preserved? Has the responsibility for the other constitutive of subjectivity been respected?) that move the work of politics beyond that which particular communities are willing, or not, to grant at a given moment of decision. Why such norms are of importance will again be reinforced by an examination of the history of the Shoah, in this context as it unfolded in relation to asylum in France.

'TWISTED ROAD TO VICHY': JEWISH ASYLUM IN FRANCE DURING THE SECOND WORLD WAR

In his memoir *Asylum*, Moriz Scheyer, an Austrian Jewish refugee, recounts that upon arriving at the French border, the guard at the checkpoint 'smiled at me and said: "Maintenant vous pourrez respirer". Now you will be able to breathe again'.[53] For a brief time Scheyer shares in this optimism, yet after a while his expectations of France are dashed. Disappointments, betrayal, and incidents of bureaucratic cruelty or indifference multiply; 'the Nazi seed had fallen on fruitful ground', in either indifference or active persecution, yet the kindness of individuals and of organizations, secular and Christian, ultimately result in the rescue of Scheyer and his family and protection for the duration of the war.[54]

In microcosm, the experience of Scheyer would be an apt descriptor for the plight of Jewish refugees in France during the years of looming darkness in the 1930s, ending with the arrival of the dark with Vichy in 1940, were it not for the fact that he survived, which was an uncommon fate. In the 1930s, France was both the 'major haven' (Caron) for German and Central European Jewish refugees (in contrast to the United Kingdom and the United States 'it had never imposed an anti-immigration statute') and was the 'foremost nation of asylum in the world', owing not only to the presence of European Jewry but also half a million Spanish Republicans.[55] Initially, in 1933, France adopted a generous and welcoming attitude towards Jewish refugees from the Nazis, however this quickly altered to a less generous, even exclusionary stance, which waxed and waned with the rapidly changing governments of the dying Third Republic. Under conservative governments, measures became harsher, while Leon Blum's socialist Popular Front opted for more humane methods for those refugees present on French soil (while maintaining exclusions against those not yet arrived). France quickly moved from being a *terre d'asile* to a *gare de triage*, a sorting-house or way-station for refugees on their way to elsewhere. Concerns about 'absorption capacity'[56] led to absurd fears of children and the elderly, that the former would be a burden and that the latter 'threatened [!] national security since there were already too many Germans in the border provinces'.[57] In this context, the tradition of asylum of Republican France was a useful tool to be utilized by asylum advocates against the restrictive policies of the day;[58] however, ultimately the struggle was lost – Greg Burgess refers to the 'end' of asylum in France: 'The refugee depot [which had hospitably sheltered 18th and 19th century political refugees] and the concentration camp mark the opposing ends of the path of the principles of the right of asylum across the years since the French Revolution . . . It seems appropriate to mark this down as the end of asylum because the responses to the Spanish republican refugees of 1939 showed how devoid of principle asylum had become.'[59] Caron argues that apropos of Jewish refugees, the deportations were related to a failure by the Vichy authorities to enforce emigration policies: 'Laval's decision to collaborate with the Germans in the deportations of Jewish people from both zones, a decision finalized in July 1942, must be understood against the background of this emigration impasse.'[60] Laval attempted to blame other Western powers for the consequences by pointing out that they did not help France with its refugee problem, which as Caron notes, is a claim not to be entirely dismissed, despite its self-exculpatory exigency (and Laval's terrible crimes, for example, his responsibility for the deportations and the infamous 'La Rafle').[61] The consequences that attend the failure to provide refuge are stark in this history, and liberal-democracies worldwide, and not France alone, bear much of the responsibility.

Refugees were forced to negotiate a complicated system of applying for permission to remain in France, which did not guarantee their right to asylum but kept them in limbo.[62] Hannah Arendt, herself a Jewish exile in Paris in these years who aided other exiles, wrote in dry prose of the enthusiasm 'we refugees' had for attempting to become 'French', such 'that we could not even criticize a French governmental order; thus we declared it was all right to be interned'.[63] Circumstances continually changed throughout the 1930s with the rise and fall of different governments in rapid succession; generally, refugees fared better under socialist governments than by right-wing governments, although the socialists, including luminaries such as Leon Blum, were also constrained by political reality and at times reluctant to admit more refugees than had already entered France. Governments wrestled with political instability, the logic of appeasement of both domestic and foreign actors, and economic uncertainty during the Depression.[64] During the 'Conservative Crackdown' of 1934–1935, following the more liberal period of 1933, the minister of the interior argued that 'it was his "mission" to ensure that France not "become the refuge for the rest of the world's undesirables"'.[65] Challenged on whether this meant an end to asylum for refugees, the minister responded: '"If they don't have the means to live, yes. We don't have to nourish them. There are plenty enough unfortunate Frenchmen without our having to ensure the existence of foreigners".'[66]

Yet this economistic logic, even within the context of the Great Depression, was self-defeating. There was a great fear of refugees becoming 'public charges' during a time of economic downturn, yet the criminalization of refugees, who had to negotiate a Byzantine system of applying for visas and permission to work and so on, meant that they ended up in French prisons, 'supported' by the French state regardless. (This could readily be compared to the billions of dollars Australia spends to sustain a few hundred refugees in offshore detention conditions that the UN has said violates the torture convention, or the three billion dollar deal Europe shamefully concluded with Turkey to prevent Syrian refugees from travelling past the Turkish border. State praxis reveals it is never really a question of resources or money or economics; real concerns are elsewhere, in political calculation or a pathological fear of numbers, or if not pathological or resistant in the psychological sense, then ideology in its purest form, the logic of an idea divorced from the real.) Caron notes the 'Malthusian' logic of opponents of asylum who believed that the economy was bounded by certain limits and was incapable of further growth;[67] yet where refugees were permitted to set up businesses, the results were positive, including the hiring of French workers: 'In the Alsatian district of Haguenau, for example, a newly created refugee-owned shoe manufacturing firm had, according to the subprefect there, created hundreds of new jobs and had "thoroughly eliminated all fear of unemployment in this important locale".'[68] Similarly, agricultural work schemes were successful and an important contribution to the French economy (indeed, following the slaughter of the First World War France had actively sought migrants to renew its population and workforce).[69] To the extent that France did not take in refugees and Britain did, the latter was a huge beneficiary in terms of economic outcomes.[70]

Consequently, it is apparent that the exclusionary fears driving (particularly conservative or right-wing) politics during this period were manifestly unjustified. And yet even if they had been – if deleterious economic consequences had attended the reception of thousands of refugees – as a moral question, that is not dispositive; from a universal perspective, the safeguarding of human dignity and life surely trumps the relative prosperity of an extant community; to deny work rights was equivalent to a sentence of death by hunger, as advocates maintained. Leon Blum argued against the linking of asylum with wealth, for do this was to build 'the wall of money of the exile'.[71] Blum, in a moving speech, argued that it was an 'elementary human duty' to provide asylum, and even reproached his fellow Jewish citizens (some of whom had sought, in a logic of appeasement, to exclude European Jewry from France): 'There is nothing in the whole world as painful and dishonorable to me as to see French Jews today attempting to close the doors of France to Jewish refugees from other countries . . . Perhaps your house is already full, it's possible, but when they knock on your doors, let them in and don't ask them for their identity papers, judicial records, or vaccination certificates.'[72] Yet even Blum reinforced the logic of the *gare de triage*, suggesting that 'asylum for one night' was necessary until permanent relocation could be found elsewhere; thus he was closer to Kant in endorsing a right of visitation, even in the context of asylum, rather than to an Arendtian notion of belonging.[73] What is denied, even in some arguments of the Socialists, is a right of refugees to belong in order to secure their rights (Arendt), and the moral imperative of providing for the other, even if it means a sacrifice on the part of oneself and those nearest, the tearing of 'the bread from one's mouth' to give to the other (Levinas).[74] The leaders of France, left or right, did not think that France could accommodate 'the rest of the world's undesirables' – a curious, exorbitant (in the negative sense) objection to asylum, which requires deconstructing, and hence an examination of the work of Jacques Derrida.

'ALL THE WRETCHED POVERTY OF THE WORLD'

In an address delivered at the Sorbonne in 1882, Ernst Renan asked: 'What is a Nation?' In quick order he dismisses several possible predicates of the nation: it is, for him, neither bound up with race, nor language, nor shared interest, nor religion, nor is it even delimited by a geographical principle. He summarizes it as a community of 'moral conscience': 'A great aggregation of men, in sane mind and warm heart, created a moral conscience that calls itself a nation'.[75] This universalism was a consistent theme of the progressive vision of asylum in France: in 1882 Clovis Hughes, echoing the expansive Jacobinist constitution, declared: 'We are among those who think that, for France, there are no foreigners . . . those who think that after the French Revolution we have no right to speak of foreigners.'[76]

This notion of a nation being coterminous with a community of moral conscience aligns with the Republican ideal of providing shelter for asylum seekers; the 'nation' of the nation-state of France is beyond the normal predicates of nationality, on this interpretation – language, ethnicity, religion, and so on – and recast in a modality of responsibility, a shared 'moral conscience'.[77] Yet what should the limits of this moral conscience, this sense of ethical responsibility (and thus, perhaps a form of irresponsibility in relation to limits) be?

After a significant period of French presidents (including the socialist Miterrand) denying that the crimes of Vichy were the crimes of France, President Chirac accepted the responsibility of France for the deportations committed under Vichy, including the infamous 'La Rafle', or round-up, of Jewish people from Paris into the Vel d'Hiv cycling stadium: 'France that day performed the irreparable.'[78] Yet while this was an act complicitous ultimately in genocide, the denial of asylum at the time was also tantamount to a death sentence for thousands of people; Michael R. Marrus notes that Vichy was not that much different from the end of the Third Republic in relation to the politics of asylum.[79] Despite these horrors of twentieth-century French history (to which can be added French crimes in Algeria and elsewhere), French leaders continue to evince paranoid fears about 'the rest of the world's undesirables', which as will be seen is a recurrent theme in French politics, their rhetorical gift to the world which might be seen as the dark obverse to the French tradition of asylum, the 'other' France noted by Levi and Badiou. In a very short text titled 'The Principle of Hospitality' (which is in fact an interview from *Le Monde*) collected in the book *Paper Machine*, Derrida is asked about the deployment of political rhetoric concerning such limits:

LE MONDE: Some years ago now, Michel Rocard said, 'France cannot take in all the wretched poverty of the world.' What does this statement suggest to you? What do you think of the way that Lionel Jospin's government is currently working toward a partial granting of official status to illegal immigrants?

DERRIDA: I seem to remember that Michel Rocard withdrew that unfortunate phrase. Because either it's a truism (who ever did think that France, or any other country, has ever been able to 'take in all the wretched poverty of the world'? Who has ever asked for that? Or its rhetoric is that of a joke meant to produce restrictive effects and to justify cutbacks, protectionism, and reactionary attitudes ('after all, since we can't take in all the wretched poverty, don't let anyone ever reproach us for not doing enough, or even for not doing it at all any more'). This is presumably the effect – the economic, economistic, and confused effect – that some people sought to exploit, and that Michel Rocard, like so many others, came to regret.[80]

As discussed in the introduction, Derrida linked ethics as such to hospitality – 'ethics is hospitality' – via the interpretation of *ethos*, the etymological root of ethics, as pertaining to the manner of dwelling in a place. Yet Derrida's innovation is to distinguish between 'unconditional' and 'conditional' hospitality, or the Law versus the laws, plural, of hospitality – a 'Law' of hospitality that would postulate an unconditional openness to others of all kinds, that has to be negotiated against the 'laws' or conditional versions of hospitality, of calculation and limits.[81]

Derrida was prone to a certain hyperbole on the subject of hospitality, suggesting that 'yes' should be said to 'who or what turns up' – a conditionless preliminary affirmation of the other person, which will afterwards have to be negotiated.[82] Thus when Derrida asks who did think that France can take in everybody, a possible rejoinder is to say that it was precisely him! But Derrida does not call for simple irresponsibility, but rather *negotiation* between the conditioned and the unconditioned. In response to exclusionary 'economistic' rhetoric masquerading as responsibility (an exorbitant claim about what France might do, marshalled as an excuse to do as little as possible), Derrida in the same interview responds with a call for 'another kind of politics':

> Hence the anxiety of those who, without ever asking for a straightforward opening up of the frontiers, have argued for another kind of politics, with figures and statistics to support this (based on methods tried out by experts and relevant associations, who have been working in the field for years). And they have done this 'responsibly', not 'irresponsibly', as I believe one minister had the nerve to say – one of the sort who nowadays (and it's always a bad sign) make carefully controlled little slips. The decisive limit, from which a politics is judged, comes somewhere between 'pragmatism' and even 'realism' (both indispensable for an effective strategy), and their dubious double, opportunism.[83]

As a thinker of the impossible, for Derrida it is nevertheless essential to work out a practical politics in regards to refugees, 'with figures and statistics', done 'responsibly', 'without ever asking for a straightforward opening up of frontiers', even one tied to 'pragmatism' and 'realism'.

Michel Rocard, who represented the socialist party, claimed to have been misquoted, and that the second part of his statement is that France should

nonetheless take its part (however, there seems to have been different iterations of the statement by him, not all of which have this qualification present).[84] Taking Rocard at his word, it rather begs the question, as to what part
of the world's misery is France responsible for, owing to its colonial past, its
foreign interventions,[85] its role in the violence and exploitation of capitalism.
However Rocard is far from alone – his exclusionary statement was quoted
verbatim by President Emmanuel Macron in 2017.[86] These statements are
sometimes accompanied by distinctions between a duty to refugees and the
right to exclude migrants – a reasonable distinction, if one that requires careful consideration as to who constitutes a refugee in need of assistance, and
whether the current definition of persecution is not inadequate in excluding
economic suffering. As noted above, this precise sentiment was also voiced
by then minister of the interior, Marcel Régnier, during the Jewish refugee
'crisis', who declared it his own personal 'mission' that France not 'become
the refuge for the rest of the world's undesirables'.[87]

A very simple question can be asked: how do Rocard and company know
that France cannot take in every arrivant? One is tempted to venture a *psychoanalytic* reading of this repeated declaration by French leaders (a political
version of the 'repetition compulsion', which Freud linked to the death drive
in *Beyond the Pleasure Principle*), drawing upon a very French word that
doubles as a political and psychoanalytic concept: that of resistance. Derrida
writes in *Resistances of Psychoanalysis* of 'this word, which resonated in
my desire and my imagination as the most beautiful word in the politics and
history of this country, this word loaded with all the pathos of my nostalgia,
as if, at any cost, I would like not to have missed blowing up trains, tanks,
and headquarters between 1940 and 1945'.[88] However, beyond nostalgia or
admiration for the resistance to fascism in the war, in psychoanalysis this
word has an opposed meaning to its political signification: as Jacqueline Rose
has observed in her essay 'The Last Resistance', rather than in the latter case
a moral resistance to evil, in the former it represents the repression of the
psyche's path to freedom. 'If in political vocabularies, resistance is the passage to freedom, for psychoanalysis, it is repetition, blockage, blind obeisance
to crushing internal constraint'.[89] Resistance is thus in part repetition, which
Rose links to politics: 'Psychoanalysis can help us to understand the symptom
of statehood, why there is something inside the very process upholding the
state as a reality which threatens and exceeds it.'[90] That is, as human subjects
enact the formation and behaviour of states and nations, there is a need for
psychoanalysis to interpret this.[91] Rose writes that 'the mind, like the world
of the 1930s and I would say today, is a frightening and fortified place', and
she comments on the trauma of exile for European Jews during the 1930s,
and how that has been subsequently deployed in remembrance either in a
universal ethic of compassion or in exclusionary psychological resistance (as

with Butler in *Parting Ways*, her focus in this essay is Israel–Palestine) where 'trauma enters the national psyche as resistance to its own pain'.[92]

Rose argues that 'Fascism is a form of resistance, a carapace against what the mind should, ideally, be able to do with itself', thus Freud becomes a revolutionary or resistant, fighting to overcome the resistance of the world which will thus allow it to be saved, struggling, as Arnold Zweig writes to him, 'against fallacies, taboos and repressions of our contemporaries', a struggle 'comparable with the one the prophets waged against the recalcitrant nation of their day'.[93] Psychoanalysis, in displacing any vision of pure or ideal selfhood, in presenting the self-difference of oneself to oneself, underscores what Derrida in an essay on Freud called the violence of the One: 'As soon as there is the One, there is murder, wounding, traumatism . . . the One forgets to remember itself to itself, it keeps and erases the archive of this injustice that it is.'[94] Resistance takes the form of multiple deluded phantasms: a phantasm of race, of numbers, of economics, of nationalism, of one-ness.

Broadening the discussion beyond France – for both Rose and Edward Said, Freud's legacy is pertinent in the Israel–Palestine context – in *Freud and the Non-European*, Said draws on Freud's provocative thesis in *Moses and Monotheism* to point to the self-difference of Israel's origins, where a new understanding between Israelis and Palestinians might be forged.[95] The gesture of Freud/Said to open Judaism on to its purported non-Jewish origins is not to undermine Judaism or Israel but to avoid the violence of a political community seeking to be solely one with itself. For Said, the political implication of this gesture meant the possibility of forming a new understanding between Israelis and Palestinians, which Judith Butler emphasizes in *Parting Ways*. Here, it pertains to the non-closure of identity to the other who comes from without the state. This is the 'contrapuntal' insight of the outsider, that both Said and Derrida embodied in their lived experiences, that is, caught between, aware of and informed by more than one culture, and the existence of the 'psychic contrapuntal', of the self-difference of a subject to itself, means that in this sense we are all exiles of a sort, and can come to empathize with those exiled from place, community, and safety.[96] For Rose, the universal lesson of the Shoah should be applied in this context – a lesson of openness to others, rather than enclosure in resistance of the subject that, in positing itself as One, does violence to the other.[97] The pathologies of the antisemite identified in Sartre's famous essay wherein the antisemite cannot face up to themselves and projects their fears onto others are thus mirrored in the most recalcitrant and reactionary forces in Israel that would deny basic human rights, let alone belonging, to the Palestinians; it is necessary, in political terms, to undo the resistance of the nation and its orthodoxies.[98] However this undoing is the most difficult, in that the superego itself resists the uncovering of unconscious resistances

(thus the 'last resistance' of Rose's title).[99] As Derrida has argued, there is
also a resistance to psychoanalysis itself, even within the psychoanalytic
process, resistance to overcoming resistance which Freud referred to as the
repetition compulsion,[100] which can sometimes only be overcome not by
rational explanations, but moments of affect.[101] (One might posit this as the
explanation for why images of Alan Kurdi's lifeless body were able to overcome the resistances of many European states for a short while; the resistance to the standard progressive political analyses was overcome when the
latter was supplemented by the affecting images of the child.) Repetition
qua iterability, in Derrida's terms, thus requires interminable analysis, that
is to say, deconstruction.[102] And, to return to the topic of France, in the
resistance, in psychological terms, of the repeated declarations of French
leaders that they cannot take in all of the 'wretched poverty' of the world,
the same issue adheres. One needs to ask what role France has played in
making people in the Global South, from Francophone Africa to Vietnam,
'wretched'.

Bonnie Honig, in her book *Democracy and the Foreigner*, summarizes
the problem with reducing foreigners to empiricism: '[. . .] in contemporary
debates about immigration, the facts can inform but they cannot resolve the
question of whether immigrants are good or bad for the nation because the
question is not, at bottom, an empirical question'.[103] This remark, which
Honig intends in a broader sense of how foreigners relate to the life-world
of democracies, applies equally to the reduction of stateless persons to numbers. The totalizing calculability of an ethical demand for refuge would seem
to founder on the impossibility of any 'determinative judgment', as Derrida
observes in *Rogues*:

> A calculable event, one that falls, like a case, like the object of some knowledge,
> under the generality of a law, norm, determinative judgment, or technoscience,
> and thus of a power-knowledge and a knowledge-power, is not, *at least in this
> measure*, an event. Without the absolute singularity of the incalculable and the
> exceptional, no thing and no one, nothing *other* and thus *nothing*, arrives or
> happens. . . . *The unconditionality of the incalculable* allows or gives the event
> to be thought.[104]

And it is precisely on the subject of hospitality that for Derrida, unconditionality is often privileged:

> Among the figures of unconditionality without sovereignty I have had occasion
> to privilege in recent years, there would be, for example, that of an *uncondi-
> tional hospitality* that exposes itself without limit to the coming of the other,
> beyond rights and laws, beyond a hospitality conditioned by the right of asylum,

by the right to immigration, by citizenship, and even by the right to universal hospitality, which still remains, for Kant, for example, under the authority of a political or cosmopolitical law. Only an unconditional hospitality can give meaning and practical rationality to a concept of hospitality. Unconditional hospitality exceeds juridical, political, or economic calculation. But no thing and no one happens or arrives without it.[105]

Unconditional hospitality is that which exceeds calculation, but it is also related to it: '*both* calculation *and* the incalculable *are necessary*'.[106] The relation to the other is not a mathematical claim but rather the relationship to the infinite in the sense of that which exceeds the subject, per Levinas – but nevertheless, calculations are necessary, in the move from ethics to justice as the beginning of politics, of the need to weigh competing obligations and make decisions, even where, as seen in the previous chapter, this does not necessitate the abandonment of an 'anarchical', exorbitant responsibility. An unconditional demand by definition cannot be fulfilled. This ceaseless negotiation between the unconditioned demand and the necessarily conditional modes of its realization is the basis of a responsible politics (and something which Derrida and Levinas were in apparent agreement on, as in Simon Critchley's persuasive thesis that the ethics of deconstruction are heavily influenced by Levinasian ethics).[107]

What if, one day, it was suggested that France take in the entire global population of concern, on its own? That is to say, every current displaced person, refugee, and asylum seeker, every member of every refugee camp, and all those in transit. Current estimates put this total figure at a more-or-less commensurate figure with the total population of France.[108] That is, for every current citizen or resident of France, one more person would be added – an automatic doubling of the population. The likely political reaction is imaginable – this is a political impossibility at present, and probably for all time; other questions like social cohesion and attitudes to the new arrivals would be dramatized in this context. However, if one brackets political feasibility and takes up the question of economic feasibility, in the sense of a potential problem of scarcity and meeting a limit, the problem might be reconsidered. And why France alone? For Levinas, the responsible subject is not concerned with the responsibilities that others have, but only their own; while reciprocal agreements between states may meet obligations to stateless persons, the securing of such agreements should not set the limit to its own actions.

The question of economic status also engages the limitations of regarding refugees as those who suffer non-economic forms of persecution; it is this limitation that leads Badiou (as previously mentioned) to move beyond the category of refugee and refer to the 'nomadic proletariat', as encompassing a broader array of human migratory imperatives. Slavoj Žižek, in rearticulating the meaning of violence, has insisted upon the function of systemic violence, which functions 'like the dark matter of physics' as inscribed in the operation of modern political and economic systems, without being as visible as more direct, dramatic forms of persecution and violence.[109] Whether the legal category of refugee should be expanded to include people fleeing economic persecution, and how that is to be defined and determined, is a difficult matter, however one that should be faced. Nicole Loraux has observed that 'analysis of the Athenian citizen's identity has also permitted me to observe that it was probably better to be an Athenian Metic than an immigrant in 1990s France'.[110] Indeed, 'Métèques', a term redeployed in the twentieth century by the reactionary Charles Maurras, has come to denote a term of derision for unwelcome foreigners in France. The damning nature of this charge relates to the positioning of the Metic in Athens outside of citizenship, as resident foreigners, who nevertheless had access to certain rights and dignity, which led critics to charge democracy itself as being excessive in nature; Metics even had access to rudimentary treaties to claim the right to asylum, even though appearing before the law was reserved for citizens.[111] Yet the Metics often posed a challenge to democracy in obtaining significant economic or cultural status that challenged the demarcation between the free status of the citizen and their own bounded status. Conversely, as seen in the history of asylum for European Jewry in the 1930s, economics was a significant issue that was appealed to especially by right-wing political forces to justify exclusion of vulnerable refugees. As a justification for asylum, or its denial, the question of economic status and economic impact cannot be avoided in forming judgements in this context.

For Levinas, 'the other concerns me in all his [*sic*] material misery' – his ethics is based upon a phenomenology of experience: 'We live from "good soup", air, light, spectacles, work, ideas, sleep, etc. . . . These are not objects of representations.'[112] [44] Reception of millions of people will require rooms and beds, families buying the cheap bread and milk and 'good soup' to sustain the arrivants. Perhaps living rooms would need to be commandeered, laying mattresses on floors, and cramped living conditions everywhere. The organization of capitalist societies, where the legal defence of private property results in leaving empty thousands of dwellings in a city that could be used by those who need them, becomes relevant in this context; existing arrangements are not dispositive in their logic. A society that tolerates billionaires cannot speak of scarcity. If the *telos* of politics is the flourishing of plural human beings, and attendance to their needs (in the sense that Agnes Heller writes of Marx), then a reordering of society on this basis would be necessary, exposing the phantasm of scarcity within the capitalist order, in addition to putting an end the grotesque distortions of bloated military budgets, tax cuts for the very wealthy, and fossil fuel subsidies, amidst other horrors.[113]

Why this reference to practical, everyday concerns? It is due in part to the exigency of a phenomenological ethics – articulated by Emmanuel Levinas – as a basis for thinking through questions of political asylum, in order to avoid the formalism or contractual nature of liberal theories of justice and other approaches, to literally and figuratively put a 'Face' on the problem. And yet just as Arendtian politics seems incomplete without reference to Levinasian alterity as an account of responsibility, conversely Levinasian responsibility requires grounding in an Arendtian account of belonging – a move beyond taking responsibility, feeding, clothing, housing the other, a rhetorics of charity of which Levinas was perhaps too predisposed towards, yet which Arendt failed to prioritize qua the 'social question' – to allow for political membership and agency as the fulfilment of the right to have rights. It is not sufficient to engage this topic only at the level of material conditions; actualization of human beings requires belonging where human beings can appear and act amongst each other. Yet analysis of the concrete fulfilment of human need is also bound up with the deconstruction of purported limits to asylum available to a sovereign state to proffer to refugees.

The household can be seen, to repeat this phrase, as the false synecdoche of the state. Political theorists and philosophers who study hospitality are aware of the familiar and by now tired recall of its etymological root wherein 'hostis' can imply both host and hostility, the person who is at home who decides whether to admit or to deny the arrivant. Derrida refers to this when he writes that there is 'no hospitality, in the classic sense, without sovereignty of oneself over one's home'.[114] Similarly, the etymology of economics refers to 'the laws of the house' – *oikonomia*, oikos, house, nomos, law or custom, management.[115] This has been called into question throughout as problematic in relation to the limits of welcome within economic capacity. It is often on the grounds of economics that governments make claims about what they can provide to the displaced. But there may be a problem in limiting hospitality qua economics, by more significantly reference to the household, its laws and limits. Aristotle was already aware of this in the *Politics* (and this is a point of agreement with him): 'It is an error to suppose, as some do, that the role of a statesman, of a king, of a household-manager and of a master of slaves are the same, on the ground that they differ not in kind but only in point of numbers of persons'.[116]

In positing the idea of 'France Alone', reference was made to the practical level of the household, as a means of questioning economic limits. But in a nation-state, new arrivants are not simply to be housed and fed in existing household; extra people are extra workers and extra consumers, who bring extra ideas, and thus the overall economic 'pie' grows – it is not a zero-sum game. But what are the evident flaws of household economics in relation to thinking the state? Such analogies are not necessarily helpful, because a household truly has certain limits which it will quickly reach, whereas there is a certain plasticity to the expansion, contraction, debt, and earning capacities of a nation-state, which is backed in any event by its taxing power, whereas a household is not. And as mentioned above, new arrivants do not represent only a burden, but can become workers and consumers and entrepreneurs, and so on. Thus, if a nation-state's economy is viewed as akin to a household economy, we limit the possibilities of welcome based upon a false analogy. A nation-state has capacities that a household does not.

Thus – and this is a key point – when Derrida says, 'Let us say yes *to who or what turns up*', an extreme formulation of welcome for which he is often reproached – who is to say that he is in fact wrong? What is the calculus, the rigorous assessment from which this reproach is issued? *What is the limit-point, and who can say what it is*? Are there an agreed set of figures about the limits of a city or nation, of a country's population and economy, of its capacity to provide? At what point does a state reach its ideal size? Such an ideal is of course a nonsense – cities and nation-states have no set limit or finally determinable capacity beyond which one should not go. The impossible to which both Levinas and Derrida point when they admonish us to practice a greater hospitality, may in fact remain within the bounds of possibility, the limit-point of which always remains over the horizon and out of sight. Sometimes in their rhetorical flourishes, Derrida and Levinas seem to request the erasure of all limits. But they were not so foolish as to actually desire this; the concept of 'pure' hospitality in Derrida and the subjection of the ego to the other in Levinas are to my mind conceptual apparatus which are immediately mediated by context – in Derrida, the distinction between the purity of impossibility and the need for achievable possibilities is sometimes (though not always) emphasized, and in Levinas the apparition of the Third removes the possibility of total solicitude for any one other and introduces the need to make limiting choices – the moment of justice, of weighing decisions and outcomes.

In other words, even those thinkers who seem to call for the impossible recognize that it is necessary to make limiting choices. Indeed, perhaps Derrida himself is too much in thrall to the limits of hospitality as conceptualized through the metaphor of the household. Nation-states, like households, surely do have limit-points for their capacity to welcome – at some point, the notion of scarcity must come in to play. However this point is not easy to determine. Thus, the comparison with household economics should be avoided, or at least treated with more care. What indeed is this privilege that is granted to the etymological root of a word, and the signification that this root indicates concerning the concept, practice, or thing it names? Is hospitality bounded by this cleavage between host and hostility? If it is, perhaps it is not 'hospitality' but rather *belonging* which needs to be the focus of reflection – belonging as understood in the Arendtian sense of plural beings able to appear amongst each other. 'No hospitality, in the classic sense', but perhaps the 'classic sense' is inadequate. Hospitality at the national level needs to move out of the house, and perhaps, to go even further, it is necessary to have done with the notion of hospitality in the limitations it seems to establish, even when appearing ostensibly radical and generous, as in the discourse of Derrida.

What becomes interesting, and a challenge, is the way in which Derrida's logic of decision, which must occur in the night of aporetics where certainty cannot be guaranteed, is an account of responsibility that is fundamentally at odds with the notion of a guarantee, which Arendt called for without substantiating, and which has been pursued throughout this book in relation to the memory of the disappeared who were refused entry for various reasons and consequently suffered and in many cases died. For Derrida, what is called responsibility must occur via such undecidability:

> Far from opposing undecidability to decision, I would argue that there would be no decision, in the strong sense of the word, in ethics, in politics, no decision, and thus no responsibility, without the experience of some undecidability. If you don't experience you undecidability, then the decision would simply be the application of a programme, the consequence of a premiss or of a matrix.[117]

And yet the imperative to 'actively preserve' (Butler) unchosen plurality, plurality as the 'law of the earth' (Arendt) in an experience of ethico-political subjectivity where one does not choose from the position of an imperious subjectivity, but is always-already called to responsibility for others (Levinas), would seem to indicate a delimitation of decision. Attendant to this, the horrors of history also put starkly into question the logics, or aporetic illogics, of decisionism. As Simon Critchley asks in *The Ethics of Deconstruction*: 'But how exactly does this deconstructive, ethical conception of justice translate into political judgement and action? Derrida insists that judgements have to be made and decision have to be taken, provided it is understood that they pass through an experience of the undecidable. But my question to Derrida would be: *What* decisions are taken, *which* judgements are made?'[118] The problem with Derrida's account of responsibility as the necessary interplay between undecidability and decision, via a traversal of the impossible, is that it risks recapitulating the game that states already play, in positing the need to make decisions concerning asylum, when, in fact, materially, culturally, morally, in the delimited context of asylum, there is no decision to be made. The dialectic is refused, a 'premiss' is asserted – the duty to preserve unchosen plurality. While unconditional hospitality ('one of the names of deconstruction') is extremely positive in undermining quotidian versions of hospitality that posits limits in advance, and reassert the dominance of the

host, it also reinscribes a logic of negotiation, of dialectic (although deconstruction is not coterminous with the Hegelian dialectic), of an inside and an
outside. To be sure, in actuality there is an inside and outside when it comes
to persons seeking asylum – a political community that already exists, and
those who have been cast out of or forced to leave a political community,
the *heimatlosen* as Arendt put it, those without homes or belonging. But to
establish grounds of decision as a negotiation between the host and the guest,
the inside and the outside, the unconditional and conditional versions of hospitality (where it is advanced that there are conditions – but are there any, in
relation to asylum?) – is to re-establish, along ostensibly more generous lines,
the same logic already operative in the work of modern sovereign states.
Derrida's assumption is that responsibility is coterminous with undecidability and the decision, and that hospitality, in the experience of the aporia, is
self-deconstructing, and this in the name of justice; but there is nothing in
the meaning of *respondere* or responsibility that means hospitality must of
necessity be an experience of the impossible, nor that hospitality is properly
that which is at issue. It is true that decisions and choices must be made with
the arrival of strangers, but the normative implication of unchosen plurality
is that such decisions or choices are bounded but a priori considerations of
preserving or destroying the givenness of human plurality. The freedom to
act, and therefore to commit crimes, including crimes against humanity as
such – ontological crimes – remains, but is bounded by what Butler calls a
'constitutive unfreedom' where what is furnished are clear criteria of judgement concerning such acts. Responsibility, for Levinas, is not a weighing of
whether or not to come to the assistance of the other, but the questions that
are engaged with the advent of the third and the need to make decisions and
calculations between competing duties; as quoted in the previous chapter,
justice, nevertheless, is 'in no way a limitation of anarchic responsibility'.[119]
In this sense, the oscillation between host and hostility, which Derrida claims
can only be traversed by an experience of the impossible, risks reinforcing
the logics of exclusion it purports to deconstruct.[120] Perhaps Derrida would
maintain a distinction between refugees and other migrants and admit of an
unconditional hospitality for the former; however, this is not clear, on my
reading at least, from his interventions on the subject of hospitality. 'Indeed,
for an organized society that upholds its laws and wants to maintain the sovereign mastery of its territory, its culture, its language, its nation, for a family
or for a nation concerned with controlling its practices of hospitality, it is
indeed necessary to limit and condition hospitality. This can be done with
the best intentions in the world, since unconditional hospitality can also have
perverse effects.'[121] As with Badiou, a clearer distinction between asylum and
migration is needed in such discussions; to the extent that the definition of
asylum should be broadened to include categories of economic migrants – in

my view a plausible argument – well and good, but the rhetorical effect of a guarding against unconditional hospitality in general terms is worrisome. Hospitality for Derrida is the negotiation of the unconditional with the conditional, the impossible experience of the aporia of a decision that cannot be absolutely determined, though he insists that 'deconstruction is on the side of unconditionality, even when it seems impossible, and not sovereignty, even when it seems possible'.[122] Nevertheless, as with the preceding quotation, he admits of a necessary, conditional hospitality for sovereignty to be workable. Once again, in the context of asylum, this is mere assertion. The dialectic of inclusion and exclusion, in the context of asylum, should be refused. There is an absolute right to be preserved from death and misery, and to belong somewhere; such is the law of the earth qua human plurality.

CONCLUSION

Thomas Paine, the extraordinary polemicist of both the American and French Revolutions, once observed that 'moderation in principle is a species of vice'.[123] Purported moderation as the stipulation of a limit, has been a continuous theme of politics in France, akin to Aristotle's delimitation of the ideal size of the city *The Politics* (which as previously observed, Hannah Arendt explicitly countersigns). Yet France also styled itself from the Revolution on as a land of asylum. What remains of this tradition, following the failures of the 1930s–1940s, and up to the present? As seen above, Greg Burgess referred to the 'end of asylum' in France, given the depths to which it sank before and during the Second World War. Perhaps nothing is left other than that which Sophie Wahnich intimates: 'There is but a life-raft remaining, of the Revolution in the social imaginary.'[124] The *idea* of France as *terre d'asile* remains, but little more than that; France did not offer its Navy as life-raft at the time when the Italian government was begging for assistance in saving lives on the Mediterranean.

That is to say that, given the failure of the French state to pursue a persistently just policy in relation to asylum, resistance remains the principal hope for such a just politics, as enacted by activists such as Cedric Herrou, who was criminally charged for assisting migrants. Resistance is that which others the world, which as Jacqueline Rose puts it, apropos of the struggle against the Nazis, such moments 'tell us that anything is possible in conditions where mostly nothing was'.[125] That such acts are possible in extremis, let alone in the comfortable conditions of a state's ability to proffer aid, even somewhat exorbitant aid, to those who need it. However it is also a matter, in psychoanalytic terms, of overcoming resistance, of finding the 'path to freedom' which recognizes the constitutive nature of self-difference that points to the acknowledgement of difference itself, the path out of fascism and the violence of the One. The long civil war from 1789 to 1940 of which Vicki Caron writes, ended in victory for zombie-fascism (Badiou's 'transcendental Petainism') and the disaster of the Shoah as it unfolded in France. It cannot be said, following the pronouncements of politicians of both left and right concerning France's inability to take in 'all the wretched poverty of the world' – nonsensical hyperbole – that lessons have been learnt. Herrou invoked the principle of 'fraternité' of the Republic in his defence, which Levinas also held to be fundamental to a just politics (despite the problematic masculine terminology, a blind spot for him); politics is from the beginning a solidarity with others. The Constitutional Council which dismissed the charges against Herrou found that the motto of 'fraternité' as included in the French Constitution trumped the statute criminalizing assistance to migrants.[126] However, this is no more than the patina of decency that the law is – sometimes – able to provide in curtailing the worst actions of the state.

One set of responses would be to appeal to a new model of politics, based upon struggle, upon local democracy, upon 'newly created territorial entities' founded beyond nationalisms and state sovereignty, formed from unchosen plural human groups who find mutually accommodating modes of cohabitation. The emphasis can shift from the state to cities, or regions, or federations, and from the imaginary scarcity of capitalist societies to a solidarity amongst the '99%' where it is not a question of resources but of distribution. But an *ethos* of responsibility for persons seeking asylum is not delimited to any particular form of the political, and to be truly responsible, must be operative in any given political context. There would be a certain irresponsibility in a theoretical call for a simple move beyond states, whose hegemony is being reinforced and expanded worldwide. Local acts of resistance and solidarity may be too limited to address the scope of the problem, which can be better met at the level of state power. While many individuals and organizations worked to save refugees during the disaster – Moriz Scheyer refers in his memoir to the 'miracle of goodness'[127] – Arendt cautioned against the 'unpredictable hazards of friendship and sympathy, or by the great and incalculable grace of love',[128] which were insufficient materials with which to guarantee human dignity. A political guarantee is required, beyond struggles which can also be named as political, but which lack the authority and power for their effective realization.

Consequently, an *ethos* of responsibility must pertain also to the sovereign state. In *The Future of an Illusion*, Freud refers to the notion of a culture having an ideal of itself being based on a narcissistic pride in its achievements, which are then compared to the achievements of other cultures.[129] Arendt observed that to the Ancient Greeks, great deeds were as real as physical things, were alive and vibrant in the life of the polis and gave it meaning.[130] What is the political identity of a state that should be appealed to? Perhaps it is a matter, in Derrida's phrase, of 'choosing one's heritage'. Derrida refers to Europe in

The Other Heading in the guise of exemplarity: 'The idea of an advanced point of exemplarity is the idea of the European idea',[131] and that '[. . .] it is necessary to make ourselves the guardians of an idea of Europe, of a difference of Europe, but of a Europe that consists precisely in not closing itself off in its own identity and in advancing itself in an exemplary way toward what it is not'.[132] In France, a self-image as a hospitable nation has often conflicted with the realities and pressures of responding to refugees, and with reactionary policies and rhetoric. The tradition of France around asylum has been a civil war between two competing traditions, the radically open and the violently closed, and the struggle continues; from the horrors of the 1930s to the occupation of the Church of St Bernard in the 1990s to the Calais 'Jungle' in the mid-2000 teens to the recent occupation of the Pantheon by stateless persons, the realization of a *terre d'asile* for all who need it remains to come.

What then is the value of such cultural ideals? The appeal to a political formalization of a right to asylum at the level of the state remains fecund in thinking through the stakes of an *ethos of responsibility*. It is to instantiate within the state something beyond the state, a principle transcending the state that informs the sense of *Fraternité* as Levinas understood it, a criterion against which politics can be judged:

> Should not the fraternity that is in the motto of the republic be discerned in the prior non-indifference of one for the other, in that original goodness in which freedom is embedded, and in which the justice of the rights of man takes on an immutable significance and stability, better than those guaranteed by the state?[133]

Just as Robespierre thought that the people should be subject to justice, this is precisely in alignment with Levinas's statement: 'It is the responsibility for the other that determines the legitimacy of the state, that is, its justice.'[134] While there are international agreements, agencies, and laws that relate to stateless persons, nevertheless much of the effective operation of asylum occurs at the level of the state, and thus asylum continues to need to be thought in relation to the state for that thought to be a responsible engagement. Indeed, despite the violence of state borders, state sovereignty need not always be seen in a negative light in regard to asylum. Towards the end of *Rogues*, Derrida offers a justification for a certain privileging of the state:

> Nation-state sovereignty can even itself, in certain conditions, become an indispensable bulwark against certain international powers, certain ideological, religious, or capitalist, indeed linguistic, hegemonies that, under the cover of liberalism or universalism, would still represent, in a world that would be little more than a marketplace, a rationalisation in the service of particular interests

. . . responsibility would consist in orienting oneself without any *determinative* knowledge of the rule.[135]

The right to have rights is pointless if political communities, especially sovereign states, will not respect them, and will remain a utopian cry to the extent that other forms of political community do not gain hegemony. What then stands in the way of sovereign states respecting the right to have rights? As seen in previous chapters and again here, the problem of numbers is often advanced as a limit upon the right to asylum. As an asylum response, an *ethos* of responsibility would represent a move beyond humanitarianism, which has a proud tradition in France – as Didier Fassin observes, despite this tradition, and the founding of many leading humanitarian organizations in France, a rupture is observable in the French (and American) responses to the Haitian earthquake, where some very generous humanitarian efforts were also attended by very low admission of Haitian asylum seekers.[136] It is perhaps symbolically ironic that during the refugee 'crisis' in Europe from 2015 onwards, France's neighbour, Germany, enacted a version of expansive hospitality that goes some way towards what has been discussed as possible above – admitting one million refugees or more in 2015 alone. Yet this is dwarfed by the responsibility already engaged by states in the Middle East such as Lebanon, where one in four residents are refugees, produced partly by the violence of imperial invasions and settler-colonialism.[137] (It should not be forgotten that Syria itself, despite 50% of its population being forced to flee following the recent conflict, was from the nineteenth century on a great state of asylum and refuge for many different peoples; France is not alone in having such a tradition, though perhaps alone in having the most explicit articulation of it – as has been seen, with this articulation having mixed efficacy when put under pressure.)[138] Subsequent to this decision by Merkel, Germany struck a deal with Turkey designed to limit the continued flow of Syrian asylum seekers into Europe, thus the laudable nature of this gesture has its limits.[60] But Germany's initial gesture tilts – and not necessarily in Quixotic fashion – at the possibility of the impossible discussed in this chapter, the possibility that states, especially powerful and wealthy states, can negotiate the limits of welcome in an expansive modality without coming to harm, and indeed attracting benefits to themselves. That is to say that the seemingly impossible – to take in 'all the wretched poverty of the World', and not only the poor but the politically vulnerable – those without the rights afforded by citizenship – can be broached as *possible*. Whether one wealthy nation alone could do it, the extreme example given in this chapter, will probably never be established[61] – but once the numbers were divided over a greater number of states, say all of the members of the OECD – wealthy and relatively stable states – the total number of arrivants for each would be significantly diminished, and the problem of the guarantee of human dignity for all the stateless of the world could be comprehensively addressed. But such a gesture requires a modality of politics that recognizes hospitality as a kind of allowing, a mode of justice that informs by a grace that precedes it. Noam Chomsky has written recently of the refugee crisis, indicating that he believes powerful states could 'easily accommodate' the numbers of refugees requiring safe-haven, 'but the reaction of the states is a moral disgrace, even putting aside their considerable responsibility for the circumstances that have compelled people to flee for their lives'.[139]

In 'We Refugees', Arendt writes that 'the comity of European peoples went to pieces when, and because, it allowed its weakest member to be excluded and persecuted'.[140] The novel force of this argument is its inversion of political risk – the risk was not the admission, but rather the exclusion of refugees, and the failure to do so attended the fall of political regimes and the disaster of the deportations.[141] The violation of unchosen plurality, the precondition and mediating factor of all politics, is the undoing of politics, not only morally but in this case, literally (the collapse of the tremulous French Third Republic and more generally, European 'comity'). In any case, a security dependent upon the death and suffering of others is indefensible. In this context, what is compelling in the idealism of Robespierre and the Jacobinist constitution of 1793 is the appeal to universality; Frenchness equals humanity as such (less the tyrants!). Nationalism in this guise is always-already internationalism. One answer might be a move beyond the sovereign state, yet as noted above, the European Union has in recent times been equally as guilty of exclusion as the French state of the 1930s was. Having federated entities has not changed this equation; whether a state, or a federation, or a local community, what matters is the delimitation of nationalist and particularist claims to membership owing to the respect due to plurality as the 'law of the earth'; which is to say, the Montesquieu-ian principle or 'spirit' in which the laws of a society move.

Subsequent to writing *The Last of the Just*, André Schwarz-Bart, after a long hiatus, took up writing once more, but moved beyond the confines of Europe to a more universal portrait of resistance to oppression. France was not the answer, despite the wrenching hopefulness of those few pages of his first novel; Schwarz-Bart will ultimately gesture towards a tradition of the oppressed that traverses national cultures and becomes a universal remembrance of the victims of history. It is this notion of a universal history of the victims and the disappeared that must now be articulated, as the normative 'ghost in the machine' of an *ethos* of responsibility, where unchosen plurality and responsibility pertain not just to the living but to the dead and to those not yet born, of disasters past, disasters unfolding, and disasters to come.

NOTES

1. Sudhir Hazareesingh, *How the French Think: An Affectionate Portrait of an Intellectual People* (New York, NY: Basic Books, 2015), p. 6.

2. Vicki Caron, *Uneasy Asylum: France and the Jewish Refugee Crisis, 1933–1942* (Stanford, CA: Stanford University Press, 1999), p. 202.

3. Gershom Scholem notes that Schwarz-Bart alters the legend of the Just Men, which does not refer in Jewish tradition to any family lineage; the Just Men are usually anonymous, unknown to others and even themselves. See the essay 'The Tradition of the Thirty-Six Hidden Just Men' in Gershom Scholem, *The Messianic Idea in Judaism and Other Essays on Jewish Spirituality* (New York, NY: Schocken, 1995). One should also note that they are also, at least traditionally as well as in Schwartz-Bart's rendering, all men, though in the short story 'Valaida' by John Edgar Wideman, whom Kathleen Gyssels argues was heavily influenced by Schwarz-Bart, the Lamed-Vav is a Black woman, bringing the different experiences of oppressed groups into proximity. I explore this theme more fully in the concluding chapter. See Kathleen Gyssels, 'A Shoah Classic Resurfacing: The Strange Destiny of The Last of the Just (André Schwarz-Bart) in the African Disapora', *Prooftexts*, Vol. 31, 2011, pp. 229–62.

4. Schwarz-Bart, *The Last of the Just*, pp. 150–51.

5. Walter Benjamin, 'Central Park', in *Walter Benjamin: Selected Writings 1938–1940*, eds. Howard Eiland and Michael W. Jennings (Cambridge, MA: Harvard University Press, 2003), p. 185.

6. Avinoam Patt, 'No Place for the Displaced: The Jewish Refugee Crisis', in *Refugee Policies from 1933 until Today: Challenges and Responsibilities*, eds. Steven T. Katz and Julian Wetzel (Metropol: Berlin, 2018), p. 104. A publication of the International Holocaust Remembrance Alliance.

7. I take this syntagm from the work of Andrew Benjamin. A 'caesura of allowing' can be understood as a form of interruption that occasions the othering of a human world concerned with being-in-common and being-in-place, that allows for the inter-articulation of justice and the law where 'what it occasions is a sense of commonality'. In other words, in the Schwarz-Bart narrative, it is the allowing qua belonging, of a placedness and a being-in-common that is accomplished, albeit temporarily, by the asylum granted to this refugee family. See Benjamin, *Place, Commonality and Judgment*, pp. 5–6 and 19–20. This syntagm also figures throughout many of his other works concerned with the establishment of a philosophical anthropology and his writings on Walter Benjamin, as discussed in chapter 1.

8. Schwarz-Bart, *The Last of the Just*, p. 278.

9. Schwarz-Bart, *The Last of the Just*, pp. 278–79.

10. Caron, *Uneasy Asylum*, p. 2.

11. See the interview at: https://www.versobooks.com/blogs/3156-revolution-still-the-stuff-of-dreams-a-conversation-with-sophie-wahnich, retrieved 16 November 2019.

12. Karl Marx, 'On the Jewish Question', in *Karl Marx: Selected Writings*, ed. Lawrence H. Simon (Indianapolis, IN and Cambridge: Hackett Publishing Company Inc., 1994), pp. 1–26.

13. Karl Dietrich Bracher, *The German Dictatorship* (Fort Worth: Holt, Reinhart, 1970), p. 10.

14. Rachel Bowlby, trans., *Questioning Judaism: Interviews by Elisabeth Weber* (Stanford, CA: Stanford University Press, 2004), p. 1.

15. Shanti Marie Singham, 'Betwixt Cattle and Men: Jews, Blacks, and Women, and the Declaration of the Rights of Man', in *The French Idea of Freedom: The Old Regime and the Declaration of Rights of 1789*, ed. Dale Van Kley (Stanford, CA: Stanford University Press, 1994), pp. 122–23.

16. See Maurice Samuels, 'The Emperor and the Jews', *Judaism*, New York, NY, Vol. 54, No. 1/2, Winter 2005, note 5. I thank Suzanne Hampel for bringing this to my attention.

17. Primo Levi, *The Complete Works of Primo Levi*, Vol. 2, ed. Ann Goldstein (New York, NY and London: Liveright, 2015), p. 1271.

18. Alain Badiou, *The Meaning of Sarkozy*, trans. David Fernbach (London and New York, NY: Verso, 2008), pp. 2–3.

19. Badiou, *The Meaning of Sarkozy*, p. 16.

20. Alain Badiou, 'Questions of Method', in *Greece and the Re-Invention of Politics*, trans. David Broders (London and New York, NY: Verso, 2013), p. 5.

21. Alain Badiou and Alain Finkielraut, *Confrontation: A Conversation with Aude Lancelin*, trans. Susan Spitzer (Cambridge: Polity, 2014), pp. 4–5.

22. Caron, *Uneasy Asylum*, especially chapters 1 and 2, and passim.

23. Frantz Fanon, *The Wretched of the Earth* (London: Penguin, 1990), p. 251.

24. C. L. R. James, *The Black Jacobins: Toussaint L'Ouverture and the San Domingo Revolution*, 2nd edition (New York, NY: Vintage, 1989), p. 374.

25. For a fascinating defence, see Sophie Wahnich, *In Defence of the Terror* (London and New York, NY: Verso, 2015).

26. Lucas Kowalczyk and Mila Versteeg, 'The Political Economy of the Constitutional Right to Asylum', *Cornell Law Review*, Vol. 102, No. 5, July 2017, pp. 1261–62. The first state to enshrine a right to asylum in their constitution that went into effect was Colombia in 1811.

27. See Angeliki Tzanetou, *City of Suppliants: Tragedy and the Athenian Empire* (Austin, TX: University of Texas Press, 2012).

28. Jacques Derrida and Elisabeth Roundinesco, *Of What Tomorrow . . . A Dialogue*, trans. Jeff Fort (Stanford, CA: Stanford University Press, 2004), p. 5. Although I do not have room for an extended biographical reading in this chapter, it is of note that the disaster of Nazism personally affected the three primary thinkers of this book – Arendt, Levinas, and Derrida – personally. Arendt fled from Germany to France, then had to flee again to avoid capture by the Nazis, escaping from Gurs concentration camp, ultimately taking a boat from Portugal to the United States; Levinas was interned as a Jewish French prisoner of war in a work camp (i.e. he was separated from other French soldiers as a Jewish person but was protected by his military personnel status from deportation); Derrida was thrown out of school on the antisemitic orders of the Vichy authorities in Algeria. Derrida often noted that while Germans never set foot in Algeria, the Vichy French authorities carried out antisemitic actions

all the same, and revoked the 1870 Crémieux Decree which had naturalized Jewish residents of Algeria as citizens.

29. Caron, *Uneasy Asylum*, p. 362.

30. Caron, *Uneasy Asylum*, p. 363.

31. Michael R. Marrus and Robert O. Paxton, *Vichy France and the Jews* (New York, NY: Basic Books Inc., 1981), p. 343.

32. Peter McPhee, *Liberty or Death: The French Revolution* (New Haven, CT and London: Yale University Press, 2016), p. 103.

33. Greg Burgess, *Refuge In the Land of Liberty: France and its Refugees, from the Revolution to the End of Asylum, 1789–1939* (Hampshire and New York, NY: Palgrave Macmillan, 2008), p. 1.

34. Burgess, *Refuge In the Land of Liberty*, p. 4.

35. Kant, 'The Philosophy Faculty', p. 153.

36. Slavoj Žižek, *Slavoj Žižek Presents Robespierre: Virtue and Terror* intro. Slavoj Žižek, text selection and annotation Jean Ducange, and trans. John Howe (London and New York, NY: Verso, 2007), p. 93.

37. McPhee, *Liberty or Death*, p. 102.

38. Hazareesingh, *How the French Think*, chapter 1.

39. Peter McPhee, *Robespierre: A Revolutionary Life* (New Haven, CT and London: Yale University Press, 2012), p. 92. See also p. 150 – when Robespierre published his own draft Declaration, it was a restatement of his internationalism and universalism.

40. Žižek, *Slavoj Žižek Presents Robespierre*, p. 47.

41. Žižek, *Slavoj Žižek Presents Robespierre*, p. 68.

42. Text of the 1793 Constitution can be found at https://chnm.gmu.edu/revolution/d/430/, retrieved 8 January 2020. It should be noted that while the constitution was adopted it was never implemented and its radical proposals were not actualized.

43. Alain Badiou and Alain Finkielkraut, *Confrontation* (Cambridge and Malden, MA: Polity Press, 2014), p. 8.

44. https://revolution.chnm.org/d/430/, retrieved 20 January 2021.

45. Burgess, *Refuge in the Land of Liberty*, p. 143.

46. Burgess, *Refuge in the Land of Liberty*, p. 143.

47. McPhee, *Robespierre: A Revolutionary Life*, pp. 172–173.

48. James, *The Black Jacobins*, p. 77. James further notes that Robespierre made an 'ass' of himself on this point (p. 116).

49. Singham, *The French Idea of Freedom*, pp. 122–23.

50. Wahnich, *In Defence of the Terror*, pp. 8–9.

51. Wahnich, *In Defence of the Terror*, pp. 12–13.

52. See Rancière, 'Who is the Subject of the Rights of Man?', pp. 297–310, as well as Rancière, *Hatred of Democracy*; and Balibar, 'Man and Citizen', pp. 99–114. Rancière in 'Who is the Subject', p. 307: 'I think that we had rather leave the ontological destiny of the human animal aside if we want to understand who is the subject of the Rights of Man and to rethink politics today'. Balibar, 'Man and Citizen', p. 105: 'Equaliberty' means that 'the *basic right of man* . . . is *a right to politics*'. And: 'We may say that the identification of liberty and equality is the internal prerequisite

of the universal identification of man and citizen. A man is a citizen if and only if liberty and equality become identified. Therefore a man is a citizen inasmuch as liberty equals equality'. Thus, the solutions offered by Rancière and Balibar emphasize the political character of rights, not the ontological precondition of human plurality or a Levinasian account of the dignity of human beings via the perception of their vulnerability qua the epiphany of the face, the 'precarity' (Butler) of human life. This is a consistent tendency in many political theorists and is a central point being opposed in the present argument.

53. Scheyer, *Asylum*, p. 20.
54. Scheyer, *Asylum*, p. 74.
55. Caron, *Uneasy Asylum*, pp. 1–2.
56. Caron, *Uneasy Asylum*, p. 123.
57. Caron, *Uneasy Asylum*, p. 209.
58. Caron, *Uneasy Asylum*, p. 5.
59. Burgess, *Refuge in the Land of Liberty*, p. 214.
60. Caron, *Uneasy Asylum*, p. 338.
61. Caron, *Uneasy Asylum*, p. 339.
62. Burgess, *Refuge in the Land of Liberty*, p. 166.
63. Hannah Arendt, 'We Refugees', in *The Jewish Writings*, ed. Jerome Kohn (New York, NY: Schocken, 2007), p. 270.
64. Caron, *Uneasy Asylum*, pp. 354–55.
65. Caron, *Uneasy Asylum*, p. 50.
66. Caron, *Uneasy Asylum*, p. 50.
67. Caron, *Uneasy Asylum*, p. 22.
68. Caron, *Uneasy Asylum*, p. 23.
69. Caron, *Uneasy Asylum*, pp. 215–16.
70. Caron, *Uneasy Asylum*, p. 26.
71. Caron, *Uneasy Asylum*, p. 49.
72. Caron, *Uneasy Asylum*, p. 307.
73. Caron, *Uneasy Asylum*, p. 212.
74. Levinas, *Otherwise Than Being*, p. 74.
75. Ernst Renan, *Qu'est-ce qu'une nation?* (Paris: Presses-Pocket, 1992).
76. Burgess, *Refuge in the Land of Liberty*, p. 217.
77. Andrew Jacob, 'An Alternate Nationalism: A Comparative Study of D.R. Ambedkar and E. Renan', in *Beyond Imagined Uniqueness: Nationalisms in Contemporary Perspectives*, eds. Joan Burbick and William Glass (Newcastle: Cambridge Scholars Publishing, 2010), p. 134.
78. Quoted in Jacques Derrida, *On Cosmopolitanism and Forgiveness*, trans. Mark Dooley and Michael Hughes, Preface Simon Critchley and Richard Kearney (London and New York, NY: Routledge, 2001), p. 36.
79. Michael R. Marrus, 'Vichy Before Vichy: Antisemtic Currents in France During the 1930's', *Wiener Library Bulletin*, Vol. 33, No. 51/52, 1980, pp. 13–19.
80. 'The Principle of Hospitality', in Jacques Derrida, *Paper Machine*, trans. Rachel Bowlby (Stanford, CA: Stanford University Press, 2005), pp. 68–69.

81. Judith Still, *Derrida and Hospitality: Theory and Practice* (Edinburgh: Edinburgh University Press, 2013), p. 10.

82. Anne Dufourmantelle and Jacques Derrida, *Of Hospitality: Ann Dufourmantelle Invites Jacques Derrida to Respond*, trans. Rachel Bowlby (Stanford, CA: Stanford University Press, 2000), p. 77.

83. Derrida, *Paper Machine*, p. 69.

84. https://www.liberation.fr/societe/2009/09/29/la-misere-du-monde-ni-tronque e-ni-mutilee_584555, retrieved 29 January 2020.

85. Even where an intervention seems laudable, as in Mali in 2013, this must be seen in the context of the destabilizing impacts in the region of the 2011 Libyan intervention in which France took part. See the debate at https://www.aljazeera.com /programmes/headtohead/2015/03/transcript-bernard-kouchner-150331163703721. html, retrieved 29 January 2020.

86. https://www.newstatesman.com/world/europe/2018/01/macron-s-visit-calais -shines-light-his-theresa-may-immigration-policies, retrieved 24 February 2020.

87. Caron, *Uneasy Asylum*, p. 50.

88. Jacques Derrida, *Resistances of Psychoanalysis*, trans. Peggy Kamuf, Pascale-Anne Brault, and Michael Naas (Stanford, CA: Stanford University Press, 1998), p. 2.

89. Jacqueline Rose, *The Last Resistance* (London and New York, NY: Verso, 2017), p. 21.

90. Edward Said, *Freud and the Non-European* (London and New York, NY: Verso, 2003), p. 60.

91. Rose, *The Last Resistance*, p. 35.

92. Rose, *The Last Resistance*, pp. 7 and 29–30.

93. Rose, *The Last Resistance*, p. 21.

94. Jacques Derrida, *Archive Fever: A Freudian Impression*, trans. Eric Prenowitz (Chicago, IL and London: University of Chicago Press, 1998), p. 78.

95. Said, *Freud and the Non-European*, p. 55.

96. Said, *Freud and the Non-European*, p. 8.

97. Rose, *The Last Resistance*, p. 8.

98. Rose, *The Last Resistance*, p. 13.

99. Rose, *The Last Resistance*, pp. 29–31.

100. Derrida, *Resistances of Psychoanalysis*, p. 23.

101. Derrida, *Resistances of Psychoanalysis*, pp. 18–20.

102. Derrida, *Resistances of Psychoanalysis*, especially pp. 31–32.

103. Bonnie Honig, *Democracy and the Foreigner* (Princeton, NJ: Princeton University Press, 2001), p. 6.

104. Jacques Derrida, *Rogues: Two Essays on Reason*, trans. Pascale-Anne Brault and Michael Naas (Stanford, CA: Stanford University Press, 2005), p. 148.

105. Derrida, *Rogues*, p. 149.

106. Derrida, *Rogues*, p. 150.

107. This thesis has been denied, for example, by Martin Hägglund in *Radical Athiesm: Derrida and the Time of Life*. Hägglund attempts to 'disjoin' (his word) these thinkers, favouring Derrida, despite the multiple affirmative statements and

declared fidelities between these thinkers: Derrida once observed that he was ready to subscribe to everything in Levinas's work, even if he posed deconstructive questions to that work.

108. The total number of displaced people in the world is about 70 million, and the population of France is between 65 and 70 million. See the UNHCR 2018 Global Trends Report, https://www.unhcr.org/5d08d7ee7.pdf, accessed 28 January 2020. France's population can be obtained from multiple sources such as the World Bank; figures vary slightly but are within the range noted here.

109. See Žižek's foreword to Wahnich, *In Defence of the Terror*, p. xv.

110. Nicole Loraux, *Born of the Earth: Myth & Politics in Athens*, trans. Selina Stewart (Ithaca, NY and London: Cornell University Press, 2000), p. 128.

111. Loraux, *Born of the Earth*, pp. 133 and 138.

112. Levinas, *Totality and Infinity*, p. 110.

113. Agnes Heller, *The Theory of Need in Marx* (London and New York, NY: Verso, 2018).

114. J. Derrida, *Of Hospitality: Anne Dufourmantelle Invites Jacques Derrida to Respond* (Stanford, CA: Stanford University Press, 2000), p. 55. See also J. Derrida, 'Hostipitality', *Angelaki: Journal of the Theoretical Humanities*, Vol. 5, No. 3, December 2000.

115. http://www.etymonline.com/index.php?term=economy, retrieved, 9 January 2020.

116. Aristotle, *The Politics* (London: Penguin, 1981), 1252a7, p. 54.

117. Richard Kearney, *Questioning Ethics: Contemporary Debates in Continental Philosophy* (London and New York, NY: Routledge, 1999), p. 66.

118. Simon Critchley, *The Ethics of Deconstruction: Derrida and Levinas*, 2nd edition (Edinburgh: Edinburgh University Press, 1999), p. 275.

119. Levinas, *Otherwise Than Being*, p. 159.

120. Derrida, 'Hostipitality', p. 15. For a sustained critique of Derrida's use of impossibility as the necessary experience of the interplay of the conditioned and the unconditioned, see the final chapter of Andrew Benjamin's *Virtue in Being*.

121. Jacques Derrida and Elisabeth Roundinesco, *For What Tomorrow . . . A Dialogue*, trans. Jeff Fort (Stanford, CA: Stanford University Press, 2004), p. 59.

122. Derrida and Roundinesco, *For What Tomorrow*, p. 92.

123. Thomas Paine, ed. Moncure D. Conway, *The Writings of Thomas Paine*, Vol. 3, 1895, pp. 94–95.

124. https://www.versobooks.com/blogs/3156-revolution-still-the-stuff-of-dr eams-a-conversation-with-sophie-wahnich, retrieved 6 January 2020.

125. Rose, *The Last Resistance*, p. 3.

126. https://www.nytimes.com/2018/07/06/world/europe/france-migrants-farmer -fraternity.html, retrieved 29 January 2020.

127. Scheyer, *Asylum*, p. 29.

128. Arendt, *The Origins of Totalitarianism*, p. 301.

129. Sigmund Freud, *The Future of an Illusion*, trans. J. A. Underwood and Shaun Whiteside (London: Penguin, 2008), p. 12.

130. Hannah Arendt, *Lectures on Kant's Political Philosophy*, ed. Ronald Beiner (Chicago, IL: University of Chicago Press, 1992), p. 110. See also Arendt, *The Human Condition*, p. 198.

131. Jacques Derrida, 'The Other Heading: Memories, Responses, and Responsibilities', in *The Other Heading: Reflections on Today's Europe* (Bloomington, IN and Indianapolis, IN: Indiana University Press, 1992), p. 24.

132. Derrida, *The Other Heading*, p. 29.

133. Levinas, 'The Rights of Man', p. 125.

134. 'Apropos of Buber: Some Notes', in *Outside the Subject*, p. 45.

135. Derrida, *Rogues*, p. 158.

136. Didier Fassin, *Humanitarian Reason: A Moral History of the Present*, trans. Rachel Gomme (Berkley, CA, Los Angeles, CA, and London: University of California Press, 2012), pp. xi–xii.

137. Chomsky, *Who Rules the World?*, pp. 251–52.

138. On Syria's tradition of asylum, see Dawn Chatty's history in *Syria: The Making and Unmaking of a Refuge State* (Oxford: Oxford University Press, 2017).

139. See https://chomsky.info/05052016/, retrieved 9 January 2020.

140. Arendt, *The Jewish Writings*, p. 274.

141. However, it is contradicted by her own declaration in Arendt, *Origins of Totalitarianism* (quoted in Chapter One) that the ever-increasing numbers of refugees 'threaten our political life'.

Coda

Politics of Hauntology/Of Missing Persons

We tell the story of the cabin boy who came back, we do not tell the stories of the ninety-nine sailors who drowned.

– Umberto Eco

From out of this landscape two figures emerge, those of the ghost and the child – the only witnesses at the end.

– Jean Birnbaum, introduction
to *Learning to Live Finally*

The war, the children missing Lord, it's almost like the blues.

– Leonard Cohen

LES ENFANTS D'IZIEU

Izieu is one of the most beautiful places I have ever seen. It is a tiny hamlet gathered around a crystal blue lake, nestled in a valley in the hills of south-eastern France, the snow-capped Alps forming a glorious backdrop to the peaceful, even idyllic landscape. And yet experiencing these lovely environs only confirmed for me the truth of Adorno's dictum that 'even the blossoming tree lies the moment its bloom is seen without the shadow of terror'.[1] For I had been inspired to make a pilgrimage of a kind to Izieu – train from Paris to Lyon, train from Lyon to a small town named Tour-du-Pin, and from there a long taxi ride deep into the countryside – in order to pay my respects to a group of forty-four Jewish children who were deliberately disappeared from the earth by the Nazis. I became aware of this microcosm of the Shoah because of a documentary called *Hotel Terminus*, directed by Marcel Ophuls (who had himself been a Jewish child refugee who fled with his family from the Nazis during the war). This film, so named for the hotel in Lyon that the Gestapo had commandeered as their headquarters during the Occupation, examines the crimes, flight into exile, arrest and trial of Klaus Barbie, a Gestapo agent who had operated in occupied Lyon; infamously, he captured and tortured to death the head of the Resistance, Jean Moulin. Even more infamously, it was in Izieu in April 1944 that Barbie rounded up forty-four Jewish children, who were a mix of French citizens and refugees from other European states, and who were in hiding from deportation, far from home and from their parents. Barbie went a great deal out of his way to find these children (Izieu is a small and remote place, not a major population centre, which itself is a telling sign of the absolutism of the Nazis' murderous drive to pursue that insane war-within-the-war, the Final Solution, at a time when the other war had already turned against the Nazis and D-Day was imminent); he spared no effort to find them and was successful. Consequently, all of them were murdered in Auschwitz, along with several adults deported with them.

Previously, I had had the good fortune to study on scholarship in Paris, and had been struck during my strolls through the city by the plaques that adorn the walls of so many schools within the *Périphérique*: so-and-so number of children were deported on this date in Nineteen-Forty-x; doubly jarring when from within the walls of those same schools that I would pass, the happy screams of the children at play would issue forth. Were there other screams, I wondered, when the end came for the children memorialized on the wall; or was it more like as depicted in Louis Malle's masterpiece, *Au Revoir Les Enfants*, when the arrest of the Jewish children happens mostly in a chilled silence, broken only by the barked commands of the Gestapo agent, and the few brief '*au revoirs*', before the final shot lingers on the empty doorway through which the deportees have passed. (Malle's voiceover comments that despite the passage of forty years, he has never forgotten the events of that January morning.)

After I had finished my tour of the memorial, I sat on the steps of the *Maison d'Izieu*, the boarding school where they had stayed, and looking down across that peaceful valley, I tried to conjure by hallucination the moment, in this gentlest of places, when the truck pulled up, and the Nazi soldiers and SS officers got out and started rounding up children – at one point they kicked a child hard in the stomach when he resisted, and violently threw another even younger child up into the truck (they also briefly detained one non-Jewish child, whom they released once it was established that he wasn't Jewish). I tried to imagine the faces of the forty-four children full of fear, driven to Montluc Prison in Lyon that night, then forced onto a series of trains ending in terminus Auschwitz, where one of the adults who accompanied them, the only survivor of the Izieu deportees, testified that the sky itself was blood red and seemed to be on fire, where all of the children without exception were exterminated, presumably immediately upon arrival, as was standard practice in the treatment of children in that hell.

The next day, once I had returned to Lyon from Izieu, I visited Montluc prison, where the children had been detained for a night prior to their onward journey to Auschwitz; following his capture in South America and extradition to France nearly forty years later, Klaus Barbie himself was briefly (and symbolically) returned to Montluc while awaiting trial. Later the same day I lingered on the steps of the Palais de Justice in Lyon and reflected on that trial – the first concerning crimes against humanity in the history of France – and the many issues it had raised. It was a highly controversial affair; Barbie's defenders, led by an (in)famous lawyer named Jacques Vergès, tried to put France itself in the dock by pointing out how the French had tortured in Algeria just as Barbie had done in Lyon, arguing that the horrors of its colonial crimes rendered it incapable of passing judgement on the old Nazi, a so-called 'rupture defence' strategy. That is, Vergès ranged horror against horror, victim against victim, and indicted the bourgeois French system's attempt to administer justice, in an effort to deliberately confuse matters and in the end to make it appear that the Nazi in the dock also belonged in the category of victims.[2] Finally, completing this idiosyncratic tour of unhappiness, in the twilight of dusk I walked to the Hotel Terminus itself, now operating under another name and doing business as usual. It is a large, 'grand' hotel built in a classic style, a beautiful old building. I sat under a tree opposite the hotel as the night descended, and looked up at the darkening façade, contemplating the time when the Gestapo were using it as their base, and people were being dragged across the lobby to an unknown fate. As I sat there across the way, two children, a girl and a boy, came bouncing along the footpath in front of their parents and bundled happily through the entrance into the foyer; and I thought about those other children, and that other time, while the street lights came up and the sun went down on the dark hotel.

THE DISAPPEARED

The children of Izieu are disappeared, gone from the earth. The Second World War and its final living protagonists will soon pass into history, and their story will belong to the past (notwithstanding Faulker's admonition that the past is never really past); those children could now be enjoying their old age, and the lives of their children and grandchildren. Yet they remain present in other ways, to the extent that neo-Nazis recently attacked the memorial that was erected in Lyon to their memory[3] – the 'despoiling of graveyards' being the essence of antisemitism, according to Adorno and Horkheimer,[4] or, as Walter Benjamin similarly put it, even the dead will not be safe if the enemy is victorious; even dead children will be symbolically exhumed and destroyed once more, or perhaps over and over again; or be re-destroyed by another route, by the oblivion of forgetting or the ignoring of their memory.[5] And yet despite the unassimilable nature of the horror of the story of the children of Izieu, one is struck when watching *Hotel Terminus*, by the attitudes of so many interviewees who think such crimes should be let go with the passage of time, that the criminal should not be punished, despite the fact that those children never had the chance to live the duration of the time that was their due. (Indeed, it is this question of justice across time, its realization or failure, that captivated me most upon seeing the film.) It seems that those who inhabit the present are often far too content with it and do not perceive the ghosts all around them; but it is possible to object to such people that forgiving and forgetting, and the natural amnesia that attends the passage of time, are, as Jean Améry thought, crimes against justice, and require a counter-resentment that refuses to let go of the indignation provoked by the crime and which demands, impossibly, the annulment of time itself.[6]

One could think that the deliberate hunting down and extermination of children is morally the bottom of the pit – or the revelation that in fact, there is no bottom. Yet the killing of children is a fact of political practice in every Western democracy today, and other polities besides, the only distinction being that of a neglectful letting die as opposed to an active putting to death, an evil of omission rather than commission (though sometimes that too), of thoughtlessness or worse, knowing indifference. For the fact is that there is a global undeclared war on children, from the multiple children who have died in Customs and Border Protection custody[7] (a record 70,000 migrant children have been detained in the United States)[8] to the children separated from their parents at the border in the United States (including an infant aged four months),[9] to the neglect of children in ICE facilities – 4 toddlers so ill and neglected that lawyers forced the government to hospitalize them,[10] to the 1-year-olds (70 of them) having to attend U.S. deportation hearings (1 three year old climbed up onto the table during her hearing),[11] to the school bus blown up in Yemen by a missile that was sold by the United States and fired by Saudi Arabia,[12] to the children in the Calais 'jungle' who were both harassed and neglected by French authorities and whom the UK refused to admit under the Dubs Amendment,[13] to the children in the Congo forced to dig up precious metals for Western smartphones at gunpoint by militiamen,[14] to the child soldiers in Nigeria,[15] to the children sold into sex slavery in South-East Asia,[16] to the two-year-old girl in Australian detention who was denied a birthday cake by authorities,[17] to the five year old in Australia who faced deportation because of a mild disability (god forbid that someone who needs help becomes a 'public charge!'),[18] to the thousands of unaccompanied minors driven into terrifying exile on their own,[19] to the huge mental health crisis amongst Rohingya child refugees,[20] to the drowned Alan Kurdi whose image provoked sympathy for the briefest of moments,[21] to the children denied asylum on the spurious ground that they could contract or spread Covid-19,[22] and all those other suffering and disappeared, the global diaspora of children who are invisible to the world, who do not appear at all, even to be lamented or grieved.

Contrary to Derrida's advice in *The Post Card* that the child should never be made into a symbol, children are an unapologetic focus here, in their utter vulnerability, which serves to underscore the true horror and moral bankruptcy of the age and bring it into stark relief.[23] Derrida will go rhetorically much further in the same text: '*doom*, always to prefer the child. The child in itself, in oneself'.[24] [!!] As will be made clear, it is not a matter of 'always'; yet the destruction of children most dramatically emphasizes the erasure of unrealized possibilities which every disappeared child represents, that never had even the minimal chance to actualize themselves – such a focus on children represents, to borrow Henry James' phrase, an additional 'turn of the screw'. In the Foreword to *French Children of the Holocaust*, the memorial book compiled by Serge Klarsfeld that documents all of the deported children (and is an enormous book of nearly two thousand pages, which resists the oblivion of forgetting by restoring to posterity the names, faces, and facts about their deportation of each child), Peter Hellman puzzles over why the Klarsfelds have always emphasized the children, when one day suddenly:

> I had my answer, its full force coming at an unexpected moment that recalled what Magda Bogin, who translated some of these pages, has referred to as our 'inter-changeability' with the victims. It was on a summer day in Bar Harbor, Maine, where I was strolling with my three-year-old daughter. We were two tourists among many, gazing into shop windows. Thinking that she had her eye on me, I stepped into a shop for a moment which must have turned into two or three. Suddenly, I heard a shriek from the sidewalk. I dashed out to see my daughter's face filled with the fear of having been deserted in a strange town. At that instant, I had a flash of an image of her, separated from parents and uncomforted, first in the filth of Drancy, then in a boxcar on the way to Auschwitz: the actual fate of 11,000 children arrested in France. Then I understood, not with my intellect but with a father's protective instinct, why the Klarsfelds had always emphasized the children.[25]

The evocation of 'interchangeability' here recalls the Levinasian notion of 'substitution' – the putting of oneself in the place of the suffering other: 'The ipseity [self-hood], in the passivity without arche characteristic of identity, is a hostage. The word *I* means *here I am* [*me voici*], answering for everything and for everyone . . . I exist through the other and for the other, but without this being alienation . . . [a] "substitution", in which identity is inverted.'[26] (The documentary on Eva Mozes-Kor, the child twin who survived Auschwitz, and controversially forgave her torturer Joseph Mengele, intertwines that horrific past with her relatively benign present in a poignant way, cutting between scenes suddenly so the viewer appreciates that we are all substitutes for the past world that once inhabited our present; one might think also of Walter Benjamin's claim that the past 'flashes up' in the present.)[27] In *Tell Me How It Ends: An Essay in Forty Questions*, Valeria Luiselli recounts her experience of acting as translator for undocumented refugee children from Central America in the court system of New York City, and trying to explain to her own children the plight of the other children (the title borrowed from her child's question about their fates, and the questions she has to ask the refugee children in her work), wondering if her children could endure such difficult journeys.[28] This theme is further developed in her semi-fictional account of the same saga, *Lost Children Archive*, where in one very long and moving sentence lasting several pages, the stories of the children on holiday with their parents, who have gone missing, blends and merges into that of migrant children crossing the desert.[29] Substitution perhaps becomes an especial focus around children due to their vulnerability, whether related to us or not, a commonality of affect or instinct as well as the Levinasian view of the universal human experience of exposure to the vulnerable Face and the subject as hostage. And such a focus seems more urgent than ever in the context of asylum; for a new phenomenon has emerged, linked to the hopelessness experienced by predominantly child and adolescent refugees: 'resignation syndrome', where young people denied a normalization of their circumstances, that is, a permanent exile into stress, enter a coma-like state, and where the introduction of hope – a change in their asylum status – is positively linked to recovery.[30] These resigned children are missing persons in our very midst. This might recall 'Hurbinek', the tiny child in Primo Levi's *The Truce*, who struggles in his brief existence in the liberated camp to articulate words, but dies without language, without family, and without ever being able to actualize himself in life.[31] Is there a more poignant representation of the lost, silenced voice of the disappeared child than that of poor Hurbinek? But the world is now full of Hurbineks of various kinds. 'A child is being killed', as Blanchot discusses apropos of Serge Leclaire – as though the realization of the self, including the political self, depended upon the putting to death of the child: 'that in us which has not yet begun to speak and never will speak; but, more importantly, the marvellous (terrifying) child which we have been in the dreams and desires of those who were present at our birth (parents, society in general). Where is this child?'[32] Yet whereas for Leclaire the child put to death is within, now the murdered *infans* is also without; the realization of the political community depends upon the death drive aimed at the other that is not within oneself, politics realized as *politico-infanticide*, the murder or putting to death of children, deliberately, the denial of the right to *be* a child, to enjoy their childhood free of hellish trauma. Fealty to Moloch as the essence of the political.

And thus we are compelled to ponder the deliberate construction of an anti-world, or put differently, the destruction of a human world – that is, a world in Heidegger's sense, distinct from the earth, the world as a purposive shared work of human beings – in which the child is regularly brought face to face with the worst, to wonder with Lyotard 'if what is "proper" to humankind were to be inhabited by the inhuman?'[33] Yet focusing on the plight of children is fraught; as discussed in chapter 3 in relation to the reception of children and adolescents into the United Kingdom, who were attacked in the press for not 'looking like children'; the category of the child is not a guarantee of protection, is an unstable and potentially problematic descriptor. And yet, the parental protection of the child is paradigmatic of ethical responsibility, as argued by Hans Jonas: 'Here the plain being of a de facto existent imma-nently and evidently contains an ought for others, and would do so even if nature would not succor this ought with powerful instincts or assume its job alone . . . We shall find that its distinction lies in the unique relation between possession and non-possession of being, displayed by beginning life, which demands from its cause to continue what it has begun.'[34] Recall from chapter 1 Judith Butler's critique of the liberal autonomous subject, embodied in Robinson Crusoe, who was never a child and thus never dependent. As Serge Klarsfeld writes, 'In my eyes and in the eyes of many others, crimes against humanity are above all the crimes committed against innocents, those who threaten no one.'[35] The figure of the child, while fraught, is also a reminder of the inescapable mutual dependence and vulnerability that is proper to *all* human beings. The minimal decency, the incontrovertible imperative of a global human community that guards against the violation of the safety of children is far from having been realized, even though one must simultane-ously insist on not delimiting the imperative of safety as applicable to chil-dren alone. Thus, a certain dialectic can be posited around the figure of the child as paradigm of that which requires protection. And yet can one deny the evocative power of children in images (Alan Kurdi, the naked Vietnamese running girl, the little boy in the cap with his hands held up in the Warsaw Ghetto), in film (the little girl in red in Schindler's List)? In literature too – in André Schwarz-Bart's novel *The Last of the Just*, discussed in the previous chapter, at a moment of a terrifying pogrom unfolding in his town, the child protagonist Ernie, seeking to guide his little brother to safety, pauses to look around, 'gauging the Christian world', where refuge seems non-existent.[36] (One finds a very similar scene in James Baldwin's *Tell Me How Long the*

Train's Been Gone, where a lost African-American child is confronted with a terrifying world where every person he might reach out to represents threat as much as salvation, a fear justified by the fate of Emmett Till, the murdered children of Atlanta, Trayvon Martin, and so many more.)[37] Schwarz-Bart further informs us that hundreds of Jewish-German children killed themselves during the years of persecution, as indeed Ernie attempts to do after being horribly bullied.[38] Fellow survivor Imre Kertész in *Kaddish for an Unborn Child*, explains in tortured fashion why he elected never to bring a child into the world, given 'just how foul a place the world is for a young child'; from the elemental fascism of his childhood bully torturers to his experiences in Auschwitz, the persecution had never ended: 'Auschwitz, I said to my wife, seemed to me to be just an exaggeration of the very same virtues to which I had been educated since early childhood.'[39] Similarly in *Minima Moralia*, Adorno reproaches himself with not having seen Nazism coming based on his experience at the hands of his tormentors in school.[40] (The travails and hiding places of children were a consistent theme in Adorno, as demonstrated in texts such as his essay on Kafka, where he writes of refuge, that 'whereas the interiors, where men live, are the homes of the catastrophe, the hideouts of childhood, forsaken spots like the bottom of the stairs, are the places of hope' – an image that was all too real in regard to the children who hid in attics and cupboards and behind false walls, in all the preciously marginal places, such as Serge Klarsfeld himself, who narrowly escaped detection as a child.)[41] Fascism understood in this way would have a terrifyingly omnipresent quality, unrestrained by time, its hate aimed from the beginning at the child; in *Berlin Childhood around 1900*, Walter Benjamin writes of the childhood memories and traumatisms that seemed to him to have anticipated the future crises of his adulthood, scenes from Benjamin which Adorno described as issuing from the 'gaze of the condemned man', given his well-known exile and tragic suicide; darkly and ineluctably, 'the origin is the goal', a different version of William Burroughs's stratagem of cutting up texts from the past to unveil the future.[42] In reflecting on the 'loggias', the in-between courtyard spaces of Berlin buildings that fascinated him as a child, spaces that are non-abodes, Benjamin darkly prefigured his own coming status as *heimatlosen*, homeless, 'the solace that lies in their uninhabitability for one who himself no longer has a proper abode', the loggia as a space of exile or even death, 'a mausoleum long intended just for him'.[43] For Benjamin as for Lyotard, a 'debt' is owed to childhood that requires (quoting Lyotard) a 'task of writing, thinking, literature, arts, to venture to bear witness to it'.[44] As Benjamin writes in 'On the Image of Proust', 'a remembered event is infinite, because it is merely a key to everything that happened before it and after it'.[45] The mutual imbrication of past and present, the palimpsest nature of experiences, the horror built into the pleasant present; this is the reality hidden in the night of being, undisclosed by the daytime of appearances, of mere contemporaneity and the ready to hand. Benjamin sought signs, intimations, presentiments of the future in the past, detrital traces of what is to come, of the man prefigured in the child, and in a certain way their shared fate, the security of a childhood that was lost and irrecoverable. Benjamin thought that in the effort of recollection, there was some possibility of rescue, as indicated by the signed copy he gave to his sister Dora where he describes *Berlin Childhood* as an 'ark'.[46]

Arks, however, are in short supply, now as then. The phenomena of the disappeared, the missing, is already a legal category ('enforced disappearance'), a historical and contemporary phenomenon (the '*Desaparecidos*' of Argentina, Mexico and across Central and South America, victims of political and gang and gender-based violence), and an academico-journalistic theme (e.g. Amartya Sen's famous and disturbing thesis about the 'missing women' who never came on to the earth because they were aborted or selected against or killed on the basis of their sex).[47] This theme is painfully resonant in the context of asylum – there are millions of missing children, and millions of missing adults also – dead at the bottom of oceans because no one rescued them, or stranded or imprisoned in camps where they cannot 'appear', in the Arendtian meaning, cannot fully and meaningfully exercise political agency. For while the plight of missing and miserable children brings the contemporary nightmare into poignant relief, this should by no means entail a forgetting of adults, as could be seen when all children were evacuated to the Australian mainland from offshore detention, but many adults were forced to remain behind (which separated some families).[48] Behrouz Boochani has written powerfully of their struggles in his memoir *No Friend But the Mountains*.[49] Horrors multiply – it is often adult males who are perceived as threatening outsiders ('they don't look like children'), and who are subject to exclusion thereby; yet it is also women and children who are particularly vulnerable to harm in refugee camps.[50] Women seeking asylum are vulnerable to abuse, violence, sexual assault and rape or kidnapping for the purpose of human trafficking.[51] Valeria Luiselli writes that 80% (!!) of all women and girls from Central America are raped while in transit as asylum seekers in Mexico, and given the likely inevitability of this experience, many take contraceptive precautions in advance.[52] LGBTIQ+ persons qualify as a persecuted class of refugees, as 'members of a particular social group' under the 1951 convention and face persecution at home and when in transit.[53] The family unit, normally such a cause célèbre of the political right (and protected under many aspects of international law), is not exempt either; family separations at the U.S. border have been horrific, adjudged by experts to constitute torture and enforced disappearance,[54] yet nothing historically new, the same thing occurred during the Shoah, perpetrated not just by the Nazis but including, for example, the French police (Derrida often pointed out that there was never a German on Algerian soil, yet antisemitic measures went into effect regardless).[55] Reporting at the time of this writing suggests that due to administrative failures ('no way to link' the parent and the child), many of the recently separated families will be unable to ever reunite, as the infant children will simply have no way of finding their parents when they grow up, and vice versa; a disaster, the deliberate undoing of the family bond that anchors the individual from isolation, the creation of the 'permanently orphaned' whose parents still live and the denial of the right to a *name*, a family, or an identity, the deliberate production of 'ethical loneliness' (I return to this further on).[56] Indeed, a Trump administration official wanted to destroy the one list that was kept that would enable parents and children to be linked, due to the embarrassment of the list being leaked and contradicting the administration's denials of the existence of a separation policy.[57] Even babies and very young children were not spared, removed from their parents and sent to 'tender-aged shelters'.[58] During the recent debate in the United States concerning those camps where both children and adults are concentrated, and whether they should be considered 'concentration camps' (which many commentators failed to distinguish from extermination camps) where many have died from the poor conditions and refusal of authorities to provide medicine (the administration had to be taken to court to force them to provide basic necessities such as towels and toiletries),[59] it was pointed out that one of the most famous victims of the Shoah, Anne Frank, died not from gassing but likely from typhus, and certainly from the poor conditions in Bergen-Belsen.[60] Holocaust scholar Timothy Snyder's important intervention in this debate was to point out that 'to forbid analogies makes the Holocaust irrelevant to future generations'.[61] Analogy is a vital educative function in guarding against iterations of similar horror, which of course have to be contextualized in their particular uniqueness, what Derrida referred to as the negotiation of responsibility each time in a singular context. Conditions in the United States have been appalling, traumatizing children and their adult family members alike in unnecessary and cruel separation; the effects of this 'toxic stress' causing permanent, irreversible damage to children.[62] Yet Orwellian wrangling about the appropriate way of naming conditions can be lifted verbatim from the news sites of today or the history books concerning yesterday: 'The regime declared that the camps should henceforth be called "shelter centers" rather than internment or concentration camps.'[63] This describes Vichy's response in 1940 to international criticism, 'especially in the United States',[64] of French camp conditions. 'Some of these families were deported together. Others were split so that children separated from their parents were forced to make the horrific journey uncomforted by loved ones.' This refers to the deportation of Jewish families from France to Auschwitz.[65] In *No Place to Lay One's Head*, Françoise Frenkel, a Jewish woman hiding in Occupied France, records that 'a new measure was instituted: Jewish children were to be removed from their parents. They were thrown into trucks, their papers torn up on the spot'. Frenkel reserves special scorn for the French police who went at this task with vigour.[66]

Multiple 'tradition[s] of the oppressed'[67] thus persist: an unabated war on vulnerable children, a second war on vulnerable adults; and yet a third war on those who would help them. Horror redux – in the 1990s, Derrida expressed his horror at the criminalization of aiding asylum seekers:

> I remember a bad day last year: it just about took my breath away, it sickened me when I heard the expression for the first time, barely understanding it, the expression crime of hospitality [délit d'hospitalité] . . . This 'crime of hospitality' (I still wonder who dared to put these words together) is punishable by imprisonment. What becomes of a country, one must wonder, what becomes of a culture, what becomes of a language when it admits of a 'crime of hospitality', when hospitality can become, in the eyes of the law and its representatives, a criminal offense?[68]

A quarter of a century later, many continue to assert that hospitality and the proffering of refuge are crimes. In France, Cédric Herrou was charged for helping migrants (charges activists characterize alternatively as 'crimes of solidarity') though he was acquitted. In Italy, rescue ship captain Carola Rackete was found not guilty on similar charges (a country where the politics have swung from the active solicitude – *ethos* of responsibility – exemplified by the search and rescue operations of the Italian Navy's 'Mare Nostrum' programme – to outright xenophobia; yet the imperial assertion of Mare Nostrum was magnificently inverted, for a temporary, exemplary period, when they rescued thousands of people from the sea). In the United States, Scott Warren of 'No More Deaths' in Arizona was prosecuted for assisting migrants who had crossed the desert, which border policy deliberately forces people into, with lethal consequences.[69] Other activists have been prosecuted for leaving food and water in the desert for migrants who might otherwise die.[70] (Arguments that such efforts might represent a dangerous 'pull-factor' need to contend with that which people are fleeing – terrible gang violence and sexual violence, the destruction of societies in part caused by meddling by the United States.)[71] These heroes are anti-Barbies, or rather, not concatenating his name to theirs, at the antipodes of Barbie – instead of the active effort to destroy, they engage in active solicitude, of seeking out and caring for others in distress; they embody what I have called an *ethos* of responsibility, in them the spirit of Raoul Wallenberg is not dead. Mercifully, courts have thus far upheld the law in ways that shield these actors from the reach of imprisonment, an at least minimally humanizing effect of legalism in opposition to the violence of politics. That any half-way decent society should favour these actors should be obvious – Derrida, as discussed earlier in the book, defined ethics itself as hospitality, as bound to the *ethos*, the manner of living in the place of one's residence; but those politicians and citizenry that would permit of a 'crime of hospitality' can be called, without hyperbole, *tacit Barbies* – here the terrible appellation is maintained in its apposite conjuncture – as they must be confronted with the lethality of their determinate failure to help and to stop those who do help. For while rounding people up for extermination represents the outer limit of an anti-refuge politics, other forms of destruction continue in family separation, offshore detention, this criminalization of rescue and assistance, from Arizona to Italy, very often with death as the end result. The 'drownings argument' and talk of 'pull-factors' are the cynical last refuge of those who would deny the need for rescue, but the bankruptcy of this position, in the Australian context, for example, is manifest in the failure to concatenate to the turn-back policy (arguably justifiable to prevent such drownings) a meaningful regional resettlement programme to bring people safely and provide them with the 'queue' which does not in fact exist.

Patrick Modiano, writing of the tracking of Dora Bruder, a Jewish girl, by the French police, to her arrest and ultimately deportation and death, refers to the 'sentinels of oblivion', remarking the horror of an anti-world where 'the very people whose job it is to search for you are themselves compiling dossiers, the better to ensure that, once found, you will disappear again – this time for good.'[72] (In the French the meaning is even more resonant – *'sentinelles de l'oubli'*, where *'oubli'* can mean both *oblivion* and *forgetting*, perhaps the oblivion *of* forgetting.)[73] The distinction between making and letting die is not so clear here either, as borders can be lethal, as in the aforementioned example of the deliberate forcing of migrants transiting from Mexico into Arizona via the Sonoran desert.[74] While those who implement such barriers describe it with another Orwellian term, that of deterrence, these are in fact lethal practices and thus arguably represent a deliberate putting to death, and not simply a leaving to die, and thus a *version* of what can be accurately termed extermination. Resistance to such practises would thus seem to meet the criteria of the morally justifiable invocation and operationalization of 'never again', where never again is not the impossible prevention of a history that has past and will never return in precisely the same form, but the impetus to guard against future iterations that will have their own form; the negotiation of never again each time in a singular and unique context, an imperative nevertheless informed by the lessons of the past. Jeremy Slack has documented in his recent book *Deported to Death* that migrants expelled from the United States (in violation of its legal obligation to uphold the principle of *non-refoulement*) into the border towns and cities of Mexico are often killed (one commentator has suggested that is necessary to begin talking about *migranticidio*, migranticide), attacked, raped, and exploited, and they cannot return home to Central America without enormous risk to their lives, or in the case of women often a return to the domestic violence they were fleeing in the first place.[75] *Feminicidio* (Femicide or feminicide, a form of gendercide), the killing of women, is the term for the horrific targeting of women for death in Mexico (particularly bad in dangerous border communities such as Ciudad Juárez), but is also the reality facing women seemingly everywhere, symbolized in the rallying cry of Argentinian women activists: '*Ni una menos*', not one more.[76] Nevertheless, the previous U.S. administration removed domestic violence from its list of categories that qualify for asylum.[77] (A similar book in the Australian context, *Following Them Home*, tracks the incredible dangerous consequences of the deportation from Australia of Afghan, Iraqi, and Iranian asylum seekers, the traumatic psychological effects, homelessness and dislocation, and indeed the impossibility of fully accounting for some who cannot be traced, who have disappeared once they return.[78]) The United States has also denied visa stays to victims of the Haitian earthquake due to supposed improvements in conditions in camps in Haiti, but those 'improvements' in numbers have been shown by reporting to be linked to people dying in the camps.[79] As with the denial of asylum for European Jewry, exclusion equals death for many people in Central America and in Mexico – they cannot be turned back even to Mexico given the way they are preyed upon by gangs, and the rape and murder that follows, and they cannot go home without enormous risk. The same can be said of those people seeking asylum now trapped in appalling conditions in Libya, in Bangladesh, and elsewhere.

Thus, the linking of exclusion to a lethal outcome is vitally important to highlight, in that it underscores the moral bankruptcy of 'moderate' considerations that would delimit the scope of asylum, or the taking seriously of the liberal-democratic paradox, the tragedian's vision of a tension between self-determination and rights in its modern form. While not extermination or cattle cars, these practises are nevertheless forms of *necropolitics* or *thanatopolitics*, the allowing to die or the tacit putting to death of the vulnerable. Such are the Barbies and the tacit Barbies: sentinels of oblivion, practitioners of extermination, forcing or letting the vulnerable die. And the present work has adumbrated the same argument apropos of political theorists and philosophers who argue vaguely in favour of limits and self-determination for political communities that would keep the vulnerable out, or whose generous arguments nevertheless do not go nearly far enough – these theorists too should have the lethal consequences of their arguments pressed upon them, to insist, as Foucault once did with such eloquence, that the '"great rage of facts" should serve to "plaster onto ideas the death's-heads that resemble them"'.[80] To take the example of any one child, separated from its parents, perhaps with no name or family that they can properly recall, a life, however brief, filled with filth and rape and abuse, before a hideously violent death, never to be seen or heard of or thought of again, and realize this is always going on at every moment en masse and always has, that one benefits from a system that ensures that all this happens, and that none of this is hyperbole or emotional blackmail, but is simply *the case*, or an infinite number of cases, that will never be solved. Never again, in this context, is too often inverted in practise into the eternal recurrence of the horrific same, and the proof of the damage caused is (not) all around us.

WHAT IS A POLITICS OF HAUNTOLOGY?

Following the outline of the *ethos* of responsibility in the preceding chapters, to conclude I want to argue that a thinking of the disappeared – those already disappeared and those *still to come who are already disappeared because no one will help them* – should inform the *telos* of the political as such, under-stood as an ethical solicitude towards others, including the non-members of a political community. What I am proposing is a politics of hauntology, a phrase borrowed from Derrida, which puts into question a too-easy confi-dence that the world simply is as it appears. What would it mean to think the ways in which the world could have been, or could be, rather than to accept it as it is? And what implications might this have for the politics of asylum?

Ontology is a term in philosophy referring to the study of *ontos*, existence, of what exists. As argued in chapter 1 in relation to Levinas, a philosophi-cal thinking of the political will often rest upon a particular conception of ontology – what is the nature of existence, of human experience, and so on. A 'hauntology', on the other hand, is a neologism and portmanteau coined by Derrida, which sounds like ontology but differing from ontology which describes what is, hauntology describes what isn't, what isn't yet or what is no longer. This term is intended to trouble all certainty concerning the limits of what exists, of the living and the dead, past and present, and those yet unborn. A hauntology, in other words, is a kind of poetics of ghosts, a thinking of the ghost, the spectre, the revenant, the figure that is not a figure, that trembles on the edge of ontological signification and certainty, like the trace or the cinder, which is and is not at the same time, a continuation of Derrida's theme of the deconstruction of the metaphysics of presence. This concept of hauntology, of spectrality and the spectre, is linked to that of the trace, which plays a sig-nificant role in Derrida's writings; as he observes, the trace and spectrality are inseparable.[81] The trace is that which functions as a reminder, troubling the distinction between inside and outside. For example, the cinder that is left after a fire or holocaust. What is a cinder? Does it have an ontological signification? Is it a 'thing' in any real sense? It seems to inhabit that destabilized position of the trace, as much hauntology as ontology. In French, because the h is silent, hauntology and ontology are homophones, sounding the same; akin to his celebrated 'differance', Derrida highlights with this neologism that ontology is always-already hauntology. In *Specters of Marx* he writes:

> If I am getting ready to speak at length about ghosts, inheritance, and genera-tions, generations of ghost, which is to say about certain others who are not present, not presently living, either to us, in us, or outside us, it is in the name of justice. Of justice where it is not yet, not yet there, where it is no longer, let us understand where it is no longer present, and where it will never be, no more than the law, reducible to laws or rights. It is necessary to speak of the ghost, indeed to the ghost and with it, from the moment that no ethics, no politics, whether revolutionary or not, seems possible and thinkable and just that does not recognize in its principle the respect for those others who are no longer or for those others who are not yet there, presently living, whether they are already dead or not yet born. No justice – let us not say no law and once again we are not speaking here of laws – seems possible or thinkable without the principle of some responsibility, beyond all living present, within that which disjoins the living present, before the ghost of those who are not yet born or who are already dead, be they victims of wars, political or other kinds of violence, nationalist, racist, colonialist, sexist, or other kinds of exterminations, victims of the oppres-sions of capitalist imperialism or any of the forms of totalitarianism.[82]

Allow me to digress for a moment to comment on my own process: when I first typed out this passage, I committed a horrific transcription error which stopped me in my tracks. The correct phrase was as follows: 'the ghost of those who are not yet born or who are already dead'. But the phrase that I typed was: 'the ghost of those who are not yet born who are already dead'.

Those not yet born who are already dead. It is a terrifying phrase, but one that is an ineluctable fact of the future to come. There are people who are not yet born, who are already dead, not simply because everything dies, but precisely because governments, and Western governments especially, given the power they wield, will have (borrowing the future anterior tense that Derrida so favoured) failed to save their lives, from boats that will sink to the bottom or the Mediterranean sea or the Indian Ocean, to the lives lost in the actualization of their potentiality by being immiserated for decades in refugee camps, to deaths at dangerous border crossings, dying of thirst in the desert from the Sahara to the Sonoran Desert (Mexico-Arizona). People not yet born, who are already dead, because of a lack of responsibility-taking, because the world could have been other than what it was, but this other world did not materialize.

In other words, these are ghosts, or spectres, to use Derrida's phrase (itself a reference to the first line of the Communist Manifesto – 'A specter is haunt-ing Europe – the specter of Communism!'), that are still to come, who aren't even born and are already ghosts. And this in a world already replete with ghosts, of those who could have been saved but were not. In *Cinders*, a text which enacts an haunted, fragmented circling around of the theme of disappearance, ashes, and traces, Derrida quotes Nietzsche: 'Our entire world is the cinder of innumerable living beings'.[83] The cinder is 'what remains without remaining from the holocaust, from the all-burning, from the incineration'.[84] He also quotes Nietzsche to the effect that: 'Let us guard against saying that death is opposed to life. The living being is only a species of what is dead, and a very rare species'.[85] Life and death are traces of each other. Derrida, in explaining the trace, writes the following:

> The trace, as we know, both "constitutes the self-presence of the living present" and introduces into self-presence from the beginning all the impurity putatively excluded from it". It is thus the intimate relation of the living present to its outside, the opening to exteriority in general" that impels us beyond present life . . . its empirical or ontological actuality: not toward death but toward a living-on . . . of which life and death would themselves be but traces . . . a survival whose possibility in advance comes to disjoin or dis-adjust the identity to itself of the living present".[86]

The cinder as philosophical theme, from a twentieth-century Jewish philosopher, cannot but make the reader think of the Shoah, even if Derrida mostly addressed this enormous topic obliquely, his near-silence perhaps a different form of addressing what can scarcely be comprehended. The reference to impurity in discussing the trace recalls what Primo Levi writes in *The Periodic Table*, using chemistry as an analogy, about the danger of purity, of its alliance with fascism, and the necessary good of impurity, of foreign agents introduced into an environment.[87]

So what does this mean, these strange meditations on ghosts and ashes, cinders and traces, purity and impurity, and disappearance? It serves to recall to mind that the world can always be different to how it appears, in fact it always-already is. One could invert the poetics of othering here – that we already live in the *other* world, the unrealized world, the world where the children of Izieu never grew up and had children of their own. Benjamin too reminds us that the world can always be othered, but the fact is that the diversion has already occurred – such as, to refer again to Primo Levis's image, a railway switch sending the world down a different track, the world has been othered, permanently othered, that is, radically reconfigured.[88] It is a question of how politics should other the world, in what direction, down which track.

Such a reminder should serve to inform what this book has argued for in the form of an *ethos* of responsibility – that which enacts the realization of the political, but understood, in addition to the perspective of unchosen responsibility of the living, an additional claim made upon the living by the memory of the lost and the presentiment of those to come. It is to remind us that we are *inheritors*, and for Derrida responsibility necessarily entails inheritance; we are the inheritors of everything, including the worst, all the failures to act that have been, and those to come. We are always-already the inheritors of the disasters to come. In other words, the 'future anterior' – 'I will have done this, I won't have done that' – the anticipation of future events in the present. 'We will not have saved them'. In other words, it is necessary in considering politics, to listen to the ghosts, to be attentive to the traces, to the cinders of the past and the cinders of the future.

This destabilization of the real by the unreal is explicitly linked by Derrida in *Of Hospitality* to the plight of outsiders with reference to the 'Foreigner' in Plato's Sophist: 'The Foreigner shakes up the threatening dogmatism of the paternal logos: the being that is, and the non-being that is not.'[89] But the foreigner can also be the dead other; Derrida will insist upon the possibility of hospitality towards the dead: 'There is no hospitality without memory . . . What kind of hospitality would not be ready to offer itself to the dead one, to the revenant?'[90] According to Derrida, this is the condition of sovereignty, which is divided and cannot settle into place because it is haunted: 'Ghosts haunt places that exist without them; they return to where they have been excluded from'.[91] In the Preface to *Totality and Infinity*, Levinas asks, 'Is relationship with Being produced only in representation, the natural locus of evidence?', a question he answers in the negative – hence the 'night of being', the way that things not present to consciousness nevertheless form and inform lived experience.[92]

But do the disappeared, the missing, have a Face in Levinas's sense? Judith Butler, in her book *Precarious Life: The Powers of Mourning and Violence*, links Levinas's notion of the face to her own emphasis on precarity – the vulnerability of others, as faces that we need to acknowledge;[93] but in *Frames of War* it is not just a matter of the face but of the 'frame'; she writes about the way in which recognition of the other (here Hegel comes into view) is determined by the way in which that recognizability is framed and the norms which govern that framing, which disturbs the given sense of reality.[94] In *Precarious Life*, Butler writes: 'The public sphere is constituted in part by what cannot be said and what cannot be shown. The limits of the sayable, the limits of what can appear, circumscribe the domain in which political speech operates and certain kinds of subjects appear as viable actors.'[95] Yet hegemonic frames of representation do not exhaust possibility: in *Frames of War*, she argues that living figures fall 'outside the frame furnished by the norm, but only as a relentless double whose ontology cannot be secured, but whose living status is open to apprehension', a 'specter that gnaws at the norms of recognition'.[96] This is not unrelated to her work on queer studies; Butler has written on the expendability of the lives of homosexuals, prostitutes, and others deemed superfluous; Christopher Peterson links this to Sharon Holland's claim in *Raising the Dead: Readings of Death and (Black) Subjectivity*, that 'bringing back the dead is the ultimate queer act', that is, a deliberate destabilization of hegemonic norms so that other forms of precarious life, or even those already dead, might gain recognition.[97] Butler makes the point of highlighting the expendability of Palestinian children, who are 'framed' as 'duplicitous shrapnel', as expendable human shields.[98] And yet periodic outrage, even concerning children, does not convert into meaningful, sustained political activity, as can be seen from the effect of the images of Alan Kurdi, which caused only the briefest disturbance to Europe's exclusionary business-as-usual (here the unstable moral impact of the image in the public imaginary, as analyzed by Susan Sontag in *Regarding the Pain of Others*, is also a vital consideration).[99] Thus while Butler is mostly convincing in engaging the critique of given frames as well as the possibility of the production of new frames, of recognizing precarious life, of the vulnerable body, the political efficacy of these gestures is somewhat limited. Nevertheless, they underscore the setting of political loneliness, of abandonment outside of a frame that allows for appearance in Arendt's sense, for both those who are outcast and indeed the lonely but included members of the dominantly framed society. Peterson, referring to Derrida writes: 'We might consider that all bodies live in the "shadowy regions of ontology," – all bodies are hauntological, not ontological. Only by virtue of the fiction of ontology do certain bodies appear to be more present than others. The social existence of the majority, of those white, male bodies that supposedly matter, is conditioned by a certain disavowal and projection of the body's finitude. The socially dead are thus made to stand in for the death that haunts each and every life.'[100] Butler has also been criticized for reinstating a metaphysics of presence in her emphasis on corporeality and the lived presence of the body, even if, according to her, it is constituted through language and discourse.[101] A hauntology, on the other hand, is not delimited to corporealization, though Butler is right to also emphasize the real suffering, precarious bodies in need of protection and refuge.

In Shirley Jackson's superb novel *The Haunting of Hill House*, haunting and ghostliness are overtly linked to *loneliness*: the story's introduction and conclusion end with the same words: 'whatever walked there, walked alone'.[102] The ghost wants to go home, to find someone who will listen, to be somewhere it belongs, to be wanted. The strong intimation of the story (spoiler!) is that the haunting is the psychic projection of one of the visitors to the house, Eleanor, who towards the end refuses to take leave of her fellow guests, and of the house itself; 'journeys end in lover's meeting', she tells herself throughout the story, but the anticipated happy end does not arrive, and she fears her return to exile, her disappearance as subject, she who has come alive and become somebody in the company and conversation of others, in a shared project and experience.[103] The others refuse to take responsibility for her, even though they have heard her plaints projected throughout the house, and the busybody characters of Mrs Montague and Arthur are unable even to hear the nocturnal manifestations of the ghost that is haunting the house, in their surety that they have missed nothing in their comprehension. But they, and perhaps less attentive readers, miss the fundamental loneliness, the home-lessness of haunting, of being a ghost – a ghost that cannot go home, cannot come to rest, cannot be admitted or accepted, that is 'walled up alive'.[104]

Could it be that perhaps Arendt was writing a hauntology without real-izing it? If one does not 'appear' *amongst others*, one does not truly appear, one does not truly exist – this seems to be the heart of the Hill House story. Subjectivity in the condition of statelessness is experienced as *aphanisis*, as the disappearance of the human being qua subject when it is forced into exile. In Arendt's unfortunate phraseology, the stateless risk becoming barbarians, but perhaps spectral or ghostly is less pejorative, understood as their non-appearance in the political sense. To be is to appear; subjectivity is welcoming the other, who is prior to and constitutes the self. I need the other to become myself. Responding to the haunting of the other, enabling the encounter with the ghost, requires the ethical insomnia of which Levinas wrote, attentiveness in the night; Eleanor professes guilt that she may have failed to wake in the night and provide her mother with life-saving medicine (or that she might have heard the cries and gone back to sleep).[105] In this case, it is the child who failed to save the parent, who left them alone and ends up lonely themselves. The first line of the novel: 'No live organism can continue for long to exist sanely under conditions of absolute reality.'[106] Here can be recalled Jean Améry's combat against the isolation of the individual and the non-forgetting of the indignity – that as he wrote, revolt against reality is rational so long as it is moral.[107]

Loneliness was an important theme in Arendt. Jennifer Gaffney has writ-ten on Arendt's critique of that loneliness which is engendered by liberalism, which leaves citizens isolated in a condition of worldlessness and superfluity, and thus susceptible to the domination of totalitarianism.[108] The legacy of the past, the practise of listening to the ghosts, might be considered the redemp-tion of the lonely liberal subject, perhaps especially those who reside in set-tler-colonial societies. Bonnie Honig in her book *Public Things: Democracy in Disrepair*, insightfully links two moments of despair and emptiness that de Tocqueville records in *Democracy in America*: on the one hand, that of a displaced Choctaw band whose animals seem to ventriloquize their suffering by proceeding to 'set up a dismal howl' on the bank of the Mississippi as their masters leave the shore; and on the other, the 'strange melancholy' of white settlers regarding a 'ghostly disappointment that never quite materializes into something real', the 'strange melancholy often haunting inhabitants of democracies in the midst of abundance'.[109] This may recall Kubrick's brilliant rendition of *The Shining*, where blood gushes from the depths of the Overlook Hotel via its elevator shaft (the hotel, the viewer learns at the beginning, is built atop an American Indian burial ground). A hotel too is a space that receives the other, but in a space that has been brutally taken from an-other other, that is, the Overlook Hotel is very the image of the liberal settler-colonial state. The question of proffering asylum, hospitality, welcome on stolen land, in settler-colonial liberal-democratic societies, might produce an uncanny or uneasy feeling, what the historian Henry Reynolds, apropos of the dispossession of Indigenous Australians, has called 'this whispering in our hearts'.[110] (Recall from chapter 1 that Aboriginal groups in Australia have symbolically issued Aboriginal Passports to asylum seekers in detention as a show of solidarity with other oppressed peoples). Indeed, in *Bury My Heart at Wounded Knee*, Dee Brown refers to the Indians who had suffered through the 'trail of tears' as *refugees*.[111] It is not just that liberal-democratic societies are lonely, as Arendt thought, referring to the decline of political life amongst plural beings; it is that they are *haunted* by that loneliness, and by the ghosts that lie both under their foundations and outside the city walls, dual traditions of the oppressed. More such traditions, such as slavery, can also be added in many cases – the oppressed or the 'wretched', to borrow the well known yet in some ways inadequate translation of Fanon – better translated as the 'damned' of the earth (*Les Damnés De La Terre* – I owe this insight to Lewis Gordon).[112] In Poe's 'The Fall of the House of Usher', the reclusive Roderick lives in constant trepidation at the thought of the crime he has committed against his sister – 'we have put her living in the tomb!' – and a house built on such crimes and such fearfulness, in that tale literally cannot stand.[113]

Anya Topolski also discusses loneliness in her book on Arendt and Levinas, where she argues that both thinkers recognize that such loneliness contributes to the loss of both community and individuality which can lead to dehumanization.[114] More recently, the theme of loneliness has been developed in an explicitly ethical register by Jill Stauffer. Stauffer brings Jean Améry into proximity with Levinas in exploring the effects of persecution and abandonment – she defines it thusly:

> Ethical loneliness is the isolation one feels when one, as a violated person or as one member of a persecuted group, has been abandoned by humanity, or by those who have power over one's life's possibilities. It is a condition undergone by persons who have been unjustly treated and dehumanized by human beings and political structures, who emerge from that injustice only to find that the surrounding world will not listen to or cannot properly hear their testimony – their claims about what they suffered and about what is now owed them – on their own terms.

So ethical loneliness is the experience of having been abandoned by humanity compounded by the experience of not being heard. Such loneliness is so named because it is a form of social abandonment that can be imposed only by multiple ethical lapses on the part of human beings residing in the surrounding world.[115]

Stauffer emphasizes, as does Arendt, the role of storytelling in a 'shared world'; 'selves and worlds are built by human interactions – affective, reasoned, chosen and unchosen'.[116] Robert Bernasconi, commenting on Stauffer's work, emphasizes the importance of hearing as well as listening, while also noting that one should take care not to assume that one has really heard properly the intended message:

> I attribute to her the idea that we have the responsibility not just to listen but to hear, even though we might lack the power to hear. My responsibility to hear is independent of my ability to do so and this must be so especially when it is a question of hearing the testimonies of those who suffered in ways I cannot even imagine. Levinas's philosophy is not a philosophy of communication but of a saying that transcends the said. That is why in *Existence and Existents* Levinas highlighted the failure to communicate in love as what in fact constitutes the positive character of the relation: in the proximity of the Other in eros 'the absence of the other is precisely his presence as other'.[117]

This work of listening, hearing, remembering, and recalling applies also to the past, to the children of Izieu as much as their late contemporary Alan Kurdi – Stauffer: 'The past cannot be changed, but it can resound in the present moment in vastly different ways, some of them more hospitable to human thriving than others. It is everyone's job to author conditions where repair is possible.'[118] As Jerome Kohn writes, for Arendt, 'thinking about an event is remembering it, that "otherwise, it is forgotten", and that such forgetting jeopardizes the meaningfulness of our world'.[119] But how to make meaningful, appropriate connections between different histories and stories, between living and dead, between different peoples, between fiction and non-fiction? Is there a means by which such worlds can be brought into proximity, without being conflated or compared, without being weighed against each other as to their gravity, without speaking for those who can often no longer speak for themselves, but which might nevertheless cast mutual illumination, a storytelling that underscores an ethics?

TRADITION(S) OF THE OPPRESSED

The chapter on France reflected on André Schwarz-Bart's novel, *The Last of the Just*, which depicts the plight of a Jewish family over time, culminating in the death of the 'last of the just' men in Auschwitz. What is most *dis-graceful* – the word is apposite – in contemporary politics of asylum, especially that practised by states of the Global North, is the complete failure to absorb the moral lesson of past calamities, the Shoah being among the most significant in both scale and degree of horror. As Schwarz-Bart laments, what good does it do to sense the evil of the world, if nothing changes?[120] As one reviewer put it in *Commentary*, responding to the various controversies that the book elicited, 'If there is a point one wants to discuss, it is that millions of defenseless men and women and children lived and died horribly after the Western democracies had declined the chance to take them in'.[121]

As seen in the previous chapter, Nicole Loraux analysed the pejorative term 'Métèques' as deployed by the far-right in France to analyse the comparative situations of Metics in Ancient Greece and migrants in 1990's France. This interpretive gesture evinces the possibility of marking a continuity across history and across societies of the oppression of the exiled, displaced, or migratory human being that need not be thought in isolation but can be brought into meaningful proximity. Walter Benjamins's notion of the 'tradition of the oppressed' is important in understanding the meaning of *ethos* of responsibility as being informed by different histories of oppression: 'The tradition of the oppressed teaches us that the "state of emergency" in which we live is not the exception but the rule. We must attain to a conception of history that accords with this insight.'[122] *Traditio*, from Latin, means to 'hand down', to receive; the present claim is that such a tradition is evinced by the experienced of exiles and the persecuted across time, a continuity which can be marked even while attending to the singularity and uniqueness of disparate experiences. As the preceding chapters have demonstrated, the experience of Jewry in the 1930s and 1940s is instructive for contemporary asylum politics for many reasons, given the scale, the murderous consequences of a failure to provide refuge, the living presence and testimony of survivors up to the present, and in highlighting the clear failure of Western states to provide refuge, which continues in contemporary politics. Yet other calamities before and after these experiences need to be placed alongside them, to make clear that as Benjamin asserts, the 'enemy has never ceased to be victorious'.[123]

In 'On the Concept of History', Benjamin argues for the nostalgic use of the past as a means of providing a radical critique of contemporary problems, that the past and present are mutually imbricated.[124] Benjamin refers to the ability of those inhabiting the present to draw upon a 'weak messianic power':

> The past carries with it a secret index by which it is referred to redemption. Doesn't a breath of the air that pervaded earlier days caress us as well? In the voices we hear, isn't there an echo of now silent ones? . . . If so, then there is a secret agreement between past generations and the present one. Then our

coming was expected on earth. Then, like every generation that preceded us, we have been endowed with a weak messianic power, a power on which the past has a claim.[125]

This (weak) messianism is linked to Benjamin's Marxism; as Michael Löwy comments in *Fire Alarm*, 'True universal history, based on the universal remembrance of all victims without exception – the secular equivalent of the resurrection of the dead – will be possible only in the future classless society'.[126] The future society, or the politics to come, will be that which 'resurrects the dead' by remembering all victims, recounting missed possibilities and unfulfilled hopes or potential,[127] where, as Benjamin writes, remembrance is 'the only consolation afforded to those who no longer have any hope of being consoled'.[128]

This recounting of the past as caesura within the present also recalls Levinas's interpretation of 'eschatology', discussed in chapter 1, which interrupts history *within* the course of its flow, yet which also provides a criterion of judgement over that history:

Eschatology institutes a relation with being *beyond the totality* or beyond history . . . It is reflected *within* the totality of history, *within* experience. The eschatological, as the 'beyond' of history, draws beings out of the jurisdiction of history and the future; it arouses them in and calls them forth to their full responsibility. Submitting history as a whole to judgment, exterior to the very wars that mark its end, it restores to each instant its full signification in that very instant: all the causes are ready to be heard. It is not the last judgment that is decisive, but the judgment of all the instants in time, when the living are judged. The eschatological notion of judgment (contrary to the judgment of history in which Hegel wrongly saw its rationalization) implies that beings have an identity 'before eternity', before the accomplishment of history, before the fullness of time, while there is still time [. . .].[129]

As Andrew Benjamin comments apropos of Walter Benjamin, 'Once the present is no longer defined within the continuity of historicism then it becomes the site in which the irreducibility – the irreducibility that defines a politics of time – can be said to be always already at work', an irreducibility which opens up existing power relations to 'the possibility of their own radical transformation'.[130] And one might add, to the possibility of judgement, which Andrew Benjamin emphasizes in relation to Kant and Arendt (discussed in chapter 1) as that which philosophy provides as insight into the political. For Arendt, judgement was linked to the faculty of thought but was also a matter of memory, of the way in which a political community tells stories about itself to itself: 'Imagination alone enables us to see things in their proper perspective . . . Without this kind of imagination, which actually is understanding, we would never be able to take our bearings in the world.'[131] While the judgement of history can only be applied backwards (Hegel's dictum concerning the Owl of Minerva), it might also furnish criteria of judgement that can apply in the future. Max Horkheimer wrote that:

> What has happened to the human beings who have fallen no future can repair. They will never be called to be made happy for all eternity . . . Amid this immense indifference, consciousness alone can become the site where the injustice suffered can be abolished [aufgehoben], the only agency that does not give in to it . . . Now that faith in eternity is necessarily breaking down, historiography [Historie] is the only court of appeal [Gehor] that present humanity, itself transient, can offer to the protests [Anklagen] which come from the past.[132]

Horkheimer was critical of the theologism present in Benjamin's work (as was Brecht, while conversely, Scholem decried his Marxism). However, it is not that the victims can actually in some way be mystically restored, but that their memory might provide criteria for judgement for future political praxis, to the possibility of radical transformation noted above.

Such an effort of historical remembrance also involves different traditions of oppression being brought into proximity with each other, and is worked through not just in historiography but also, for example, in literature. In Schwarz-Bart's second novel, *A Woman Named Solitude*, the terrible experience of an African woman born into the slave-service of French plantation owners in Guadeloupe is recounted. In the epilogue, Schwarz-Bart invokes a phenomenal hauntology, of wandering around the ruins of the old plantation and encountering ghosts of the past there:

> Conscious of a faint taste of ashes, the visitor will take a few steps at random, tracing wider and wider circles around the site of the mansion. His foot will collide with one of the building stones, concealed by dead leaves, which were dispersed by the explosion and then over the years buried, dug up, covered over, and dug up again by the innocent hoes of the field workers. If he is in the mood to salute a memory, his imagination will people the environing space, and human figures will rise up around him, just as the phantoms that wander about the humiliated ruins of the Warsaw ghetto are said to rise up before the eyes of other travellers.[133]

Here there is an evocation of ruins, of ashes and phantoms, of the past retaining traces in the present, of one calamity echoing another, of the 'image of enslaved ancestors', to quote from thesis twelve of Benjamin's famous late work, of the Middle Passage and the Shoah brought into proximity as melancholic subjects for reflection.[134] Indeed, hauntology has been fruitfully engaged in postcolonial studies, beyond the limits of European concerns.[135] In the book *Facing Black and Jew*, Adam Zachary Newton makes explicit reference to Levinas and Walter Benjamin in staging an encounter between Jewish and African American literature in the United States; for Newton, the notion of allegory in Benjamin and ethics in Levinas provides for the possibility 'to contrive a space or appearance of proximity for them to draw near without coinciding'.[136] Emily Budick in *Jews and Blacks in Literary Conversation* refers to a similar proximity which she terms 'mutuality', the mutual exchange of experiences enacted through writings, dialogues, and correspondences between Jewish and Black authors.[137] These gestures appear to be at work in Schwarz-Bart's second novel, as well as the incomplete work he undertook with his wife Simone Schwarz-Bart, who was of Guadeloupean origin; he was also aware of the work of Emmanuel Levinas, and that this work, qua description of the human encounter, enabled mutual understanding between members of different ethnic and racial groups.[138] Kathleen Gyssels notes the influence of Schwarz-Bart on African American novelists such as John Edgar Wideman and Caryl Phillips who 'write back' to Schwarz-Bart, co-signing his conviction of the necessary dialogue between cultures that are linked by an experience of trauma.[139] Michael Rothberg in *Multidirectional Memory: Remembering the Holocaust in the Age of Decolonisation*, counters what he sees as the problematic possibility of a competitive, zero-sum game amongst different narratives of horror, with a 'countertradition in which remembrance of the Holocaust intersects with the legacies of colonialism and slavery and ongoing processes of decolonization', a way of approaching differing narratives 'premised on hospitality to histories of the other'.[140] This intersectional work is thus well underway; what I want to focus on here is how these different narratives intersect specifically around questions of the memory of the victims, especially in relation to the theme of asylum. However, it is necessary to proceed with some care: as Toni Morrison writes in *Playing in the Dark: Whiteness in the Literary Imagination*: 'I am a black writer struggling with and through a language that can powerfully evoke and enforce hidden signs of racial superiority, cultural hegemony, and dismissive "othering" of people and language which are by no means marginal or already and completely known and knowable in my work . . . The kind of work I have always wanted to do requires me to learn how to maneuver ways to free up the language from its sometimes sinister, frequently lazy, almost always predictable employment of racially informed and determined chains.'[141] The risks are surely magnified when writing about victims for whom one has no right to speak, or who can no longer speak, the troubling and controversial aporia that Agamben reflected upon, apropos of Primo Levi, in *Remnants of Auschwitz: The Witness and the Archive*.[142] In *Witnessing Witnessing: On the Reception of Holocaust Survivor Testimony*, Thomas Trezise resists the paralysing effects of the discourse of Agamben and other thinkers, arguing that bearing witness is a matter of *reception*, of receiving the message of the witness, as well as the witness receiving the witness of the receiver, and the importance of self-awareness in 'how listeners hear themselves'.[143] If the ineffability of transmission of the story, the message, the plea of the witness is maintained, then what lessons can be drawn? But how to draw lessons without running the risk of speaking for the witness, especially when the survivors are gone and can no longer speak for themselves?

Another problem: Can, or should, the disparate experiences of different oppressed groups be brought together in reflective proximity, or this a fundamentally invidious exercise? Is there a risk here of a levelling of all events down to the same, or the counter-risk of a comparison, a weighing of relative horrors, of magnitude, of severity, a competition of the victims? Or rather, does the Benjaminian 'tradition of the oppressed' thus become manifest in a way that might inform politics? In her masterpiece *Beloved*, Toni Morrison dedicates her ghost story to the 'Sixty Million and more' estimated victims of the Middle Passage. Levinas dedicates *Otherwise Than Being* to 'the closest among the six million, the victims of the same hatred of the other man, the same anti-semitism'; the same hatred, beyond the particularity of anti-semitism, the hatred of other human beings, is here deliberately emphasized. Franz Fanon argued:

> I sincerely believe that a subjective experience can be understood by others; and it would give me no pleasure to announce that the black problem is my problem and mine alone and that it is up to me to study it . . . Is there in truth any difference between one racism and another? Do not all of them show the same collapse, the same bankruptcy of man?[144]

Fanon shared with Levinas the equation of antisemitism as dehumanizing of all: 'Colonial racism is no different from any other racism. Anti-Semitism hits me head-on: I am enraged, I am bled white by an appalling battle, I am deprived of the possibility of being a man. I cannot disassociate myself from the future that is proposed for my brother. Every one of my acts commits me as a man. Every one of my silences, every one of my cowardices reveals me as a man.'[145] Achille Mbembe, a great reader of Fanon, elucidates a similar logic, while linking it to 'phantasmatic' fears (recall Butler from chapter 1) as well as to the refugee and to the border:

> The enthusiasm for origins thrives by provoking an affect of fear of encountering the other – an encounter that is not always material but is certainly always phantasmatic, and in general traumatic. Indeed, many are concerned that they

have preferred others over themselves for a long time. They deem that the matter can no longer be to prefer such others to ourselves. Everything is now about preferring ourselves to others, who, in any case, are scarcely worthy of us, and last, it is about making our object choices settle on those who are like us. The era is therefore one of strong narcissistic bonds. In this context the functions that an imaginary fixation on the stranger, the Muslim, the veiled woman, the refugee, the Jew, or the Negro play are defensive ones. There is a refusal to recognize that, in truth, our ego has always been constituted through opposition to some Other that we have internalized – a Negro, a Jew, an Arab, a foreigner – but in a regressive way; that, at bottom, we are made up of diverse borrowings from foreign subjects and that, consequently, we have always been *beings of the border* – such is precisely what many refuse to admit today.[146] (Emphasis added)

Jane Marks, author of *The Hidden Children* (about Jewish children hidden during the war), remarks on her surprise when at a gathering of these survivors she spots an African American woman attending the proceedings. A survivor shows Marks a letter sent by the woman:

2/21/91 To whom it may concern: I'm Black, a woman, 36 years old. I'm in medical school. I just finished reading 'The Hidden Children', New York magazine, Feb. issue. I want to come to the gathering May 26 and 27. I have to be there. I don't know exactly why. I have trouble sorting out and explaining my strong feelings about the Holocaust experience. It's almost as if I were there. Perhaps 36 years of being Black in America has caused me to feel like a survivor too. I identify with what it feels like to be ashamed of who you are, to feel others hate so powerfully that it causes your heart to beat faster. No, there's something more. I, like the others, know that there is something in my soul – a will, a destiny to live, to tell.[147]

The African American singer Paul Robeson, while visiting the Soviet Union, performed the song of the Warsaw Ghetto 'Zog Nit Keynmol' which was broadcast to millions, in an overt display of solidarity with Russian Jews at a time of their persecution under Stalin. When one visits the Elsternwick Holocaust Memorial in Melbourne, Australia, amongst the sad displays is a heartening installation outlining the solidarity evinced by William Cooper, the famed Aboriginal activist, who led a march of first nations people to the German Consulate in Melbourne in 1938 to protest the German treatment of the Jews (and whose political insight and compassion thus far outstripped all of the assembled states at the Evian conference who were determinedly failing to do anything about the same events). As victims of settler-colonialism and murderous destruction, Australian aboriginals, dispossessed of their land, could be compared to exiled Jewry, but also to other victims of settler-colonialism such as the Palestinians, and contemporary refugees. In Australia, the destruction of families occurred via the Stolen Generations, dispossession, ethnocide, and direct massacre (the documentation of the sites of such massacres has barely begun). As Sonia Tascón writes in her essay 'Refugees and the coloniality of power: border-crossings of postcolonial whiteness':

> It is indeed almost uncanny, if it were not also following a kind of perverse logic, that there is a parallel between the treatment of Aboriginal peoples historically and presently, and that of onshore refugees: both groups have been exiled, one internal and one external to their place of origin; both have been non-citizens at some point; both have been subject to laws that mandatorily detain them; and both have been subjected to racialised treatment. Both have endured intense state surveillance that has sought to exclude, contain and reject. It is also worth noting that the issue of land, and fears surrounding the issue of land, has become significant in the treatment of both groups of people – one because of the manner in which they enter the land; the other because their presence highlights a dispossession of land that continues at the centre of a colonial struggle that fails to be resolved ten [*sic*] years after the Mabo High Court ruling. Both groups have collided most forcefully with colonial power relationships that were established over 200 years ago in Australia. Race and whiteness, as the set of knowledges that invisibly confers privilege or marks for exclusion, have been integral parts of the power/knowledge nexus of colonial practices.[148]

In chapter 1, the solidarity of Aboriginal peoples with refugees housed in offshore detention by Australia was noted; however, the differing relations to place as experienced between Indigenous and non-Indigenous persons also needs to be marked. As Aileen Moreton-Robinson eloquently expresses it:

> Indigenous people cannot forget the nature of migrancy and position all non-Indigenous people as migrants and diasporic. Our ontological relationship to land, the ways that country is constitutive of us, and therefore the inalienable nature of our relationship to land, marks a radical, indeed incommensurable, difference between us and the non-Indigenous. This ontological relation to land constitutes a subject position that we do not share, and which cannot be shared, with the postcolonial subject whose sense of belonging in this place is tied to migrancy.[149]

Thus, solidarity is evinced even in conditions where some arrivants, not only migrants but refugees, necessarily have an 'incommensurable' way of relating to the site where asylum is proffered, with those who proffer it, which does not forestall the proffering. Such generosity of cohabitation could be seen as an exemplar of what has been termed throughout as an *ethos* of responsibility, where being-in-common and being-in-place are realized in a space where the original inhabitants, who provide refuge, would be recognized as such, as Toula Nicolacopoulos and George Vassilacopoulos write: 'Place is fundamental to all these ways of presenting one's being as one's own but equally so is the willingness to dwell in such a place, whether as one's own or with the acknowledgement that it belongs to another.'[150]

Perhaps the starkest drawing into proximity of traditions of the exiled-oppressed in literature occurs in a remarkable act of self-naming that occurs in Kafka's first novel, '*Der Verschollene*', which translated means the 'Missing Person' or the 'Disappeared One'. The protagonist of the novel, Karl Rossmann, is an exile, who upon entering the harbour of New York, sees that (in Kafka's world), the Statue of Liberty is holding aloft a sword rather than a torch, a menacing, threatening figure, and the novel depicts Rossmann's descent into a deeper and deeper disappearance, that is, he is being forced by circumstance, to borrow a phrase from the Radiohead song, to learn 'how to disappear completely'. There is an entire poetics of disappearance in the novel which illustrates the fate that can often befall those who arrive, without protection or welcome, in a new country. In other words, the figure of the exile or the refugee is very often coterminous with that of the disappeared person. Kafka died in 1924, the year the United States passed the restrictive Johnson-Reed (Immigration) Act, and the current revanchist politics of that country is a reminder that the ghosts of the past can always return. Towards the end of the novel, Rossmann gives his name to the 'Nature Theatre of Oklahoma' (he deliberately preserves the misspelling of a picture from a German photographer's book, 'idyll aus Oklahoma' that depicts the lynching of an African American in Oklahoma) as 'Negro', to the stunned amazement of the registrar. This adoption of the name of the oppressed becomes that much more startling when Rossmann-Negro is sent with thousands of other people *on trains without their luggage*, into the interior of the United States; it is evident from Kafka's diary that he intended for Rossmann to be put to death.

Kafka's train seems to represent the dark, menacing aspect of American modernity, that portends destruction and not liberation, not an 'underground railroad' to freedom, but an above-ground passage to destruction. Perhaps Kafka intends his 'Negro' Rossmann to be a *Jewish* 'Negro', that is, that he is marking an affinity between Jewish people and African Americans in their mutual experiences of oppression at the hands of white Europeans. There is similarly a brief passage in Kafka's writings when he expresses the desire – while possibly just a romantic notion common in the European imaginary – to be a Native American, which read more charitably might also suggest the desire for an advancement, to borrow a Derridian formulation, towards *what one is not*, as the more exemplary possibility of the European tradition, the obverse of the will to colonial domination. It may be that in this way, the taking of the name 'Negro' is a kind of performative gesture, in line with Baldwin's thesis that it is the white man who invents the Negro – hence the title of the recent documentary, 'I am not your Negro'; perhaps akin to Sartre's thesis (despite its elision of a multi-millennial-old culture) that the Jew is the invention of the antisemite.

The fear of a final solution visited upon African Americans was a persistent theme of the non-fiction of James Baldwin: 'The truth is that this country does not know what to do with its black population, dreaming of anything like "the final solution".'[151] Baldwin's comment on the Second World War was that it was not fought to save the Jews, but for the West to save itself and for no other reason.[152] For Baldwin, America, as a child of Europe, is capable of the same crimes: 'There is nothing in the evidence offered by the book of the American republic which allows me really to argue with the cat who says to me: "They needed us to pick the cotton and now they don't need us anymore. Now they don't need us, they're going to kill us all off. Just like they did the Indians." And I can't say it's a Christian nation, that your brothers will never do that to you, because the record is too long and too bloody. That's all we have done. All your buried corpses now begin to speak.'[153] When multiple African American children were disappearing in Atlanta or turning up murdered, Baldwin, in *The Evidence of Things Not Seen*, suspected wider forces at play, even if there was a direct perpetrator or perpetrators, in the context of a socio-political system designed to endanger the children regardless. References to genocide, Final Solution, Holocaust, America as the Fourth Reich, the shadow of the gas chamber, are replete throughout his work. *In The Evidence of Things Not Seen*, he suggests that African Americans have less reason to be reassured about their fate than did assimilated German Jewry, and that 'the truth concerning the White North American experience is to be deciphered in the hieroglyphic lashed onto the Black man's back';[154] in *The Fire Next Time*, referring to the Holocaust, he writes: 'I could not but feel, in those sorrowful years, that this human indifference, concerning which I knew so much already, would be my portion on the day that the United States decided to murder its Negroes systematically instead of little by little and catch-as-catch-can.'[155] Interestingly, in the French Resistance the notion of an 'underground railroad' was the appellation used to describe the underground to get Jewish people over the frontier from France to Switzerland, whose predecessors in a different but equally vital struggle were the extraordinary heroes of the American anti-slavery resistance such as Harriet Tubman.[156]

Given these fears, the question of asylum in reading across traditions of oppression becomes of heightened importance. In *Beloved*, Toni Morrison poignantly demonstrates how often African Americans could only rely upon each other in their flight from enslavement.[157] Morrison makes plain how escape from slavery is bound up with the need for asylum: the character Paul D reflects on all those 'who, like him, had hidden in caves and fought owls for food; who, like him, stole from pigs; who, like him, slept in trees in the day and walked by night; who, like him, had buried themselves in slop and jumped in wells to avoid regulators, raiders, paterollers, veterans, hill men, posses and merrymakers . . . Move. Walk. Run. Hide. Steal and move on'.[158] When Paul D is later hiding out and needs refuge but will not ask for it, the character Stamp Paid indignantly exclaims: 'Why? Why he have to ask? Can't nobody offer? What's going on? Since when a blackman come to town have to sleep in a cellar like a dog?'[159] The guiding assumption in this exclamation is that the proffering of asylum amongst the oppressed goes without saying: 'they followed secondary routes, scanned the horizon for signs and counted heavily on each other. Silent, except for social courtesies, when they met one another they either described nor asked about the sorrow that drove them from one place to another. The whites didn't bear speaking on. Everybody knew'.[160] Indeed, the reader is struck by the immediacy of the refuge granted to the title character Beloved, a complete stranger, by those who do not yet know she is of their family, but dead, or returned from the dead, the living dead, a totally unknown revenant.[161] Here is immediate, virtually unconditional hospitality granted to the wholly other, up to and including the dead: the very enactment of the apparently impossible purity of Derrida's injunction to 'say yes to who or what turns up . . . [including] a living or dead thing'.[162] The tradition of the oppressed is here enacted as a *solidarity* of the oppressed (in terms of rescuers as part of this tradition, as discussed above, one thinks here also of the extraordinary abilities and courage personified in Harriet Tubman); whether by choice or necessity, one theme of the novel is that the oppressed have to live with their exiles and their ghosts, in a way that the dominant stratas of society do not, as well having to live with the memory of the disappeared, often not knowing their fate. Indeed in *Beloved*, hell, that is, the slave plantation, is depicted as a pretty place, of genteel environs that for the former slaves are nevertheless full of ghosts: 'Fire and brimstone all right, but hidden in lacy groves. Boys hanging from the most beautiful sycamores in the world'.[163] Morrison coins the neologism 'rememories' in the novel to describe this process of working through memory as a working through of the often unbearable. In a later essay entitled 'Rememory' she explains:

It was in *Beloved* that all of these matters coalesced for me in new and major ways. History versus memory, and memory versus memorylessness. Rememory as in recollecting and remembering as in reassembling the members of the body, the family, the population of the past. And it was the struggle, the

pitched battle between remembering and forgetting, that became the device of
the narrative. The effort to both remember and not know became the structure
of the text. Nobody in the book can bear too long to dwell on the past; nobody
can avoid it.[164]

The first ever U.S. Congressperson from a Palestinian background,
Rashida Tlaib, made remarks concerning the Israel–Palestine conflict
that she felt pride in the fact that it was her people, the Palestinians, that
had been able to provide a refuge for Jewish people in the aftermath of
the Shoah. While her comments were perhaps awkwardly phrased (she
indicated that it gave her a 'calming feeling', an infelicitous expression),
and her account of the history was immediately challenged, it underscores
Butler's argument of the possibility of a common understanding being
forged between displaced people, and a polity in Israel–Palestine based
on a mutual recognition of a history of exile and the possibility of comity
grounded in the common rights of the refugee (which would necessitate a
law or right of return applicable to all).[165] Levinas, often reproached for his
apparent hostility to Palestinians (in an interview where in fact he broke
his silence on Israel to condemn the Sabra and Shatila massacres), nevertheless obliquely recognized the injustice of their treatment, writing that
'next to a person who has been affronted, this land – holy and promised
– is but nakedness and desert, a heap of wood and stone'.[166] Edward Said
gestured in a similar direction (and this was a major influence on Butler)
in his short text *Freud and the Non-European*, where he takes up Freud's
provocative thesis that Moses was a non-Jew to argue for the recognition
of different peoples across their claimed particularisms, a deconstruction
or abolition of nationalism.[167] Thus, contrary to the scandalous stratagems
of Jacques Vergès in defending the Nazi Klaus Barbie by ranging horror
against horror (you French colonial criminals cannot judge Nazi criminals), forms of continuity and resonance can be marked in the traditions
of oppressed peoples. 'Multidirectional memorialism' need not be seen as
violently reductive of disparate traditions, but of pointing to the shared
experience of trauma and suffering that might evince a way of thinking
through current predicaments.[168] The same society that separated families
under slavery, as so harrowingly depicted in *Beloved*, continues to do so at
its border with Mexico. Just as the Saint Louis was turned away from every
harbour of refuge, boats containing Rohingya refugees are left to languish
on the Andaman Sea. On and on it goes, the enemy has not ceased to be
victorious. Arendt was surely correct to write in *Eichmann in Jerusalem*
that 'the unprecedented, once it has appeared, may become a precedent
for the future'.[169] The mass stateless which to her generation was unprecedented has become a permanent state of exception.

In her incredibly influential yet controversial work, *Hegel, Haiti and Universal History*, Susan Buck-Morss uses the example of the successful revolution in Haiti by the enslaved as illustrative of the possibility of a 'universal history', both of horror and of resistance to that horror. (Links could be drawn between this text and Schwarz-Bart's account of a slave revolt in Guadeloupe in the above-mentioned *A Woman Named Solitude*, where both gesture towards a universal history by noting resonances across different histories of oppression.) Universal history is not simply a product of European philosophy and appeals to the French Revolution, but is marked by those moments of discontinuity when an oppressed people is pushed beyond the limits of the tolerable.[170] Buck-Morss writes:

> The definition of universal history that begins to emerge here is this: rather than giving multiple, distinct cultures equal due, whereby people are recognized as part of humanity indirectly through the mediation of collective cultural identities, human universality emerges in the historical event at the point of rupture. It is in the discontinuities of history that people whose culture has been strained to the breaking point give expression to a humanity that goes beyond cultural limits. And it is our empathic identification with this raw, free and vulnerable state, that we have a chance of understanding what they say. Common humanity exists in spite of culture and its differences. A person's nonidentity with the collective allows for subterranean solidarities that have a chance of appealing to universal, moral sentiment, the source today of enthusiasm and hope. It is not through culture, but through threat of culture's betrayal that consciousness of a common humanity comes to be.[171]

What Benjamin means by the tradition of the oppressed can thus be linked to Buck-Morss's account of a universal history, where the latter has little to do with the European inculcation of its liberationary values (although the 'Black Jacobins' certainly invoked France's ideals against its brutal hypocrisy), but to resistance to its oppression. (Does not Europe's earliest story, the *Iliad* – the 'poem of force', as Simone Weil described it – already reveal the will to violent domination, the refusal of mercy and the destruction of societies, the necropolitics of which Achille Mbembe writes, that will constitute the essence of its history?) Walter Benjamin, reviewing a book on modern fairy-tales which he suggested reveals the blood-thirsty dark heart of the German imaginary, expressed the heavily ironical hope that the dying Weimar Republic 'will still find the energy to block the path of this fun-loving reformism, for which psychology, folklore and pedagogy are only flags under which the fairy tale as an export commodity is freighted to a dark corner of the globe, where the children in the plantations yearn for its pious mode of thinking'.[172] Here is where an important difference – and disagreement – with Levinas must be

marked, who once observed in an interview: 'I am sceptical with regard to a
literature that seeks to show that all humanity is one, since I would not build
the future of humanity on exotic cultures'; in the same interview, he remarks,
'humanity is Biblical', that is, in his standard formulation, the Bible and the
Greeks.[173] This cultural myopia and ethnocentrism must be opposed, even if
it can and should be opposed in the terms of Levinas's own thought where
respect for the other is primary and of universal significance – in the face, as
he argued, a right is to be found. And it is not a matter of reducing humanity
to 'one', but of noting the 'universal' history of oppression of different groups
with unique experiences. No Levinasian should evade his evident failings in
these matters, which is a different way of remaining faithful to the importance
of his work than discipleship, a matter of 'faithful unfaithfulness', or 'unfaith-
ful faithfulness', to borrow Derrida's expression.

   Yet even if it can be maintained that disparate traditions of oppression can
be brought into meaningful proximity in ways that might inform an *ethos* of
responsibility, further difficulties remain. How is it possible to take responsibility for those you cannot even name, for the disappeared, the drowned at
sea, all those who never managed to escape? From the Mediterranean to the
Mexican borderlands, the nameless victims multiply: as Todd Miller writes
in *Empire of Borders*, 'Father Alejandro Solalinde, a priest who ran a migrant
shelter in nearby Ixtepec, Oaxaca, calls this Mexican borderlands region a
"cemetery for the nameless"'.[174] This problem of naming the disappeared
underscores the literary genius of Toni Morrison's gesture in giving her
protagonist the non-name of 'Beloved', a headstone signifier that was never
completed with a proper name:

> Everybody knew what she was called, but nobody anywhere knew her name.
> Disremembered and unaccounted for, she cannot be lost because no one is look-
> ing for her, and even if they were, how can they call her if they don't know her
> name? . . . It was not a story to pass on. They forgot her like a bad dream.[175]

Yet the violence of forgetting is mirrored by a violence of remembrance: the
difficulty of memorializing the unknown, the unnamed, the already missing
or disappeared or long dead, is further complicated by the moral problem of
how to memorialize that which resists memorialization or indeed making of
the memorial a use-value, an instrumentalization which risks deploying the
memory of the dead for one's own purposes. There may be limits or context
that determine (but how to determine them?) the right one has, or does not
have, to tell someone else's story. Rebecca Comay has written on the moving exhibitions of Doris Salcedo, whose work encompasses multiple victims
of oppression, from the disappeared in Colombia, to the unnamed drowning
victims of migrant sea crossings.[176] Comay notes that Salcedo's installations

do not contain any overt call to political action – 'any solidarity is with the dead'.[177] Comay refers to Adorno to encapsulate the challenges provoked by Salcedo's work:

> Salcedo thus seems to confront the predicament that Adorno expressed so brutally. On the one hand, it is the task of art to commemorate suffering. On the other hand, art, by its very existence – its status as a thing among things – is complicitous in this suffering. Furthermore, every attempt to withdraw from this complicity only compounds it: in its flight to otherworldliness art colludes in reinforcing the divisions of class-dominated society. And further yet, every attempt to give voice to this predicament, even to state or unpack the aporia philosophically, also risks embellishing suffering by producing the thrilling distractions of – merely – intellectual upheaval. And this guilty pleasure, or this pleasurable discomfort, intensifies with every subsequent theorisation.[178]

Comay leaves the reader faced with several antinomies or aporias, concerning the paralysis that attends the effort to memorialize the unnamed (a risk haunting every sentence of this chapter) – risks of narcissistic identification, catharsis, pity.[179] But perhaps it is necessary to resist this mode of aporetic thinking (which nevertheless opens the space of true responsibility-taking, as Derrida has explained, for where there is nothing to be decided there is no true responsibility), to be somewhat more direct and uncompromising; the response to Comay/Salcedo might be something like this, that ironically, it may be possible to break out of the (negative?) dialectic with some help from Adorno, who stipulated that the protection of suffering bodies is the *sine qua non* of an acceptable politics: 'The *telos* of such an organization of society would be to negate the physical suffering of even the least of its members.'[180] In this sense, biopolitics is not simply to be dismissed as a dangerous corralling of the human animal, but also affirmed in its protective modalities, as has been developed by Judith Butler around the precarity of bodies, the actual suffering of lived humanity. Perhaps what must be guarded against is a *speaking for*, and instead to emphasize a practice and ethics of *listening*: as Adorno also emphasized, the condition of truth is to allow suffering to speak.[181] The Berlin Memorial to the Murdered Jews of Europe might be seen as staging a certain dialectic concerning the antinomies of memorialization – on its surface, blank grey blocks, like graves with no names; yet inside, in 'The Room of Names', the names of victims are continuously read out. The Klarsfeld's immense tribute to the French children of the Holocaust is a similar effort, as are memorial and works of history in many places and contexts worldwide: Serge Klarsfeld referred to this rescue of the memory of the children 'who did not grow up' as like 'taking someone from the night and bringing him to the light'.[182] Klarsfeld: 'This book is born of my obsession to be sure that these children will not be forgotten. Twenty years ago, when reconstructing the lists of Jews deported to death from France, I found that some of the deported children were listed only by number – the infants were too young to know or say their names – and I felt a deep shame that they died nameless to the world.'[183] This 'necronominalism'[184] resists the oblivion intended by the Nazis, and tacitly intended by the mean-spiritedness of the liberal-democracies: 'the disaster is . . . the disappearance of the proper name' (Blanchot).[185] The monument to Walter Benjamin, built at the site of his grave in Spain where he was buried after committing suicide as a refugee fleeing the Nazis, contains the following quotation: 'It is more arduous to honour the memory of the nameless than that of the renowned. Historical construction is devoted to the memory of the nameless.'[186] In Ciudad Juárez, murals of the faces of the disappeared and murdered women, the victims of *feminicidio*, adorn the city walls, serving multiple functions as a performative warning to the still-living women of the city, a memorial to the dead as well as a reproach of the government's failure to act, and the neoliberal capitalist system that produces the environment of exploitation in which such crimes are manifested: the faces looking 'directly at NAFTA, consequently haunt[ing] neoliberalism itself as a culpable agent'.[187]

Such remembering, rememory, memorialization, however fraught, remains essential – for remaining in the antinomies of witnessing would do violence to the indignation of many survivors, just as archiving itself, as Derrida wrote, carries within it the archive 'fever' that risks destruction: 'If there is no archive without consignation in an external place which assures the possibility of memorization, of repetition, of reproduction, or or reimpression, then we must also remember that repetition itself, the logic of repetition, indeed the repetition compulsion, remains, according to Freud, indissociable from the death drive.'[188] Archiving can be violent, even work against itself, and in so doing 'verges on radical evil' (Derrida).[189] Yet the risk must be run; a responsible politics of memory must be attentive to what Elias Canetti called the 'invisible crowd of the dead'.[190] The survivor often implores others to listen – indeed, Primo Levi's nightmare was that no one would listen. He wrote of an experience in Poland wherein he tried to convey his experience, but that no one understood: 'I had dreamed something like that, we all had, in the Auschwitz night: to speak and not be listened to, to find freedom again and remain alone.'[191] This fear of 'ethical loneliness' is also reflected in the Preface to *If This Is a Man*, where he writes that 'the need to tell our story to "others", to make "others" share it, took on for us, before the liberation and after, the character of an immediate and violent impulse, to the point of competing with other elementary needs'.[192] The poem 'Shema' (named after the Jewish prayer), which serves as epigraph to that work, carries the exhortation that doubles as threatened condemnation, that those who live in safety must 'carve into your hearts' the memory of the horror, or else be deserving of ill-tidings themselves.[193] Toni Morrison notes in her introduction to Levi's complete works that Levi's poetry contain 'accusatory ghosts', such as his: 'Song of the Crow 1', where the crow travels a great distance 'to sit in your heart each evening' and trouble the quiet repose of the contented.[194]

The ghost, in Levi's poems as in Morrison's *Beloved* and in *Hamlet* and elsewhere, *returns to accuse*. The audience are exhorted to listen, to carve these memories into their hearts; yet Salcedo/Comay are right to warn against complacency in the assumption of this as an ethical duty; as Blanchot put it, 'The wish of all, in the camps, the last wish: know what has happened, do not forget, and at the same time never will you know'.[195] As Morrison observed in *Beloved*, anything dead coming back to life hurts.[196] Perhaps the messages from the dead are, in the words of T. S. Eliot, 'tongued with fire beyond the language of the living'.[197] One of the children of *La Maison d'Izieu*, Liliane Gerenstein (eleven years old), wrote a 'letter to God' that was found in the abandoned house after she and her brother Maurice had already been deported to their deaths:

God? How good You are, how kind and if one had to count the number of
    goodnesses and kindnesses You have done, one would never finish.
God? It is You who command. It is You who are justice, it
    is You who reward the good and punish the evil.
God? It is thanks to You that I had a beautiful life before, that I was
    spoiled, that I had lovely things that others do not have.
God? After that, I ask You one thing only: Make my parents come
    back, my poor parents protect them (even more than You protect
    me) so that I can see them again as soon as possible.
Make them come back again. Ah! I had such a good mother and such a
    good father! I have such faith in You and I thank You in advance.[198]

Her mother at that point had already been deported and murdered, and her father never learned of his children's fate.[199] The already-dead child's admonition to 'make them come back', to un-do the irreparable, is difficult to bear. A God to whose name was repeatedly appended, by the pleading, soon-to-be-murdered child, a question-mark. Erich Auerbach's thesis that Dante is a poet of the secular world (recall also Arendt's reference to Hell coming to earth, discussed in the Introduction) is here apposite – Dante journeys with Virgil to the dark place, but the hellish other world is in fact a representation of our own.[200] It shows a human protagonist, an exile (Dante himself), engaging with so many formerly living human beings who have no possibility of return to life or continuing on in the afterlife (as do those in the *Purgatorio*) and whose deepest desire is that they not be forgotten. Yet one is tempted by a Beckettian formulation here: the dead cannot come back, they must come back, if only in memory and 'rememory', in remembrance and mourning, in melancholy yet as impetus to future action. However, memory can also produce paralysis, the mounting pile of bodies and detritus (how could death have unmade so many?) in Benjamin's image is not something the angel of history can act upon, being that it is helplessly propelled backwards. Recall the last passage of Melville's celebrated short story, 'Bartleby the Scrivener', who has been reduced to a state of total inaction (the famous 'I would prefer not to'), where one is given a clue as to the cause of his torpor:

> The report was this: that Bartleby had been a subordinate clerk in the Dead Letter Office at Washington, from which he had been suddenly removed by a change in the administration. When I think over this rumor, hardly can I express the emotions which seize me. Dead letters! Does it not sound like dead men? Conceive a man by nature and misfortune prone to a pallid hopelessness, can any business seem more fitted to heighten it than that of continually handling these dead letters, and assorting them for the flames? For by the cart-load they are annually burned. Sometimes from out the folded paper the pale clerk takes a ring:-the finger it was meant for, perhaps, moulders in the grave; a bank-note sent in swiftest charity:-he whom it would relieve, nor eats nor hungers any more; pardon for those who died despairing; hope for those who died unhoping; good tidings for those who died stifled by unrelieved calamities. On errands of life, these letters speed to death.
>
> Ah Bartleby! Ah humanity![201]

Is there not a sense of paralysing futility in my own gesture of homage to dead children from seventy years ago in a country not my own, to insist, as Améry does, that the moral person demands annulment of time, for all time, in all times? 'Sufficient unto the day are the evils thereof' (Matthew 6:34); and yet while it is true that contemporary events continually press upon political decision-making, to focus only on the present is to do an injustice to the victims of the past. Améry laments that 'the social body is occupied merely with safeguarding itself and could not care less about a life that has been damaged'.[202] In Michael Mann's gripping film *Heat*, the detective Vincent Hanna, played by Al Pacino, is relentless in his pursuit of wrongdoers, but won't share his confronting work with his wife, explaining to her: 'Because I gotta hold on to my angst. I preserve it. Because I need it.' She reproaches him with the destruction of their common life (their marriage is falling apart): 'You don't live with me. You live among the remains of dead people.' There is a representation in this dynamic of the unnatural resistance of the indignant one, the just person as resentful or angst-filled, to the natural passage of time (what Améry called 'my personal protest against the antimoral natural process of healing that time brings about'), and their need to tarry with the dead, their memory, the gruesome tableau of their murder scenes.[203] Hanna/ Pacino, in the famous diner scene where he meets Robert De Niro's character, recounts a recurring dream where he is seated at a big banquet table where all the murder victims from his cases are staring at him with their black eyes, and who nevertheless do not speak.[204] Yet the obligation of responding to their unspoken demand risks the destruction of a common world, the world of family and connection, social commonality that perhaps requires forgetting and moving on in order to sustain the necessary bonds that make life liveable; this was Primo Levi's reproach to Améry's philosophy of resentment, that it would ultimately only bring harm to the resenter: 'A man who gets into fist-fights with the whole world regains his dignity but pays a very high price because he is certain of his own defeat.'[205] *Fiat iustitia et pereat mundus*, the destruction of the world as the commonly shared world of human personal and social cohabitation, for a vision of justice that requires fidelity to those who can no longer voice their demand, who are no longer in the world, if the world is construed solely according to the categories of presence and the dictates of clock-time. Améry had 'the desire that time be turned back and, with it, that history become moral'.[206] His justification: 'Whoever submerges his individuality in society and is able to comprehend himself only as a function of the social, that is, the insensitive and indifferent person, really does forgive. He calmly allows what happened to remain what it was. As the popular saying goes, he lets time heal his wounds. His time-sense is not-dis-ordered, that is to say, it has not moved out of the biological and social sphere into the moral sphere.'[207] In other words, those who merely conform to the preservation of the social and the unchallenged progression of clock-time are dangerous, because they may forgive and forget anything on that basis. A murder or massacre or a boat that sank at sea, if it happened only yesterday, is literally *yesterday's news*, already competing impotently from the beyond with the more pressing demands of the immediate. In this sense, justice requires an unnatural resentment that defies the bonds of time.

And yet how one contends with the memory of the victim is also fraught – danger lurks even in memorialization; Marcel Liebman in his memoir *Born Jewish*, wrestles with this problem in refusing to simply memorialize his deported brother, but keeping the trauma of this memory open as a question. As with Judith Butler, he refuses a reading of this history that would justify the actions of the State of Israel against the Palestinians, but rather universalizes the lesson into one of anti-racism, in addressing his disappeared brother: 'Any obligation I have felt to the dead of the war and, if one wished to personalise this, to one of them in particular, is a duty that comes down to this: holding the racism that murdered them to be a crime in which one never colludes . . . If one could imagine what duty the living have to the dead, I really believe that my brother could not ask for anything more.'[208]

It is possible to draw the wrong lessons from the past, or morally dubious lessons; perhaps this is what Samuel Moyn means when he writes that 'sometimes the present should only be haunted by itself, its own novelty'.[209] However, the 'sometimes' must be marked here, as it is difficult to agree totally. It is true that there is nothing I can do for the children of Izieu now to make them come back to life, and there are urgent calamities of the present and those still coming, or of the horrors committed in my own society, closer to home to me than the south of France. Yet the privilege I feel they are owed is also a universal privilege, applying also (and with greater temporal urgency) to the children of Palestine, the children in camps, the incarcerated Indigenous children of my own society, and the child that once was, in every adult. One can remember, try to understand, knowing one never will truly understand, try to draw the appropriate moral lessons for future political praxis, to not forget the victims, *any* of the victims, as much as humanly possible, to listen to those who speak, or spoke, and those who interpellate as best they can the memory of the disappeared. Remembrance of those who are near, and remembrance of those who are far off, especially given that 'it can happen anywhere', that the horrors of the far-off may *become* the horrors of the near. For André Schwarz-Bart, writing in *The Morning Star* (the book which provides the epigraph to the present book), 'the point was to stay in touch with the dead, make a living space for them on earth, in his mind, day after day, until he departed this life, here below. . . .'[210] As his widower Simone Schwarz-Bart writes in the introductory note to that book, the difficulty he faced in finishing this unfinished work was 'for him, that would mean abandoning the dead, whereas he wanted to keep them there inside him till the end: "Finishing anything is always treason, high treason"'.[211] Schwarz-Bart evinced a horror of failing to remember the disappeared: In *The Last of the Just*, in wondering how one accounts for all the suffering of the world, one of his characters exclaims: 'It gets lost, oh my God, it gets lost!'[212]

In *Kaddish for an Unborn Child*, addressed to the ghost of a child that was deliberately not conceived owing to the horrors of Kertész's experience – from the hands of childhood tormentors through to the Nazis – Kertész suggests that being ought not to be[213] (a question all the more fraught when considering the arrival of children into a world threatened by climate change, millions of whom may become refugees); a question posed also by Levinas ('is it righteous to be?'),[214] and by Adorno's revision of his dictum concerning poetry after Auschwitz, a semi mea-culpa in *Negative Dialectics*, which is followed by an even more devastating question concerning the permissibility of living at all following that disaster.[215]

Memory, grief, mourning, and melancholia, accusatory charges against being as such; can politics be formed upon such matter, or are they inherently unproductive experiences which can only lead to a state of withdrawal and torpor? In *Philosophy and Melancholy*, Ilit Ferber notes that melancholy, while it can be depressive, can also be productive (it is often linked to works of genius).[216] Yet this genius is not to be interpreted as simple madness, but is related also to what Andrew Benjamin calls the 'ineliminability of measure', that is, a certain dialectic between madness and measure.[217] Ferber analyses Walter Benjamin's idea of the history of melancholy encapsulated in the image of the whirlpool in which "'the prehistory and posthistory of an event, or better, of a status, swirl around it'".[218] This is linked to the emphasis upon mood (*stimmung*) in Heidegger, which discloses rather than conceals the world (and determines philosophy's encounter with the world, contrary to other accounts of epistemology), and that this attunement to mood is linked to wakefulness. While Ferber acknowledges that Benjamin is no Heideggerian, she suggests that mood as crucial to the philosophical is of decisive importance in 'the understanding of melancholy's place in Benjamin's thought'.[219] Benjamin challenges Freud's distinction between mourning and melancholia in a way that moves these concepts from a psychological pathology to a social normativity; as Ferber writes, 'What is so evocative about the *Trauerspiel* for Benjamin is its continuous state of death or, put differently, the way it makes constant reference to its own state of being the object of loss.'[220] Mood is thus not simply constitutive of a particular human subject, not a property of a subject but constitutes one's very being in the world.[221] (One might link this to that noted above concerning the experiences of mourning and melancholia evinced in the dispossessed and the new settlers, respectively, in the United States, as observed by de Tocqueville.)

Concatenating a further thought to Ferber's, there is a deep resonance with Levinas here. Similar, though distinct, from Heidegger's writings on *Stimmung* (often translated as mood), is Levinas's reflections in his earlier work on the '*il y a*' and insomnia. The *il y a*, 'there is', is the impersonal rumbling of existence, the empty night in which nevertheless something silent stirs.[222] The awareness of this *il y a* leads the subject to a kind of wakefulness, an insomnia; this can be understood as both a phenomenological description of human experience and an ethical claim. For Levinas, insomnia is the non-sleep of the ethically watchful, a nightwatchman at the antipodes of Robert Nozick's libertarian minder, who rather watches out for the welfare of the other, and responds with 'me voici', 'here I am', in affirmative reply, a promise of assistance, to the cry of distress. To mood, melancholy, mourning, memory, watchfulness, can also be added Levinas's use of 'presentiment' – he once defined his work as defined by both the presentiment and the memory of the Nazi horror, and his essay 'Reflections on the Philosophy of Hitlerism' was indeed remarkably prescient in already understanding in the early 1930s that Nazism portended a challenge to the 'very humanity of man'.[223] Thus to Derridian hauntology,

Benjaminian melancholy and the Arendtian critique of loneliness must be added Levinasian wakefulness and presentiment; as Shakespeare seems to suggest at the beginning of Hamlet, it is those who are standing watch in the night who will encounter the ghost (although not only scholars!). The 'night of being', a consistent theme in the arguments of this book, means that 'ultimate events of being' are not those disclosed to the daylight of consciousness, but to other states of awareness or non-awareness – melancholy or insomnia, hauntedness or presentiment, and so on; the other meaning of 'unchosenness' that must inform the new concept of the political concerning the right to asylum. René Char's masterpiece of poetry, *Hypnos*, uses the metaphor of night to depict both the darkness of Occupied France with the night that enabled the movements of his partisans and himself; to this he opposes the 'daytime of Nazism', which he curiously links to economics: 'The hideous flower, the outlined flower [the swastika], revolves its black petals in the mad flesh of the sun. Where is the source? Where the remedy? When will the economy finally change its ways?'[224] The trading hours of the light of day are undermined by the moral clarity effectuated under cover of night, where Hypnos, god of sleep 'took hold of winter and dressed it in granite', an endless ordeal but where the dark provides cover and clarity, and where the 'moon of Hypnos' represents hope in the form of resistance to oppression: 'resistance is nothing but hope'.[225] 'If only life could be disappointed sleep', Char reflects.[226] Insomnia as the awareness that ultimate events of being are not reducible to the light of comprehension or calculation, to the readily observable or already chosen.

In the conclusion of the *The Last of the Just*, André Schwarz-Bart, who admits of having reached a limit ('I am so weary that my pen can no longer write'), ends the book with a strange recollection: 'At times, it is true, one's heart could break in sorrow. But often too, preferably in the evening, I cannot help thinking that Ernie Levy, dead six million times, is still alive, somewhere, I don't know where . . . Yesterday, as I stood in the street trembling in despair, rooted to the spot, a drop of pity fell from above upon my face; but there was no breeze in the air, no cloud in the sky . . . there was only a presence.'[227]

Examples of this claim multiply in literature and in memoir. In his simply titled slim volume *Paris*, Julian Green recounts a visit to Notre Dame Cathedral in 1940, where a gale is tearing at the canvas that has been put in place of the stained glass window that has been removed as a precaution against the impact of bombing. At the front of the cathedral were several men and women who, Green wrote, seemed to be keeping a vigil: 'It was as if the wind, the gathering dusk, the pillars and vaults, and the entire cathedral had been shouting a terrible warning to us all, which we could not hear. I left the building almost immediately, having no idea that it would be five years before I saw Notre Dame again'; by the time he returns, after the war, the question he had been asking, 'but whose vigil are they keeping?', seems to find its answer in a cross now placed in the Cathedral dedicated to the victims of Buchenwald.[228]

Returning to Patrick Modiano's novel *Dora Bruder*, concerning his attempts to establish the lost history of a deported Jewish girl who had lived in Paris, the reader is confronted with a world full of stillborn stories, recollections of people that are lost, that can never be fully recovered or known. Modiano's sense of haunting permeates the book, from the intimations he had of looking for something that he can't quite name, to his feeling, in traversing the paths once tread of those who have disappeared, of an obscure sense of connection: 'At the time, I knew nothing of Dora Bruder and her parents. I remember that I had a peculiar sensation as I hugged the wall of Lariboisière Hospital, and again on crossing the railway tracks, as though I had penetrated the darkest part of Paris'.[229] Modiano's Paris is a Paris of ghosts that are almost felt, that, as with Schwarz-Bart, in some way, a presence lingers: 'Ever since, the Paris wherein I have tried to retrace her steps has remained as silent and deserted as it was on that day. I walk through empty streets. For me, they are always empty, even at dusk, during the rush hour, when the crowds are hurrying toward the mouths of the métro. I think of her in spite of myself, sensing an echo of her presence in this neighbourhood or that. The other evening, it was near the Gare du Nord'.[230] Modiano reflects on how real streets in Hugo's *Les Misérables* suddenly divert into fictional streets: 'It is the same sense of strangeness that overcomes you when you find yourself walking through an unfamiliar district in a dream. On waking, you realise, little by little, that the pattern of its streets had overlaid the one with which, in daytime, you are familiar.' But buildings and streets change, taking with them the memory, but perhaps leavings a trace: 'And yet, from time to time, beneath this thick layer of amnesia, you can certainly sense something, an echo, distant, muted, but of what, precisely, it is impossible to say.'[231] Judith Butler refers similarly to the 'amnesiac surface of time, so that what seems to be moving toward us . . . is a memory as it acts upon the present, a memory that takes fragmented and scattered form . . . We do not seek to redeem that past . . . Things have to remain undone', but in a way that allows 'for a different now-time', a Benjaminian resistance to 'the swifter resolutions of Hegelian desire', wherein the 'history of oppression might break through the history of the victor, destabilize the claim to progress'.[232] The point, that is, is to remain haunted, not to resolve matters, or even to reassure, via means of a meditative hauntology, that one has understood. The dead take their secrets with them, as Modiano reminds us so movingly at the end of his meditations upon Dora: 'I shall never know how she spent her days, where she hid, in whose company she passed the winter months of her first escape, or the few weeks of spring when she escaped for the second time. That is her secret. A poor and precious secret that not even the executioners, the decrees, the occupying authorities, the Dépôt, the barracks, the camps, History, time – everything that defiles and destroys you – have been able to take away from her.'[233]

Scott Warren of No More Deaths believes that the dead linger in the place where they fell, in the Arizona desert that he patrols with his fellow rescuers, as a sentinel of aid.[234] A proper understanding of human relationality and that which is proper to the being of human beings would see the efforts of No More Deaths as the fundamental work of political life. Indeed, the very name of this group – No More Deaths – would seem to represent the enactment of a politics of hauntology, of memory and remembrance that keeps the deaths that have occurred at the front and centre of their political project. Natasha Lennard, in her recent book *Being Numerous: Essays on Non-Fascist Life*, discusses the notion of hauntology in relation to her experience of a 'ghost' that she has always felt lived in the bathroom of her family home. To apply a rigorous epistemology to such an experience and dismiss it as nonsense is, she argues, to lock oneself into 'stable, unmovable categories that could never allow for ghosts'.[235] Lennard links this resistance to the searching light of the ghost-busting sceptic with a political imperative: 'To believe (impossibly) that another world is possible, while necessarily being unable to explain that world from the confines of this one.'[236]

Ghosts, phantoms; but in a thoroughly disenchanted world, do drops really fall from the air, does the heart really whisper, do the dead really linger in place, do ghosts hang around in bathrooms? But it can hardly matter that these images and metaphors, while poetically evoking a resonant meaning, do not speak to anything real; as Derrida wrote of ghosts: 'Of course they do not exist, so what?'[237] One does not have to share the metaphysics expressed by Modiano or Lennard or Warren, to realize that it is it is profoundly unserious not to believe in ghosts, that (Derrida) 'haunting is the state of proper being as such'.[238] The true error is the apparently real: as Levinas pithily puts it in *Totality and Infinity*, 'The presence of the Other dispels the anarchic sorcery of the facts'.[239] In Oscar Wilde's 'The Canterville Ghost', the staunchly secular house-buyer will have no truck with the ghostly – even insisting pragmatically that it oil the chains it rattles. The new residents of the mansion mock and disdain the ghost, despite a blood stain left by the ghost that will not dissipate. The comic elements of this particular ghost story notwithstanding, the symbolic denial of the non-material is telling as the metaphysical attitude of liberal bourgeois societies. The ghost complains about those it is supposed to haunt: 'They were evidently people on a low, material plane of existence, and quite incapable of appreciating the symbolic value of sensuous phenomena.'[240]

In the face of such myopia, storytelling thus becomes an active duty; indeed, just as the human being is the political animal, it is just as fundamentally the storytelling animal.[241] In *What Ought I To Do*, an examination of Kant along-side Levinas, Catherine Chalier reminders the reader that Kant thought human dignity requires 'every political community to endeavor to shape the hearts and minds of its citizenry'.[242] Here both history and storytelling are of deci-sive importance, their import relating to Kant's hope that eventually humanity will not have to be '"forced to turn our eyes from [the history of mankind] in disgust"', which, as Chalier notes, can only be accomplished when it is con-ceivable (quoting Kant again) '"how our descendants will begin to grasp the burden of the history we shall leave to them after a few centuries"'.[243]

That politics must shape the self-understanding of a political community in relation to memory, inheritance, and generations was also articulated by Arendt (storytelling is consistently emphasized in *The Human Condition*), why conceived of the polis as 'a kind of organised remembrance'.[244] The polis, for Arendt, 'is not the physical state in its physical location; it is the organization of the people as it arises out of acting and speaking together [. . .] 'Wherever you go, you will be a polis".[245] The creation of a shared world is also a world of memory and remembrance: 'To be deprived of it means to be deprived of reality, which humanly and politically speaking, is the same as appearance. To men the reality of the world is guaranteed by the presence of others, by its appearing to all: "for what appears to all, this we call Being" [quoting Aristotle], and whatever lacks this appearance comes and passes away like a dream, intimately and exclusively our own but without reality.'[246]

And yet here again – a theme throughout! – Aristotle must be resisted. In *Herodotus and the Origins of the Political Community*, Norma Thompson argues that Aristotle's opposition to the fabulations, if such they were, of Herodotus, has led to an 'academic enclosure of the human commons', 'a triumph of rigorous intellectualization over a way of inquiry more willing and able to comprehend uncertainty, contingency, inconsistency, and the varied sources of human constancy and change'.[247] Thompson argues that 'Much of political thought as we know it today exists in a universe designed by Aristotle', but that in Herodotus a different way of approaching politi-cal matters can be discovered, that mixes factual history with stories, that 'link knowledge with life'.[248] Storytelling is consequently an endless pro-cess 'that is at the root of any political community . . . To be human is to engage history, for history is all we have. What we make of it will shape a common destiny'.[249] As mentioned in the introduction, the original political philosophers, Plato and Aristotle, were silent on the theme of refuge as a political question, whereas the tragedians of the fifth century BCE made it an explicit theme (such as in *The Suppliant Maidens* and *Oedipus at Colonus*). Storytelling may do the work of staging the problem of asylum in a way that leads to understanding, something that political philosophy may fail to do; here Heidegger's remark may be applied (without the emphasis being the same), that 'The tragedies of Sophocles – provided such a comparison is at all permissible – preserve the ēthos in their sagas more primordially than Aristotle's lectures on "ethics"'.[250] One might also consider Maurice Blanchot's *Awaiting Oblivion*, where the distinction between philosophy and narrative is blurred to the point of indeterminacy, where finally, 'It is not a fiction, although he is incapable of pronouncing the word "truth" in connection with all of that. Something happened to him, and he can say neither say that it was true, nor the contrary. Later, he thought that the event consisted in this manner of being neither true nor false'.[251]

Thompson quotes Benjamin's essay 'The Storyteller', where he argues that a story endures in a way that the information of any given present moment will not: 'It [a story] does not expend itself. It preserves and concentrates its strength and is capable of releasing it after a long time'.[252] For Benjamin, the storyteller has a moral purpose, and offers counsel to the reader, and is thus distinguished from information or mere explanation.[253] Storytelling is the act of repetition, and whereas 'bourgeois society seeks "to make it possible to avoid the sight of the dying"', the very importance of the storyteller is derived from the dead: 'Death is the sanction of everything that the storyteller can tell. He has borrowed his authority from death'.[254] Repetition of events sanctioned by the authority of the dead – this is storytelling, where, distinct from historians, 'they [the chroniclers] have from the very start lifted the burden of demonstrable explanation from their own shoulders. Its place is taken by interpretation, which is not concerned with an accurate concatenation of definite events, but with the way these are embedded in the great inscrutable course of the world'.[255] If chroniclers have historically been concerned with religious eschatology, the storyteller is the inheritor of the eschatological task of the chronicler;[256] while Benjamin uses eschatology in its more traditional sense in this essay, this could be related to the discussion of eschatology as advanced by Levinas where moral judgement that interrupts the course of history becomes actualized, though via a different means, not the experience of ethics (Levinas) but a storytelling that is itself ethical or 'righteous': ultimately, Benjamin's bold claim is that the 'storyteller is the figure in which the righteous man encounters himself'.[257]

In this sense it may be possible to reorient the meaning of Arendt's claim that the polis is a kind of organized remembrance; rather than the polis simply celebrating the deeds of the members of that society, a remembrance of another history, a ghostly history, or even stories that go beyond but speak to the realities of history, also lies at the source of the polis, or shadows it.[258] To think about something is to remember it, Arendt counselled – to be responsible for history and its implications for the present requires that memory or what Toni Morrison called 'rememory', the deliberate revisitation of memories, yet where rememory, in her stories, becomes embodied in figures like

Beloved, where the dead return to press their demands. In relation to refugees, storytelling enables refugees to be recognized as unique individuals (here Arendt's own emphasis upon plurality as equality and distinction is important), not a mass called 'refugees', even if this group terminology cannot be entirely avoided. The intellectual process of understanding cannot remain bound to rational thought, but accommodate what Edward Said termed 'surrationalism', an effort 'to generate thought in order to activate itself beyond the bounds and limits set by the mere historical conventions of reason'.[259] The polis is also always a necro-polis, a being-with-the-dead, cohabitation with those who precede us as messengers of a truth unveiled in the past that irrupts within the present. Arendt, in a poem written in memory of Walter Benjamin, is close to his thought when she writes of the voices of the dead sent as 'messengers ahead, to lead us into slumber'.[260] The reference to slumber here might recall Arendt's chilling remarks in 'We Refugees', where those still living come to envy the dead exiles in the cessation of their struggles against an indifferent world.[261] Yet the dead return to deliver their message, to accuse and remonstrate, encountered in the night of being where it is not a matter of slumber but of wakefulness, of insomnia as a duty.

CONCLUSION

In *The Eighteenth Brumaire of Louis Bonaparte*, Marx writes that 'the tradition of the dead generations weighs like a nightmare on the minds of the living'.[262] Marx was referring to the burden of inherited circumstances that cannot be avoided when dealing with present matters. (There is much talk of spirits and ghosts in *The Eighteenth Brumaire* as in much of Marx's work, such as the famous spectre invoked in the opening lines of the *Communist Manifesto*, which influenced Derrida's insight regarding the importance of ghosts for Marx; hence Derrida's development of 'hauntology', related also to the deconstruction of the metaphysics of presence, of the privilege granted to immediacy over the absent.) Marx was doubtless correct about the inheritance of circumstances as somewhat mediating the possibilities of the present; and yet the concern evinced in this coda, apropos of the politics of asylum, is precisely the opposite: that the tradition of the dead weighs far too little upon the minds of the living. The multiple traditions of the dead (Marx), the oppressed (Benjamin), the disappeared (Modiano and co.) – these have scant issue in informing the politics of asylum.

I have just emphasized the importance of mourning and remembrance, of the power of history and storytelling in preventing the victims from disappearing a second time. However, it's important to go beyond storytelling, even where such stories evoke a tradition of hospitality (as in the example of France, even such a tradition has its limits) to a reworked concept of the political. It is necessary to shift the very ground on which all this operates, not just tell encouraging, or haunting, stories, or refer back to a tradition of hospitality. These are elements of the *ethos*, that should inform it and guide it, but ultimately politics itself must be rethought in relation to unchosen plurality and ethical responsibility. Indeed, the reason for terming this final chapter a Coda and not a conclusion, is that the argument is separate to the overall argumentation of the book that precedes it, but which should nevertheless animate it, inform, and undergird it, dare I suggest, *haunt* it. The argument for an *ethos* of responsibility for people seeking asylum as a *telos* of the political, read via Arendt, Levinas, Derrida, Butler, the two Benjamins and others, has its own logic, which had not yet been expressed in the manner in which it has now been described. Yet equally important is to underscore why those preceding arguments are so important, and why throughout it has been necessary to argue that so much political theory is unserious, to insist upon the moral weight of all this. Moralism requires that certain *mores* (Latin for rules of behaviour) be operative in human commonality as it is lived out, an insistence which has leaped the bounds of a no-longer-fashionable irony that would pour scorn on a moralism which is now all the more pressing with the piling up of bodies and victims, the nothing that never ceases to expand. The 'intermittent flare of the event', to quote but refashion the sentiment of the historian Braudel, obscures as much as it illuminates, in that one must finally recognize the fundamental inadequacy of responding to the individual Alan Kurdis who gain prominence for just a moment in an exemplary flash of an image, before politics collapses back in upon its usual sorry state of affairs.[263] In the fifth thesis of 'On the Concept of History', Walter Benjamin also refers to the precarity of the image 'which threatens to disappear in the any present that does not recognize itself as intended in that image'.[264] At the conclusion of *The Trial*, in the moment before execution a strange 'flash' occurs above the quarry, and Josef K. wonders in the moments before his death whether it is someone who wants to help: 'The casement window flew open like a light flashing on; a human figure, faint and insubstantial at that distance and height, forced itself far out and stretched its arms out even further. Who was it? A friend? A good man? One who sympathized? One who wanted to help? Was it one person? Was it everybody? Was there still help?'[265] This moment has been interpreted by Carolin Duttlinger and Howard Caygill in relation to photography.[266] Yet reliance on such images risk the same poverty of theory (*theoros*, spectator), in failing to impact those who, from the safety of the shore, witness the peril of those in danger on the sea. Hence Hans Blumenberg's insistence that the metaphor of the shipwreck be taken not as an end point but a point of departure: 'The metaphorics of embarkation includes the suggestion that living means already being on the high seas, where there is no outcome other than being saved or going down, and no possibility of abstention'.[267] But as a matter of rescue missions, Horace's ship of state is not embarked, and no help arrives for Josef K. Arendt is surely correct in her essay 'Personal Responsibility Under Dictatorship' to warn against morality understood as mores that are 'customs and manners' which can be changed as a set of table manners can be changed, the surface chatter of a society which collapsed totally within a hitherto civilized society.[268] Yet the meaning of morality here relates back to that discussed in chapter 1, the meditations by Levinas in the Preface to *Totality and Infinity*, where 'ultimate events of being' are moral events, that is, the revelation of a world shared in common, where human subjectivity is always-already called to responsibility for its counterparts. Morality or *mores* are not just customs and manners, thus understood, nor the naïve obverse of a world dominated by the reality of war and conquest, but a fundamental account of human inter-relationality that is opposed to that which so often undergirds political theory, be it Hobbesian pessimism, or liberal social contractualism unrelated to moral considerations, and even Arendtian intellection where *mores* are a matter for reasoned judgement.

In *Politicide* (a book that is ostensibly an indictment of the record of Ariel Sharon, but is more broadly, an examination of the Israel–Palestine conflict), Baruch Kimmerling writes that 'were it not for the economic depression that began in the late 1920s and the subsequent immigration restrictions, it is highly probable that most European Jews would have emigrated to America in the 1930s, thus reducing the scope of the Holocaust and possibly preventing the establishment of the Jewish state in Palestine. But history does not recognise ifs'.[269] Whether a matter of creating a state or not, the key point here is the othering of history that was possible if Western immigration restrictions had not locked European Jewry into a deadly trap.

'History does not recognise ifs'. But must this be the case? Perhaps it is a matter of going beyond history and empiricism. The othering of history, the articulation of a counter-history of *what could have been*, is also a political gesture, which Benjamin understood; how one interprets the events of the past and the story a society tells itself (Derrida: 'There is no political power without control of the archive, if not of memory'.)[270] To really understand responsibility requires works of imagination and even forms of counter-factual storytelling – here there is a strong link between Arendt and Walter Benjamin – in imagining that the world can be other than it is or could have been. Yet on this point the tension in Arendt's work, discussed in chapters 1 and 2, comes to the fore – the stability of the human political community as resting upon moderation ('one of the political virtues par excellence', in her words) may come into conflict with her call for a new law on earth which would safeguard the dignity of all human beings. In othering the world in the direction of safety and dignity, moderation and bounds *must* be called into question. Thus, it is necessary to make counterfactual links between historical events: there would be no story of the children of Izieu if they had all been on the Kindertransport; it was the fact that they were trapped on the continent that sealed their fate. If more nations had had a Kindertransport, more could have been saved. If the 'Kinder' transport had not only contained *die Kinder*, the adults would have been saved. The scope of the rescue of both children and adults by the British alone (who must be credited for what they did indeed do, even if bordering states like France received far greater numbers of refugees) would have entailed an enormous reduction in the dimensions of the Shoah if the pathological resistance to 'numbers' and cultural cohesion, economic scarcity and dangerous elements, and so on were recognized as so many phantasms (where links to political economy must also be made: to the extent that one billionaire exists in a society, there is no legitimate question of capacity or resources; such a society is by definition not set up to meet genuine human need), even in a time of war (in similarly desperate post-war circumstances, Great Britain inaugurated enormous social welfare programmes like the NHS, and as noted in the previous chapter, benefited economically from receiving refugees). Of the six million Jewish victims of the Shoah, 1.5 million were children; why not a Kindertransport of this size? Why not all six million? Why not the ten million victims of the Holocaust, including the non-Jewish victims? Why not all the exiles of today? Why should there ever be a limit to asylum? What is the limit, and who can say what it is, and prove it? Which societies have been destroyed or even seriously harmed by receiving too many people seeking asylum?

Nor is it simply a matter of hindsight being 20/20, and now we know enough to have acted better had we knew. The failure continues into the present, make remarkably clear by the appalling failure of the Dubs Amendment to be respected, as discussed in chapter 3. Thousands of Syrian children have also been left stranded on the continent, with Great Britain refusing to accept more than a few hundred as refugees. 'So what is it with the British government, why won't they let us in?', Abu Anas, a refugee in the 'Hara Hotel', the refugee camp in Greece, asks. The author and volunteer Teresa Thornhill responds by explaining the irrational fear of terrorism after terrorist attacks in Europe.[271] Does one really need to yet again rehearse and patiently explain once more the statistics on the low rates of crime and terrorist acts amongst refugees compared to domestic populations, that the Jewish people were also portrayed as threats in the 1930s, and so on?

In her essay 'Understanding and Politics', Arendt, in wrestling with the comprehension of totalitarianism – an irruption of the new, in the worst sense, within politics – argues that 'the trouble with the wisdom of the past is that it dies, so to speak, in our hands as soon as we try to apply it honestly to the central political tendencies of our time'.[272] While this may be apposite as regards totalitarianism, and she is right to emphasize the open-ended work of understanding, the wager of the present work is precisely the opposite: the wisdom of the past, the tradition of the oppressed, are absolutely instructive; indeed there is a sense of responsibility in some thinkers, including both Arendt and Derrida, that has become intellectually *de rigueur*, which one could argue is too overly-cautious in producing hesitations around decision. What more, to paraphrase Adorno, are we waiting to learn? René Char, in a fragment of *Hypnos* that could serve as an important addendum to Arendt, wrote that 'Action, which has meaning for the living, only has value for the dead, is only complete in the minds of those who inherit it and question it'.[273]

As discussed in chapter 1, political theorists are very often constrained by fears of what would eventuate from undermining political self-determination: Arendt, in *Origins*, shares in this worry when she writes of the 'ever-increasing numbers [of stateless persons] who threaten our political life, our human artifice, the world which is the result of our common and co-ordinated effort'.[274] In Chapter 1, the antinomy of a guarantee for stateless persons is evinced in her own work where she is at once committed to the rights of the excluded, and the Aristotelian commitment to moderation and the delimitation of the polis. But the disaster has already taken place for so many millions of people; the victims of exclusion are already piled up. What is the counter-evidence concerning disaster that would also result within, from a greater commitment to asylum? Politicians and even political theorists consider these matters as does the paranoid Prince Prospero in Poe's 'The Masque of the Red Death', except that there is no red death to be kept out. The right attributes the fall of the Roman Empire from an invasion of 'barbarians', language, as we have seen, that Arendt was not immune to, but this is a nonsense talking point that has been debunked. What are the justifications for the fearful prudence of the wise, that wisdom mocked by Adorno and inculcated by Aristotle that moderation is the virtue appropriate to reasonable people?

Of the utmost urgency is a concept of the political at the antipodes of Klaus Barbie and all of the sentinels of oblivion. That the most elementary imperative of a politics which prevents the putting to death of children remains unrealized, is why one must insist that nothing has changed. Instead of actively seeking out children to destroy them, or less evil yet still outrageous, doing nothing to help those in need, an *ethos* of responsibility would entail an active seeking out of those who need help (in the language of human rights, asylum as a *positive* right of assistance and not simply a negative right of allowing movement), who need asylum, who need a refuge but more than that, who need a place to belong. Such a politics would entail active respect for unchosen plurality, in recognition of what Martin Luther King in his 'Letter

from Birmingham Jail' called our 'inescapable network of mutuality'.[275] Here
the idea might be risked, *pace* Arendt, of a politics of love, the politics that
James Baldwin sought in combatting the American terror against his people,
where he feared the very worst. While Arendt wrote to Baldwin criticizing
him for including love within the realm of the political – for her, it was too
uncertain a quality to be a matter of public affairs – in contrast Baldwin and
also King emphasized its necessity (King famously preached that love and
power separated from each other were no more than empty sentimentality and
brute force, respectively, though his parsing of the term power is of course
different to Arendt's).[276] Love or tenderness, where it does not lapse into
identitarian violence, is also, as Adorno maintained, a resistance to the sway
of economics and calculation, the inauguration of the possibility of 'relations
without purpose'.[277] Love, however, should be understood in the sense that
Levinas gives it, inverting the traditional meaning of philosophy – from the
'love of wisdom' to the 'wisdom of love': 'philosophy is the wisdom of love
at the service of love', but a love without concupiscence, an attachment to
the others that is not romantic or tied to kinship but rather obliged by bonds
of shared humanity.[278] Luce Irigaray has maintained the necessity of not
speaking simply about others, but speaking to them, engaging in dialogue,
especially those voices and perspectives such as those belonging to women
who have been traditionally excluded by a philosophy that privileges the subject–object relation, rather than a 'wisdom of love' that emphasizes the relation itself.[279] This is the *just* meaning of the political, if, following Levinas,
justice is understood as originating in love – responsibility as a responding
to the other which refers both to memory – the tradition of the oppressed, as
well as to the demands of the present and those of the future, to an anticipation of need.[280]

A politics only attentive to the immediate and to what merely seems to
be, to the apparently living present, to the ontologically ready-to-hand, is
not only foolish but an irresponsible politics, as it does not account for the
memory of the dead, nor the anticipation of those still to come, nor those
who are amongst us but who are not allowed or able to appear in Arendt's
sense. A politics of presentism and surface phenomena, of immediacy and
contemporaneity, is like an animal that assumes that only those beings can
exist, have existed, or will exist, which currently fall within its present field
of perception. But the absent, the missing, the disappeared, the hidden and
marginalized, exiles in the dark, the unchosen and the far away may be invisible, yet always shadow the daytime of appearances as its other reality – the
night-time of being. William Golding's *Pincher Martin* depicts a hallucinated
other life where Martin found safety, which turns out to be but the dream of
a dying man, as he drowns. Indeed, the opening pages of the book present a
terrifying phenomenology of drowning, of being lost at sea and thrown about,

like Odysseus, at the mercy of the endless force of the 'idiot water'.[281] Just
as Adorno's trees were lying to him, just as Izieu in its loveliness seemed
to lie to me about the past, the blue tranquility of the ocean's surface lies to
the spectator on the shore, concealing those whose bones brush against the
ocean floor because they were not saved: as Hans Blumenberg wrote, 'Both
progress and sinkings leave behind them the same peaceful surface'.[282] So too
the quiet streets of the peaceful urban neighbourhoods in the lands of plenty,
of those who believe they have a right to choose who to share the earth with,
their state with, their neighbourhood with, that politics is a matter of contracts and consciously willed agreement. In *Lost Children Archive*, Luiselli
describes the moment following a meeting with a lawyer who declines to
defend two migrant children because their case is 'not "strong enough"',
which will mean their deportation: 'We walked out onto Broadway, into the
late morning, and the city was buzzing, the buildings high and solid, the sky
pristine blue, the sun bright – as if nothing catastrophic were happening.'[283]

The constant theme of political theory and of much refugee scholarship is:
how can we get states to accept responsibility? How can we have a more just
politics, better respect for international law, how do we balance the needs
of residents and foreigners?, and so on. But legalism and the negotiation of
the liberal-democratic paradox are concepts which should be shot into space
because they have manifestly failed to articulate a politics that would attend
to the safeguarding of the lives of those who needed help, and the very idea
of moderation (as Blanchot put it, 'moderation's mediocre morality') should
come with a warning label: contents may kill.[284] Yet perhaps philosophy,
thinking, has always been in tacit alliance with the exile (even if it seems
largely to have *failed to think refuge as a philosophical problem*), from the
expulsion of the moderate Aristotle from Athens, to Dante's expulsion from
Florence, Spinoza's double-exile from Spain and his own refugee community in Lisbon, Arendt's flight from Germany, then France, Derrida's double
expulsion 'out of school and into prison', Levinas's stint in an internment
camp, and so on. Voltaire maintained that the writer should live near a border so as to be able to hop across it at the first sign of trouble. Despite this
constant affinity between the fate of the thinker and the fate of the exile, it
is difficult to locate in any political theory, indeed in the canon of political
philosophy as such, the claim that asylum is proper to the inner meaning of
politics. Arendt, and Judith Butler reading her by way of Levinas, perhaps
come closest to articulating this, but do not, on my reading at least, move
beyond the right to have rights or an ethics of cohabitation to take the decisive step of equating the realization of the purpose of politics as such with
asylum.

In the verso pages of *Of Hospitality*, commenting on Derrida's work, the
philosopher Anne Dufourmantelle (who died in 2017 while trying to save

drowning children at a beach) asked: is an oath possible after the Shoah?[285] What value can be found in a promise or oath after such events? For Arendt, a promise is one of the binding commitments that makes possible the actualization of human community commensurate with the human condition, that is, of the ability of plural beings to converse with and perform actions amongst each other in a position of relative trust. But it is precisely the value of promise that has broken down, perhaps irretrievably – or perhaps it was never anything but a myth, or a vague hope, what Jean Améry called, in describing what he lost after being tortured, 'trust in the world', the 'certainty that by reason of written or unwritten social contracts the other person will spare me – more precisely stated, that he will respect my physical, and with it also my metaphysical, being'.[286] Levinas, as discussed in chapter 1, pointed out that the Jewish people of Europe had placed their trust in liberalism to protect them, which turned out to be an empty promise of belonging, including in those states, such as France, that even proclaimed themselves as exemplars of asylum and had emancipated the Jewish people in the Revolution by making them full citizens – the antipodes of Nazism. One chooses to make a promise that is then kept or not kept. For a guarantee to be actualized, then – here we return to the beginning – for all its violence against self-determination, it must be insisted that asylum is no longer a matter of choice, nor simply a duty, but rather pertains to the actualization of political life. The guarantor does not promise nor will a decision, even if pragmatic decisions must be taken – the guarantor is already chosen, already called by the other, already operating within the context of unchosen plurality. Politics is the always-already having been chosen by the unchosen. The guarantee is a normative absolute that admits of no exceptions, if one is within the sphere of politics (coterminous with the active preservation of plurality as the law of the earth) as defined in this book. To repeat and once more forestall the obvious objection: this state of chosenness by the unchosen, of being the other's hostage, can be denied, forsaken, rejected, abandoned, but then one is no longer within the sphere of politics, and judgement is clear. At present, in the pall cast by moderantism and self-determination and social contracts and the definition of politics as freedom, such judgements are not are clear as they should be.

On the one hand, a truly just politics concerning human relationality and belonging would recognize asylum as the realization of the political, in that unchosen plurality is the ineluctable condition of human planetary cohabitation and thus the *telos* or *conditio per quam* of politics as such; and asylum can therefore be understood from the earliest inception of democratic politics as its proper work (the persistent theme of asylum in the Greek tragedies, from the society that birthed the very notion of democracy, seems a telling clue, even if the present work has rejected the dialectics at work in such tragedies). On the other hand, if politics does not take into account the tradition of the oppressed, the disappeared, those that should or could be here (here amongst the living or here amongst those included within a society) but are not, then politics is a falsity – to repeat Adorno's inversion of Hegel, the whole is the false – based only on the apparently visible. In the words of Sebald, we have appointments to keep in the past,[287] and one might add, in the future, with those unborn generations with whom we 'take turns' to share the earth, which forms the context where the preservation of plurality, refugees, and climate change are understood as inseparable demands.[288] Here we return to the metaphor of night. In chapter 1 it was argued that political theory often depends upon a false sense of ontology. That which is given over to intellection does not constitute ultimate events of being, where human subjectivity is transformed by the event of the infinite, revealing, in the Face of the other, a world shared in common. One can make a similar claim for history, that the real of history is not that which is most readily apparent; the children of Izieu are not here, but they could be. The nature of reality is the permanent possibility of it being othered, and indeed, one must realize that it has always-already been othered, diverted from a path it could have taken if the dignity of the victims of history had been honoured; the disaster has already taken place, is taking place, will have taken place, disaster in the place where the other should be, or disaster that removes the place for the other to be. Disaster as dis-placed-ness, dis-astrum, unchained from the fixity of place, denying the other their place, taking their place, a 'substitution' realized not as responsibility but as murder and indifference.

But to recall this has to do with more than a memorializing impulse, which nevertheless remains essential, but with the self-understanding of political theorists and political practitioners, of what they think they are doing and why they are doing it. It may be that philosophy or political theory can do no more than provide criteria of judgement for assessing the real of politics. Yet can it be claimed that the above criteria have figured sufficiently in refugee politics? There is little evidence that they have; theory remains the spectator on the shore, perhaps its rightful place, but have its claims been strong enough to challenge politics in its essence? From the poverty of the shameful Evian conference in 1938 to the shameful 2016 conferences on refugees, nothing was done, and that is when confining oneself to the criminal misdeeds of liberalism, even before one confronts the growing authoritarianism in the world where often asylum is not only treated as a crime, but where little short of a war has been declared on the vulnerable. The disaster that Benjamin saw prefigured in his childhood, which arrived not only for him and so many other victims, is also a rolling disaster, hence the continuously growing pile of wreckage that falls under the gaze of his angel driven backwards into the future. And yet as Judith Butler points out, vulnerability is a feature of shared lives, and the human community (though constituted by exclusions which haunt it), and exists in mutual relations of interdependency and precarity; disaster respects no border.[289] (This could be seen in the horrific Australian bushfires of 2019-2020, which produced displaced persons within a prosperous and developed country, when the fire front left many stranded on the beach, requiring rescue by the Navy.) The *Aeneid* turns (somewhat) aside from the rapaciousness of its Homeric antecedents by reminding the reader that the glory of Rome begins in the exodus of a desperate and defeated band of refugees, who insist upon the 'sailor's right to shore', and the welcome due to 'we who have drunk deep of every disaster'. (Arendt, in reference to judgement as the faculty for dealing with the past and with history, quotes Cato: 'The victorious cause pleased the gods, but the defeated one pleases Cato', which aligns her with the Benjaminian concept of history as seen from the standpoint of the defeated, which she saw as a means to reclaim our human dignity, where capital-H History as the dogmatic triumphalism of the victor is undermined.)[290] All lives matter, but not all lives are equally exposed to danger, and some lives must therefore be highlighted as those that require safeguarding (the interesting move to recapitulate the movement for saving lives on the Mediterranean as another iteration of 'Black Lives Matter', given the phenomenal impact of this movement, is cause for hope).

All puerile talk of trying to get states to maybe make some better decisions, to think about a nicer degree of hospitality, a nicer weighting of the liberal-democratic paradox, a tilting to the more unconditional end of the conditional–unconditional hospitality polarity, must cease. Enough with this nonsense. There is nothing to negotiate, no problem of numbers, no outsized risk of terrorism (there are already domestic terrorists, refugees commit crimes at a lower rate than citizens, and so on), no problem of social cohesion that is society-threatening, nothing; the only delimitation to open borders and only concession to the respect for political self-determination that the present argument has conceded, is the necessity of continuing to privilege the right to asylum in conditions of emergency and danger over other arguably less urgent modes of migration (while remaining open to the systemic causes of migration and the possible need to expand the definition of refugee to accommodate ecological, economic, and other modes of oppression), and thus to avoid the present political unfeasibility concerning open borders in that context. Judith Butler puts it well (and with more 'patience' than myself):

> Critical patience is required, in the face of impending nihilism, to expose the forms of phantasmagoria according to which someone is 'attacking' when they are not, or when that same person is, indeed, being attacked. This inversion is enacted by the view, the policy, that considers that the migration of people from the Middle East or North Africa will destroy Europe and humanity and so

should be refused and abandoned, even left to die, if necessary . . . That form of defensive aggression is quite far from the insight that this life is not finally separable from another, no matter what walls are built between them. Even walls tend to bind together those they separate, usually in a wretched form of the social bond.[291]

Charles Péguy poetically envisioned hope itself as a little girl, who runs the whole world. But, one must add, she needs allies to transform her into action, those to whom hope, *pace* Kafka, has been given. 'We can't let everyone in!' 'We', that is, all members of the international community but perhaps those best able and/or most responsible, can let in everyone who needs somewhere *to be safe and to belong*. The shared surface of the earth, as Kant observed long ago, implies a common right of belonging. In terms of asylum, there is no limit to the number who can be received, 'no numerus clausus for arrivants' (Derrida).[292] To return to the beginning, the in-dignation of which Arendt wrote concerning the denial of dignity, that nothing was done in other calamities and other times – indeed, the indignation of those enduring calamities today – has driven the arguments of this book. *Nothing has changed, nothing has been learned, nothing has been remembered.* This in-dignation of survivors past and protagonists present concerning the denial of their dignity, the indignation that runs from Schwarz-Bart to the living exiles of today and those not even born yet who will not be saved, an indignation received here as veritable *command*, can be simply put: Let them in. There is no reason not to. Trials await (in fact they are, to borrow from Kafka, always in standing session) that will put to the test Kafka's wager in his tortured letter to Milena: 'I consider all human beings to be good . . . My body, however, simply cannot believe these people will stay that good once they really have to; my body is afraid and would rather crawl slowly up the wall than await this trial, which really would – in this sense – redeem the world.'[293] In that brief scene of hope in *The Last of the Just*, where the refugee family finds temporary respite in Paris prior to being deported to their deaths, Schwarz-Bart, who lost his entire family in the disaster, provides a glimpse of what the actualization of that other, redeemed world can be:

No one insulted them, and no one seemed to be holding back a desire to spit in their faces. Coming back, they could go into any old bakery, now one and now another, to vary the pleasure, and without the slightest hitch buy some of those milk rolls so fragrant with French flour, so intoxicating to savour on top of a rackety little train while the countryside unrolls at your feet like an honorific carpet. And then, heartwarming thing, sometimes an old commuter would nod amiably; and they would return his greeting, all airs and graces; and Benjamin would squeeze his son's hands tightly (both of them were a head taller than he was), as he whispered in Yiddish, in a tone implying that this was the ultimate revelation: 'My little pigeons, this is the life'.[294]

NOTES

1. Adorno, *Minima Moralia*, p. 25.

2. Alain Finkielkraut, with whom I otherwise have serious political disagreements, has written movingly and powerfully of this trial and its effects in *Remembering In Vain: The Klaus Barbie Trial & Crimes Against Humanity* (New York, NY and Oxford: Columbia University Press, 1992).

3. https://www.france24.com/en/20170809-memorial-deported-jewish-children-vandalised-france-wwii-anti-semitism, retrieved 21 December 2019.

4. Adorno and Horkheimer, *Dialectic of Enlightenment*, p. 150.

5. Löwy, *Fire Alarm*, p. 42.

6. Améry, *At the Mind's Limits*, p. 72.

7. Jacob Soboroff, *Separated: Inside An American Tragedy* (New York, NY: Customs House, 2020), p. 365.

8. https://apnews.com/015702afdb4d4fbf85cf5070cd2c6824, retrieved 8 February 2020.

9. https://www.nytimes.com/2019/06/16/us/baby-constantine-romania-migrants.html, retrieved 25 February 2020.

10. https://www.huffpost.com/entry/four-severely-ill-migrant-babies-hospitalized-after-lawyers-visited-border-patrol-facility_n_5d0d3bbce4b07ae90d9cfe4f, retrieved 25 February 2020.

11. Uhlmann, *Abolish ICE*, p. 4.

12. https://www.theguardian.com/world/2018/aug/19/us-supplied-bomb-that-killed-40-children-school-bus-yemen, retrieved 25 February 2020.

13. https://www.independent.co.uk/news/uk/home-news/dubs-child-refugees-home-office-immigration-home-office-supreme-court-a8566191.html, retrieved 25 February 2020.

14. https://www.dw.com/en/child-labor-still-rife-in-democratic-republic-of-congo/a-39194724, retrieved 25 February 2020.

15. https://childrenandarmedconflict.un.org/where-we-work/other-countries/nigeria/, retrieved 25 February 2020.

16. https://www.voanews.com/archive/child-trafficking-prevalent-throughout-southeast-asia, retrieved 25 February 2020.

17. https://www.newshub.co.nz/home/world/2019/06/two-year-old-girl-in-australian-immigration-detention-centre-denied-birthday-cake.html, retrieved 25 February 2020.

18. https://www.theguardian.com/australia-news/2019/nov/02/five-year-old-boy-facing-deportation-from-australia-because-of-mild-disability, retrieved 25 February 2020.

19. https://theintercept.com/2019/10/29/mexico-migrant-unaccompanied-children-border-crossing/, retrieved 25 February 2020.

20. https://www.voanews.com/south-central-asia/1-5-rohingya-child-refugees -suffer-severe-mental-health-issues, retrieved 25 February 2020.

21. https://www.theguardian.com/world/2015/sep/02/shocking-image-of-drowne d-syrian-boy-shows-tragic-plight-of-refugees, retrieved 25 February 2020.

22. https://theintercept.com/2020/04/16/coronavirus-mexico-border-children -asylum/, retrieved 30 April 2020.

23. Jacques Derrida, *The Post Card: From Socrates to Freud and Beyond*, trans. Alan Bass (Chicago, IL: University of Chicago Press, 1987), p. 25: 'A child is what one should not be able to "send" oneself. It never will be, never *should* be a sign, a letter, even a symbol'.

24. Derrida, *The Post Card*, p. 145.

25. Peter Hellman, *French Children of the Holocaust*, Foreword to Serge Klarsfeld, French Children (New York, NY: NYU Press, 1996), pp. ix–x.

26. Levinas, *Otherwise Than Being*, pp. 114–15.

27. *Forgiving Mengele*, documentary film, directed by Bob Hercules and Cheri Pugh, 2006.

28. Luiselli, *Tell Me How It Ends*.

29. Valeria Luiselli, *Lost Children Archive* (London: 4th Estate, 2019), pp. 326–27. This beautiful and moving novel is written as a meditative, complex 'autofiction' travelogue.

30. *Life Overtakes Me*, documentary film, directed by Kristine Samuelson and John Haptas, 2019.

31. Primo Levi, *The Truce*, in *The Complete Works of Primo Levi*, Vol. 1, ed. Ann Goldstein (New York, NY: Liveright, 2015), pp. 226–28.

32. Blanchot, *The Writing of the Disaster*, p. 67.

33. Jean François-Lyotard, *The Inhuman: Reflections on Time* (Cambridge: Polity Press, 1993), p. 2.

34. Hans Jonas, *The Imperative of Responsibility: In Search of an Ethics for the Technological Age* (Chicago, IL and London: University of Chicago Press, 1984), p. 131.

35. Hellman, *French Children of the Holocaust*, p. xv.

36. Schwarz-Bart, *The Last of the Just*, p. 151.

37. James Baldwin, *Tell Me How Long the Train's Been Gone* (London: Penguin, 1994), p. 37.

38. Schwarz-Bart, *The Last of the Just*, p. 261.

39. Imre Kertész, *Kaddish for an Unborn Child* (London: Vintage, 2017), pp. 100 and 112.

40. Adorno, *Minima Moralia*, pp. 192–93.

41. Derrida commented on this theme when he received the Adorno prize; one could also make similar claims about Derrida and the theme of childhood (e.g. his recollections in *Circumfession* and Derrida, *The Post Card*) despite his disavowal of childhood qua philosopheme, as noted above. For Derrida's remark on this theme in Adorno, see Jacques Derrida, 'Fichus', in *Paper Machine*, trans. Rachel Bowlby (Stanford, CA: Stanford University Press, 2005), p. 171. For Adorno's quote, see Theodor Adorno, 'Notes on Kafka', in *Can One Live After Auschwitz? A*

Philosophical Reader, ed. Rolf Tiedmann (Stanford, CA: Stanford University Press, 2003), p. 238.

42. Walter Benjamin, *Berlin Childhood around 1900*, trans. Howard Eiland (Cambridge, MA and London: The Belknap Press of Harvard University Press, 2006), p. 23.

43. Benjamin, *Berlin Childhood Around 1900*, p. 42.

44. François-Lyotard, *The Inhuman*, p. 7.

45. Walter Benjamin, 'On the Image of Proust', in *Walter Benjamin: Selected Writings, Vol. 2: Part 1, 1927–1930*, eds. Michael W. Jennings, Howard Eiland, and Gary Smith (Cambridge and London: The Belknap Press of Harvard University Press, 2005), p. 238.

46. Benjamin, *Berlin Childhood Around 1900*, pp. 32–33.

47. https://www.nybooks.com/articles/1990/12/20/more-than-100-million-women-are-missing/, retrieved 26 February 2020. This article is many decades old, one shudders to think what the number of missing women, in his sense, would be by now.

48. https://www.theguardian.com/australia-news/2018/nov/10/many-families-remain-separated-amid-ongoing-nauru-medical-transfers, retrieved 26 February 2020.

49. Behrouz Boochani, *No Friend But the Mountains* (Sydney: Pan MacMillan, 2018).

50. Parekh, *Refugees and the Ethics of Forced Displacement, is this shortening a referencing convention?*, pp. 34–35.

51. https://www.cfr.org/blog/sex-trafficking-and-refugee-crisis-exploiting-vulnerable, retrieved 26 February 2020.

52. Luiselli, *Tell Me How It Ends*, p. 25.

53. Arzu Güler, *LGBTI Asylum Seekers and Refugees from a Legal and Political Perspective*, eds. Maryna Shevtsova and Denise Venturi (New York, NY: Springer International Publishing, 2019).

54. https://theintercept.com/2020/02/25/family-separations-border-torture-report/, retrieved 27 March 2020.

55. Jacques Derrida, *Monolingualism of the Other; or, the Prosthesis of Origin*, trans. Patrick Mensah (Stanford, CA: Stanford University Press, 1998), pp. 16–17, p. 17: 'One never saw a German uniform in Algeria. No alibi, denial or illusion is possible: it was impossible to transfer the responsibility of that exclusion upon an occupying alien'.

56. Soboroff, *Separated*, pp. xix and 278.

57. Soboroff, *Separated*, p. 158.

58. Soboroff, *Separated*, pp. 262–63.

59. https://www.nytimes.com/2019/08/15/us/migrant-children-toothbrushes-court.html, retrieved 26 February 2020.

60. https://theintercept.com/2019/06/29/concentration-camps-border-detention/, 26 February 2020. A shamefully distracting debate on whether 'concentration camps' was the apposite term for the U.S. camps ensued, and many eminent scholars, including Deborah Lipstadt (who is at other times luminous in combatting antisemitism), wittingly or unwittingly provided political cover to the administration by denying that this was a relevant term, failing to distinguish between concentration camps and

extermination camps. Others such as Andrea Pitzer, the author of *One Long Night: A Global History of Concentration Camps* argued that this term was indeed relevant.

61. https://slate.com/news-and-politics/2019/07/holocaust-museum-aoc-detention-centers-immigration.html, retrieved 20 February 2020.

62. Soboroff, *Separated*, p. 245.

63. Caron, *Uneasy Asylum*, p. 344.

64. Caron, *Uneasy Asylum*, p. 344.

65. Hellman, *French Children of the Holocaust*, p. ix.

66. Françoise Frenkel, *No Place to Lay One's Head*, Preface Patrick Modiano (London: Pushkin Press, 2018), p. 132.

67. I am here using (and pluralizing) Walter Benjamin's phrase, which I examine further below.

68. Jacques Derrida, 'Derelictions of the Right to Justice (But What Are the "Sans-Papiers" Lacking?)', in *Negotiations: Interventions and Interviews 1971–2001*, ed./trans./intro. Elizabeth Rottenberg (Stanford, CA: Stanford University Press, 2002), p. 133.

69. https://theintercept.com/2019/05/04/no-more-deaths-scott-warren-migrants-border-arizona/, retrieved 26 February 2020.

70. https://www.washingtonpost.com/nation/2019/01/20/they-left-food-water-migrants-desert-now-they-might-go-prison/, retrieved 24 February 2020.

71. See Óscar Martínez, *A History of Violence: Living and Dying in Central America* (London and New York, NY: Verso, 2016).

72. Patrick Modiano, *Dora Bruder*, trans. Joanna Kilmartin (Berkeley, CA, Los Angeles, CA, and London: University of California Press, 1999), pp. 11 and 68.

73. Patrick Modiano, *Dora Bruder* (Paris: Éditions Gallimard, 1999), p. 16.

74. See, for example, Jason de Léon, *The Land of Open Graves: Living and Dying on the Migrant Trail*, photographs by Michael Wells (Oakland, CA: University of California Press, 2015). In this book 'necroviolence', distinct from Mbembe's necropolitics, names the deliberate mistreatment of corpses.

75. Jeremy Slack, *Deported to Death: How Drug Violence is Changing Migration on the US-Mexico Border* (Oakland, CA: University of California Press, 2019), p. 132 and passim, especially Chapter Six.

76. For more on the dangerous conditions facing women at the U.S.–Mexico border, see Nina Maria Lozano, *Not One More! Feminicidio on the Border* (Columbus, OH: The Ohio State University Press, 2019). The importance of Lozano's account is to provide a systemic analysis of the neoliberal context in which violence against women becomes operable.

77. For the administration's decision and its consequences, see https://www.latimes.com/opinion/story/2019-11-22/asylum-immigration-women-violence-congress, retrieved 26 February 2020.

78. David Corlett, *Following Them Home: The Fate of the Returned Asylum Seekers* (Melbourne: Black Inc., 2005).

79. 'Erasing the Dead', https://theintercept.com/2019/10/22/haiti-tps-earthquake-displacement-camps/, retrieved 27 October 2019.

80. Daniel Zamora and Michael C. Behrent, eds., *Foucault and Neoliberalism* (Cambridge: Polity Press, 2016), p. 9.

81. Jacques Derrida et al., *Ghostly Demarcations: A Symposium on Jacques Derrida's Specters of Marx*, ed. Michael Sprinker (London and New York, NY: Verso, 1994), p. 268.

82. Derrida, *Specters of Marx*, p. xix.

83. Jacques Derrida, *Cinders*, trans. Ned Lukacher and intro. Cary Wolfe (Minneapolis, MN and London: University of Minnesota Press, 2014), p. 51.

84. Derrida, *Cinders*, p. xv.

85. Derrida, *Cinders*, p. 51.

86. Derrida, *Cinders*, pp. xiii–xiv.

87. Levi, *The Periodic Table*.

88. Levi, *The Periodic Table*, p. 803.

89. Dufourmantelle and Derrida, *Of Hospitality*, p. 5.

90. Dufourmantelle and Derrida, *Of Hospitality*, p. 144.

91. Dufourmantelle and Derrida, *Of Hospitality*, p. 152.

92. Levinas, *Totality and Infinity*, p. 24.

93. Butler, *Precarious Life*, pp. xvii–xix.

94. Judith Butler, *Frames of War: When is Life Grievable?* (London and New York, NY: Verso, 2016), pp. 4–7 and 9.

95. Butler, *Precarious Life*, p. xvii.

96. Butler, *Frames of War*, pp. 8 and 12.

97. Christopher Peterson, 'The Return of the Body: Judith Butler's Dialectic Corporealism', *Discourse*, Vol. 28, No. 2 and 3, Spring and Fall 2006, p. 154. Peterson argues that Butler neglects spectrality, but as I quoted above (to be fair to Peterson, following her previous book and the critique of that book) the term spectre is explicitly used.

98. Butler, *Frames of War*, p. xxvii.

99. Butler, *Frames of War*, p. xiv.

100. Peterson, 'The Return of the Body', p. 157.

101. Peterson, 'The Return of the Body', p. 161 and passim.

102. Shirley Jackson, *The Haunting of Hill House* (London: Penguin, 2009), pp. 3 and 246.

103. Related to the prior meditations, I note that it is the presentation of the haunting as the suffering of a child that initially engages the solicitude of the house guests.

104. Jackson, *The Haunting of Hill House*, p. 240.

105. Jackson, *The Haunting of Hill House*, p. 212.

106. Jackson, *The Haunting of Hill House*, p. 3.

107. Améry, *At the Mind's Limits*, p. 72.

108. Jennifer Gaffney, 'Another Origin of Totalitarianism: Arendt on the Loneliness of Liberal Citizens', *Journal of the British Society for Phenomenology*, Vol. 47, No. 1, 2016, pp. 1–17.

109. Bonnie Honig, *Public Things: Democracy in Disrepair* (New York, NY: Fordham University Press, 2017), pp. 8–9. See also the book which Honig comments upon at length: Jonathan Lear, *Radical Hope: Ethics in the Face of Cultural*

Devastation (Cambridge, MA and London: Harvard University Press, 2006). Lear examines the strategies of the Chief of the Crow Nation, Plenty Coups, in leading his people through a time of dispossession and profound change. Honig takes issue with Lear's privileging of Plenty Coup's somewhat pragmatic strategy over that pursued by Sitting Bull and the Sioux: 'For Lear, Sitting Bull lacks the realism to face his people's true circumstances, which demand radical, not messianic hope. But as Jason Frank argues, "It is worth remembering that Sitting Bull's Ghost Dance so worried U.S. Authorities for its subversive potential that they actively tried to suppress it, and that Sitting Bull also attempted to organize a pan-Indian alliance . . . Who is to say whether such a strategy – indicated a state of denial or acting out on the basis of a false messianic promise?"' (Honig, *Public Things*, p. 70). What is staged here is two ways of confronting the disruption of a world – one which leads pragmatically beyond it into a form of survival in a new form (Plenty Coups), the other which reached for liberation via a messianic performativity but arguably failed in pragmatic terms. I will not form any judgement, except to note the role that 'haunting' plays in Honig's understanding of politics in settler-colonial societies, and the 'hauntology' of the approach pursued via the 'Ghost Dance', where an evocation of the dead played a leading and threatening role against the hegemonic forces of the state. One final note on the theme of hauntology, the film in which Derrida appears as himself and explains much of his thinking on ghosts is also entitled 'Ghost Dance', though no explicit references to the American Indian experience (to my knowledge) are made; perhaps meaningful research bringing the history of the American Indian Movement and/or other indigenous struggles into proximity with resources of Continental Philosophy (and the questioning of the latter implied due to its provenance in the same countries of many colonial powers) on the theme of hauntology would prove insightful. See also Nick Estes, *Our History is the Future* (London and New York, NY: Verso, 2019), pp. 122–24.

110. Henry Reynolds, *This Whispering in our Hearts* (Sydney: Allen & Unwin, 1998).

111. Dee Brown, *Bury My Heart at Wounded Knee: An Indian History of the American West* (London: Vintage, 1991), pp. 7–8.

112. See the interview with Professor Gordon in https://www.versobooks.com/blogs/3775-revisiting-frantz-fanon-s-the-damned-of-the-earth-a-conversation-with-lewis-r-gordon, retrieved 25 August 2020.

113. Edgard Allan Poe, 'The Fall of the House of Usher', in *The Portable Edgar Allan Poe*, ed. J. Gerald Kennedy (London: Penguin), p. 143.

114. Topolski, *Arendt, Levinas, and Politics of Relationality*, p. 50.

115. Jill Stauffer, *Ethical Loneliness: The Injustice of Not Being Heard* (New York, NY: Columbia University Press, 2015), pp. 1–2.

116. Stauffer, *Ethical Loneliness*, pp. 2–3.

117. Robert Bernasconi, 'Invisible Tears and Voices Unheard: On Jill Stauffer's Ethical Loneliness', *Philosophy Today*, Vol. 62, No. 2, Spring 2018, pp. 679–80.

118. Stauffer, *Ethical Loneliness*, p. 4.

119. Arendt, *The Promise of Politics*, p. xxii.

120. Schwarz-Bart, *The Last of the Just*, p. 179.

121. https://www.commentarymagazine.com/articles/the-last-of-the-just-by-andre-schwarz-bart/, retrieved 27 February 2020.

122. Löwy, *Fire Alarm*, p. 57.

123. Löwy, *Fire Alarm*, p. 42.

124. Löwy, *Fire Alarm*, p. 2.

125. Walter Benjamin, 'On the Concept of History', in *Walter Benjamin: Selected Writings, Vol. 4: 1398–1940*, eds. Michael W. Jennings, Howard Eiland, and Gary Smith (Cambridge, MA and London: The Belknap Press of Harvard University Press, 2003), p. 390.

126. Löwy, *Fire Alarm*, p. 67.

127. Michael G. Levine, *A Weak Messianic Power: Figures of a Time to Come in Benjamin, Derrida and Celan* (New York, NY: Fordham University Press, 2014), p. 3.

128. Löwy, *Fire Alarm*, p. 84.

129. Levinas, *Totality and Infinity*, pp. 22–23.

130. Benjamin, *Working With Walter Benjamin*, p. 38.

131. Hannah Arendt, 'Understanding and Politics', in *Essays in Understanding 1930–1954*, ed. Jerome Kohn (New York, NY: Schocken Books, 1994), p. 323. For an extended treatment of Arendt on storytelling and imagination in relation to political understanding, see Margaret Canovan's book *Hannah Arendt: A Reinterpretation of Her Political Thought*.

132. Löwy, *Fire Alarm*, p. 31.

133. André Schwarz-Bart, *A Woman Named Solitude* (New York, NY: Atheneum, 1973), pp. 178–79.

134. W. E. B. Du Bois similarly made connections between the experiences of African Americans and Jewish people in his essay 'The Negro and the Warsaw Ghetto'.

135. See, for example, Ayo A. Coly, *Postcolonial Hauntologies: African Women's Discourses of the Female Body* (Lincoln, NE: University of Nebraska Press, 2019).

136. Adam Zachary Newton, *Facing Black and Jew: Literature as Public Space in Twentieth-Century America* (Cambridge: Cambridge University Press, 1999), p. xiv.

137. Emily Muller Budick, *Blacks and Jews in Literary Conversation* (Cambridge: Cambridge University Press, 1998), p. 2.

138. Neil R. Davison, 'Schwarz-Bart, Levinas, and Post-Shoah-Postcolonial Ethics', *Modern Fiction Studies*, Vol. 60, No. 4, 2014, p. 768.

139. Gyssels, 'A Shoah Classic Resurfacing', pp. 229 and 251.

140. Michael Rothberg, *Multidirectional Memory: Remembering the Holocaust in the Age of Decolonization* (Stanford, CA: Stanford University Press, 2009), pp. xiii and 137.

141. Toni Morrison, *Playing in the Dark: Whiteness and the Literary Imagination* (New York, NY: Vintage, 1993), pp. x–xi.

142. Giorgio Agamben, *Remnants of Auschwitz: The Witness and the Archive*, trans. Daniel Heller-Roazen (New York, NY: Zone Books, 1999).

143. Thomas Trezise, *Witnessing Witnessing: On the Reception of Holocaust Survivor Testimony* (New York, NY: Fordham University Press, 2013), p. 3 and passim. The literature on the subjects of witnessing and testimony is vast: see also, for example, Shoshana Felman and Dori Laub, *Testimony: Crises of Witnessing in Literature, Psychoanalysis and History* (New York, NY and London: Routledge, 1992). It is impossible to do justice to all of the potentially relevant material here.

144. Franz Fanon, *Black Skin, White Masks*, trans. Charles Lam Markmann, intro. Zlauddin Sardar and Homi K. Bhabha (London: Pluto Press, 2008), pp. 63–64.

145. Fanon, *Black Skin, White Masks*, pp. 65–66.

146. Achille Mbembe, *Necropolitics*, trans. Steve Corcoran (Durham, NC and London: Duke University Press, 2019), p. 30.

147. Jane Marks, *The Hidden Children: The Secret Survivors of the Holocaust* (New York, NY: Random House, 1995), p. xviii.

148. Sonia Tascón, 'Refugees and the Coloniality of Power: Border-Crossings of Postcolonial Whiteness', in *Whitening Race: Essays in Social and Cultural Criticism*, ed. Aileen Moreton-Robinson (Canberra: Aboriginal Studies Press, 2004), p. 239. Thanks to Rachel Joy for this and the related references on indigenous perspectives below.

149. Aileen Moreton-Robinson, 'I Still Call Australia Home: Indigenous Belonging and Place in a White Postcolonising Society', in *Uprootings/Regroupings: Questions of Postcoloniality, Home and Place*, eds. Sara Ahmed, Claudia Cataneda, Ann Marie Fortier, and Mimi Shellyey (London and New York, NY: Berg, 2003), pp. 23–40.

150. Toula Nicolacopoulos and George Vassilacopoulos, *Indigenous Sovereignty and the Being of the Occupier: Manifesto for a White Australian Philosophy of Origins* (Melbourne: Re.press, 2014), p. 9. Nicolacopoulos and Vassilacopoulos refer to the way in which White Australian society has constructed the non-white migrant as the other of the white property-owning insider (p. 91) and the refugee in detention as the threat to be feared, now that ethnic difference is everywhere in the community. Thus despite their differing ontological relationship to the land, a tradition of solidarity between first nations peoples and refugees, in recognition of the 'tradition of the oppressed' to which both are subjected by the dominant society, is possible – as evidenced by the gestures that run from Cooper's solidarity with European Jewry to the issuance of Aboriginal passports to refugees in detention.

151. James Baldwin, *I Am Not Your Negro*, compiled by Raoul Peck (New York, NY: Vintage, 2017), p. 48.

152. James Baldwin, *The Evidence of Things Not Seen*, foreword Derrick and Janet Bell (New York, NY: Owl Books, 1995), p. 45.

153. Baldwin, *I Am Not Your Negro*, p. 81.

154. Baldwin, *Evidence of Things Not Seen*, pp. 44–45 and 47.

155. James Baldwin, *The Fire Next Time* (London: Penguin, 2017), p. 50.

156. Robert Gildea, *Fighters in the Shadows: A New History of the French Resistance* (London: Faber and Faber, 2015), pp. 200–1.

157. Toni Morrison, *Beloved*, intro. A. S. Byatt (London: Everyman, 2006), pp. 64–65.

158. Morrison, *Beloved*, p. 80.

159. Morrison, *Beloved*, p. 215.

160. Morrison, *Beloved*, p. 65.

161. Morrison, *Beloved*, pp. 62–69.

162. Dufourmantelle and Derrida, *Of Hospitality*, p. 77.

163. Morrison, *Beloved*, p. 13.

164. Toni Morrison, *The Source of Self-Regard: Selected Essays, Speeches and Meditations* (New York, NY: Alfred A Knopf, 2019), p. 324.

165. For Tlaib's comment, see https://www.theguardian.com/us-news/2019/may/14/rashida-tlaib-holocaust-israel-palestine-comments-democrats-defend-context-republican-attack, retrieved 27 February 2020.

166. Derrida, *Adieu to Emmanuel Levinas*, p. 4.

167. Said, *Freud and the Non-European*.

168. Gyssels, 'A Shoah Classic Resurfacing', p. 252.

169. Arendt, *Eichmann In Jerusalem*, p. 273.

170. Susan Buck-Morss, *Hegel, Haiti and Universal History* (Pittsburgh, PA: University of Pittsburgh Press, 2009), pp. 133–34.

171. Buck-Morss, *Hegel, Haiti and Universal History*, p. 133.

172. Walter Benjamin, *The Storyteller: Tales Out of Loneliness* (London and New York, NY: Verso, 2016), p. 178.

173. 'Humanity is Biblical', interview in (Bowlby, *Questioning Judaism*), pp. 82 and 85.

174. Todd Miller, *Empire of Borders: The Expansion of the U.S. Border Around the World* (London and New York, NY: Verso, 2019), p. 21.

175. Morrison, *Beloved*, p. 315.

176. R. Comay, 'Material Remains: Doris Salcedo', *The Oxford Literary Review*, Vol. 39, No. 1, 2017, pp. 42–64.

177. Comay, 'Material Remains', p. 44.

178. Comay, 'Material Remains', pp. 44–45.

179. Comay, 'Material Remains', p. 53.

180. Theodor Adorno, *Negative Dialectics* (New York, NY and London: Continuum, 2007), pp. 203–4.

181. Adorno, *Negative Dialectics*, pp. 17–18.

182. https://www.nytimes.com/1996/12/05/books/the-holocaust-children-who-did-not-grow-up.html, retrieved 13 March 2020.

183. Hellman, *French Children of the Holocaust*, p. xi.

184. I take this term from Thomas W. Lacquer. See his *The Work of the Dead: A Cultural History of Mortal Remains* (Princeton, NJ and Oxford: Princeton University Press, 2015).

185. Blanchot, *The Writing of the Disaster*, p. 40.

186. Michael Taussig, *Walter Benjamin's Grave* (Chicago, IL and London: University of Chicago Press, 2006), p. 16.

187. Lozano, *Not One More!*, p. 87.

188. Derrida, *Archive Fever*, pp. 11–12.

189. Derrida, *Archive Fever*, p. 20.

190. Taussig, *Walter Benjamin's Grave*, p. 25.

191. Levi, *The Truce*, pp. 252–53.

192. Primo Levi, *If This is a Man*, in *The Complete Works of Primo Levi*, Vol. 1, ed. A. Goldstein, intro. T. Morrison (New York, NY: Liveright, 2015), p. 6.

193. Levi, *If This Is a Man*, p. 7.

194. Toni Morrison, 'Introduction', in *Complete Works of Primo Levi*, Vol. 1 (New York, NY: Liveright, 2015), p. xii.

195. Blanchot, *The Writing of the Disaster*, p. 82.

196. Morrison, *Beloved*, p. 46.

197. In the poem 'Little Gidding'.

198. http://www.izieu.com/new_page_5.htm, retrieved 27 February 2020. Thanks to Rozemund Uljée for bringing this to my attention.

199. See online source at note 172.

200. Erich Auerbach, *Dante: Poet of the Secular World*, intro. Michael Dirda (New York, NY: New York Review Books, 2007).

201. Hermann Melville, *Billy Budd, Bartleby and Other Stories* (New York, NY: Penguin, 2016), p. 54.

202. Améry, *At the Mind's Limits*, p. 70.

203. Améry, *At the Mind's Limits*, p. 77.

204. *Heat*, Film directed by Michael Mann, 1995.

205. Primo Levi, *The Drowned and the Saved*, in *The Complete Works of Primo Levi*, Vol. 3 (New York, NY: Liveright, 2015), p. 2510.

206. Améry, *At the Mind's Limits*, p. 78.

207. Améry, *At the Mind's Limits*, p. 71.

208. Marcel Liebman, *Born Jewish: A Childhood in Occupied Europe* (London and New York, NY: Verso, 2005), pp. 180–81.

209. Samuel Moyn, *A Holocaust Controversy: The Treblinka Affair in Postwar France* (Lebanon, NH: Brandeis University Press, 2005), p. 167.

210. André Schwarz-Bart, *The Morning Star: A Novel*, trans. Julie Rose (New York, NY: Overlook Press, 2011), p. 191.

211. Schwarz-Bart, *The Morning Star*, p. 13.

212. Schwarz-Bart, *The Last of the Just*, p. 74.

213. Kertész, *Kaddish for an Unborn Child*, p. 12.

214. Levinas, *Is It Righteous To Be?*.

215. Adorno, *Negative Dialectics*, pp. 362–63.

216. Ilit Ferber, *Philosophy and Melancholy: Benjamin's Early Reflections on Theater and Language* (Stanford, CA: Stanford University Press, 2013), p. 2.

217. Benjamin, *Working With Walter Benjamin*, pp. 233–34.

218. Ferber, *Philosophy and Melancholy*, pp. 2–3.

219. Ferber, *Philosophy and Melancholy*, p. 7. For more on the unrealized Benjamin-Heidegger encounter (Benjamin and Brecht had planned a reading group in which to 'demolish' Heidegger), see Andrew Benjamin and Dimitris Vardoulakis, eds., *Sparks Will Fly: Benjamin and Heidegger* (New York, NY: SUNY Press, 2015).

220. Ferber, *Philosophy and Melancholy*, p. 27.

221. Ferber, *Philosophy and Melancholy*, p. 29.

222. Emmanuel Levinas, *Existence and Existents*, trans. Alphonso Lingis and foreword Robert Bernasconi (Pittsburgh, PA: Duquesne University Press, 2001), pp. 51–53.

223. Emmanuel Levinas, 'Reflections on the Philosophy of Hitlerism', trans. Seán Hand, *Critical Inquiry*, Vol. 17, No. 1, Autumn 1990, p. 71.

224. René Char, *Hypnos*, trans. Mark Hutchinson (London, New York, NY and Calcutta: Seagull Books, 2015), p. 14.

225. Char, *Hypnos*, pp. 2 and 46.

226. Char, *Hypnos*, p. 54.

227. Schwarz-Bart, *The Last of the Just*, p. 383.

228. Julian Green, *Paris* (London: Penguin, 2012), pp. 47–51.

229. Modiano, *Dora Bruder*, pp. 21–22.

230. Modiano, *Dora Bruder*, p. 119.

231. Modiano, *Dora Bruder*, p. 109.

232. Butler, *Parting Ways*, pp. 106–7.

233. Modiano, *Dora Bruder*, p. 119.

234. https://theintercept.com/2019/05/04/no-more-deaths-scott-warren-migrants-border-arizona/, retrieved 7 November 2019.

235. Natasha Lennard, *Being Numerous: Essays on Non-Fascist Life* (London and New York, NY: Verso Books, 2019), p. 28.

236. Lennar, *Being Numerous*, p. 30.

237. Derrida, *Specters of Marx*, p. 174.

238. Lennar, *Being Numerous*, p. 31.

239. Levinas, *Totality and Infinity*, p. 99.

240. Oscar Wilde, *The Complete Short Stories of Oscar Wilde* (New York, NY: Dover, 2006), p. 177.

241. See Yuval Noah Harari, *Sapiens: A Brief History of Humankind* (London: Vintage, 2016). Harari explains why storytelling made Homo sapiens effective at organizing, but notes that this was not often to moral ends, but usually in the service of modes of domination.

242. Chalier, *What Ought I To Do?*, p. 10.

243. Chalier, *What Ought I To Do?*, pp. 10–11. The quotations are drawn from Kant's essay 'Idea for a Universal History from a Cosmopolitan Perspective'. See Immanuel Kant, *Towards Perpetual Peace and Other Writings on Politics, Peace and History* (New Haven, CT and London: Yale, 2006), pp. 3–16.

244. Hannah Arendt, *The Human Condition*, intro. Margaret Canovan (Chicago, IL: University of Chicago Press, 1998), p. 198.

245. Arendt, *The Human Condition*, p. 198.

246. Arendt, *The Human Condition*, p. 199.

247. Norma Thompson, *Herodotus and the Origins of the Political Community: Arion's Leap* (New Haven, CT and London: Yale Press, 1996), p. 8.

248. Thompson, *Herodotus and the Origins of the Political Community*, p. 29.

249. Thompson, *Herodotus and the Origins of the Political Community*, pp. 164–67.

250. Martin Heidegger, 'Letter on Humanism', in *Basic Writings* (London: Routledge, 2011), p. 174.

251. Maurice Blanchot, *Awaiting Oblivion*, trans. John Gregg (Lincoln, NE and London: University of Nebraska Press, 1997), p. 4. Blanchot's complex and difficult text also, as the translator John Gregg notes, performatively demonstrates the difficulty in retelling stories without losing track of the attempt to master the situation by understanding, though this can be understood as ethically positive, in that the attempted mastery over alterity is continually undone – yet another paradox for the ethics of storytelling in the present context.

252. Thompson, *Herodotus and the Origins of the Political Community*, p. 145.

253. Walter Benjamin, 'The Storyteller', in *Illuminations: Essays and Reflections*, intro. and ed. Hannah Arendt (New York, NY: Schocken, 1968), p. 86.

254. Benjamin, 'The Storyteller', pp. 93–94.

255. Benjamin, 'The Storyteller', p. 96.

256. Benjamin, 'The Storyteller', p. 96.

257. Benjamin, 'The Storyteller', p. 109.

258. Arendt, *The Human Condition*, p. 198.

259. Abdirahman A. Hussein, *Edward Said: Criticism and Society* (London and New York, NY: Verso, 2004), p. 86.

260. Elisabeth Young-Bruehl, *Hannah Arendt: For Love of the World* (New Haven, CT and London: Yale University Press, 2004), p. 163.

261. Arendt, 'We Refugees', p. 266.

262. Karl Marx, 'The Eighteenth Brumaire of Louis Bonaparte', in *Surveys From Exile: Political Writings*, Vol. 2 (London and New York, NY: Verso, 2010), p. 146.

263. Thompson, *Herodotus and the Origins of the Political Community*, p. 59.

264. Löwy, *Fire Alarm*, p. 40.

265. Franz Kafka, *The Trial*, trans. Idris Parry (London: Penguin, 2000), p. 178.

266. See Carolin Duttlinger, *Kafka and Photography* (Oxford: Oxford University Press, 2007), p. 205; and Howard Caygill, *Kafka: In Light of the Accident* (London and New York, NY: Bloomsbury, 2017), pp. 143–44.

267. Hans Blumenberg, *Shipwreck with Spectator: Paradigm of a Metaphor for Existence* (Cambridge, MA and London: MIT Press, 1997), p. 19.

268. Arendt, 'Personal Responsibility', p. 43.

269. B. Kimmerling, *Politicide: Ariel Sharon's War Against the Palestinians* (London and New York, NY: Verso, 2003), p. 20.

270. Derrida, *Archive Fever*, p. 4.

271. Teresa Thornhill, *Hara Hotel: A Tale of Syrian Refugees in Greece* (London and New York, NY: Verso, 2018), p. 185.

272. Hannah Arendt, 'Understanding and Politics', in *Essays in Understanding: Formation, Exile and Totalitarianism 1930–1954*, ed. Jerome Kohn (New York, NY: Schocken Books, 1994), p. 309.

273. Char, *Hypnos*, p. 51.

274. Arendt, *The Origins of Totalitarianism*, p. 302.

275. King, *Letter from Birmingham Jail*, p. 3.

276. For Arendt's letter to Baldwin, see http://www.hannaharendt.net/index.php/han/article/view/95/156, retrieved 27 February 2020. I have always found it curious, to say the least, that in a text (Baldwin, *The Fire Next Time*) where Baldwin evinces fears of a coming Final Solution for African Americans, Arendt's focus is to chastise him for introducing love into the sphere of politics – another example of her fear of normative direction within politics, preferring the activity of politics itself, which seems to risk an implicit conservatism or aestheticism.

277. Adorno, *Minima Moralia*, p. 41.

278. Levinas, *Otherwise Than Being*, pp. 162 and 123.

279. Luce Irigaray, *The Way of Love* (London and New York, NY: Continuum, 2003).

280. Levinas, *Is It Righteous To Be?*, p. 169.

281. William Golding, *Pincher Martin* (London: Faber and Faber, 2015), p. 14.

282. Blumenberg, *Shipwreck with Spectator*, p. 59.

283. Luiselli, *Lost Children Archive*, pp. 18–19.

284. Blanchot, *The Writing of the Disaster*, p. 56.

285. Dufourmantelle and Derrida, *Of Hospitality*, p. 116.

286. Améry, *At the Mind's Limits*, p. 28.

287. W. G. Sebald, *Austerlitz*, trans. Anthea Bell (London: Penguin, 2011), p. 360.

288. On Climate Change from a Continental Philosophy perspective (that also utilizes a great deal of Analytic work), see Matthias Fritsch, *Taking Turns with the Earth: Phenomenology, Deconstruction and Intergenerational Justice* (Stanford, CA: Stanford University Press, 2018).

289. Butler, *The Force of Non-Violence*, p. 59 and passim.

290. Hannah Arendt, *The Life of the Mind* (New York, NY: Harcourt, 1978), p. 216.

291. Butler, *The Force of Non-Violence*, pp. 145–46.

292. Jacques Derrida, *Politics of Friendship*, trans. George Collins (London and New York, NY: Verso, 1997), p. x.

293. Franz Kafka, *Letters to Milena*, intro. and trans. Philip Boehm (New York, NY: Schocken, 1990), p. 182.

294. Schwarz-Bart, *The Last of the Just*, p. 280.

Index

Adorno, Theodor, 4, 58–59, 94, 132–33, 195; on anti-Semitism, 198, 202; on art, 229, 234; the failure of thought, 8; philosophy's dominance by number, 148–49, 153

Aeneid (Virgil), 249

Afghanistan, 207

Agamben, Giorgio, 22, 62, 162, 219–20

American Revolution, 20, 55

Amèry, Jean, 63, 132, 198, 213–14, 232–33, 248

Anderson, Benedict, 25; imagined communities, 47, 97n20

Antigone (Sophocles), 12

Arendt, Hannah, 3–9, 11–13, 16–29, 31–34, 47–51, 54–68, 85–88, 91–94, 105–14, 149, 153, 179, 184, 187, 213–14, 217, 226, 239–40, 243–46, 249–50; and Aristotle, 134, 137; on Brecht, 117; and Denmark, 107–8, 111–17, 120–21; and Edmund Burke, 88; her exile in Paris, 170, 189n28, 247; and James Baldwin, 263n276; and Judith Butler, 70–77, 168; on Kafka, 123, 125; and Kant, 66, 87, 166; and Marxism, 56, 58, 125; natality, 6, 19, 55; plurality, 4, 13, 18–24, 26–28, 38n22, 47–48, 57, 65–77, 87, 89–90, 118, 121–23, 165, 181, 241; and Serena Parekh, 52–53,

97n19. *See also* dignity; guarantee; responsibility

Aristotle, 5–6, 18, 20, 29, 32, 61, 68, 81, 92, 95, 111, 179, 239; and Levinas, 130–34, 141–48; moderation, 10, 42n80, 132–39, 142, 144, 147–53, 243–47; the political animal, 16, 30, 49

Arizona. *See* Mexico; Warren, Scott

Australia, 25, 33, 206–7, 259n150; Aboriginal Australians, 43n101, 214, 221–22; off-shore detention, 69–70, 170, 198

Badiou, Alain, 15, 54, 97n21, 130, 162–63, 167, 177, 182–84

Baldwin, James, 201, 224, 245–46, 263n276

Balibar, Étienne, 26, 64, 168, 190n48

Barbie, Klaus, 196–97, 205–7, 226, 245

Benhabib, Seyla, 11–12, 52, 61–62, 71–73, 118

Benjamin, Andrew, 4, 16, 25, 28, 49, 54, 89–93, 188n7, 217, 235; and Derrida, 103n175, 193n116; on evil, 122

Benjamin, Walter, 1–4, 35, 91, 160, 198, 200, 202–3, 210, 230, 235, 249; the Angel of History, 32–33, 232; the concept of history, 216–19, 240–42,

www.ingramcontent.com/pod-product-compliance
Lightning Source LLC
Chambersburg PA
CBHW021811270326
41932CB00007B/139